ALSO BY WILL IRWIN

The Jedburghs: The Secret History of the
Allied Special Forces, France 1944

ABUNDANCE OF VALOR

ABUNDANCE OF
VALOR

RESISTANCE, SURVIVAL, AND LIBERATION: 1944–45

Will Irwin

BALLANTINE BOOKS / NEW YORK

Published in the United States by Presidio Press, an imprint of The Random House Publishing Group, a division of Random House, Inc., New York.

PRESIDIO PRESS and colophon are trademarks of Random House, Inc.

LIBRARY OF CONGRESS CATALOGING-IN-PUBLICATION DATA

Irwin, Will
Abundance of valor: resistance, survival, and liberation: 1944–1945 / Will Irwin.
p. cm.
ISBN 978-0-345-50176-9
eBook ISBN 978-0-345-51908-5
1. Arnhem, Battle of, Arnhem, Netherlands, 1944.
2. World War, 1939–1945—Aerial operations, British.
3. World War, 1939–1945—Aerial operations, American.
4. Jedburgh (Program)—Biography.
5. Parachute troops—Biography.   I. Title.
D763.N42A73525 2010   940.54'219218—dc22   2009052986

Printed in the United States of America on acid-free paper

www.presidiopress.com

2 4 6 8 9 7 5 3 1

FIRST EDITION

Book design by Casey Hampton

One powerful full-blooded thrust across the Rhine and into the heart of Germany, backed by the whole of the resources of the Allied Armies, would be likely to achieve decisive results.

—Field Marshal Sir Bernard Law Montgomery

I think we might be going a bridge too far.

—Lieutenant General Sir Frederick A. M. Browning

"Not in vain" may be the pride of those who have survived, the epitaph of those who fell.

—Sir Winston S. Churchill, on Operation Market-Garden

CONTENTS

LIST OF MAPS

PROLOGUE

On the evening of Monday, September 11, 1944, three men
strapped on parachutes and climbed aboard a snub-nosed
British Stirling, a specially modified four-engine bomber, at a secret airfield in England. Months of rigorous training and painstaking preparation had brought the men to this point. In recent days, they had endured
detailed briefings in London, outlining their mission of arming and
training the Dutch underground, even last-minute guidance and a personal farewell from Prince Bernhard of the Netherlands' royal family.[1]

Bernhard, a German by birth, had married the Dutch princess Juliana in 1937, and although the German national anthem and the "Horst
Wessel" had been sung at the wedding reception, Bernhard held a fer-
vent hatred for the Nazis. When the royal family had fled the Netherlands* at the time of the German invasion, he had prudently seen to his

---

* The formal name of the state commonly referred to as Holland is the Netherlands. The name "Holland" correctly identifies two provinces in the western region of the country. In informal usage, the name "Holland" is customarily used by
English speakers in referring to the entire country. While the more formal form,
"the Netherlands," is used in this book when it is most appropriate, the more colloquial "Holland" is used, in most cases, when referring to the entire country.

family's safe removal to Canada before returning to London to head the Dutch resistance movement.

Days of nervous anticipation followed for the parachutists as their mission first was postponed because of high winds, then was aborted two days later after their plane reached Holland and survived heavy German flak,* only to have the pilot turn back when he failed to locate the drop area.

The men made themselves as comfortable as possible in the plane's long, slender interior. At ten that night, the Stirling roared down the runway, the four huge Bristol engines on the short wings straining to lift the enormous plane from the runway, then leveling to a steady drone as the bomber headed toward the English Channel. The men tried to relax as the flight continued over the water. Before long, the plane crossed the Dutch coast over the fishing town of IJmuiden, northwest of Amsterdam, and encountered light flak but was not hit.

At twenty minutes past midnight, twenty-nine-year-old Major Henk Brinkgreve, wearing the brown uniform of the Royal Netherlands Army, dropped through the opening in the floor of the Stirling. As eager as the other two members of the team were to get their mission under way, Brinkgreve's fervor was more personal, more emotional; he was returning to his homeland for the first time since the 1940 German invasion. The Dutch officer was quickly followed by Sergeant John Austin, the team's British radio operator. Last to leave the plane was Major John Olmsted, an infantry officer from the United States Army who had come to be called "Pappy" by the others because of the year or two of age he had on them.

The three men were unaware that nearly all of the agents previously dropped into the Netherlands by Britain's Special Operations Executive—more than fifty men since 1941—had been captured and imprisoned or executed by the Germans. Recent operations had been more successful, but no one could be sure what awaited the three men now approaching Dutch soil.

The reception committee—members of the underground gathered to meet the team at the drop zone and help remove the parachutists and their accompanying supplies from the area as quickly as possible to avoid detection or capture by the Germans—had extinguished the lights marking the drop zone as soon as the three parachutists had jumped.

---

* Antiaircraft fire.

NORTH
SEA

ZUIDER
ZEE

Jedburgh team Dudley
insertion on the night of
September 11–12, 1944

Zwolle

Raalte

Almelo

Borne

Epe

Deventer

Hengelo

HOLLAND

Apeldoorn

Ijssel

Amsterdam

The Hague

Ede

Delft

Neder Rijn

Oosterbeek

Arnhem

Rotterdam

Waal

Nijmegen

Groesbeek

Rhine

Maas

Grave

Veghel

St.Oedenrode

Son

Eindhoven

GERMANY

Antwerp

Roermond

Allied front line, September 16, 1944

Meuse

BELGIUM

30 kilometers

Brussels

30
miles

Brinkgreve and Olmsted had anticipated this unwelcome action, having been briefed that this reception committee was receiving its first drop. The inexperienced resistance fighters were unaware that special operations planes typically required two passes over the small drop zones to deliver both the parachutists and the cargo of twelve man-size cylindrical containers packed with weapons, ammunition, explosives, and other gear that accompanied most special forces teams deploying behind enemy lines. Because of this, Brinkgreve and Olmsted had persuaded the aircrew to reverse the normal procedure, dropping the parachutists on the first pass and the long steel containers on the second.

As the three men drifted toward the farmland of eastern Holland, near the town of Wierden and less than six miles from the German border, they spotted a truck convoy not far away. With the nearest Allied ground forces still more than a hundred miles to the southwest, the convoy was certainly German.

Brinkgreve hit the soft pasture turf, collapsing and rolling to one side, leaped to his feet, freed himself from his parachute harness, and quickly located the reception committee chief. He informed the resistance man that the Stirling would be circling for another pass over the field to drop the twelve metal containers. The lights, the major explained, needed to be turned on again at once for the pilot to find the drop zone on the second pass.

Not far away, Major Olmsted and the radio operator gathered up their parachutes. Sergeant Austin's carbine had caught on the edge of the opening as he exited the plane, jarring the weapon from his grasp and causing it to become tangled in his parachute. He had somehow managed to descend safely but had landed within only a few feet of Olmsted.

Major Olmsted set out in search of Major Brinkgreve while the radio operator buried their parachutes. The American had not gone far when a shadowy form approached him in the dark. As the figure drew nearer, Olmsted could just make out what appeared to be a German uniform. He drew his forty-five-caliber automatic and cocked the hammer, ready to shoot the intruder.

But the stranger suddenly said, "Hallo, pal."[2]

Startled at first by the strange greeting, Olmsted challenged the man for the planned recognition signal and then relaxed when the man gave the correct response. Olmsted lowered the pistol, easing the hammer forward with his thumb, and returned the weapon to its holster. The uniform that had appeared to Olmsted to be German was, in fact, that of a Dutch constabulary force, or gendarmerie, called the Marechaussee. The policeman, in this case, was also an active member of the underground.

Olmsted followed the policeman to a spot where Brinkgreve and the reception committee chief were awaiting the container drop. Along the way, the two men were joined by another man, a Dutchman who had been trained in Great Britain to organize resistance groups in the Netherlands. He and his radio operator had parachuted into the Veluwe region, to the south, nearly two weeks earlier, but they had lost all of their equipment on the jump. The two had since made their way northward into the province called Overijssel (the "ij" is pronounced like the English word "eye").

Brinkgreve had successfully gotten the reception committee to relight the drop zone by the time Olmsted and the two Dutchmen found him. Soon the Stirling could be heard approaching the field on its second pass. As the lumbering, roaring shadow soared overhead, less than eight hundred feet above the men, twelve parachutes opened, one after the other, blossoming against the night sky. The drop was a good one, and in a matter of seconds the containers thudded to the ground.

Olmsted smiled as one of the Dutch boys on the reception committee, unacquainted with the use of containers, scampered through the darkness of the almost moonless night, darting from one parachute to the next. As each man-size container hit the ground with a thump, the Dutchman called out, "Hallo, boys!"[3]

—————

On the following Sunday morning, September 17, 1944, British, American, and Polish forces kicked off history's largest airborne assault to date, dropping three parachute divisions into German-occupied Holland. The bold operation, called Market-Garden by Allied planners, was a high-risk assault into enemy-held territory that began amid lofty hopes of ending the war by Christmas. The ensuing battle has been the subject of many books in the years since World War II, and in 1977 it was vividly portrayed on film by an all-star cast in Joseph E. Levine's production of *A Bridge Too Far*, based on the bestselling book of the same name by Cornelius Ryan (Simon & Schuster, 1974).

More Allied soldiers and airmen died during the battle known as Operation Market-Garden than died on D-Day of the Normandy invasion three months earlier. In the currency of Allied casualties, the cost of the week-long operation ran to some seventeen thousand men killed, wounded, or missing. Of the roughly ten thousand paratroopers of the British 1st Airborne Division alone, dropped near Arnhem at the opening of the battle, all but about two thousand were killed or captured.

One part of the Market-Garden legend, though, has never been told. It is the gallant story of the handful of three-man Jedburgh teams— Allied special forces—that parachuted into the Netherlands in support of the operation. This book tells their story, focusing especially on the three teams dropped farthest behind enemy lines in support of the Allied operation. Of the nine men who made up those three teams, three were killed in action, three were wounded, and two were captured. One of those captured was later executed by the Germans. Two of the teams would have only one man come out alive. It would be two months before one of the men made it back, evading capture by German search parties until finally reaching friendly lines. The other would not return for more than seven months—months spent slowly starving as a prisoner of war in Poland and Germany—until, after many attempts, he eventually escaped from his German captors.

This is the true story of how these courageous men prepared for the mission, how they fought, how some of them died, and how two men survived different but equally harrowing ordeals to make their way back to friendly territory. These men fought the enemy, dealt with fear and isolation, and defied overwhelming odds—overcoming countless obstacles, dangers, and hardships—to survive and return home. The book is based, in part, on the firsthand testimony of the survivors of these three teams. Further details are taken from recently declassified documents, including mission after-action reports, communication records, and personnel files.

The Jedburghs were elite, highly trained three-man teams formed from a pool of British, American, Free French, and Dutch volunteers. Ninety-three such teams were parachuted throughout occupied France during the Allied campaign to liberate that country in the summer of 1944. Dropped well behind German lines, these teams organized and armed thousands of French resistance fighters and ensured that the sabotage and guerrilla warfare activities of these groups contributed to the overall Allied ground campaign. Meanwhile, a handful of Jedburgh teams stood by, prepared to make a similar contribution to the liberation of the Netherlands.

ABUNDANCE OF VALOR

ONE

THE ENGLAND GAME

A string of events that would have a profound impact on the Jedburgh teams dropped into the Netherlands began more than two years earlier in the coastal Dutch city of The Hague, the nation's bustling political center.

On the cold, damp evening of Friday, March 6, 1942, Lieutenant Hubertus Gerardus Lauwers prepared to transmit a coded message to London on his clandestine radio from a building near the center of the city. He had often used this second-floor apartment at 678 Fahrenheitstraat, the home of a newly married couple named Teller, as a place to operate his radio. In fact, he had fallen into a routine of transmitting from the Teller home at six-thirty on alternate Friday evenings. It was from here that he had arranged his first drop of weapons and explosives for the Dutch underground, which had arrived only a week earlier. Now Lauwers set up his transmitter on a table in an unheated room of the apartment.[1]

Lauwers, thin-faced and bespectacled, rather frail-looking, was a twenty-six-year-old native of the Dutch East Indies, where he had been a journalist before the war. After the German invasion and occupation of the Netherlands, he had gone to England to join the exiled Dutch forces in the fight against the Nazis. There he had been recruited by Britain's

Special Operations Executive (SOE), trained as a behind-the-lines radio operator, and parachuted into Holland in 1941.

SOE had been organized early in the war to carry out Prime Minister Winston Churchill's plans to build an immense armed resistance movement in the German-occupied countries of Europe. To organize and train resistance fighters and saboteurs, SOE had begun parachuting highly trained agents into Norway, France, Belgium, Denmark, and the Netherlands. Working as resistance organizers, they arranged for parachute drops of weapons, ammunition, explosives, and other supplies. They also trained the partisans in their use and in the age-old tactics of guerrilla warfare. When the time came for the Allies to launch an invasion aimed at liberating the occupied countries of Western Europe, well-timed sabotage and interdiction efforts by such groups could cripple German communications and delay German reinforcements from reaching the invasion area. Each SOE organizer, typically, was accompanied by a radio operator.

To orchestrate such activities in the Netherlands, SOE had established its Dutch Section in 1941. As one of a number of country sections, Dutch Section was charged with recruiting and training Dutchmen in the United Kingdom to serve as agents—organizers and radio operators—to be parachuted into the Netherlands. Prospective agents were found among the many Dutch citizens who had escaped their homeland at the time of the German invasion and found their way to England.

Upon completion of his training in England, Lieutenant Lauwers had been assigned as radio operator for an agent named Thijs Taconis; and on the night of November 7, 1941, the two men, dressed in civilian clothes, had jumped into Holland from a modified British Whitley bomber.[2]

Four months later, sitting in his winter overcoat in the cold room in the Tellers' apartment, headphones to his ears and a blanket draped over his knees, Lauwers prepared to tap out his message on the radio's Morse key.

Not far away that evening, a French car bearing Dutch plates pulled to the curb on Cypresstraat, near the intersection with the broad thoroughfare called Fahrenheitstraat. In the car was a balding, stern-looking man in civilian clothes—Major Hermann J. Giskes of the Abwehr, Germany's military intelligence organization. He had been posted to The Hague only two months earlier to serve as chief of the Abwehr's III-F department (counterespionage) for the Netherlands and Belgium. Already he had formed a close working relationship there with the head of the counterespionage and countersabotage office of the Sicherheitsdienst, or SD (German Security Service), a melon-headed Bavarian named Joseph Schreider.

Soon another car pulled to the curb—a huge gray Mercedes with an ominous black-and-white SS pennant sprouting from the passenger-side fender. In this car sat Schreider, his dumpy form bedecked in the menacing dark uniform of his branch, a coal black collar tab bearing the four silver pips of an SS-Sturmbannführer (major). Other police cars, each containing armed men, also pulled to the curb on Cypresstraat.

Giskes and Schreider were acting on a tip from an informer, a fat and often inebriated diamond smuggler named Georges Ridderhoff, who had penetrated the Dutch resistance in December 1941. Since that time, he had provided information to the Germans for payment of five hundred guilders a month. Ridderhoff had identified several radio operators and, under German direction, had fed the radiomen false information to transmit to London. One of the operators he had betrayed was Lieutenant Hubertus Lauwers.

Ridderhoff had saved the Germans much time and effort in locating Lauwers's transmitter by providing information that indicated the general neighborhood in which Lauwers operated. Giskes had alerted a radio-monitoring unit, which used radio direction–finding equipment to attempt to identify the particular building from which radio transmissions originated. Before long, the men operating the direction finders had narrowed down the transmitter's location to a block-long, three-story red brick apartment building on Fahrenheitstraat, near the intersection with Segbroeklaan.

As Lauwers prepared to send his message on the evening of March 6, Teller entered the room and reported to the radioman that several police cars had gathered down the street near the Cypresstraat intersection. Lauwers did not seem alarmed, however; police were often seen in the area. He was concerned, however, that German radio direction–finding scanners might be searching the area for a transmitting signal. To be on the safe side, Lauwers decided to pack up his radio and leave the apartment. He quickly reeled in his antenna and ground wire, packed the radio and headset back in their case, and pocketed a couple of pieces of paper containing unsent messages. Teller and Lauwers decided that they would casually exit the apartment building and walk down the street, chatting innocently to appear unconcerned with the police presence.

Snow was falling as the two men left the building through the front doorway, sauntered down the half-dozen stone steps, and began walking along the sidewalk, talking quietly and being careful not to appear suspicious by looking around. A brisk wind out of the northwest drove the snow through the chilled sea air. It was nearly dusk; what daylight remained seeped through low, somber clouds. At the corner, Teller and Lauwers turned onto Cypresstraat in the opposite direction from where the police cars sat. Lauwers was able to steal a quick glance back and was satisfied that the police were paying no attention to them. But as the men picked up their pace, the two cars carrying Giskes and Schreider began following slowly, creeping along the icy cobblestones, as if stalking the men.

Lauwers and Teller, uncertain of what was happening behind them as they dared not look back, tried to appear innocently unconcerned, even unaware; but they felt the eyes of the Germans on them. When would they pounce? *Would* they pounce?[3]

As the two men reached the next corner, the Mercedes suddenly shot forward and pulled sharply to the curb next to them, followed quickly by the French car. Armed men sprang from both cars, shoved the two Dutchmen against the wall, frisked them for weapons, handcuffed them, then threw Teller into the security police car and Lauwers into the car with Giskes. The car carrying Lauwers, who was lodged between two Germans in the backseat, turned around and headed back toward the Teller apartment. Schreider's car drove off with Teller, who would eventually meet his death in a concentration camp.

Teller's wife had suspected trouble as soon as her husband left with Lauwers. Anticipating that a police search of the apartment might soon follow, she took the small suitcase containing Lauwers's radio and threw it out behind the house from the balcony in back. Not long afterward, the Germans arrived, conducted a search of the apartment, inside and out, and found the radio. Already, in searching Lauwers, they had found three enciphered messages in one pocket.

Lauwers was then interrogated harshly, though not tortured, and was coerced into giving up the code he used for enciphering his messages. Lauwers was not overly distraught, though. Hadn't the SOE instructors back in England told him that after resisting to a reasonable point, he could give up his code, as long as he did not reveal his security check?[4]

Communications specialists at SOE, those responsible for briefing radio operators and providing them with their codes prior to deployment, were fully aware of how the "radio game" was played—how captured operators could be coerced into transmitting messages back to England under duress and German supervision. Such messages were carefully crafted by German intelligence officers to mislead and manipulate Allied planners—reporting inaccurate "intelligence," inviting additional delivery of arms and agents into the hands of the waiting Abwehr or Gestapo, Germany's state security police.

As a defense against this, all Allied radio operators sent to the field were given a "security check" to be used in all messages sent back to England. This usually consisted of a particular and deliberate mistake that was to be inserted into every message. Radio operators were instructed that in the event they were ever captured and forced to transmit messages back to England, they were to omit the deliberate mistake. Thus, when an operator's security check was missing from a message, it was a signal to the recipients in London that the operator had been arrested and was transmitting under duress for the enemy.

Upon completion of his initial interrogation, Lieutenant Hubertus Lauwers was taken to a prison just outside The Hague. There, Giskes further questioned the Dutchman in his cell for more than an hour. The Abwehr man was in his forties, with penetrating blue eyes and a thin mustache over equally thin lips. Sometimes he spoke in German, other times in Dutch, using his ample powers of persuasion to try to convince Lauwers that many of his comrades had already been captured and were now working for the Germans. Other Dutch SOE radio operators, Giskes lied, had opted to use their radios to transmit German-prepared messages to London rather than face a firing squad.

As Lauwers knew, the Germans could not simply use their own radio operators to communicate with London over the SOE wireless sets. Every radio operator's touch on the Morse key was unique, like a fingerprint, and the girls receiving the messages at the base station back in England would quickly detect a message that was sent by an impostor. If the Germans wanted to send false messages to mislead SOE, they would need to coerce the Dutch operators into doing the transmitting.

———

By March 15, nine days after his arrest, Lauwers had missed three scheduled transmissions to London, and his next was to be at two that afternoon. That morning, Major Giskes took him to a building housing the Abwehr's radio section in The Hague, a large house on Parkstraat. Giskes made a deal with Lauwers. If the Dutchman would make his scheduled transmission at two o'clock, he and Thijs Taconis, who also had been arrested, would be saved from the firing squad. All other captured radio operators, Giskes once again glibly assured Lauwers, had agreed to cooperate. Why, then, should Lauwers persist in his stubborn loyalty to a British organization and lose his life as a result? Finally, Lauwers consented.[5]

Perhaps the German was telling the truth about the other radio operators, thought Lauwers. Certainly he had been rather well treated, under the circumstances, since his arrest. Lauwers pretended to go along with Giskes's proposal. Privately, though, he still hoped that by omitting his security check from any message he sent, as he had been trained to do in a circumstance such as this, he could alert London to the fact that he was now under enemy control.[6]

Lauwers's assigned security check was to be a deliberate error in every sixteenth character in each message he sent. The presence of this error told SOE that all was okay; its absence signaled danger.

Lauwers realized that because he had surrendered his code, the Germans undoubtedly had already deciphered the three messages they had discovered in his pocket. In two of those messages, by coincidence, the sixteenth character had been the letter "O" in "STOP"—the word used in Morse code messages to indicate a period at the end of a sentence. Accordingly, when writing the messages before his capture, Lauwers had employed his security code, inserting deliberate errors in the sixteenth character of each message by changing the word "STOP" to read "STEP" in one message and "STIP" in the other.

So when Giskes, who had already learned of SOE's use of security checks through interrogation of other prisoners, asked Lauwers for his security check, the clever Dutchman explained that his check consisted of misspelling the word "STOP" in every message. He further explained his failure to do so in the third message as a simple oversight. Luckily, Giskes seemed satisfied with this answer.

When the time came for Lauwers to transmit, he began a procedure that he would follow in every message he sent for the Germans throughout his captivity. In every message, he was careful to use "STIP" or "STEP" in place of "STOP" to satisfy Giskes, but he also omitted his true security check—a spelling mistake in every sixteenth character.

Surely the decoders back in England would catch the omissions and know that he was sending under the eyes of the Germans.

When messages from SOE's field agents arrived in London, they were delivered by motorcycle messenger to a team of decoders at a country house just outside the city. After decoding, the messages from the Netherlands were taken to Dutch Section's offices at Norgeby House on London's Baker Street.

When Lauwers's messages were deciphered, they were correctly stamped "SECURITY CHECK OMITTED" and forwarded on to Norgeby House. Upon their arrival at Dutch Section, the deciphered messages were handed to Major Charles Blizzard, a regular army officer who had been attached to SOE only three months earlier and made chief of Dutch Section in February 1942.[7] Blizzard, for reasons that have never been adequately explained, decided to ignore Lauwers's omission of the security check.

Lauwers was shaken, then, when he received the next message from London, announcing the pending arrival of another agent by parachute during the next full moon. When the agent, Lieutenant Arnold Baatson, jumped from a British plane on the night of March 27, German security police were waiting on the ground and arrested him immediately upon landing. Lauwers was then made to signal to London that the agent had arrived safely.

Germany's radio game with SOE's Dutch Section had begun. Within months, some thirteen SOE agents were captured in the same way, including five radio operators.[8]

———

In the summer of 1942, a talented twenty-two-year-old code maker named Leo Marks began working for SOE's Signals Branch. Marks proved to have an unusual gift for code and cipher work, and soon he was putting his skills to work decoding what were called "indecipherables," those messages that, because of a coding error by the radio operator in the field, were scrambled and unreadable when they arrived in London. Virtually every radio operator transmitting from France and other occupied countries of Western Europe, Marks learned, occasionally made such errors.

But never the Dutch operators. Dutch Section seemed to be blessed with radio operators who never made mistakes. There simply were no indecipherables coming from the Netherlands. It was as if, thought

Marks, someone was double-checking every message from Dutch operators before transmission. To Marks, that "someone" could only be the Germans. Moreover, as Marks investigated further, he found that three Dutch Section radio operators—one of them Lieutenant Hubertus Lauwers—were now omitting their security checks, and in all three cases the omissions continued to be ignored by the officers in Dutch Section. Marks, however, young and impetuous, and often viewed by his superiors as a clever but impertinent civilian in uniform, was unable to convince anyone in SOE that there was a problem.[9]

There were other indicators that something had gone terribly wrong in Holland. The most serious warnings came from Great Britain's other secret service. While SOE was responsible for establishing sabotage networks to conduct special operations throughout the Netherlands, it was the task of Britain's Secret Intelligence Service, or SIS, to send espionage agents into the country to spy on the Germans and send intelligence reports back to London. These SIS agents were accompanied by their own radio operators, and a few of these had also been arrested. But when these operators first made contact with London and omitted their security checks, SIS knew they'd been arrested and immediately broke all contact with the operators. Messages soon reached SIS from their agents in the field indicating that the Dutch underground reported at least eight of SOE's agents captured. SIS passed this information on to SOE, but SOE was still not convinced.[10]

By the end of 1942, the Germans had collected forty-three SOE agents—nearly all of the men SOE had put into Holland—and were controlling all communications back to England from fourteen radio operators. By April 1943, another thirteen agents had arrived straight into the hands of the waiting Germans.[11] Through interrogation of these prisoners, all of whom were held at a Catholic seminary in Haaren that was being used as a prison, the Germans had gained extensive knowledge of the operations of SOE's Dutch Section.

Then, on August 30, 1943, two Dutch agents—Lieutenant Johan Ubbink and Sergeant Pieter Dourlein—escaped from Haaren and, after evading the Germans for three months, arrived at the Dutch legation in Berne, Switzerland. There, the two men told of the number of Dutch agents who had been arrested and reported that the Germans knew everything about SOE operations in the Netherlands. Incredibly, when Dourlein and Ubbink returned to London and repeated their story, SOE still refused to believe that their operations in Holland had been compromised, choosing instead to view the escape of the two men as some sort of German trick.

Fortunately, the men of Britain's Special Duty Squadrons—those responsible for flying missions to drop agents and supplies for SOE—had by this time become suspicious enough to halt further operations into Holland.[12]

Major Giskes had enjoyed a bountiful string of successes at the expense of SOE's Dutch Section, even after the section came under a new chief, Seymour Bingham, in February 1943. Not until February 1944 did SOE finally accept the truth, and the total damage was assessed. From ninety sorties flown into Holland by the Special Duty Squadrons over a twenty-month period, the Germans had collected fifteen tons of weapons and supplies and half a million guilders in cash. More than four thousand radio messages had been exchanged between the Dutch Section of SOE and the enemy. Even more devastating, though, was the loss of more than fifty agents, all now imprisoned at Haaren.[13]

SOE's Dutch Section had fallen prey to a counterespionage technique of which the Germans had become masters, a technique they liked to call the *funkspiel* (radio game). Officially, the German counterespionage coup conducted against Britain from Holland was called Operation North Pole. Unofficially, though, Giskes and his men knew it as *das Englandspiel*—the England game. Realizing now that the game was up, Giskes, appropriately on April Fools' Day 1944, used all of the British radio sets still in contact with London to send a final, mocking farewell message to SOE.[14] The Dutch agents held at the Haaren prison were sent to Mauthausen concentration camp, where some were made to work in a quarry while the rest were shot. Only four would survive the war.[15]

The haunting impression left on the British by the North Pole disaster, the shameful stigma of professional incompetence it left, hung like an incubus over the planning offices of SOE and especially the Dutch Section. For the remainder of the war, it would negatively affect how special operations would be conducted in the Netherlands, especially in the 1944 operation to seize a bridgehead over the Lower Rhine at the city of Arnhem.

TWO

THE MAN FROM WASHINGTON

To the men of the 541st Parachute Infantry Regiment at Camp Mackall, North Carolina, it was apparent in the early fall of 1943 that the unit would not soon be going anywhere. The 541st had been created only weeks earlier at Fort Benning, Georgia, and many of its men had only recently completed parachute training. From its inception, the 541st was to be unlike other parachute regiments; its purpose would be to test new airborne warfare equipment and techniques. Because of this, or so it was rumored at the time, the regiment was filled with men chosen for the high scores they had received on the army's intelligence test. Organized on August 12, the regiment quickly filled its ranks through the final sweltering weeks of Georgia summer and into the autumn, and in October the unit moved to Camp Mackall.

Not far from Fort Bragg, a sprawling artillery post built during the last war, Camp Mackall had been carved out of the state's heavily pine-forested Piedmont region during the winter of 1942–43 to accommodate America's new and rapidly expanding airborne force. Well over a thousand wood-frame buildings had gone up—recreation halls, chapels, day-rooms, orderly rooms, mess halls, movie theaters, post exchanges, and canteens. Prefabricated tarpaper-sided huts served as barracks. These stood along unpaved streets that were barely wide enough to accommodate formations of paratroopers running four abreast, doing the airborne shuffle in the dust and the heat and chanting paratrooper ditties that they wouldn't want their mothers to hear.

The men of the 541st learned that other parachute regiments had come to Bragg and Mackall, had joined the new 82nd and 101st Airborne Divisions, and had shipped out to Europe to prepare for combat, the 82nd leaving in April 1943, the 101st in September. Two more recently formed airborne divisions—the 11th and the 17th—continued to fill their ranks with battalions of paratroopers fresh from jump school. But there were no indications that the 541st would join either of these divisions; it seemed destined to continue in its role as a test bed for the new Airborne Command headquartered at Mackall.

On a slow and unseasonably warm October afternoon, shortly after the 541st arrived at Mackall, a telephone rang in the office of Captain John M. Olmsted, the 2nd Battalion's operations officer. The twenty-nine-year-old officer had been busy drafting a training schedule for the following month.

Olmsted picked up the receiver, identified himself, and listened as the caller from regimental headquarters asked if the battalion had any-one who might be interested in hearing about an opportunity for some mysterious assignment. An officer from Washington, it seemed, had ar-rived in camp and wished to speak with any officers interested in leav-ing the 541st. About the only information the caller was able to provide was that the visitor was particularly interested in officers with knowl-edge of a foreign language, especially French. Captain Olmsted quickly spread the word throughout the battalion and soon found three or four interested officers who seemed to fit the requirements.

Officers from throughout the regiment, responding to the an-nouncement, gathered at regimental headquarters to listen to the man from Washington. One of those who attended the briefing, an eager young West Point second lieutenant named Bill Pietsch, soon returned to battalion headquarters, clearly excited by what he had just heard. Pietsch urged Captain Olmsted to go check it out. Although Olmsted did not speak French, he decided that there was no harm in hearing what the stranger had to say.

When his turn came for an interview, Olmsted was ushered into a small room with a plain army desk and two chairs, where he met a tall, rugged-looking, rufous-haired major with shiny parachute wings on his chest just above the ribbon of the Purple Heart. The major invited

Olmsted to sit down and then proceeded, in a very articulate manner, to explain that he was seeking volunteers for an assignment that would involve operations behind enemy lines. Though the likable major made no mention of it, he was from the Office of Strategic Services, or OSS. For the next twenty minutes, he answered Olmsted's questions as best he could. Constrained by the secret nature of the project, he could offer few details about the job. One startling bit of information that the man did share was his judgment that the chances for any volunteer's survival were roughly fifty-fifty. Nevertheless, Olmsted volunteered to be included.

At the conclusion of the interview, Olmsted returned to his office while the major completed his report on the captain. He assessed Olmsted's character to be "excellent" and noted that he "wants action."[1] He further explained that the captain was "capable enough to handle any mission. If not used for one job—should definitely be used for others."[2]

Born in Lake Crystal, Minnesota, on September 23, 1914, John Olmsted had grown up on the move, migrating with his family as his father, a minister, served at one church after another in Nebraska, Kansas, and Colorado. After graduating from high school in Holyoke, Colorado, in 1932, he attended Ottawa University, in Ottawa, Kansas, and later transferred to the University of Wyoming. Then came four years of teaching math and science at the junior and senior high schools in Gering, Nebraska, where he also coached the freshman football, basketball, and track teams. His summers were spent working as a lifeguard at the municipal swimming pool.

In the fall of 1939, at the age of twenty-five, Olmsted joined Company F of the 134th Infantry Regiment, 35th Infantry Division, Nebraska National Guard. The division was called to active federal service in December of the following year and grew from cadre size to full strength at Fort Robinson. It was there, in May 1941, that John Olmsted was commissioned as a second lieutenant.

Immediately after the Japanese attack on the United States base at Pearl Harbor, Hawaii, on December 7, 1941, John Olmsted moved with the 35th Division to Fort Ord, California, where its troops patrolled a sector of the California coast while preparing for service somewhere in the Pacific.

Olmsted remained in California less than a year. He had been promoted to first lieutenant by the time he volunteered for the paratroops in August 1942. After completing jump training at Fort Benning in early

October, he was given command of a company in the 507th Parachute Infantry Regiment, earning a further promotion to captain in early December. He remained with the regiment as it participated in the army's large-scale maneuvers along the Texas-Louisiana border in early 1943, and in May of that year received orders sending him back to Fort Benning to attend the Infantry Officers Advanced Course. He had been assigned to his current job as a battalion operations officer in the newly formed 541st Parachute Infantry Regiment upon graduation in early August.

Since his call to active duty, Captain Olmsted, like the rest of the action-seeking men of the 541st, had remained stateside, following the war only in the papers, gleaning cryptic images of the fighting from the movie newsreels that preceded feature films at theaters. By October 1943, he had been a paratrooper for a year and was eager to get overseas; to him, the assignment the secretive major spoke of seemed a terrific opportunity, regardless of the inherent risks. He accepted the challenge and volunteered.[3]

If action was what Olmsted and the other volunteers sought, they had decided wisely in signing on for the assignment about which the man from Washington was able to tell them so little. Although they didn't know it at the time, the 541st would remain in "strategic reserve," never seeing combat, until being shipped out to the Philippines in July 1945 and immediately disbanded upon its arrival. The men who stepped forward for the work that the major had described as hazardous were seeking action, even the extreme action called for in the elite new units this war had spawned. They were not deterred by talk of the risks involved; rather, they were drawn by the enigmatic nature of the assignment, lured by the uninformative responses to their questions, the secretive manner of the elusive major. The attraction had an almost occult quality, and men who wanted to be the best, and to serve with the best, were drawn to it like raccoons to a sweet corn patch.

All those at Camp Mackall who volunteered for the mysterious assignment, Olmsted included, soon received orders to report to Washington, D.C., for temporary duty. Ahead of them lay weeks of assessment by the OSS staff—an elaborate and demanding process that served as something of a special operations job interview. Qualifications would be tested, motivations examined, and abilities measured to determine who among them would be allowed to enter training for a new special forces unit to be called the Jedburghs. Those who failed to make the cut would be sent back to their units. Captain Olmsted never returned to Camp Mackall.

———

Like John Olmsted, Lieutenant Harvey Allan Todd* had been a high school teacher and football coach before the war. A native of Decatur, hub of the agriculture industry in central Illinois, Todd had graduated from high school in 1934 and gone on to Eureka College, a small Christian school in Illinois, where he majored in history and mathematics. Not a large or widely known school, Eureka did have one alumnus—former student body president Ronald Reagan—who already had become a big name in Hollywood. In fact, Todd played football at Eureka under the same coach Reagan had played for.[4]

Todd received his BA degree from Eureka in 1939 and found a job, at a salary of twelve hundred dollars per year, teaching high school math and science and serving as assistant football coach in the southern Illinois town of Marion.

In May 1941, the twenty-five-year-old Todd found an envelope from the War Department in his mail. The letter he withdrew informed him that he had been selected by the local draft board to represent his friends and neighbors in "the Great National Emergency." He had been drafted. Orders to report for active duty followed a month later, and in late June, Todd entered the army in Chicago. After being officially sworn in as twenty-one-dollar-per-month soldiers, he and the other recruits were trucked to a reception center at Camp Grant, near Rockford, Illinois, where they drew an issue of khaki uniforms and experienced their first mess hall meal. The next morning, the men boarded a troop train bound for Camp Roberts, California, where they were to take their basic training. They settled into their barracks six days later on a hot Fourth of July.

What followed were three months of tough training and maneuvers in the sand and sun-burned grass of central California, where the camp lay in the Salinas River floodplain, its garrison area as flat as a skillet and surrounded by bleak, almost treeless hills. Obstacle courses and grueling road marches with full field packs hardened the men, and Todd lost thirty pounds in the process. He also learned how to use and maintain

———

* In the army, Todd was known as Harvey, but to his family and close friends he was always Allan.

the weapons of the infantryman, qualifying as an expert with the rifle and bayonet, the light machine gun, and the sixty-millimeter mortar. By November, Todd had completed training, earned a second stripe on his sleeve, and was assigned as an instructor with the camp cadre.

Corporal Todd was on a weekend pass when he awoke at a Los Angeles hotel late on the morning of Sunday, December 7, 1941. He soon learned of the Japanese attack on Pearl Harbor and heard that all leaves and passes had been canceled; all military personnel were to report back to their bases immediately. Civilians were eager to help, and when Todd began hitchhiking back to camp, he had no trouble getting a ride.

In the months following America's entry into the war, Californians, as well as officials in Washington, feared that a Japanese attack on the West Coast could come at any time. With the entire coastline exposed and vulnerable, Corporal Todd and the other instructors at Camp Roberts began a tiring routine of drilling recruits during the day and guarding key points along the coast at night.

Then, in May 1942, Todd was shipped across the country to Fort Benning, Georgia, to attend Officer Candidate School. He graduated at the end of August with an infantry second lieutenant's commission, remained at Benning another six weeks to complete the Cannon Company Officer Course, and then was off to join the 8th Infantry Division at Fort Jackson, South Carolina.

For the next seven months, Lieutenant Todd served in a rifle company, learning how to lead troops, as the 8th Division journeyed from one training locale to the next. First came the large Tennessee Maneuvers that fall, more training through the winter at Fort Leonard Wood, Missouri, then off in the spring of 1943 to Camp Laguna, near Yuma, Arizona, for six months of desert training. But Todd yearned for something more challenging, and he soon took an interest in the new airborne divisions then being formed. In short order, he volunteered for jump school and returned to Fort Benning, where the army's parachutists were made, at the end of May.

By August, Lieutenant Todd had completed parachute training and a follow-on two-week camouflage course. He received orders assigning him to the newly formed 541st Parachute Infantry, joining the regiment at about the same time as Captain John Olmsted.

Parachute jumping and camouflage techniques were not all that occupied Allan Todd's mind, though. He also thought of Mandy.

Allan Todd had been raised in the Baptist faith and had attended church regularly throughout his life. One Sunday morning in 1939, back in Marion before he'd entered the army, he attended services at the town's Baptist church. Sitting in the first row of the choir loft were several young, single women. One of them was a local schoolteacher and minister's daughter named Amanda Carlton. Marion was a small place, and the congregation was such that everyone knew all the other members. So when Allan Todd, a stranger in town, walked into church late that Sunday morning all by himself, all the young women in the congregation noticed him. He was tall and handsome and athletically built and didn't appear to be attached. In the front row of the choir loft, young women whispered back and forth, "Who is that?"[5] But no one knew who the stranger was. Todd had caused such a stir that the young women paid little attention to the sermon. At the conclusion of the service, when everyone filed out of the church, he could not be found.

A few weeks later, Todd appeared in church again, and this time Amanda Carlton's father was also present. Though her father was a Baptist minister, he conducted services at churches outside Marion. On this Sunday, the minister conducting the service introduced Allan Todd, the stranger who had caused such a stir during his last visit. When Amanda's father, William Carlton, heard the name, he wondered if the young man was related to another Baptist minister he had known, a much older man named Todd who was no longer alive. After the services, he found the young Todd and introduced himself and asked him if he knew of the minister of the same name. Allan Todd said that the man he was referring to was his grandfather. Todd and Mr. Carlton took a liking to each other and soon became friends.

Amanda Carlton next heard of Allan Todd from a different source. High school football practice had begun, and Amanda's young brother, Bill, often came home telling stories of their new coach, the young man named Todd.

Amanda Lee Carlton was born in Marion, Illinois, where she graduated from Marion Township High School before attending Southern Illinois Normal University, in Carbondale. For the past three years, she had been teaching at a small school just outside Marion. Amanda still lived in her parents' home at 1012 West Main Street, along with her two younger sisters and a younger brother. Her brother, a tall, gangly kid, was just entering Marion High School in the fall of 1939 and was looking forward to playing basketball and football there. Amanda was introduced to

Todd that fall, and she liked the young man's subtle, dry sense of humor. The two began seeing each other regularly.

Allan and Amanda talked about getting married someday, but then Allan was drafted. They made no firm plans because they assumed he would be shipped overseas before long. But by the fall of 1943, Allan Todd had come to the conclusion that he was going to be stuck stateside and might never get to the war. He therefore saw no reason to further delay their marriage. During his time in the army, Allan Todd had gone home on leave often, but by September he had used up all of his accrued leave. So Amanda traveled to Fort Benning, and she and Allan were married in the parsonage of the First Baptist Church in Opelika, Alabama, on September 8, 1943. Later, the officers of Todd's unit hosted a supper in the couple's honor back in Columbus, Georgia, where the newlyweds found a place to live. Five days after their marriage, Todd was allowed a short leave, and the couple went to Atlanta for a brief honeymoon.

By the twentieth of the month, Lieutenant Todd was back in training, this time in Parachute Demolition School, which lasted into October. At about this time, Todd responded to a notice on a bulletin board and attended a briefing given by an officer from Washington who spoke of some exciting assignment opportunity. Fearful that he was destined to spend the entire war attending schools and training troops, Todd added his name to the list of volunteers. Training at the demolition school concluded in October, and soon thereafter Lieutenant Todd and the rest of the 541st Parachute Infantry made the move to Camp Mackall, North Carolina.

In late October, the men who had volunteered for the Jedburgh project began receiving their orders to report to Washington, D.C. At about two o'clock one afternoon, while involved in a field exercise at Camp Mackall, Lieutenant Todd was handed a telegram directing him to report to an address in the nation's capital. He was to leave immediately and should expect to remain in the Washington area on temporary duty for at least three weeks. In fact, he had scarcely more than two hours to pack some things and get to the airport to catch a plane.

Amanda Todd had been out walking around Fayetteville that day, looking for an apartment that she and Allan could move into in order to get out of the boardinghouse where they had temporarily taken a room. She returned to the rooming house that afternoon and was startled to find Allan packing his clothes. He had one large suitcase already packed.

"What are you doing?" she asked.

"I need to leave immediately," said Todd.

"Where are you going?"

"I just received orders to report to Washington, and my plane leaves in about an hour. I have to be on that plane."

"Why do you have to go to Washington?"

"I don't know."

"What will you be doing there?"

"I don't know." Todd had little knowledge of what lay ahead, no notion of the dangers to come. He knew only that his urgent call to Washington was in some way related to the hazardous assignment for which he had volunteered. But he had little understanding of what that job entailed, knew nothing yet of a Dutch city called Arnhem.

"When will you be back?" asked Amanda.

"I don't know."

Suddenly Amanda realized that she would be left in a strange town, without Allan and without any friends and with a car she had never driven. And she had no way of knowing how long he would be gone. "What am I supposed to do?" she asked.

"I don't know that either," replied Todd.[6]

THREE

HAZARDOUS DUTY

S econd Lieutenant George M. Verhaeghe was a twenty-five-year-old midwesterner of Flemish descent, a native of Mishawaka, Indiana, just east of South Bend. Before joining the army in May 1943, he had worked as a guard at a defense plant and as a cellar man in a brewery. Shortly after enlisting, he had gone to Officer Candidate School at Fort Benning, Georgia, and was commissioned in the infantry in July 1943. Like Allan Todd, George Verhaeghe was married. His wife, Hermina, remained at their home on South Nash Street in South Bend.

In September, Lieutenant Verhaeghe arrived at Camp Fannin, near Tyler, Texas, and was assigned to an infantry training battalion. Fannin was one of the scores of new camps that had sprung up across the United States in the first years of the war to train the millions of young men and women who would enter the service until victory was won. At its peak, the Infantry Replacement Training Center at Fannin, which opened in the spring of 1943 and was only one of several such training centers, produced between thirty-five thousand and forty thousand soldiers every four months to replace combat losses in frontline units overseas.[1]

Verhaeghe was summoned to camp headquarters on October 22, 1943, for an hour-long interview with a civilian from Washington. The man asked several questions about Verhaeghe's background and interests, and he inquired about the young infantry officer's foreign language ability. (Verhaeghe was a Flemish speaker.) Then he spoke of an elite unit that was being formed, and he told of the difficult and dangerous training that those selected for the unit would go through. He very generally described the hazardous nature of the combat missions the unit would carry out behind enemy lines. When asked if he was interested in being considered for assignment to the unit, Verhaeghe volunteered at once. He soon received orders to report to Washington for a three-week period of temporary duty.

Verhaeghe reached Washington on October 24, just two days after his interview at Camp Fannin; Captain John Olmsted arrived two days later. Lieutenant Harvey Allan Todd arrived at the Washington airport on a flight from Fayetteville, North Carolina, that same week.

All Jedburgh officer volunteers were instructed to report to the adjutant general's office in room 1048 of the Munitions Building. Construction on the huge, impressive new limestone-faced Pentagon building on the south bank of the Potomac had begun in August 1941 and was completed in January 1943. Although the War and Navy Departments had begun occupying the building as early as April 1942, many of their administrative offices were still located in a complex of three-story white concrete buildings surrounding the Reflecting Pool near the Lincoln Memorial. Two of these buildings, stretching from 17th Street to 21st Street along the south side of Constitution Avenue, were the Main Navy and Munitions Buildings. Officers recruited by OSS for the Jedburghs in the fall of 1943 entered a part of the Munitions Building that occupied the same general area where the Vietnam Veterans Memorial sits today. There, in room 1048, a major representing OSS saw to their administrative processing.

The next stop for the Jedburgh officer candidates was a place called Q Building, a few blocks away at 25th and E streets, where they found a white two-story structure with marble columns. The handsome building, once home to the National Institute of Health, now served as OSS headquarters. It was here that most of the new men first heard of the Office of Strategic Services.

All men recruited for the Jedburgh project were attached to OSS for three weeks' temporary duty. Before they were selected for permanent assignment to OSS, they would undergo a few weeks of assessment. Designed to test their physical condition as well as their mental abilities, the period of assessment determined who among the volunteers was deemed suitable for the Jedburgh project.

The idea for the type of organization these volunteers had joined began in the minds of government and military officials in England in the early years of World War II. Great Britain had suffered terribly in World War I, with nearly a million young men killed and more than two million wounded in savage trench warfare. As another war loomed in the late 1930s, several officials sought an alternative form of warfare, one that might offer greater economy in terms of national treasure and lives.

In July 1940, the British War Cabinet approved the charter for an organization called the Special Operations Executive, or SOE. It was an endeavor with one purpose, that of supporting underground resistance movements that were beginning to form in the German-occupied countries of Western Europe. Prime Minister Winston Churchill, seeing this as a means for the people of occupied Europe to take an active part in their own liberation, provided succinct instructions to the organization's newly appointed director, Dr. Hugh Dalton, then serving as minister of economic warfare. Churchill said simply, "And now, set Europe ablaze."[2]

As SOE quickly grew from a concept to a working enterprise, a country section was formed to coordinate support to resistance groups in each occupied nation of Europe. Busiest among the country sections from the start was F Section, responsible for providing arms, training, and organizational advice to the many resistance groups within France. Responsibility for such activities in the Netherlands fell to D Section. Both sections soon began parachuting agents into the two countries to organize networks of trained and equipped saboteurs. At the same time, another British organization, the Secret Intelligence Service,* bore the responsibility of infiltrating agents into these countries for the purpose of espionage.

A similar effort was under way across the Atlantic, where President Franklin D. Roosevelt invoked several measures in conjunction with his declaration of a limited national emergency in late May 1941. One such measure was the establishment, in July, of an organization titled the Office of the Coordinator of Information. The purpose of COI, as the developing organization was known, was that of both secret intelligence

---

* SIS, also known as MI-6.

and special operations, thus combining in one establishment the functions of both the British SOE and SIS. Roosevelt appointed fifty-eight-year-old William Joseph Donovan, the man who had recommended the creation of such an organization, to be director of the COI. Donovan had earned a Medal of Honor and a Distinguished Service Cross as a battalion commander in the famed "Fighting 69th" Infantry Regiment in World War I. A Columbia Law School classmate of Roosevelt's, Donovan had become a successful Wall Street attorney and millionaire in the postwar years.

During the 1930s, Donovan embarked on several secret fact-finding missions for the president, traveling around the world to visit countries soon to be embroiled in war, observing military exercises, witnessing the employment of new weapons systems, and meeting with leaders in countries soon to be at war with America. In July 1940, Donovan went to England for a firsthand look at Britain's war preparations and to report back to Roosevelt with his assessment of that country's readiness to fight Nazi Germany, which had just invaded, defeated, and occupied France and the Low Countries—Belgium, Luxembourg, and the Netherlands. He met with King George VI and with Prime Minister Churchill, and he learned much in discussions with Colonel Stewart Menzies, head of SIS, and Colonel Colin Gubbins of the newly formed SOE. Based on what he learned, Donovan returned to the United States and prepared a report to the president in which he recommended that America establish an organization to replicate the capabilities of the two British entities.

Development of the organization known as COI was well under way by May 1942, when Colin Gubbins, by then a brigadier, met with senior British Army officials to discuss the role SOE might play in the liberation of Western Europe. A concept prepared by SOE's staff was the main topic of conversation. Lieutenant Colonel Peter Wilkinson, principal author of the concept, proposed the formation of several three-man teams of specially trained soldiers to be parachuted deep behind enemy lines. These special forces would operate in uniform, in contrast with the normal practice employed by SOE and SIS of dropping agents in civilian clothing. Their purpose would be that of organizing, arming, and training bands of resistance fighters to conduct guerrilla warfare against German occupation forces. Equally important, they would serve as a liaison between such groups and Allied headquarters, coordinating resistance operations with those of Allied ground forces following a cross-Channel invasion of occupied Europe.[3]

Given the go-ahead, SOE proceeded with plans for the special force, and in July the code name "Jedburgh," selected at random from a list of preapproved code names, was applied to the project. As the Jedburgh plan evolved, it eventually called for 150 teams, each including a British officer and a French, Belgian, or Dutch officer, depending on the country where the team would operate, as well as an enlisted radio operator.

In the United States, the COI received a new name in June 1942. William Donovan's organization was now the Office of Strategic Services. In December, a month after Anglo-American forces went ashore in North Africa to battle Hitler's Afrika Korps, OSS was activated as a military organization and placed under the direction of the Joint Chiefs of Staff. A formal agreement with SOE, completed a month later, gave OSS access to SOE's training facilities and led to full collaboration between the two organizations in the secret war against Germany. The agreement also called for OSS to begin fielding its own language-qualified special forces.

Initial OSS recruiting efforts were aimed at building thirty-man operational groups, each group oriented toward operations in a particular country. Recruiters found many men for the operational groups among the thousands of soldiers who came from recent immigrant families, first- or second-generation Americans who were raised in homes where English was a second language. With such men, OSS formed Italian, French, Norwegian, and Greek groups. And when SOE invited their OSS counterparts to participate in the Jedburgh project, a new recruiting effort was launched to find fifty officers and fifty enlisted radio operators to serve as the American contingent. Rather than each team including a British officer, as originally planned, each would now include a British or an American officer.

A staff officer from the London OSS branch, Major Franklin Canfield, an attorney in civilian life, traveled to the United States to organize the American Jedburgh recruiting effort. In Washington, OSS headquarters provided officers to assist with the search for qualified men. To find officer volunteers, recruiters in September 1943 circulated among the many U.S. Army camps in the southern states as far west as Texas. They sought men who were physically athletic, men who had some knowledge of languages such as French or Dutch or Flemish, men who were self-reliant, confident in their own abilities.

For the radio operators, recruiters visited three schools operated by the U.S. Army Signal Corps—the High Speed Radio Operator School at

Fort Monmouth, New Jersey; the Morse Code School at Camp Crowder, Missouri; and the Army Air Forces Radio Operator and Mechanics School at Scott Field in Illinois.

As a result of this recruiting effort, around one hundred prospective Jedburgh officers and more than sixty enlisted radio operators received orders to report in October for temporary duty in Washington, D.C.

Meanwhile, Britain's SOE ran its own Jedburgh recruiting campaign. More than sixty radio operators volunteered, primarily from the armored regiments. Following a round of testing and screening at a camp near Oxford, about fifty radiomen reported to Special Training School No. 54, west of London, in October.[4]

Recruiting of British officers didn't begin until late October, when volunteers were beckoned by notices posted on unit bulletin boards throughout England. Those who expressed interest underwent physical and psychological screening, after which fifty-five candidates were selected and sent to Milton Hall, a mansion north of London near the town of Peterborough.

One more component of the three-man teams remained to be found. According to the Jedburgh plan, each team was to include an officer who was a native of the country in which the team would operate. Accordingly, requests went out to the relevant Allied governments in exile for suitable volunteers. French officers and radio operators came mostly from Free French forces in North Africa; Dutch and Belgian candidates were found among the forces of those countries formed from the hundreds of men who had been able to reach England at the time of the German invasion of their homelands.

In Washington, officer and enlisted volunteers arrived through October, individually or in small groups, by train at Union Station or by plane at the city's new National Airport. Once they had completed their administrative in-processing, military vehicles transported the men to a site in the Maryland countryside just northwest of the city. Army trucks, buses, or jeeps dropped the Jedburgh candidates in front of the impressive clubhouse at the Congressional Country Club.

Opened nearly twenty years earlier as a playground for government officials and business leaders, the club had played host to many golf tournaments, tennis matches, social events, and horse shows. In March 1943, the government leased the property for the duration of the war, and the club became Area F, a training site for OSS. Almost overnight, the elegant four-story early Italianate clubhouse was transformed into the nerve center of a military installation. The building's palatial grand ballroom became an expansive classroom furnished with folding chairs and blackboards. The main dining room emerged as an army mess hall, the bar an officers' lounge, and the magnificent indoor swimming pool, boarded over, provided additional work space for the training staff.

Captain John Olmsted, along with the other officer candidates, found that their billets at Area F were pyramidal army tents with wooden floors, rows of which stood on ground covered with crushed cinders. The tents, along with several Quonset huts, masked an area that once was a well-maintained lawn and tennis courts. An obstacle course and training grounds now occupied the 406-acre golf course, and across River Road to the north stood pistol and machine-gun ranges.

During their stay at Area F, the Jedburgh candidates underwent physical testing and psychological assessment by a staff whose job it was to weed out those judged to be unsuited for unconventional warfare. For several days, the men filled out questionnaires and sat through interviews conducted by a staff of psychologists and psychiatrists. Those determined to be unsuited for the job at hand would be returned to their regular units.

Physical training, patterned after that of the British commandos, provided a welcome break from the paperwork and interviews. Training days began early and often lasted until midnight, and they were anything but dull. Mornings began with runs of up to five miles, rope climbing, chin-ups, and push-ups. Then came training in tasks such as building rope bridges over a stream. Classes on map reading, orienteering, and similar topics filled the day's schedule. Later, darkness was a time for challenging night compass runs, exercises in raids and ambushes, and training in stealthy infiltration techniques.

On an evening in early November, those selected to remain in the program boarded army trucks with canvas cargo-compartment covers tightly buttoned down. Of the roughly one hundred Jedburgh officer candidates who had reported to Area F in October, only fifty-eight remained. Among those selected were Captain Olmsted, Lieutenant Todd, and Lieutenant Verhaeghe.[5] Now trucks carried them northward on Highway 15.

Near the town of Thurmont, around sixty miles northwest of Washington, the trucks turned onto a dirt road that ran through a heavily wooded area of the Catoctin Mountains. They passed through a gate guarded by a U.S. Marine and continued along the narrow trail until they came to a place called Camp Greentop, once a camp for handicapped children. Like the Congressional Country Club, Camp Greentop had been taken over by OSS as a training area.

It was now known as Area B, a place for advanced training in hand-to-hand combat, surreptitious infiltration, close-quarters shooting, and demolitions. Nestled in the scenic Catoctin Mountain ridge of northern Maryland, Greentop was awash in the reds and oranges and yellows of autumn. The camp itself consisted of log cabins, complete with stone fireplaces and indoor plumbing, and a superb mess hall.

Training days began at the crack of dawn and often continued until well after dark. The Jedburgh trainees received instruction on explosives and demolitions, communications, fieldcraft, first aid, hand-to-hand combat, tradecraft, weapons, night patrolling, map reading, and cross-country navigation.

Instructors and trainees alike were careful to steer clear of an adjacent camp farther up the road to the east. It was a camp that had been used for Boy Scout and Girl Scout outings in the prewar years. But now it was enclosed by a ten-foot fence with a barbed-wire overhang. Sentry booths equipped with telephones and floodlights stood at regular intervals along the perimeter. Marines, accompanied by intimidating guard dogs, continually patrolled the area surrounding the camp. This was President Franklin D. Roosevelt's secret weekend retreat, a place he called Shangri La. A decade later, President Dwight D. Eisenhower would rename it Camp David.

Hand-to-hand combat instruction at Area B was given by Major William Ewart Fairbairn, a British officer on loan to OSS. The fifty-eight-year-old Fairbairn was a thirty-year veteran of the Shanghai police force in China, where he had learned the fighting skills needed to survive in the city's tough waterfront district. To the surprise of the strong young Jeds, the five-foot-ten-inch, 170-pound Fairbairn could toss them around with relative ease. In addition to unarmed fighting, the deceptively strong and agile man with the horn-rimmed glasses trained the men in silent killing techniques, shooting, and knife fighting with a specially designed foot-long stiletto.[6]

Fairbairn's weapons-training method featured forest trails where spring-loaded silhouette targets jumped up from behind bushes and a house where cardboard German soldiers sprang from doors in dimly lit hallways. Students learned to react instinctively, firing two quick shots into the target with their forty-five-caliber automatic pistols and, when necessary, rapidly changing magazines on the move.

The men learned how to handle explosives safely and acquired demolition skills by blasting trees and walls and old cars. Physical training continued throughout the stay at Area B, as the men pushed themselves to break personal records in push-ups and obstacle course runs.

On Thanksgiving Day, the men enjoyed a five-course meal with all the trimmings. Then December came, and the training days became less strenuous. Men found more time to relax, even enjoying occasional passes to visit Washington or New York or Baltimore. Athletes among the trainees took advantage of their free time to compete in sports.

In a pickup football game one day, Lieutenant Verhaeghe was playing end, a position he had once played at the University of Notre Dame. On one play, the big midwesterner went out for a pass. Just as he was about to catch the ball, a wiry young man in the defensive backfield came up from behind Verhaeghe, leapt up the lieutenant's back, and reached over him to knock the ball away before it could be caught. The man making the terrific defensive play was a Jedburgh radio operator, Technician 3rd Grade Willard W. "Bud" Beynon, a much smaller man than Verhaeghe. Later in the game, another pass came to Verhaeghe. This time, Beynon tracked Verhaeghe as he ran his pass pattern. Just as the lieutenant went into the air to make the catch, Beynon dropped to his hands and knees behind the receiver, causing Verhaeghe to come crashing to the ground on his back, jarring the ball loose. Verhaeghe leapt to his feet, glared at Beynon, and said, "You son of a bitch; I'll get you for that!"[7] Beynon just laughed, but Verhaeghe would remember the scrappy little noncom.

During their final weeks at Area B, the Jedburgh officers and men—the group was now down to about half the number of those who had arrived at Area F back in October—underwent administrative and medical processing for overseas assignment. They received inoculations and drew equipment, including special cold-weather clothing, wristwatches, Fairbairn knives, and forty-five-caliber pistols. They were not told when they would be moving out.

One night in early December, the Jedburgh officers went to bed after enjoying a steak dinner, only to be awakened at two in the morning. Trucks arrived and carried the officers to a railroad station, where they boarded a northbound train. In accordance with orders, the men wore their newly issued cold-weather gear and kept the window curtains in the railroad cars drawn. At around ten, the train arrived at New York's Grand Central Terminal, where the men got off and marched with packs and full combat gear across 42nd Street to board "deuce-and-a-halves"—army two-and-a-half-ton trucks—that carried them to the New York Port of Embarkation at Fort Hamilton in Brooklyn.

After a few days of further processing and waiting, the officers were mustered on a cold, overcast night and put aboard a ferry that took them up the Hudson and delivered them to Pier 90 at Manhattan's West Side passenger ship terminal.

Docked at the pier was the Cunard–White Star line's HMS *Queen Elizabeth,* one of several peacetime ocean liners that had been converted to troopships for the duration of the war. The *Queen Elizabeth* and her sister ship, the *Queen Mary,* were used to transport thousands of American servicemen to the British Isles. Each of the great luxury liners was more than a thousand feet in length. They had been stripped of their luxurious furnishings and carpeting, though the huge map of the North Atlantic that adorned a wall of the first-class dining room in both ships, used to track the progress of peacetime voyages, remained. Passenger cabins, even the drained swimming pools, had been fitted out with rows of wooden and metal bunks stacked three or four high. Added to these were more than twelve thousand fold-down canvas bunks called "standee" berths. Additional lavatories and showers had been added to accommodate the large numbers of troops. The *Queens* had each been designed to carry slightly more than two thousand passengers and a crew of a thousand in peacetime. With the wartime conversion, each was capable of carrying a full fifteen-thousand-man division. The roughly two thousand portholes on each ship had been blackened, and the ship exteriors had been painted entirely in battleship gray.

The fifty-five Jedburgh officers shouldered their duffel bags and formed a line to board the *Queen Elizabeth.* Each man received a mess card and a card indicating his berthing assignment. When they located their cabins on board, lieutenants found that rooms built to accommodate two people in peacetime now quartered six to a dozen men in bunk bed–style steel cots. Barracks bags and other gear quickly filled what space remained. Lieutenant George Verhaeghe found himself in a crowded six-man cabin; Lieutenant Allan Todd was in a cramped berth amidships.

Early the next morning, December 14, 1943, tugboats pushed the

Queen Elizabeth back into the Hudson. The giant ship's funnels billowed smoke into the cold and rain-threatening darkness as the *Queen* drifted down the river and into the Atlantic.

Although the North Atlantic was always rough in December, and the ship plowed through heavy seas at times, there were no storms during the crossing and the voyage was relatively smooth. The Jedburgh officers ate well and spent much of their time clannishly congregating in the officers' lounge.

Daily lifeboat drills broke some of the tedium, confused officers and troops falling out in life jackets, the ship's crew manning antiaircraft guns, deck guns, and rocket launchers that had been installed throughout the ship. Some men were concerned about the U-boat threat, but the *Queens'* cruising speed of around twenty-eight knots was more than double that of a surfaced submarine and four times a U-boat's submerged speed. As an added defensive measure, the *Queens* steamed in a zigzag pattern.

A destroyer escort met the *Queen Elizabeth* as she approached the British Isles. The troopship entered the Firth of Clyde, on Scotland's west coast, and anchored off the seaside town of Gourock. On the afternoon of December 20, the American Jedburgh officers debarked in the chilly air and were taken to a warehouse in town. After dark, they climbed aboard trucks that carried them to a railroad siding where they boarded a northbound train. A day later, having changed trains twice, the men arrived at a British commando training area near the coastal town of Arisaig, in northwestern Scotland. The officers were divided into three groups and billeted in three large, comfortable old homes maintained as trainee barracks by Britain's Special Operations Executive—Garramoor House, Inverie House, and Traigh House—nestled in the picturesque but barren Scottish countryside.

Shortly afterward, the American Jedburgh radio operators arrived aboard the *Queen Mary* and were immediately transported to a communications school west of London.

FOUR

HIGHLANDS INTERLUDE

On Christmas Eve, the American Jedburgh officers enjoyed a game of touch football and later walked four or five miles to a village to celebrate the holiday. There, at a charming resort hotel, they found drink and female companionship. The locals welcomed them to a lively Christmas party, followed by a three-mile hike to a charming old stone church for midnight services.[1]

British officers and men assigned as instructors for the Americans also served as the staff at the three houses where the men were billeted. The newcomers were surprised on Christmas morning when a batman, as the British called their orderlies, woke them and offered cups of strong English tea. Crawling from bed, Captain John Olmsted found the hot beverage a welcome contrast to the cold floor.

The next few days were spent in basic commando training, with hours of pistol firing, hand-to-hand combat drills, and long hikes through the Scottish hills. When Sunday arrived, Olmsted and some of the others hiked to nearby Torbet Bay, where they crossed in a boat to visit their buddies staying at Inverie House.

British officers on the Jedburgh staff in London insisted that all non-British Jedburgh candidates pass through the same assessment and selection process as the British candidates, regardless of similar assessments conducted previously. On the last day of December, the American officers traveled by truck and train to London to appear before the SOE Jedburgh assessment board.

After their arrival in London that evening, Captain Olmsted and a group of fellow Jeds wandered the blacked-out streets, seeing what little they could of the great city and ending up at one of the Red Cross clubs that catered to servicemen and -women from all branches. Later that night, the Luftwaffe* staged a small air raid on the city, and the Jeds watched as British antiaircraft batteries went into action. To Olmsted, the raid seemed a distant threat until one bomber dropped pathfinder flares nearby, and the Americans soon experienced a stick of bombs "walking" down the street, the nearest exploding about a hundred yards from where the Jeds were billeted. In the morning, Olmsted and several others searched the streets for antiaircraft shell fragments to keep as souvenirs of their first bombing.

———

At a place the Jeds called "the booby hatch," the Americans underwent the screening by SOE's assessment board to satisfy the British that they were fit, physically and psychologically, for the work ahead.

SOE assessments were aimed at determining a candidate's character and his ability to operate in stressful situations. They typically included three components—the stress interview, the construction problem, and the brook test. The stress interview, conducted under conditions simulating a hostile interrogation by captors, evaluated the candidate's emotional stability under severe strain. At the conclusion of the interview, the subject might be told that he had failed, allowing the examiner an opportunity to study the candidate's physical and emotional reaction to rejection.

The construction problem assessed an individual's tolerance of frustration. The candidate was given a number of large wooden blocks and dowels of various lengths that fit into circular holes in the blocks. The examiner instructed the student to build a cube of specific dimensions. Two enlisted soldiers (actually members of the assessment board) were available to assist the candidate, but they operated under secret instructions to obstruct progress and to annoy the officer in other ways, being anything but helpful.

* German air force.

Finally, the brook test evaluated how innovative and resourceful a candidate could be. Four to seven candidates were taken to a shallow meadow stream about eight feet in width. The examiner pointed out a pile of short boards, none of which was long enough to bridge the stream, lying near the bank. There were also three lengths of rope, a log, a pulley, and a small boulder. The candidates learned that the log replicated a "delicate range finder" and the boulder a "box of percussion caps." The stream, they were told, was a raging torrent too deep to ford and too wide to jump across. The group was given ten minutes to devise a method of transporting the range finder and the percussion caps to the far side of the stream. In making his assessment, the examiner considered the time it took to reach a solution. Extra points were awarded to anyone displaying exceptional initiative and leadership.[2]

At the conclusion of these tests, the assessment board developed an amazingly accurate profile of each officer's characteristics. As a result, only thirty-three of the American officers remained in the Jedburgh project.[3] Additional candidates were recruited from U.S. forces in Great Britain and the Mediterranean to round out the American contingent.

Those officers chosen to continue in the Jedburgh program returned to London, where they spent another night before moving on to their next training site. The entire pool of Jedburgh officer selectees—British, French, Dutch, Belgian, and American—was divided equally among the three locations, where they would train until the Jedburgh training center at Milton Hall, near Peterborough, was completed and ready for them to occupy. The three groups were reunited briefly at the British Airborne School for an abbreviated five-day course in parachute jumping.

Those among the Americans who had already completed the U.S. Army's parachute training at Fort Benning had to adopt Britain's different style of jumping. Paratroopers in the U.S. military jumped from a door in the side of the airplane's fuselage. Jumpers wore two parachutes—a main chute on their backs and a backup "reserve" chute on their chests. Now these men had to learn the art of dropping through a hole in the floor of the aircraft while wearing only one parachute.

Also new to the Americans was the array of training apparatuses used at the British school. One device, called an air brake, introduced jumpers to the British method. A platform stood thirty to forty feet above the ground. In the center of the platform was a hole the same size as the exit hole in an aircraft. Each trainee, in turn, sat at the edge of the hole, just as they would do in a plane. The jumper wore a harness that was connected to a slender cable wrapped around a free-running windlass. At either end of the axle of the windlass was a huge paddlelike fixture. On order, the trainee pushed off, snapping to a rigid position of attention as he dropped through the hole. As the paddles spun on the axle, the wind resistance created a braking action, allowing the jumper to hit the ground only about half as hard as if he had jumped without being connected to the contraption.

Instructors ensured that each man grasped the sides of his trousers and threw back his head as he dropped through the hole. Grasping the trousers reduced the chance, during an actual parachute jump, of flailing arms and legs that could cause the jumper to somersault through the air before the chute opened, possibly becoming entangled in the parachute's suspension lines. To ensure that the jumper kept his knees together, instructors placed a handkerchief between the jumper's knees; the handkerchief had to be held in place until it was removed by an instructor on the ground after the trainee landed.

Throwing the head back when dropping through the hole was of grave importance. If this was not executed and timed perfectly, the jumper's feet would catch the plane's slipstream and be thrown backward, violently forcing the head forward. When the nose smacked into the forward rim of the hole, there was a resounding whack. This the British termed "ringing the bell."

The Jeds made their first actual jump from an old "Wimpy," a Vickers Wellington twin-engine bomber converted for parachute operations. Trainees left the plane in "slow pairs"—two men jumping on each pass of the plane over the field.

A new challenge was ahead of the Jeds the next day, as they were scheduled to make a night jump from a tethered balloon. Parachutists dropped one at a time through a hole in the floor of a basket suspended from a balloon floating six hundred feet above the ground. Americans who had gone through jump training at the U.S. Army Parachute School at Fort Benning were accustomed to the definite jolt to the shoulders that was felt when their chute opened. As jumpers stepped from the plane into the slipstream, they were thrown rearward, and the parachute opened comparatively quickly, within sixty to ninety feet of the plane, aided by the slipstream. Jumpers were trained to count, "One thousand, two thousand, three thousand . . ." and were prepared to pull the ripcord on their emergency chute if the main chute didn't soon open. On a balloon jump, the parachutist fell straight down, uninterrupted, for a distance of 150 to 200 feet.

Captain John Olmsted's four-man group climbed into the basket and began the ascent. Little was said on the way up. When they reached the established drop height, the first jumper took his place in the hole. Almost at once Olmsted realized that numbers one, two, and three were gone, and he found himself sitting in the jump position. He pushed off and dropped through the hole. Olmsted instinctively began to count and reached seven thousand before giving up hope of his chute opening. He was sure he had "bought it." Suddenly, with barely a tug at all, his chute opened and he drifted slowly to earth.[4]

The group's third and final training jump was again made from the "Wimpy" and proved somewhat anticlimactic. Jump training concluded on January 27, and all officers were released for another two-day pass to London before moving on to Milton Hall.

February began with all Jedburgh trainees convening at Milton Hall, the newly completed Jedburgh training center near Peterborough, some seventy-five miles north of London. Many officers were billeted in the estate's old mansion; the remainder occupied newly constructed wooden barracks on the grounds. Joining the officers were the radio operators, who had remained at the wireless operator school west of London since their initial selection. Representatives of SOE's assessment board had gone to the school to conduct an assessment of all radio operator candidates at that location. Milton Hall would be the Jeds' home until most missions had returned from the field in the fall.

Early on their first morning at Milton Hall, British batmen entered the officers' sleeping area with morning tea. Some greeted the batmen with a grumpy "Good morning," while others responded with "Get the hell out of here with that blasted tea."[5]

The men were directed outside to stand muster in the damp, cold darkness of the early morning, with the British sergeant major of the training center shouting unintelligible orders to men of five nationalities. All but the British Jeds largely ignored him. Another attempt at getting the group into a military formation, this time by the commanding officer, proved equally unsuccessful. The Jeds later speculated that the fact that they had volunteered for what was considered by many to be a suicide mission was the only reason they were allowed to get away with such behavior.

During the next few days, friendships began to form among the different national groups. Initially, indications were that all of the Jeds would operate in France, even the Belgian and Dutch personnel, many of whom spoke French fluently. There had been no mention of operations in their homelands.

Through the month of February, the men underwent physical training and basic commando-type instruction. There were classes in silent killing, clandestine radio, Morse code, map reading, and fieldcraft. Even nights were often spent in demanding training exercises.

In demolition classes, the men learned how to use plastic explosives—tying the end of a length of explosive Primacord into knots and embedding the knotted end in the puttylike substance, molding the explosive around the knot. As training progressed, students learned the most effective methods for destroying railway tracks and trestles, bridges and canal locks, and key nodes of electrical distribution systems such as transformer stations and high-tension-wire pylons.

Weapons training familiarized the men with the American Browning light machine gun and a French machine gun, as well as the American Thompson, German Schmeisser, and British Sten submachine guns. In a newly built shooting house, the men fired automatic pistols and revolvers from several countries.

The staff at Milton Hall resorted to an unusual method of forming the operational three-man Jedburgh teams, allowing the men to find their own teammates. Each team began with a partnership formed by a British or American officer and a French, Belgian, or Dutch officer. Later, the two officers would select a radio operator to join them. As the weeks of training progressed, tension rose as the men competed continuously for the partner of their choice. French officers were in high demand because their homeland was, as far as any of the men knew, the only projected area of operations. As this "courtship" period continued, officers who agreed to be partners were officially recognized as such when their "marriage" was announced on the bulletin board. If a marriage didn't work out, notice of a "divorce" was posted and the officers involved sought new partners.

On several field exercises, Captain John Olmsted had worked alongside a twenty-nine-year-old Dutch officer, Major Henk Brinkgreve, who had come to the Jeds from No. 2 Dutch Troop of No. 10 Inter-Allied Commando. The two became good friends and spent much time together. When the men learned that the Jedburgh plan would be extended to include Belgium and the Netherlands, Brinkgreve asked Olmsted to go to Holland with him, and Olmsted agreed.

That same day, the remaining Dutch officers—Captain Jaap Staal, Captain Arie Bestebreurtje, and Captain Jacobus Groenewoud, all of the Royal Netherlands Army—also found teammates.

Captain Staal formed a partnership with Captain McCord Sollenberger of the U.S. Army. Born on September 24, 1920, Sollenberger was a public relations man in Maryland before the war. He enlisted from Baltimore in May 1942, began Officer Candidate School in September, and received a commission as a cavalry officer upon graduation in December of that year. A fluent French speaker, Sollenberger served as a troop officer and troop commander at the Cavalry Replacement Training Center at Fort Riley, Kansas, through 1943 until volunteering as a Jedburgh candidate. The thirty-three-year-old had a wife, Katherine, back in Baltimore.

Lieutenant George Verhaeghe, the big Flemish-speaking American, linked up with the twenty-eight-year-old Bestebreurtje. The rusty-blond Dutch captain was born in Rotterdam in 1916, in the middle of World War I. His family had also lived in Berlin for a time, and in 1935 his father, a businessman named Anton D. Bestebreurtje, moved the family to Zurich, Switzerland, because of a job transfer. Arie Bestebreurtje had twice qualified for the Olympics as a speed skater and was an alternate on the Dutch team at the 1936 games, though he did not compete. He graduated from the University of Zurich with a degree in international law in 1940 and married Australia-born Gertrude Maud Bersch that same year. At the outset of the war, Anton Bestebreurtje and his family left Switzerland and made their way to England by way of Portugal. While Arie's parents and three sisters continued on to New York, he and his new bride remained in England. There, he joined the exiled Dutch army in the spring of 1941, serving with the Royal Netherlands "Princess Irene" Brigade, a unit attached to the British Army. He attended the Royal Military College in London from 1941 to 1942.

Last, the youthful-looking Captain Jacobus "Jaap" Groenewoud paired off with Lieutenant Allan Todd. Groenewoud, who wore thick-lensed spectacles, came to the Jedburghs in the most roundabout way. Born in Amsterdam on November 8, 1916, Groenewoud was drafted into the Royal Netherlands Army in 1935 but was immediately discharged when he failed the physical examination because of poor eyesight. Two years later, he was declared unfit to ever serve in his country's armed forces. Shortly before the Germans invaded the Netherlands in May 1940, he left his homeland to live in South Africa, where he took a job as an accountant in December of that year. But on September 25, 1941, he was declared to be fit for duty in the United Kingdom. He arrived in England in February 1942, where he joined the Princess Irene Brigade. Shortly afterward, Groenewoud underwent training to be a reserve officer and received his commission in October 1942. He was then assigned as a liaison officer to the British Army and was attached to a Canadian battalion of the Black Watch. He began an officer training program at Aldershot in December, and in August 1943 he transferred to the 76th Home Guard Division. He was promoted to first lieutenant in February 1944 and assigned as a platoon commander in the 18th Welsh Regiment, where he served briefly before being selected for Jedburgh training.

Each pair of officers chose a radio operator, usually after working briefly in the field with several different operators. When they found a man they particularly liked and who worked well with them, they invited him to join their team.

Brinkgreve and Olmsted chose nineteen-year-old British Sergeant John "Bunny" Austin, who had served previously with Brinkgreve in the No. 10 Inter-Allied Commando unit. Austin was born in Castleconnell, Ireland, on August 27, 1923. He enlisted in the British Army at age eighteen and served initially with the Royal Berkshire Regiment. In 1942, he joined the Small Scale Raiding Force (SSRF, or No. 62 Commando) and participated with that unit in a raid on the Channel Islands. Late the following year, he volunteered for the Jedburghs.[6]

Twenty-nine-year-old Technical Sergeant James R. Billingsley, an American, joined the team of Sollenberger and Staal. Billingsley, the son of a minister, was born in Romney, West Virginia, on February 25, 1915. After graduation from high school, he attended college for a year, studying preengineering. He worked for two years as a broadcast transmitter operator, radio repairman, and studio engineer for radio station WWNY in his hometown of Watertown, New York. He enlisted in July 1943, leaving his wife, Doris, in Philadelphia, and volunteered for the Jedburghs in October while in training at the U.S. Army Signal Corps Replacement Training Center, Camp Crowder, Missouri. In February 1944, Billingsley was promoted to technical sergeant.[7]

When George Verhaeghe and Arie Bestebreurtje went to find a radio operator, Verhaeghe remembered the scrappy noncom named Beynon from their encounter during a football game at Area B in Maryland. Verhaeghe and Bestebreurtje went to the hut where Beynon was quartered and asked the radioman to join their team. Beynon was glad to do so.[8]

Technician 3rd Grade Willard W. "Bud" Beynon was the son of a Scranton, Pennsylvania, police captain. He had spent two years in the Citizens Military Training Corps (CMTC) program at Fort Meade, Maryland, having lied about his age to join. CMTC enlistees were issued surplus uniforms from World War I, including campaign hats and wraparound leggings, but Beynon's legs were so skinny that the leggings refused to stay up. He spent his first year learning infantry skills and his second year serving in a heavy-machine-gun company. He was on track to receive a commission after two more years when officials discovered that he was too young to be in the program.

After being released from the CMTC program, Beynon began working as a tool-and-die machinist for Westinghouse, hoping to earn a Westinghouse scholarship to college. He also did some tinkering with radios. After the attack on Pearl Harbor, he enlisted in the army in Philadelphia and was sent to the Signal Corps Replacement Training Center at Camp Crowder. One day, while training as a radio operator, he noticed a posting on the bulletin board calling for volunteers for the paratroops. He signed up and went to Fort Benning for the parachute course. While at Benning, he again responded to a bulletin board notice, this one seeking anyone interested in what appeared to be an adventurous and immediate reassignment opportunity. He attended the briefing by the OSS Jedburgh recruiter and immediately volunteered.

The partnership of Captain Groenewoud and Lieutenant Todd selected as its radio operator another American, Technician 3rd Grade Carl A. Scott of Columbus, Ohio.

The family of Dutch Jedburgh teams now included four Dutch officers, four American officers, three American noncommissioned officers, and one British noncom. Because the group was so small in comparison with the majority of Jeds who made up the French teams, it was more tightly knit. From this point on, the men in the Dutch teams did everything as a group.

Training continued through the final cold and snowy days of February. During late March, the days grew milder and the Jeds participated in their first extended field exercise. Included were parachute drops to reception committees, coding and transmitting radio messages, encounters with "enemy" roadblocks, and raids by mock Gestapo men. Teams continually moved across the English and Scottish countryside, scaring the wits out of farmers and causing many alerts among members of Britain's Home Guard. Team members learned much about their teammates—what they could contribute, what could be expected of them, what their strengths and weaknesses were. They came to know one another better than their spouses knew them. All signs indicated that the date for the cross-Channel invasion was approaching, and it seemed to the Jeds that there was so much to do yet in their preparation. Constantly badgering the staff at Milton Hall, the Jeds at times half-jokingly accused the training cadre of conspiring to keep them out of the war. Some even believed the Jedburghs might soon be disbanded and not used at all.

By this time, Pappy Olmsted, Henk Brinkgreve, Allan Todd, and "Jaap" Groenewoud shared a room at Milton Hall. Olmsted and Brinkgreve spent many warm April evenings walking through the greening countryside, sharing thoughts and expectations of life and the war. They talked of everything from their childhoods to the types of girls they enjoyed spending time with, and they discussed the war and what they thought the Jedburgh teams could realistically expect to accomplish. They held little doubt of the dangers that lay ahead. Holland was overrun with German forces, and the country's flat topography offered little to support guerrilla warfare. There were no hills or mountains to provide sanctuary when things got hot.

Major Brinkgreve remained in close contact with the Dutch Section of Special Force Headquarters (SFHQ), and he succeeded in arranging a trip to London for the entire Dutch Jedburgh group for information briefings during the third week of April. In London, the Jeds met all the officers of the Dutch Section, studied maps and reports, and learned all they could of the organization and activities of the Dutch underground. Kaas de Graaf, a young member of the Amsterdam underground, arrived in London at about this time, having come to England by way of Belgium, France, Spain, and Portugal. He eagerly shared his knowledge and experience with the Dutch Jeds.

Work continued on completing the kit of uniform and equipment to be worn and carried by each Jed when deploying to the field. All Jeds wore American jump boots along with the field uniform of their national army. Each man carried the American forty-five-caliber automatic pistol and M1 carbine, and each carried a British oil compass.

Morse code speeds continued to improve, with radio operators sending twenty to thirty words per minute, and officers, who had to be capable of performing the task in emergency situations, grew capable of sending around sixteen words per minute and receiving twelve.[9]

Families back home wrote to the Jeds, curious about what exactly it was they were doing. Security constraints prevented the Jeds from telling loved ones what kind of unit they belonged to and what type of warfare they were preparing for, and the general censorship that applied to correspondence from all service members, regardless of the branch of service, further limited what a Jedburgh might be able to share with his family. Allan Todd, like the others, received letters from home asking him about the training he was receiving and expressing concerns about his safety. Todd responded with a letter to his family in April:

> In regards to our training here—it's the best of its kind in the world. As much as I thought of the paratroop training (in the States) our training here is even better. About equal physically (for those who can keep up), and far better technical training than I have ever had before.
>
> As for demolitions, yes, I handle them a lot—so do a lot of others in the army; however, I've had the schooling and a *lot* of practical work, therefore I'm much safer than otherwise would be. I consider myself most fortunate to have gained what knowledge I have. I'm far better trained than 80% of the other officers in the army. I've just been lucky enough to have the opportunity of much more practical work than [the] average soldier has time for. I'm qualified to do jobs that others are not, and that's the only reason I'm still around.
>
> Demolitions are dangerous, but only if you don't understand them. I have pretty well mastered them and have proven it in the field. Parachuting is a little hazardous, but 90% of the danger is in the first 10 to 12 jumps. I'm well beyond that—both in British and American schools and field work. As far as fieldcraft is concerned, I've been on 5 maneuvers, when most have had only one or two—So, what are you worried about?[10]

The first of May was a beautiful spring day that provided an opportunity for the Jeds to take a break from training and enjoy some friendly athletic competition. Filling the day's schedule were events such as a track and field meet, a basketball tournament, tugs-of-war, and boxing matches. Beer and soft drink concessions provided refreshments, and there was even a large betting pavilion operated by a British officer from the Welsh Regiment wearing a colorful waistcoat.

The Jeds competed as individuals in the track and field meet, with a silver loving cup, provided by the commander, going to the overall high scorer. Arie Bestebreurtje, the former Olympic athlete, was considered by most to be the favorite, but at the end of the day the prize went to an American officer, Bob Montgomery.

Boxing matches, held in a makeshift ring in the courtyard in back of the old mansion at Milton Hall, always drew a crowd. One match involved Bud Beynon of the Dutch Jedburgh group. Beynon had gotten on the wrong side of the British sergeant major of the Jedburgh training center, a large brute of a man. The sergeant major resented the fact that the American noncommissioned officers, so young and relatively inexperienced for their rank, were paid much better than were their British counterparts. On one occasion, he got into a heated argument with Beynon. When he had taken enough from the much younger American, he challenged Beynon to a fight. It was agreed that the matter would be settled in the boxing ring, with Lieutenant Verhaeghe serving as referee.

When the signal came for the bout to begin, the two men touched gloves, and Beynon immediately punched the sergeant major in the face, bloodying his nose. With the initial blow landed, Beynon then tried to stay out of the larger man's reach, but the Brit proved as agile as he was strong, and he pummeled the American. When the sergeant major landed a strong hook squarely in Beynon's chest, the younger and smaller man went down. With Beynon struggling to breathe and in noticeable pain, the fight was over. Later, the sergeant major dropped by Beynon's quarters to visit the tough and brash young American and shake his hand. The sergeant major explained that Beynon was the first man to accept a challenge for a fight with him in his twenty years of service. A newfound respect developed between the two men, and they became good friends.[11]

————

As training continued through the hot month of May, a group of fifteen Jedburgh teams packed up for a move to North Africa, where they would stage out of Algiers for insertion into southern France. Those teams remaining at Milton Hall, including the Dutch teams, took part in a ten-day commando hike in Scotland. Instructors assigned a different route, from one hundred to two hundred miles in length, to each team, and each man was issued rations for just three days.

On occasion, when on training exercises such as this, the Dutch Jed teams would pass near a British Army officers' club, where enlisted men were not allowed. Pappy Olmsted, newly promoted to major, would remove one of his gold oak leaves and loan it to Sergeant Beynon, who would then accompany his teammates, Captain Bestebreurtje and Lieutenant Verhaeghe, into the club, appearing to outrank both of them.[12]

Next, the Dutch teams attended a ten-day British Commando small-boat course in the beautiful lakes region of Scotland. The men trained in the use of one- and two-man kayaks, two- and four-man skiffs, and the longboat. They learned the difficult art of sculling, how to rig emergency sails, how to use a sea anchor, how to assemble and use a folding kayak called a Norwegian Folbot, and the intricacies of making rock landings. As a result of their previous Jedburgh training, the men had developed strong legs and good wind; now they built powerful arms and backs.

After returning to Milton Hall, the Dutch Jeds joined those bound for France or Belgium in a ten-day field exercise beginning on the last day of May. One week into the exercise, on June 6, Allied forces landed on the Normandy coast of France on D-Day of Operation Overlord, beginning the liberation of occupied Europe. On the eve of the invasion, some Jed teams were pulled out of the training exercise for operational briefings and deployment to enemy-occupied France. By the time the field problem ended, morale sank to a new low for those teams still remaining at Milton Hall.[13]

SFHQ's Dutch Section also continued to dispatch a few agents to occupied Holland to begin attempts at further organizing and preparing the Dutch resistance. Infiltrating operatives into German-occupied Holland, though, remained a high-risk activity. Two agents dispatched on the last day of May were shot down over the Dutch countryside.[14]

Jedburgh teams operating in France sent a continuous stream of wireless Morse code messages to SFHQ, providing intelligence and reports of sabotage and guerrilla warfare operations conducted. Scraps of information from these reports filtered back to Milton Hall, further contributing to the unhappiness of those so far left behind. Between June 10 and 24, 1944, SFHQ's agents and their resistance cohorts carried out 153 successful sabotage operations.[15] Clearly, though, it was becoming evident that one of the greatest contributions the resistance would make was providing intelligence information that was available from no other source.

Additional Jedburgh teams departed for France through July and August. Dropped well behind German lines, these teams organized and armed thousands of French resistance fighters and ensured that the sabotage and guerrilla warfare activities of these groups contributed to the overall Allied ground campaign. Some eighty-seven teams had been formed for service in France, and all of them eventually made it into the field, some on more than one mission.[16] Some members of the Dutch teams left behind at Milton Hall began to harbor doubts that they would ever see action in Europe and began studying languages of the Far East, hoping for a transfer to that theater when the European war concluded.

But the time had come for the Dutch Jed teams to deploy to Holland.

FIVE

FIRST JEDS INTO HOLLAND

General Dwight D. Eisenhower had an unusual problem in the late summer of 1944. With ground operations in France meeting with such great success in driving Hitler's armies back to the German frontier, the supreme commander now sought ways to use his strategic reserve to reinforce that success in a way that could give the Allies an even greater edge. His strategic reserve consisted of airborne forces—paratroopers and glider-borne troops—who had been held in preparation in England following their highly successful employment in Normandy in support of the initial D-Day landings of Operation Overlord.

Beginning in the middle of July, Eisenhower encouraged his planners to find an opportunity to use this airborne reserve in some bold operation to further exploit the successful breakout and pursuit of the enemy. Added to his own desire to use these forces was the pressure Eisenhower received from General George C. Marshall, the U.S. Army chief of staff, and General Henry H. Arnold, commander of the U.S. Army Air Forces, for a large-scale airborne operation.

In anticipation of such an operation, and to facilitate its planning and execution, SHAEF* formed the First Allied Airborne Army on Au-

* Supreme Headquarters Allied Expeditionary Force, the headquarters of General Eisenhower.

gust 16. Command of the army went to an American, fifty-five-year-old Lieutenant General Lewis H. Brereton, who had been a senior air force commander in the Pacific and the Middle East and had arrived in England to command the Ninth Air Force. The airborne army included British, American, and Polish forces amounting to two airborne corps of six divisions and a separate independent brigade. By the end of August, the Allied high command was eager to put this new airborne army to use, but time seemed to be running out.

The army's American contingent consisted of the newly formed XVIII Airborne Corps, commanded by Major General Matthew B. Ridgway, and the IX Troop Carrier Command. Under the operational control of the corps were the combat-experienced 82nd and 101st Airborne Divisions and the more recently formed 17th Airborne Division.

The British I Airborne Corps, under the command of Lieutenant General Frederick A. M. "Boy" Browning, included the 1st and 6th Airborne Divisions and the 52nd Lowland Division (Air-transported), as well as two troop carrier groups (No. 38 and No. 46) of the Royal Air Force's Transport and Troop Carrier Group. The corps also had operational control of troops of the Special Air Service, or SAS. The forty-seven-year-old Browning doubled as Brereton's deputy army commander.

Rounding out the airborne army was the Polish 1st Independent Parachute Brigade, commanded by Major General Stanislaw Sosabowski.

Hitler's armies, severely mauled in France by the rapidly advancing Allied armies through the month of August, were in full retreat. So decimated were they that even an orderly withdrawal proved almost impossible. To many on the staff of Eisenhower's headquarters, the war appeared to be all but over. Major General Kenneth W. D. Strong, the G-2, or chief of intelligence, at SHAEF, suggested on August 11 that the war would be finished within three months.[1] In an August 23 intelligence summary, Strong's staff claimed that the "August battles have done it and the enemy in the West has had it," further declaring that an Allied victory in Europe was "almost within reach."[2] The supreme commander echoed the general belief in Germany's impending collapse in a cable to General Marshall on September 2 when he wrote, "All reports show that the enemy is routed and running on our entire front."[3] Eisenhower's chief of staff, Major General Walter Bedell Smith, told the press that the war was already won militarily, and post exchange officials prepared notices announcing that Christmas presents arriving from the United States would be returned.[4]

Through the late summer of 1944, the new Allied airborne army planned no fewer than eighteen separate operations, all designed to drop airborne divisions ahead of the advancing armies in France or Belgium to capture bridges or other key terrain. Most operations planned in late August and early September sought to gain a foothold across the Rhine at a time when logistical challenges were threatening to bring the Allied war machine to a halt. Senior commanders welcomed any such operation that might provide the boost needed to maintain the momentum across the great river obstacle. But in every case, Allied ground forces advanced so rapidly that they actually overran the planned drop zones before the drops could be made.[5] At least twice, airborne divisions had assembled at the airfields and prepared for departure before the cancellation orders came down.

One ambitious Twenty-first Army Group plan in late August, code-named Linnet, called for a bold assault into Belgium with the equivalent of four divisions to establish an airhead between Lille, a northern French city near the Belgian border, and Brussels. This blocking force, it was hoped, would cut off German forces retreating through Belgium and prevent them from stabilizing a defensive line to the west.

On August 29, Special Force Headquarters produced a plan to support the assault into Belgium. Knowledge of the highly compartmented, top secret plan was restricted to a dozen officers. It called for French and Belgian resistance elements to serve as guides for Allied paratroopers, to gather intelligence, and to provide men for labor details, guard forces, and patrols. Those resistance groups outside, but within a twelve-mile radius of, the airhead were to delay any German columns approaching the airhead. All other Belgian resistance elements—those outside the twelve-mile radius—could destroy ammunition and fuel dumps and do everything else possible to harass enemy troops withdrawing through Belgium. These instructions were later amended to add that the resistance should also assist the forward movement of Allied forces by protecting, rather than destroying, those stores and telecommunications facilities that could be of use to the Allies. British General Bernard L. Montgomery, commander of the Twenty-first Army Group, was obviously concerned that unchecked demolition activity by the resistance might actually impede the Allies' advance. Operation Linnet was scheduled to kick off on the last day of August.[6]

Since this was to be a British-led operation, the SAS was to play the leading role in organizing the resistance support. Plans called for about sixty SAS men operating in parties of ten, each party working with up to five hundred resistance fighters. One Jedburgh team and two organizers were also to be used.[7]

Recognizing the difficulty of special forces operating in the densely populated and flat terrain of Holland, along with the disastrous results of the early operations that had fallen victim to Germany's Operation North Pole and the desire to avoid compromising a large-scale airborne operation, planners opted to use the Jedburgh teams much differently from the way they had been employed in France. Rather than parachuting into Holland well ahead of ground forces, the Dutch Jedburgh teams would accompany the Allied airborne and air-transported divisions. One Jedburgh team each would be attached to the American 17th and 101st Airborne Divisions and the British 52nd Division. Each team would consist of an American officer, a Belgian officer, and a radio operator. An additional team composed of a Belgian officer, a Polish officer, and a Belgian radio operator was to go with the British 1st Airborne Division, which had under its control the Polish 1st Independent Parachute Brigade.

———

Leading Montgomery's advance along the northern coast of France was XXX Corps of the Second British Army, which had pushed off from the Seine on August 26 on a drive toward Belgium. On September 3, the Guards Armored Division, spearheading the corps' drive, entered Brussels after the Germans had hastily evacuated the city. One week later, the division reached the Meuse-Scheldt Canal and seized a bridge over the canal that had been left intact. The British 11th Armored Division captured Antwerp on September 4 and, along with the city, seized the great port facilities, then the largest port in Europe and one that was badly needed by the Allies to supply their advance into Germany. Unfortunately, Montgomery's forces failed to also capture the fifty-four-mile Scheldt estuary leading to the port. German forces continued to control the estuary for weeks, making the port unusable by the Allies until the end of November.

Germany's decimated and demoralized divisions, routed from France and Belgium, now jammed the roads of Holland in their rush eastward toward the security of the Westwall, or Siegfried line. Dutch citizens who had collaborated with the occupiers now joined the exodus, desperately seeking transport out of the country for their own safety. The ensuing panic in congested Arnhem and the surrounding area coincided with bold street celebrations by loyal Dutch people who believed that liberation was finally at hand. But then the German army halted its retreat and dug in, and the people of Holland realized that their celebration had been cruelly premature. That day, September 5, would be forever known as "Mad Tuesday."

––––––

Because of XXX Corps' rapid advance, Operation Linnet, like so many other plans for use of the airborne divisions at this time, was canceled before it got off the ground. But soon another plan began to take shape, and it would adopt many of the aspects of the Linnet plan, including the use of Jedburgh teams. Operation Comet was to result in the capture of river crossings in the pastoral, fruit-growing region of the Netherlands, near the city of Arnhem in the province of Gelderland, in the path of the advancing Second British Army. Scheduled to kick off on September 8, 1944, Comet would employ the British 1st Airborne Division and 52nd Division, as well as the Polish 1st Independent Parachute Brigade, to seize bridges over three sizable rivers in Holland: the Maas (the river known as the Meuse in France), the Rhine (known as the Waal in Holland), and the Neder Rijn (Lower Rhine, pronounced Nāderrīn). The corresponding bridges were in the towns of Grave, Nijmegen, and Arnhem, respectively. With the bridges and the connecting roadway secured, the British Guards Armored Division was to race up the road to the Arnhem bridgehead.[8]

This time the Dutch, rather than the Belgian, resistance would be called on to help, taking their instructions from SFHQ via the liaison link provided by three Jedburgh teams. One team would serve as the overall Jedburgh mission headquarters and would deploy with the airborne force headquarters. Two "sub-missions" would accompany the two division command elements, where they would be known as the Dutch Liaison Mission.

Comet, though, was canceled on September 10, but that same day Field Marshal Montgomery was prepared to propose a modified and expanded form of the plan to General Eisenhower.

––––––

With Eisenhower's headquarters fully established on the Continent and the Allied forces in full pursuit of retreating German armies following the breakout from Normandy, the supreme commander assumed operational control of all Allied ground forces from General Montgomery on September 1, 1944. Also taking command of the Allied forces driving northward from southern France after landing on the Mediterranean coast on August 15, Eisenhower now controlled three army groups—Montgomery's Twenty-first and General Omar Bradley's Twelfth racing across northern France toward the German frontier and, in the south, General Jacob L. Devers's Sixth pushing northward from the Mediterranean coast.

To ensure that Eisenhower's move to take control of the ground war was not viewed as a demotion for Montgomery, which certainly was not the intention, the British promoted the Twenty-first Army Group commander to the rank of field marshal effective the first day of September. This resulted in an awkward technicality; as a field marshal, Montgomery actually outranked his superior in the Allied chain of command, General Eisenhower. To alleviate the problem, the United States Congress, in December 1944, would create the five-star rank of general of the army and immediately confer it on Eisenhower.

The day after assuming control of the ground war, Eisenhower announced his two-thrust plan for the Allied assault on Germany, an assault across a broad front, extending both north and south of the dense Ardennes forest. Only a week earlier, Montgomery had argued his case for a single, deep Allied thrust northward to Belgium and then into Germany's vital Ruhr industrial region. Such a drive, the field marshal contended, would require holding Bradley's and Devers's army groups in static positions while all logistical support was shifted to Montgomery's armies. He further insisted that one of Eisenhower's army group commanders should be given operational control of all ground forces, leaving the supreme commander to deal with larger strategic and political issues. There was little doubt that Montgomery considered himself best qualified for this role. But Eisenhower held firmly to his plan.

————

General Eisenhower's plane, a C-47 converted for VIP travel, rolled to a stop at Melsbroek airfield, outside Brussels, on the afternoon of September 10, 1944. Three days earlier, newly promoted Field Marshal Montgomery had requested a meeting with the supreme commander. Having badly wrenched a knee only days earlier and still in great pain and unable to walk, Eisenhower, a month away from his fifty-fourth birthday, had asked Montgomery to fly to his headquarters in Normandy. But Montgomery, even though he was aware of Eisenhower's injury, had insisted that the senior commander come to meet with him at his headquarters in Belgium.

Getting off the plane proved to be too painful an ordeal for Eisenhower, so Montgomery came aboard. Accompanying Eisenhower were his deputy, Air Chief Marshal Sir Arthur Tedder, and SHAEF's assistant chief of staff for administration, Lieutenant General Sir Humphrey Gale. Montgomery brought along his logistics officer, Lieutenant General Miles Graham. Now the field marshal insisted that Gale not be present for the meeting, though he was equally insistent that his own supply expert, Graham, remain.

Six days earlier, Montgomery had sent a message to Eisenhower proposing that his Twenty-first Army Group be given absolute priority of supplies to support a thrust to the northeast. Such an operation, he argued, would allow him to jump the Rhine River and would then place him in a position to strike eastward to Berlin. Montgomery was convinced that this would be the quickest means of ending the war in Europe.[9]

Eisenhower saw the prospect for future operations from a broader perspective. He believed that such a single-thrust strategy carried the risk of opening Montgomery's right flank to counterattacks. Furthermore, he knew that the current strained logistical structure couldn't support such a deep operation. Above all, the supreme commander was certain that his approval of such a plan—giving Montgomery and his British and Canadian armies the opportunity to strike out toward Berlin and perhaps end the war while the much larger American force (two army groups) stood idly by—would be met with outrage by the media, politicians, and the public back home.

Preferring instead to advance into Germany along the entire front, Eisenhower had placed a priority on operations in the north (though not absolute priority, as Montgomery wished), with plans calling for Montgomery's army group to push as rapidly as possible to the northeast. Two main objectives were the capture of the badly needed port of Antwerp and the destruction of the launching sites of the V-1 flying bombs (essentially the first cruise missiles) that were striking London and the new V-2 rockets.

Since mid-June, as many as seventy V-1 flying bombs had been falling on London each day.[10] These pilotless, jet-propelled missiles were nonballistic and very inaccurate. Traveling at a speed of nearly 350 miles per hour at an altitude of around three thousand feet, the V-1s were not infrequently shot down by fighters or antiaircraft guns. But over an eighty-day stretch as of early September, the Germans launched some 8,000 of the flying bombs toward England, with 2,300 of those hitting the London area.[11] Nicknamed "buzz bombs" because of their engine noise, they killed more than five thousand Britons. Beginning in September 1944, the more advanced and deadlier V-2, the world's first ballistic missile, carrying a ton of high explosives at 3,500 miles per hour, spelled a new danger for the people of England. The first V-2s had landed in London on September 8, just two days prior to Eisenhower's meeting with Montgomery in Brussels. Over the next six months, more than a thousand V-2s were to fall on England, killing nearly three thousand people and leaving over twice that number injured.[12]

Eisenhower explained how important it was for Montgomery to clear the estuary leading to Antwerp so that the great port could be put to use by the Allies. The supreme commander also intended General Bradley's army group to continue to attack eastward toward the Saar region of Germany. Eisenhower now wielded a force of nearly forty divisions—more than half a million men—and logistical support channels from Normandy and the Mediterranean coast of France were strained to the breaking point. Eisenhower not only saw how critically important the opening of the Antwerp port was to the Allied campaign, he also understood that he could not adopt a strategy that left two-thirds of the forces under his command in static positions in hopes that Montgomery could end the war on his own.

The field marshal ridiculed Eisenhower's plan for a double thrust—with British armies driving north of the Ardennes and American armies attacking farther to the south—declaring that it was a recipe for failure. He was adamant that his own plan for a single thrust by his Twenty-first Army Group was the only feasible strategy.

"What you're proposing is this—if I give you all of the supplies you want, you could go straight to Berlin—right straight to Berlin? Monty, you're nuts. You can't do it. What the hell! If you try a long column like that in a single thrust you'd have to throw off division after division to protect your flanks from attack. Now suppose you did get a bridge across the Rhine. You couldn't depend for long on that one bridge to supply your drive. Monty, you can't do it."[13]

Montgomery then brought up the touchy subject of command. At the time of the Allied landings in Normandy on June 6, Montgomery had been designated the overall ground force commander with an army group that controlled one American army and one British army. Since that time, the Americans had activated a second army in France and had established the Twelfth Army Group to control the operations of these two armies. By the end of August, the Allied armies had broken out from the Normandy lodgment area, liberated Brittany, swung eastward and advanced across most of northern France, and linked up with an American-led army group approaching from the south after landings on the Mediterranean coast of France and now were poised for the final push into Germany. At this time, with his operational headquarters fully established in France, General Eisenhower had taken over control of all ground forces on the Continent in accordance with preinvasion plans.

Field Marshal Montgomery's verbal assault on the supreme commander became so extreme that Eisenhower, who had been sitting silently throughout the berating, decided he had to rein in his subordinate. He leaned forward with his blue eyes fixed on Montgomery, placed a hand on the field marshal's knee, and said, "Steady, Monty! You can't speak to me like that. I'm your boss."[14] Montgomery mumbled, "I'm sorry, Ike," and promptly changed the subject.[15]

The field marshal now proposed an operation to strike northward with his Second British Army to seize a crossing over the Lower Rhine in Holland. Such a move, he argued, would put him in a position to cut off German forces holding the Scheldt estuary, begin the encirclement of the Ruhr industrial area so vital to Germany's war effort, and eventually launch an attack straight for Berlin. At first, Eisenhower thought the idea too fantastic even to consider. An operation aimed at reaching such a deep objective was improbable when the armies' supplies were still coming over the beach at Normandy. But Montgomery contended that it was a feasible plan if all supplies were given to his army group, which meant cutting off supplies from Bradley's Twelfth Army Group to the south and especially to Montgomery's archrival, General George S. Patton. In fact, Patton had already begun running out of gas more than ten days earlier when the priority of supplies was shifted to Montgomery.

After an hour of arguing for the operation and expressing his profound belief in its chances for success, Montgomery finally began to sway the supreme commander. The field marshal explained that his plan was to use his Second British Army in a bold thrust toward Arnhem, linking up with elements of the First Allied Airborne Army, which would land by parachute and glider earlier to seize a number of bridges along the route. His code name for the proposed operation was Market-Garden.

Eisenhower still thought the plan carried much risk, leaving Second Army's right flank open to attack during the northward thrust and opening a gap between Montgomery's forces and those of Bradley to the south. An even greater disadvantage was that such an operation would further delay Montgomery's mission of capturing the great port of Antwerp, which the Allies desperately needed before moving into Germany. But Eisenhower did find two elements of the plan attractive. If successful, the operation would give the Allies a bridgehead across the Rhine. Furthermore, it would provide an ideal opportunity to use the newly formed First Allied Airborne Army, still sitting near airfields back in England.

Eisenhower finally agreed to the operation. To Montgomery, it was an opportunity to regain some of the glory he had achieved earlier in North Africa and to reestablish his stature as one of the leading Allied field commanders. To Eisenhower, the decision meant committing his strategic reserve on a risky operation—an operation that, in fact, promised little advantage to the Allies even if successful. It was a decision that Eisenhower biographer Stephen E. Ambrose would later describe as Eisenhower's "worst error of the war."[16] In his eagerness to appease Montgomery, to make use of the aggressive Allied army of paratroopers, and to gain a bridgehead across the Rhine, Eisenhower had pulled transportation assets and supplies from Bradley's advancing army group and allowed Montgomery to ignore the task of capturing the approaches to the much needed port at Antwerp.

———

With the Allies still unsure as to the breadth of the German penetration of the Dutch underground, Special Force Headquarters sent a mission into Holland in July to reestablish contact with the resistance and assess the situation. The mission determined that the penetration was not as widespread as had been feared, and by August SFHQ initiated efforts to drop a few agents and a limited amount of arms and supplies to the underground. By effectively pooling their resources in Holland, SFHQ and

Britain's Secret Intelligence Service were able to establish communications with resistance groups throughout the country in August.

At Milton Hall, orders arrived on Saturday, September 2, alerting the Dutch Jedburgh teams for movement to London for preliminary mission briefings by SFHQ's Dutch Section. Only the Dutch officers would carry false papers and civilian clothing on the operation; all other team members would operate in uniform. Because extra time was required for the preparation of their false papers and to fit them with civilian clothing, the Dutch officers reported to London the following day. The other team members would join them later.[17]

On Tuesday, the remaining Dutch team members arrived in London. The team of Brinkgreve, Olmsted, and Austin was summoned to the briefing room immediately upon their arrival in the city. Known at Milton Hall simply as Team 12, the trio now received the code name Dudley, and the men learned that they were to be dropped into Holland that very night. They would parachute into the eastern Dutch province of Overijssel, near the German border. There, the Jeds were to organize and equip local underground groups and serve as a liaison party between those groups and Allied forces, who were expected to be approaching that area within weeks. The team was to select and train reception committees and air-landing coordinators, conduct sabotage, collect and report intelligence, and plan for the defense of essential bridges that the advancing Allied forces would need to use.

The men could scarcely believe that the day they had waited for and prepared for these many months had finally arrived. One briefer after another paraded through, filling in the men on every detail of the mission: communications instructions, German military and police forces known or suspected to be operating in the area, underground contacts, map reviews. The Jeds asked many questions and answered others and barely had time to think about what they were hearing or to wonder about what lay ahead.

Amid the series of briefings was a visit by Prince Bernhard of the Netherlands, who had been named head of the Dutch resistance. Bernhard, a fluent English speaker, explained to Brinkgreve, Olmsted, and Austin what he hoped could be accomplished by the resistance, and then he bade them farewell.

The briefings concluded at three in the afternoon and team Dudley departed to SOE's Special Training School No. 61 for supper, after which they went to the airfield for departure. The weather would not co-operate, however, and the mission was scrubbed that night of September 5 and again the following night.

"Go home," the men were instructed. "We'll see you tomorrow night."[18] The disappointed men returned to the holding school, ate another meal, and spent the evening talking to other teams that had also been grounded because of the weather.

Finally, on Friday, September 8, the team was trucked to Tempsford airfield, where they boarded a British Stirling and took off an hour before midnight. This time they made it as far as the coastal islands of Holland, dropping to an altitude of two hundred feet over the island of Terschelling to hopefully fly in at an altitude below the level at which German antiaircraft batteries could depress their guns. German night fighters, however, were alerted, and a sister aircraft, following twenty minutes behind the Jeds' plane and carrying a single agent and his radio operator, was shot down. Unfortunately, the pilot of the plane carrying Jed team Dudley was unable to locate the drop zone and was forced to turn back to England. After touching down at three-thirty on the morning of the ninth, the dejected Jeds unloaded their equipment from the plane and rode back to Milton Hall.

———

Still, enough uneasiness about Holland remained at SFHQ that support provided to the Dutch resistance remained meager. Allied planners hoped for nothing more than a moderate level of assistance from the resistance as ground operations approached Dutch territory. Indeed, throughout August little was accomplished in the way of sabotage in Holland; the number of SFHQ operatives and the amount of arms and supplies that had been provided to the Dutch underground had been minimal. By the time British and Canadian forces closed on the Dutch border at the beginning of September, it was already too late to build up a resistance capability in Holland similar to that which had been so effective in France.

Two SAS parties had been dropped into Holland—one to the Prinsenkamp area, the other to the Assen area in Drenthe Province. These men were not to engage in sabotage or any other offensive actions, with or without the resistance. Their mission was simply to gather intelligence and pass it to the Allies. In this they were very successful, providing up-to-date information not only on the enemy, but also on the state of the resistance in those parts of Holland.[19]

Just one week prior to the planned Market-Garden operation, SFHQ finally dropped the first Jedburgh team into Holland. Jed team Dudley was alerted again on Monday, September 11. After being taken by truck to Tempsford, Brinkgreve's team was flown in a Lockheed Hudson to another airfield. At ten that night, they took off for Holland in a British Stirling bomber converted for special operations missions. The flight crossed the Dutch coast at IJmuiden, where the plane encountered some light flak but was not hit. Shortly after midnight, the three members of the team—Major Brinkgreve, Major Olmsted, and Sergeant Austin—parachuted successfully into eastern Holland, accompanied by twelve containers full of weapons, explosives, and other items for the Dutch resistance.

As members of the reception committee extinguished the lights marking the drop zone after the last container landed, Sergeant Austin, who had been busy burying parachutes, joined the two Jedburgh officers. He was accompanied by a local man who was to serve as their guide. All equipment and containers were quickly loaded onto several farm carts that had been standing by for that purpose, and the carts swiftly dispersed, accompanied by small groups of men who would hide the valuable cargo in barns and forests. The guide took Brinkgreve, Olmsted, and Austin to a safe house about a mile from the drop zone.

At the safe house, actually a farm known as Die Kolonie, the Jeds stashed their gear in the barn and followed the guide to the farmhouse, where they were shown into the kitchen to warm up. They met the family who lived in the house, as well as some members of the Dutch underground. One, a man named Evert, introduced himself as the leader of a resistance group called the Raad van Verzet (RVV) in Overijssel Province, in eastern Holland, where the team had landed. The men were then ushered into the dining room, where they enjoyed a typically simple yet solidly nourishing Dutch meal of dried beef, boiled eggs, and black bread. They were given hot milk to drink.

Finally, at five o'clock in the morning, they accompanied Evert and four or five of his men about a mile to a moss-covered shack, hidden away in a thickly wooded area, that served as their headquarters. Although the patch of woods surrounding Evert's command post was only about 240 square yards, it was fairly well isolated from any roads or populated areas. Shrubbery had grown up around the old shack, and it was difficult to spot from the ground or from the air. Inside, the men found several bunks and two stalls, complete with straw and blankets. Exhausted from the night's adventure, the Jeds bedded down and slept. They had no knowledge of Operation Market-Garden, scheduled to kick off in less than a week, or of the role to be played in that operation by their friends on the other teams of the Dutch Jedburgh group.

SIX

OPERATION MARKET-GARDEN

General Eisenhower had given his blessing to Field Marshal Montgomery's idea for an airborne assault and armored thrust into the Netherlands to gain a bridgehead across the Rhine. Operation Market-Garden had two primary objectives: to get Allied forces across the Rhine River, the last great natural obstacle to be overcome before entering Germany; and to set the stage for the capture of the Ruhr industrial area. Gaining a bridgehead north of the Rhine would also isolate those German forces remaining in western Holland and place the Allies in a position to launch a drive across northern Germany and on to Berlin.

The initial mention of the operation at First Allied Airborne Army headquarters, a three-story ivy-walled mansion at Sunninghill Park near Ascot, west of London, was a phone call to the chief of staff, Brigadier General Floyd L. Parks, at two-thirty on the afternoon of September 10, the day Eisenhower approved the plan. The caller, Lieutenant General Browning, the deputy army commander, had just returned from Montgomery's headquarters on the Continent. Browning told Parks that Eisenhower and Montgomery wanted an operation in the same general area as in the Comet operation.[1] Lieutenant General Brereton, commander of the airborne army, had earlier directed Parks to give as many staff personnel as possible the afternoon off; now Brereton called for a conference with all commanders at six that evening.[2] Later that same night, another planning conference took place at IX Troop Carrier Command headquarters.[3]

At Brereton's meeting, he announced that Browning, who doubled as the British I Airborne Corps commander, would command the airborne operation. Major General Ridgway, commander of the U.S. XVIII Airborne Corps, was bitterly disappointed at not being given command of the force, as two of the three airborne divisions involved were his.[4] His headquarters, he learned, was to serve only in an administrative and observation capacity.

Three airborne division commanders and the commanders of the British and American troop carrier commands were among the thirty-four officers in attendance as General Browning outlined the planned operation. He indicated that the primary ground force for the operation, British XXX Corps, would control all airborne forces after linking up with them.

Unlike much of Holland along the western seaboard, the eastern part of the Netherlands that included the area of operations was nearly all above sea level, an area of lush farmland and fruit orchards interlaced with rivers, canals, and small streams. The airborne portion of the plan, labeled Operation Market, called for three and a half airborne divisions to be dropped in the areas around the Dutch cities of Eindhoven, Nijmegen, and Arnhem to seize bridges over three rivers—the Maas, the Waal, and the Neder Rijn—as well as several canals. The paratroopers would then hold the connecting highway, stretching sixty-four miles northward from the Belgian-Dutch border to Arnhem, enabling the rapid passage of the follow-on ground force.

One detail, though, would distinguish this operation from all previous combat jumps in the war: The jump into Holland would be made in broad daylight. Browning's decision to make the drop in daylight was based on two factors. First was the desire to avoid the scattering of parachutists in the dark, as happened during the Normandy invasion, when few of the troop carriers found their assigned drop zones. Another factor had to do with the threat posed by German fighter aircraft. By the summer of 1944, the Allies had attained air supremacy in Western Europe, particularly in daylight. But an airborne operation at night, especially so near the German border, would benefit the Germans because of their effective night fighters.

Major General Maxwell D. Taylor's 101st Airborne Division would

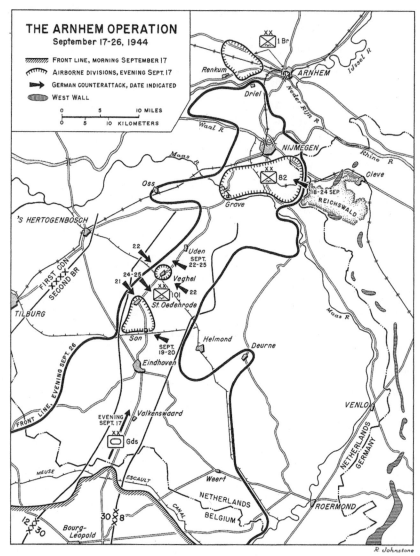

THE ARNHEM OPERATION
September 17-26, 1944

FRONT LINE, MORNING SEPTEMBER 17
AIRBORNE DIVISIONS, EVENING SEPT. 17
GERMAN COUNTERATTACK, DATE INDICATED
WEST WALL

0   5   10 MILES
0   5   10 KILOMETERS

Forrest C. Pogue, The Supreme Command, *United States Army in World War II series*
(*Washington, D.C.: Office of the Chief of Military History, 1954*), 285

land north of the industrial city of Eindhoven, between Veghel and Son (pronounced Zon), capture Eindhoven, and seize bridges over canals and rivers at Veghel, St. Oedenrode, and Son. The "Screaming Eagles" would then have to hold fifteen miles of highway, guarding against counterattacks while allowing passage of Major General Allan Adair's Guards Armored Division of XXX Corps.

Brigadier General James M. Gavin and his 82nd Airborne Division were to land south of Nijmegen, between the Maas and the Waal rivers. Nijmegen, established by the Romans nearly two thousand years earlier and an imperial city in Charlemagne's time, was the oldest city in the Netherlands. It lay on the south bank of the Waal and had a population in 1944 of nearly one hundred thousand. The Waal was the main tributary of the Rhine, wide enough to be a major shipping route linking the German industrial Ruhr area with the North Sea. The Maas, known as the Meuse in France, parallels the Waal about ten miles to the south of Nijmegen. Both the Maas and the Waal were wide rivers, deep and fast-flowing, with high banks. Roads throughout the area were narrow and either ran along the tops of dikes or stretched through flat terrain, providing little or no cover. Just west of Nijmegen stretched the Maas-Waal Canal, a predominantly north-south channel connecting the two rivers. Gavin's division had four major objectives, three of them bridges.

The "All Americans" had to seize and hold two huge steel-girdered bridges—one spanning the 250-yard-wide Maas at Grave, the other over the Waal at Nijmegen—as well as at least one of several small bridges over the Maas-Waal Canal. Added to these objectives was the responsibility of taking and holding an area of high ground called the Groesbeek Heights, a ridge southeast of Nijmegen, along the German frontier, that dominated the entire area. Indeed, at an elevation of three hundred feet, the terrain stood as one of the highest points in all of Holland. Without the necessary forces available on D-Day to seize all four objectives, Gavin planned to land his initial elements near Grave and Groesbeek. Lieutenant General Browning had directed that the Nijmegen bridge should be captured only after the other objectives had been taken; control of the bridge would be meaningless if XXX Corps was unable to get there. Finally, Gavin's division was also to secure a ten-mile stretch of the Eindhoven–Arnhem highway.

Shortly after crossing the border from Germany into Holland on its way to the North Sea, the Rhine River splits into the Waal and, branching off to the north, the Neder Rijn. The objective of Major General

Robert E. "Roy" Urquhart's British 1st Airborne Division, dropping north of the Neder Rijn, was the huge steel highway bridge spanning the river at Arnhem, sixty-four miles behind the German lines. The division was to seize the bridge, hold it, and secure a bridgehead north of the river large enough to facilitate British XXX Corps' crossing and launching a drive farther northward to the IJsselmeer. Urquhart, a six-foot, two-hundred-pound Scot, had no previous airborne experience, but he had an advantage over most senior British airborne officers by being a seasoned combat veteran, and he had the respect of the entire command. His division was to land west of Arnhem, the provincial capital on the north bank of the river, some six to eight miles west of the bridge. He and his staff and subordinate commanders would have preferred to land just south of the bridge, but Browning's planners argued against this, citing an intense concentration of flak expected around the bridge and terrain unsuitable for the landing of gliders.

Information provided to Urquhart's division indicated that opposition in the Arnhem area would not be significant. There were thought to be two thousand SS recruits in the city, some Luftwaffe personnel at an aerodrome ten miles to the north, and several antiaircraft guns near the bridges.[5] Estimates indicated that any other enemy units in the area would be manned largely by teenagers and old men and would have little ability as fighters.

Major General Sosabowski's Polish parachute brigade was to be dropped south of the Neder Rijn, just east of the town of Elden, on D plus 2, the third day of the operation. The brigade was to reinforce the British force at the bridge and, if necessary, complete the task of seizing the bridge. Once landing strips were seized or prepared in the area north of Arnhem, the British 52nd Lowland Division (Air-transported), initially held in reserve in England, was to be flown in.

In all, Operation Market, the airborne half of Market-Garden, would employ some thirty-five thousand Allied troops.[6]

The ground element, under the part of the plan known as Operation Garden, came from the Second British Army. In the main attack, British XXX Corps, with some twenty thousand vehicles, would strike northward from the Meuse-Escaut Canal on the Dutch-Belgian border toward the IJsselmeer, formerly known as the Zuiderzee, ninety-nine miles to the north. Under XXX Corps were the Guards Armored Division, the 43rd and 50th Infantry Divisions, and the 8th Armored Brigade. Supporting attacks by British VIII and XII Corps would be made on the flanks of XXX Corps.

When Montgomery had first briefed Browning on the plan in Brussels after General Eisenhower's departure, Browning asked how long the British paratroopers would be required to hold the bridge at Arnhem.

"Two days," said Montgomery. "They'll be up with you then."

"We can hold it for four," said Browning, "but I think we might be going a bridge too far."[7]

Now the original Jedburgh plan was amended to allow for the participation of four teams, one of which would be attached to the airborne corps headquarters and serve as overall Jedburgh mission headquarters. Each division involved in the airborne assault would have a Jedburgh team serving as a "sub-mission" deploying with the division headquarters. The teams attached to the airborne divisions' headquarters would each operate under the direct command of the division to which it was attached.

Dutch Captain Jaap Staal's team was to accompany the airborne corps headquarters and was designated as team Edward. Staal's teammate Captain McCord Sollenberger would serve as American liaison officer, while a British officer, Captain Mills, was attached to the team as British liaison. To provide twenty-four-hour communications capability, radio duty was to be shared by Staal's Jedburgh radio operator, Technical Sergeant James Billingsley of the U.S. Army, and Lieutenant Len Willmott, another British officer attached to the team. Team Edward was to provide liaison between the corps and the local populace and serve as advisers to the corps commander and his staff on proper utilization of the Dutch resistance. They would also provide the corps an additional communications link with England. The team would deploy with an operating fund of 10,500 guilders to be used, as needed, in paying resistance members, securing services, or obtaining supplies.

With the new plan calling for four Jedburgh teams, the total number of teams in the Dutch group, and with team Dudley already alerted for insertion well to the north of Arnhem on a separate mission, a fifth team was organized to accompany the U.S. 101st Airborne Division. Designated Daniel II,* the team consisted of British Major R. K. Wilson, British Sergeant G. W. Mason, and two Dutchmen: Lieutenant Abraham

---

* An earlier Jedburgh team code-named Daniel had deployed to France during the summer.

"Bram" Dubois and Sergeant Lykele Faber. Lieutenant Dubois, attached to the team as Dutch liaison, was not trained as a Jedburgh officer. Faber was a former Dutch telephone company employee who had joined the resistance in 1943 as a result of connections made through his fiancée's family. He had arrived in England after smuggling German defense plans for the Scheldt estuary out of Holland and making his way through France and over the Pyrenees to Spain. After being cleared by British intelligence and the exiled Dutch Secret Service in London, he was recruited for the Jedburghs and completed the training program as a radio operator.[8]

The team of Dutch Captain Arie Bestebreurtje and the two Americans—First Lieutenant George Verhaeghe and eighteen-year-old Willard "Bud" Beynon, recently promoted to technical sergeant—was designated Jedburgh team Clarence. They would deploy with the U.S. 82nd Airborne Division. Initially, this team was to drop with the British airborne division, but when General Gavin met the team he was impressed with Bestebreurtje, whom he judged to be "an extraordinary officer."[9] When the general learned that Bestebreurtje's uncle was a councilman in Nijmegen and that the Dutch captain knew the area around Nijmegen well, having hiked throughout the region during the summers of his youth, he asked the team to jump with his 82nd.[10]

Last, the team of Dutch Captain Jaap Groenewoud and two Americans, First Lieutenant Allan Todd and Carl A. Scott, now a technical sergeant, would go with the British 1st Airborne Division. They were designated Jedburgh team Claude.

These teams each had the mission of providing liaison between the airborne division and the local population in its area of operations. Furthermore, they were to make contact with local Dutch resistance elements and give them specific tasks to perform in support of the operation.

Dutch resistance to German occupation developed at a rather slower pace than that of France. The Netherlands was a neutral country when the Germans invaded on Friday, May 10, 1940. Undeterred by the nation's declared neutrality, Hitler viewed the Low Countries as a path around France's Maginot Line defenses. The sudden and unprovoked attack by Germany began with parachute assaults near the Dutch-German border and the bombing of Rotterdam, Holland's principal port.

Reservists scrambled to report for duty. With the country all but defeated by May 13, German bombers then hit the center of Rotterdam, killing some nine hundred civilians. By the end of the day, residents were working to dig out victims from the rubble of bombed-out buildings. Homes that still stood were without water or electricity, fires started by incendiary bombs left a flaxen glow over the city, and the odor of burning flesh permeated the air.[11]

The next day, with German troops only a few miles away, Queen Wilhelmina, Crown Princess Juliana, Prince Bernhard, the Dutch government, and the British ambassador and his staff boarded two British destroyers in Rotterdam's harbor and departed for England.[12] As Hitler's armies continued to march, all of the occupied countries of Europe except Denmark eventually established governments in exile in London.

The Netherlands had a small army; no wars had been fought on Dutch soil in nearly 150 years. Now, equipped largely with obsolete weapons, the Dutch army's gallant stand against the Germans lasted but five days. But on the evening of May 14, with the government in exile and with no hope of holding out against the German onslaught, General Gerard Winkelman, the commander in chief of Dutch forces, surrendered.

Almost immediately, though on a small scale, some Dutchmen began to organize themselves and hide weapons that were to have been turned over to the occupiers. Early resistance groups limited themselves to issuing pamphlets and leaflets. Leaders recruited friends, relatives, and co-workers. Dutch Communists organized mass strikes in the factories. All acted in spite of the risk of execution or shipment to a concentration camp if captured. Queen Wilhelmina and the Dutch government in exile maintained a psychological presence, serving as a symbol of hope, by keeping the people of Holland informed through BBC* broadcasts. As the months passed, more and more Dutchmen began to seek action.

In November 1940, a number of groups combined to form an organization known as Orde Dienst (Order of Service), or OD, whose main objective was to ensure the restoration of civil order and administrative services when liberation eventually came, preparing the Netherlands for the return of the Dutch government. Orde Dienst, composed primarily

---

* British Broadcasting Corporation.

of Dutch military and government officials who had been replaced by German occupation authorities, also engaged in intelligence collection.

Another group, the Landelijke Organisatie voor Hulp aan Onder-duikers (Central Government Organizations for Help to People in Hiding), or LO, was instrumental in establishing and supporting networks of agents and safe houses to assist downed aircrews and other evaders in getting out of occupied Holland.

Two additional groups provided most of the fighting elements of the Dutch resistance. The Landelijke Knok-Ploegen (Central Government Fighting Group), or KP, engaged in sabotage activities, usually targeting railways, telegraph or telephone lines, and German military supply depots and vehicle parks. By 1944, the KP had a nationwide strength of at least 550 members.[13]

The Raad van Verzet (Council of Resistance), or RVV, conducted sabotage operations but also provided protection to evaders. Numbering several thousand active members by 1944, this group maintained radio contact with the Dutch government's intelligence bureau in London and had requested arms and ammunition.[14]

Some smaller groups existed and operated on a local level, such as the Partisan Action Nederlands (PAN) in Eindhoven and surrounding towns and villages. Loosely organized groups such as this functioned like the larger groups but did not consider themselves elements of those groups. By the summer of 1944, PAN had a membership of eighty to one hundred men and women.[15]

By the spring of 1944, the three main resistance groups—the RVV, the KP, and the OD—had been brought together under an umbrella federation known as the Council for Resistance. Direction of the council and its activities came from Prince Bernhard in London, acting as commander in chief of the resistance.

The total estimated strength of resistance forces in the Netherlands by the summer of 1944 was around 107,000, only a fraction of whom were armed and organized.[16] Special Force Headquarters had been able, despite problems caused by flak and enemy troop concentrations, to drop 869 containers filled with arms and explosives to these groups between the middle of August and September 9.[17]

———

Holland was a highly industrialized country. It had been the center of world trade in the seventeenth century, with shipbuilders putting forth a fleet of ships that sailed the seven seas. The country became a prosperous world leader in international banking, insurance, diamond marketing, and trade. By the time of the German invasion in 1940, the Netherlands, with a mostly middle-class population of just over nine million, was the heart of the world's fourth largest empire and home of the seventh largest merchant marine fleet.[18]

Eastern and southern Holland, the projected venue for Operation Market-Garden, was a land of low rolling hills, lakes, and farmland, with fields of wheat and barley, potatoes, and sugar beets. It was a region that also abounded in fruit orchards. Typical farms featured thatched-roof buildings and sturdy woven-reed fences. The people were warm and generous and largely Catholic. Culturally, many southern Dutch were closer to the Belgian Flemish people than they were to the Hollanders of the north.

Geographically, though, the Netherlands was not a country well suited to guerrilla warfare. Its predominantly flat terrain did not provide the kind of mountainous sanctuary that became so vital to the survival of guerrilla fighters in France, Yugoslavia, Greece, Italy, and Norway. Movement was restricted by the many rivers and canals that crisscrossed the countryside. With movement confined largely to roads, railroads, and bridges, the Germans found it an easy matter to control and monitor such movement by establishing roadblocks and checkpoints and by limiting the availability of gasoline and tires to civilians.

Northeast of Arnhem, in an area near the German frontier, Jedburgh team Dudley was learning how difficult it would be to conduct guerrilla warfare in the Dutch provinces.

SEVEN

GERMANS EVERYWHERE

On Tuesday morning, September 12, Major Brinkgreve of Jedburgh team Dudley met with Evert, the resistance chief, and his subordinate leaders. Following the conference, the Jeds began distributing the weapons that had been dropped with the team by parachute the previous night. A supply room was established to facilitate further issue and storage of equipment. The packages with the Jedburgh team's radios had not been located, but the Jeds were assured that they would arrive later.

Members of the local resistance arranged for false papers and civilian clothing to be obtained for the Jeds. Although the planners back in London had intended for them to operate in uniform, the heavy concentration of Germans in the area made that impractical. The Dutch people then served the Jeds a breakfast of black rye bread, called *roggebrood,* tomatoes, and a cheese containing caraway seeds.

The Jeds tried to learn all they could from Evert and his men about the situation in eastern Holland, but they soon realized that these men had few contacts outside the immediate area and knew little of the strength, location, and activities of German forces. Major Olmsted and Sergeant Austin helped some of the resistance men bury parachutes and containers during the afternoon. They also dug a few foxholes in the woods in case they were surprised by the enemy. Later that evening, the three Jeds pulled on some overalls and accompanied one of Evert's men, Jan, across the fields to a farm, where they enjoyed a hearty supper.

———

Allied planners at SHAEF called for Dutch resistance groups to support operations in Holland in two phases. The first phase would focus on the area south of the Waal River and would include the sabotage of rail lines, canals, and telecommunications lines. The underground was also asked to do all they could to help prevent the destruction of port facilities by the Germans. Phase two operations would be similar but would be conducted in the area north of the Waal.[1]

Elements of the KP did succeed in sabotaging some priority rail lines and bridges during the first week of September, causing sufficient damage to require several days of repair work by the Germans. Team Dudley reported successful strikes on rail lines and the sabotage of five main canals in their area near the town of Almelo. Rail traffic throughout Holland was further disrupted when SHAEF directed a general railway strike throughout the country. So effective was the ensuing strike, with thirty thousand Dutch railway workers taking part, that by the end of September, the Germans had to take over all rail operations.[2]

———

One week before the commencement of Operation Market-Garden, SHAEF's intelligence staff estimated that the Germans had a total of forty-eight divisions on the Western Front, though they judged that the depleted divisions probably had a true strength equivalent to twenty infantry and four armored divisions. General Browning's airborne corps headquarters staff estimated the enemy to have few infantry reserves in Holland and probably no more than fifty to one hundred tanks. Most of the German troops in the area around Nijmegen and Arnhem were judged to be of low quality.[3]

Reports received from the Dutch resistance in Arnhem at this time, however, were painting a different picture. They indicated the presence of crack SS armored units in and around the city, and subsequent aerial photo reconnaissance by the Royal Air Force (RAF) corroborated this. Strewn among the forests surrounding Arnhem were signs of a concentration of tanks and other armored vehicles.

Field Marshal Montgomery did not put much stock in reports from the Dutch resistance; he had even told his staff that the resistance could not be trusted. Prince Bernhard visited the field marshal on September 9 and began briefing Montgomery on details included in the resistance reports, but he quickly realized that Montgomery believed none of it. When Bernhard explained that the underground could be very helpful whenever the Allies began operating in the Netherlands, he was surprised to hear Montgomery say, "I don't think your resistance people can be of much use to us. Therefore, I believe all this quite unnecessary."[4]

As D-Day for Market-Garden approached, British Major General Kenneth W. D. Strong, Eisenhower's intelligence chief, delivered disturbing news to Lieutenant General Walter Bedell Smith, SHAEF's chief of staff. Strong reported that there were additional indications of understrength German armored divisions in the vicinity of Arnhem, near the planned drop zone of the British 1st Airborne Division. The SHAEF G-2 presumed these to be the 9th and 10th SS Panzer Divisions and reported that the divisions were likely being reequipped with new tanks.[5] There was no hard evidence of this, only the intuition of an experienced intelligence officer and the fact that the divisions in question could not be located elsewhere. Smith urged Strong to repeat this estimate to the supreme commander at once.

Eisenhower knew Strong well enough to respect his hunch. He did not feel, however, that he could override Montgomery's decision to go ahead with the operation without some hard evidence. He sent Smith and Strong to see Montgomery at the field marshal's headquarters. The two men repeated their concerns to Montgomery and concluded with the recommendation that if the operation was to proceed, two airborne divisions should be dropped at Arnhem instead of the one as currently planned. Montgomery, as Smith later described it, "ridiculed the idea and waved my objections airily aside."[6]

An added threat developed during the two weeks leading up to Market-Garden. On September 4, Hitler recalled sixty-eight-year-old Field Marshal Gerd von Rundstedt to take command of all armies on the Western Front, the same post the Führer had relieved von Rundstedt of on July 1. The Germans also created a new army, the First Parachute Army, under Luftwaffe Generaloberst (General) Kurt Student.*

---

* In the German force structure, airborne units were part of the Luftwaffe, the German air force.

Paratroops of Student's army began arriving in the area south of the Neder Rijn. Joining the reconstituted 6th Parachute Regiment and a battalion of the 2nd Parachute Regiment were five newly formed parachute regiments, an antitank battalion, and around five thousand service troops.

The First Parachute Army, the Fifteenth Army, which occupied much of western Holland, and the Seventh Army at Aachen were all subordinate to Generalfeldmarschall (Field Marshal) Walter Model's Army Group B. Responsibility for the defense of all territory to the rear of these armies, generally north of the Maas and Waal rivers, fell to a Luftwaffe officer, General der Flieger Friedrich Christiansen, and his Armed Forces Command Netherlands.

When the monocled fifty-four-year-old Model assumed command of Army Group B on August 17, he established his headquarters at the Hotel Tafelberg in Oosterbeek, a few miles west of Arnhem. His staff occupied the nearby Hotel Hartenstein. On September 3, he directed the retreating Fifth Panzer Army to send its 9th and 10th SS Panzer Divisions to the vicinity of Arnhem for refitting and rehabilitation. Here the divisions would be equipped with new Tiger tanks, with their eighty-eight-millimeter guns, from a factory in the German town of Cleve, just across the border.

Two days later, Model ordered SS-Obergruppenführer (SS Lieutenant General) Wilhelm "Willi" Bittrich, commander of II SS Panzer Corps, to move his headquarters to the Arnhem area as well. Bittrich, tall and handsome and intelligent, was one of the best leaders in the Waffen-SS. At Arnhem, he was to oversee the rehabilitation of the 9th SS Panzer Division and two additional armored divisions, the 2nd and 116th Panzer Divisions, which were to move to Holland from the Seventh Army. The 10th SS Panzer Division was to continue movement on into Germany for rehabilitation there. They were later directed to remain near Arnhem and came under Bittrich's control.

Shortly before the launch of Market-Garden, British code breakers at Bletchley Park, who intercepted and decoded much of Germany's radio traffic and issued the resulting top secret intelligence reports to SHAEF and to field army and army group commanders, reported that they had intercepted messages that confirmed the presence of the 9th and 10th SS Panzer Divisions in the Arnhem area. What's more, they had learned that Field Marshal Model's Army Group B headquarters was also in the vicinity.

All Dutch Jedburgh teams with the exception of team Clarence gathered at British I Airborne Corps headquarters, a palatial eighteenth-century mansion that had become the clubhouse of an exclusive golf course at Moor Park, near Rickmansworth in the northwestern outskirts of London, to be briefed on their role in the upcoming operation. When the conference broke up, Captain Staal and the others of team Edward settled in to work on refining the plan over the few remaining days before the operation commenced. On Friday the fifteenth, Staal's team moved to Harwell Transit Camp and prepared for deployment.

Planners at I Airborne Corps expected that the capture of all bridges intact would depend more on surprise, and the ensuing confusion, than on hard fighting. If the airborne operations succeeded, the planners were certain that the advance of XXX Corps would be swift.[7]

As the plan developed, there were four main tasks for the Jedburgh teams. First, they were to coordinate support from local Dutch resistance groups. Second, they were to collect and report intelligence on the situation in their respective areas. Third, they were to assist in the critical task of vetting members of the local resistance to serve as guides for Allied forces or for taking part in patrols. Fourth, they were to coordinate with the resistance for any labor that might be needed by the Allied parachutists.

The staff of First Allied Airborne Army received a signal on the sixteenth from Montgomery's headquarters informing them that plans were to "limit the raising of resistance in Holland to those areas immediately affected by Operation Market and for the remainder of the country to remain underground until further instructions are issued."[8]

Team Daniel II joined the 101st Airborne at division headquarters at Greenham Lodge, located at the edge of an airfield outside Newbury, on September 12. Three days later, they attended the division operational briefing. Jedburgh team Clarence joined the 82nd Airborne Division headquarters located in a group of Nissen huts in Braunstone Park, just outside Leicester.

Captain Groenewoud's Jedburgh team Claude joined the British 1st Airborne Division, quartered in the Swinden area, and lived with the men of the 1st Parachute Brigade, to which they were attached. Over the next week, the brigade staff would come to like and respect Harvey Todd, as they called him.[9] Team Claude's three-part mission was 1) to organize a civilian work crew to clear the drop zone and help handle supplies and to round up all available civilian transportation to haul supplies and equipment from the drop zone into Arnhem; 2) to accompany the 1st Parachute Brigade into Arnhem and to contact the pre-occupation mayor and chief of police and have them assume control of the city government until Allied military government authorities arrived; and 3) once all other tasks had been accomplished, to move into the area ahead of Second British Army to gather information that would be of immediate tactical use to the commander.

Team Claude now gained a newly attached member. In an effort to ensure that an adequate number of Dutch speakers accompanied the paratroopers into Holland, members of the Dutch Commando Troop were attached to each of the airborne division and brigade headquarters to serve as interpreters. One of the Dutch commandos, Lieutenant Maarten Jan Knottenbelt, a tall young man wearing thick-lensed, rimless glasses, would accompany team Claude, even though he had never been selected and trained as a Jedburgh. The team was briefed by an intelligence officer from the airborne corps staff and by Captain Staal on Thursday, September 14.

That same morning, the three airborne division commanders, each accompanied by a couple of staff officers, met at General Browning's headquarters at Moor Park. Each commander, in turn, presented a briefing to Browning on his plan for executing his division's portion of Operation Market. As Major General Urquhart briefed his plan, he described how the British 1st Airborne Division would be dropped six to eight miles from its primary objective, the Arnhem bridge.

Upon hearing this, Brigadier General Gavin, commander of the U.S. 82nd Airborne Division, turned to his operations officer, Lieutenant Colonel John Norton, and said, "My God, he can't mean it."

Norton replied, "He does, and he is going to try to do it."[10]

As the final briefing was ending, Major General Sosabowski, the tough but emotional commander of the Polish parachute brigade, sitting right behind Gavin, asked very loudly, "But the Germans, how about the Germans, what about *them*?"[11] His question went unanswered, but Gavin shared Sosabowski's concern. To the 82nd's commander, the whole ambitious plan "seemed more like a peacetime exercise than war."[12]

In eastern Holland, radios and other supplies for team Dudley arrived on Wednesday, the thirteenth. The package included two B-2 radio sets, two Jed sets, two Eureka sets, and two S-phones.* Receivers and batteries filled another container. The Jeds gave one of the B-2 sets to Evert's radio operator, a man named Maurits. Sergeant Austin then used one of the radios to contact London and pass on the team's first report, informing Special Force Headquarters of their safe arrival, their successful linkup with the underground, and a succinct rundown on the local situation. Then, satisfied that the groundwork for a successful logistical system had been put in place, and that they were beginning to earn their keep, the men walked back to the first farm for supper.

By their second day on the ground, Majors Brinkgreve and Olmsted were beginning to doubt the efficiency of Commandant Evert. The contents of the containers that had been dropped with the team were still not fully distributed, and it had become clear that Evert had no organization worthy of the word. He had no deputy, and his intelligence net, if indeed one even existed, was incapable of providing any information on the Germans. Evert could tell them nothing of enemy troop dispositions or locations of supply depots.

Brinkgreve and Olmsted met with two young members of the Knok-Ploegen (KP) resistance organization on September 14. Johannes was the leader of a group located near the old textile town of Almelo. The other man, Cor Hilbrink, was his second in command. It did not take long for the Jeds to find themselves at ease with the KP men, and they were impressed with their grasp of resistance work. One thing they learned was that Evert and his group had taken credit for much of the KP's past operations. Johannes and Cor urged the Jeds to leave Evert and join their KP headquarters.

---

* Officially designated the Type 3 MK II, the B-2 radio was designed for use by British agents and resistance groups in occupied, or enemy, territory. The modular set consisted of a receiver, transmitter, power supply unit, a Morse key, and a spare parts box. It could operate at distances of five hundred miles or more. The Jed set was a lighter, more compact version of the B-2 designed for use by the Jedburgh teams. It included a hand-cranked power generator for use when transmitting. The Rebecca/Eureka transponder system was used by aircraft crews to locate an agent on the ground to identify where a parachute drop should be made. The Eureka ground emitter sent out a radio homing beacon in response to queries from a Rebecca interrogator mounted in the plane. The S-phone was a transceiver set that allowed voice communication between a ground operator and an aircraft up to a range of thirty miles.

To make matters worse, the situation at Evert's headquarters became one of chaos on Friday afternoon as three German army trucks, driven by unidentified Dutchmen, rolled into the woods. Evert's men learned that the drivers belonged to another resistance group and that they had stolen the trucks and had chosen this patch of woods to hide the trucks in.

The Jeds were growing uncomfortable; the situation in the area seemed unstable at best, and the Germans would surely be searching for the missing trucks. Brinkgreve and Olmsted decided that the headquarters should be moved farther to the north immediately. They began planning and preparing for the move at once, including having a photographer take their pictures in the woods so that they could have false identity papers prepared. Meanwhile, Sergeant Austin went ahead to a new safe house in Daarle.

Austin stayed at the home of a family named Dominie. The family was most accommodating and treated the British sergeant very well, although he had to remain hidden because three SS officers were also billeted in the house. At least the radioman was the only member of team Dudley with a room and bed of his own. As if sharing a house with three SS officers weren't nerve-racking enough, the entire village of Daarle was crowded with Germans.

Always careful about security, Austin asked the servant of the house if his hand-cranked generator, required for transmitting with his Jed set, could be heard downstairs. The servant replied that not only could the generator be heard downstairs, it could be heard out in the garden as well. Fortunately, the Germans were so busy that none of them paid any attention to the low whine. To be on the safe side, Austin began relying solely on his battery set for power.

———

Units of paratroopers and glidermen of all three airborne divisions began moving to their departure airfields on Friday, September 15. In all, the operation would stage out of twenty-four airfields—seven British and seventeen U.S.[13] All departure airfields were sealed that night, preventing anyone from leaving the installations without a guard escort. Paratroopers and aircrews alike were restricted to the camp. Isolation, and thus security, was further ensured as all commercial telephone service was cut off.[14]

Saturday dawned crisp and cool but grew cold and gloomy with a drizzling rain. Briefings continued throughout the morning as division, brigade, battalion, and company commanders refined their plans. Leaders and staff officers pored over maps and aerial photographs, checking every detail. General Gavin reviewed with his battalion commanders the procedure to be followed in capturing each bridge. First, all wires leading to a bridge were to be cut in hopes of preventing the Germans from blowing up the bridge with pre-planted explosives. Once all wires were cut, explosives were to be located and removed. Lastly, both ends of a bridge were to be assaulted simultaneously whenever possible.[15]

Men spent the day preparing weapons and distributing and packing rations, medical supplies, radios, antitank mines, and ammunition of all types. The British SAS provided the Jeds of team Edward a jeep and trailer, both of which were packed to the hilt and secured in the glider that would carry all of the team except Captain Staal. He was to accompany the corps G-2 on another glider.

Units of General Gavin's 82nd Airborne Division occupied airfields scattered around Fulbeck, where the U.S. 440th Troop Carrier Group was headquartered. The thirty-seven-year-old Gavin had taken command of the 82nd on August 15, when the previous commander, Major General Ridgway, had been given command of the newly formed XVIII Airborne Corps. Known throughout the division as "Slim Jim" or "General Jim," Gavin had enlisted in the army in his home state of New York at the age of seventeen and had achieved the rank of corporal before heading to the United States Military Academy at West Point, where he earned his commission in 1929. In 1941, he was a captain serving as a tactical officer at West Point.[16] Just three years later, in late 1944, he would become the youngest major general in the United States Army.[17]

Jedburgh team Clarence had joined the 82nd's headquarters staff at Cottesmore airfield, where a heavy fog hung on the morning of the sixteenth. Since General Gavin had asked Captain Bestebreurtje's team to accompany his division headquarters to Holland, the twenty-eight-year-old Dutch officer had shared his knowledge of his homeland with the 82nd's intelligence (G-2) staff. He provided valuable firsthand information, briefing the staff on the terrain in which the division was to operate, the roads and bridges and rivers in the area, and he told them about the people who lived there. As Gavin's Dutch adviser, the popular Jedburgh team leader came to be called "Captain Harry" by the men of the 82nd.

The division's plan for D-Day called for the 504th Parachute Infantry Regiment to seize the nine-span, six-hundred-yard-long bridge over the Maas River near Grave, as well as at least one of four bridges that spanned the two-hundred-foot-wide Maas-Waal Canal. The 505th Parachute Infantry Regiment was to capture the town of Groesbeek and secure the high ground south of Nijmegen, while the 508th took the high ground east of Nijmegen and then the Waalbrug, the massive 653-yard-long, steel-girdered highway bridge over the Waal at Nijmegen. Built in 1936, the bridge boasted a half-moon steel superstructure that rose nearly to the height of a twenty-story building; it was reputed to be the longest bridge in all of Europe.

Dominating the bridges over the Maas and Waal rivers was the high ground to the east, a ridge about eight miles in length and around three hundred feet in height. The German border lay along the base of the ridge's eastern slope, and beyond the border in Germany rose the forested hills of the Reichswald. Gavin realized that the high ground was his most important initial objective; seizure of the bridges counted for little if the enemy held the dominating ridgeline. But the general was also concerned about reports of German armor massing in the Reichswald. If such a force existed there, they would constitute an obvious counterattack threat.

Gavin decided that he would first concentrate on seizing the high ground and capturing the bridges spanning the Maas and the Maas-Waal Canal. That would ensure a linkup with the ground column. Although capture of the Nijmegen bridge would be a second priority, Gavin ordered Colonel Roy Lindquist, commander of the 508th Parachute Infantry, to send a battalion to the bridge immediately upon landing. If surprise offered the opportunity of taking the bridge, the division commander didn't want to pass it up.

Team Clarence was briefed on its mission of liaison between the 82nd and the Dutch resistance; the briefing included background on the resistance organizations in the objective area and a list of rendezvous points and contacts. They were also given cash totaling five thousand guilders.[18]

A light rain continued through the day, and many of the paratroopers speculated that the operation might be canceled. But the weather cleared that evening, and soon the official word came down. Basing his decision on favorable weather forecasts, General Brereton informed his staff at seven that the operation was on. D-Day was to be the next day, September 17, with H-Hour at one in the afternoon. The jump was on, regardless of the weather.

As the Jeds of team Clarence packed and rigged their gear for the jump, Sergeant Beynon worried that he would be separated from his radio during the jump.[19]

Captain Groenewoud's team, too, received more details on their mission with the British 1st Airborne Division. Upon landing in Holland, team Claude was to contact the Dutch resistance and, with their help, recruit civilian labor parties and procure local transportation to aid in clearing the drop zone and hauling supplies into Arnhem. Automobiles, trucks, horses, and wagons—nothing was to be overlooked as a possible cargo hauler. Following this, the team was to be attached to the division's 1st Brigade headquarters and would accompany elements of the brigade into Arnhem.

In spite of the reported presence of armor in the Arnhem area, the British paratroopers were told in their intelligence briefing to expect nothing more than second-rate troops—old men and boys, mostly.

Henk Brinkgreve and Pappy Olmsted had completed preparations for their move by Saturday afternoon, September 16. Once darkness arrived, men of the resistance drove a large horse-drawn hayrack close to the shack that had been serving as the Jeds' command post. The men quickly loaded all the arms and other gear aboard the hayrack, and the small group of about ten men set out on the road to their new headquarters. Two men armed with Sten submachine guns scouted well ahead of the others. Two more men with Stens led the hayrack, and another two followed as a rear guard. The few remaining men walked along both sides of the cart, carrying Stens or carbines. Everyone also carried a pistol and hand grenades. Although the huge horses made a terrible racket as they plodded across the wooden bridges spanning canals along the way, the group completed the nine-mile journey without incident.

Upon arrival at their new farm, the men unloaded the gear in the barn, and the farmer's wife served them a late snack of cookies, hard-boiled eggs, and hot milk. Then the men lay down to sleep in hay and straw that was warm and comfortable, though infested with lice.

That night, the first air strikes in support of Operation Market-Garden began under a moonless sky.

EIGHT

SUNDAY, SEPTEMBER 17

D-Day

Sunday dawned cool, with a light drizzle and a thick, ground-hugging fog. At two dozen airfields scattered about the English neighborhoods of Swinden, Newbury, and Grantham, battalions of parachutists received last minute briefings on maps and sand tables. Brief church services were available for those who wished to attend. Troops ate a breakfast of bacon and eggs and potatoes; some units even had fried chicken. At around seven, they began gathering near their assigned planes, still shrouded in mist.

As the fog cleared, men could see long rows of C-47 Skytrain troop carriers, neatly parked at a slant, side by side, lining both sides of the runway. Other long lines of planes included gliders, with tow ropes attached and laid out in large S-patterns on the ground behind each C-47. By nine, the fog had cleared, and soon the sun beamed from a cloudless sky. It was a perfect day for jumping. Men lay about near the aircraft in the midmorning sun, awaiting the time to chute up and board.

Trucks filled with parachutes pulled up near the planes, and paratroopers lined up to grab chutes from the back of the vehicles. Other trucks delivered explosives and more ammunition. When orders came down for the men to chute up, they buckled on the main parachutes with the new quick-release harnesses. At their waist, in front, went the reserve parachute, and under that hung a musette bag carrying rations for three days, extra socks, and personal items. Web belts around their waists held ammunition pouches, canteens, entrenching tools, first-aid kits, bayonets, and emergency D-rations. Packed into the large cargo pockets on their pant legs were fragmentation grenades, mines, maps, and perhaps some K-rations. Then came rifles or carbines, pistols, bandoliers of ammo clips, smoke and white phosphorous grenades, sleeping bags, knives. The men also carried Gammon grenades. Referred to as "hand artillery," they were powerful things, each containing from one to three pounds of high explosive. There were blocks of TNT and C-2 plastic explosive, along with fuses, detonating caps, and exploding Primacord. Most of the men also had to carry a couple of mortar rounds each, perhaps a can or two of machine-gun ammo, antitank mines, or bazooka rockets. Each soldier and officer grabbed a few syrettes of morphine from a wooden box and donned a Mae West life preserver, just in case they came down in water. Heavier and bulkier items were packed into containers called parapacks, which were fastened to the bellies of the C-47s, to be dropped when the paratroopers jumped.

For the men of the Jedburgh teams, pockets also carried codes, maps, and crystals for the Jedburgh radio sets. Larger items, such as the two radios themselves, the team members' rucksacks, French civilian clothing, and arms for the partisans, were all packed in supply canisters to be dropped with the team. Radio operators, of course, also carried the "one-time pads" for enciphering and deciphering messages. For the sake of security, brevity of messages was most important. To assist the radioman in keeping his traffic short, SFHQ communications personnel issued a twenty-inch-square piece of silk printed with four-letter codes for often used phrases. They also issued each team a schedule of radio contacts to be made, designating times for both sending and receiving messages.[1]

Loaded down like pack mules, inspected to ensure that everything was strapped on correctly, the men pushed and pulled one another into the planes. On average, each C-47 carried sixteen or seventeen parachutists, seated in two rows of bucket seats, facing each other, with seat belts fastened.

————

Ten miles northwest of Newbury, to the west of London, lay Welford airfield. There, the men of Jedburgh team Daniel II boarded the aircraft that would carry them to Holland with the first wave of the 101st Airborne Division. Lieutenant Dubois, who was to serve as General Taylor's interpreter and Dutch liaison officer, joined the division commander in plane number two. Major Wilson went in plane number six with members of the division headquarters staff. Sergeants Mason and Faber, the two radio operators, rode in plane number nine with more division headquarters personnel. The sergeants had packed all their radio gear into a pannier, rigged with a parachute, that was to be kicked out of the aircraft following the personnel drop. The Jeds had been briefed on the Dutch resistance in the 101st's area of operations and had been provided a list of rendezvous sites and contacts. The team carried five thousand guilders in cash.[2]

Elsewhere, paratroopers of the 82nd Airborne Division began moving to their planes at eight-thirty following a bacon-and-egg breakfast.[3] At Cottesmore airfield, Jedburgh team Clarence helped the division operations staff prepare map boards in a Nissen hut for Brigadier General Gavin's final briefing with his staff and regimental commanders. The team then joined Gavin and a few members of his staff as they prepared for the jump with the 505th Parachute Infantry Regiment. Nine planes carrying division headquarters personnel, including the Jedburgh team, would accompany the regiment's 1st Battalion and jump with them on Drop Zone N. The 505th's regimental headquarters and its remaining two battalions would depart from an airfield at Folkingham, farther to the north.

Earlier, the popular General Gavin had spoken to the assembled paratroopers at Cottesmore, encouraging the men to do their best and wishing everyone well. Listening to the general's pep talk, the 505th's regimental surgeon turned to a chaplain and remarked, "I hope he doesn't ask us to jump without parachutes, because I'm sure no man would refuse to go."[4]

Men of the 505th climbed aboard their C-47s at around ten o'clock. The 3rd Battalion was to jump first on Drop Zone N, with the mission of capturing the town of Groesbeek. They were to be followed at four-minute intervals by the regiment's other two battalions. The 1st Battalion's mission was to establish a defensive line along the southwestern portion of the division's perimeter.

Captain Bestebreurtje and Lieutenant Verhaeghe of Jed team

Clarence climbed aboard the first plane with General Gavin. Technical Sergeant Beynon, the team's radio operator, boarded the third plane, along with the equipment bundles in which his radios were packed. Beynon had never before jumped from a C-47, and he worried that he might become separated from the three packages during the jump. He had good cause to be concerned: The bundles were to be kicked out separately after the last jumper left the plane, and there would be no reception committee on the ground to keep an eye on where they came down.

At that same time, at airfields near Swinden, the British 1st Airborne Division and Jedburgh team Claude boarded their planes. Team Edward and General Browning's corps headquarters boarded aircraft at Harwell.

Just as the heat and the stench of fuel and oil and perspiration began to fill the cabins of the troop carriers, the twin engines coughed and roared to life, and the bulky airplanes taxied in line to the head of the runway to await their turn for takeoff. But they weren't to be the first aircraft to take part in Operation Market-Garden. In the early morning hours, more than 1,400 British and American bombers and escorts struck German antiaircraft gun and coastal defense positions in Holland, hoping to be as effective as possible without tipping off the enemy about the impending airborne assault.[5]

For the airborne operation itself, an armada of 1,544 troop carrier aircraft and 478 gliders prepared to carry the three airborne divisions and the airborne corps headquarters to Holland.[6] Pathfinder teams were dropped into the Dutch countryside at 10:25 A.M. to mark drop zones for the troop carriers and landing zones for the gliders. At that same time, planeloads of paratroopers began lifting off from twenty-four airfields and would continue doing so until the last plane took off at 11:55.[7] Flight time to their destinations was about two and a half hours, and the planes would be in enemy airspace for anywhere from thirty to fifty minutes.[8]

Planes carrying the 82nd began taking off at 10:19 A.M., at five-second intervals, from six airfields in the Grantham area. The lead serial contained the 505th Parachute Infantry Regiment, along with General Gavin and Jedburgh team Clarence. Next came the 504th, then the 508th, and last came 50 gliders carrying a battery of the 80th Antiaircraft

(Antitank) Battalion; in all, the division's first lift filled 480 C-47s and 50 CG-4A Waco gliders.[9] The roughly 90 planes required to carry each regiment, broken down into two serials, cleared the field in about twenty minutes and maneuvered into a long series of V-shaped formations at an altitude of fifteen hundred feet under the clear sky and bright sun.[10]

The British 1st Airborne Division lifted off from airfields in the Swinden area in 358 British and 145 U.S. troop carriers. In tow were 354 British and 4 American gliders.[11] Having been left out of the airborne operation on June 6, D-Day for Operation Overlord, the Allied invasion of Normandy, the men of the 1st Airborne Division were eager to get into action on the Continent. The Jeds of team Claude flew with the division's 1st Parachute Brigade headquarters, taking off from Barkston Heath airfield. A Horsa glider carrying Lieutenant Knottenbelt and men of the division's reconnaissance squadron lifted off from Tarrant Rushton airfield at 10:35.

At 11:20, Jedburgh team Edward departed Harwell in a glider with part of General Browning's corps headquarters.

From their aerial rendezvous points, planes carrying the British 1st Airborne Division, the U.S. 82nd Airborne Division, and the British I Airborne Corps headquarters followed the northern route toward Arnhem and Nijmegen. The massive formation of aircraft, stretching more than a hundred miles in length, took an hour and a half or more to pass a given point. The next day's London *Daily Express,* in reporting passage of the planes over the east coast of England, declared that "from 11:00 a.m. to 12:30 p.m., the fleet filled the skies."[12] People in English towns and villages gathered in the streets and waved to the planes overhead. Telephone conversations became impossible over the thunderous rumble.[13]

General Taylor's 101st, along with Jedburgh team Daniel II, lifted off from airfields in the Newbury area—Welford, Membury, Aldermaston, and Ghilbolton—in 424 C-47s and 70 gliders beginning at 10:50.[14] As the planes grouped in the skies over England and headed out on the southern route toward Eindhoven, the weather was fair, with a slight haze, visibility varying from four to six miles.[15]

Some two thousand aircraft had taken off from twenty-four airfields across the English Midlands. After climbing to altitude, the planes closed into serial formations and fell into either the northern or the southern corridor. Along each corridor, the legion of airplanes covered an area ninety-four miles in length and three miles in width.[16] Fighter cover flew overhead and on the flanks.

Soon, serials of Skytrains (called Dakotas by the British) headed east over the water where the English Channel connects to the North Sea. Paratroopers smoked cigarettes and thought of what lay ahead—or tried not to. Men leaned sideways to look out the C-47s' windows, gazing down at the vibrant cobalt waters of the Channel. They were comforted by the sight of fighters and fighter-bombers swarming in protective escort for the troop carriers. In all, more than a thousand fighters took part—British Typhoons, Mosquitoes, Tempests, and Spitfires on the northern route; American P-38 Lightnings, P-47 Thunderbolts, and P-51 Mustangs on the southern. Other planes continued to hit flak positions along the Dutch-Belgian frontier. In the water below, Britain's Air/Sea Rescue Service stood by with seventeen launches positioned along the northern route and another ten along the southern route, ready to come to the aid of aircrews or planeloads of paratroopers forced to ditch in the sea.[17]

By one in the afternoon, C-47s carrying the 101st Airborne soared over the Belgian countryside, scattering herds of cattle on the ground below. Farmers waved at the steady columns of planes passing overhead.[18] Then, just before crossing the Dutch border, the paratroopers looked down in awe at the massed British XXX Corps, with tanks and other vehicles lined up on every road and trail and scattered about the fields.[19] Some twenty thousand vehicles were poised to begin the ground operation to link up with the airborne divisions on their drive northward toward Arnhem.

The troop carriers ran into fairly intense flak as they crossed over German lines at around one-twenty, the deadly fire materializing as gray puffballs bursting in the air. One plane carrying pathfinders had already been shot down. Now, in addition to the flak, C-47s bringing in the first wave of paratroopers began taking small-arms fire from the ground. Some planes were hit, two going down before reaching the drop area, but even those that were badly damaged or burning struggled to stay on course until their loads of paratroops were released over their assigned drop zones. Pilots were determined that the scattered drops experienced at Normandy would not be repeated in Holland. Dutch people in the villages and countryside, many on their way home from church, stared skyward to watch the spectacle.

The division's 501st Parachute Infantry Regiment dropped near Veghel and accomplished all of its D-Day objectives within three hours, capturing the town and seizing rail and road bridges over the Willems Vaart Canal and the Aa River.

Men of the 506th Parachute Infantry, of later *Band of Brothers* fame, landed on the St. Oedenrode drop zone and were immediately greeted by members of the local KP resistance group. Upon learning the regiment's objectives, the resistance men led the Americans to the river bridges and briefed them on the disposition of German troops in the area. Men of the 506th secured all bridges until they reached a critical highway span over the Wilhelmina Canal south of the town of Son. Just as troops approached the bridge, the Germans blew it up in their faces.

It was nearly one-thirty when men of the division headquarters and Jedburgh team Daniel II jumped. General Taylor stood ready to follow the jumpmaster out the door of his C-47. When it came time to jump, the jumpmaster stared in awe at another plane full of paratroopers that had taken a hit and was burning. Taylor had to nudge the man out the door.[20] Planes six and nine, two of the C-47s carrying Jeds, took hits and were on fire by the time the parachutists jumped, but all the men of Daniel II landed safely on the drop zone near St. Oedenrode, five miles north of Eindhoven.

The 502nd Parachute Infantry quickly captured St. Oedenrode after a brief but intense firefight. Other D-Day tasks assigned to the regiment included the capture of a bridge over the Dommel River at St. Oedenrode and guarding the drop zones so that they could be used later as glider landing zones.

Major Wilson and Sergeants Mason and Faber quickly searched the drop zone for the package containing the team's radio equipment, but they found nothing. Apparently the fire in the aircraft had dashed all hope of having a door bundle kicked from the plane. Reporting their successful arrival in the field to Special Force Headquarters by radio was now out of the question. Most of the Jeds' remaining gear, including their spare radio, had been loaded on gliders that would arrive with the second lift, so all they could do was wait.

Team Daniel II quickly set off as German eighty-eights began shelling the drop zone. After two hours, the Jeds made their way to the division assembly area. Later, after the enemy had been cleared from the area surrounding the drop zone, the Jeds returned and once again searched for the missing radio, but still their search turned up nothing.

Lieutenant Dubois remained at General Taylor's side and would stay with him continuously through the first two days of the operation. Wilson and the others of team Daniel II settled in at the division command post near the town of Son, on the road leading into Eindhoven, part of the slender fifteen-mile stretch of concrete and macadam the division was to seize and hold, a stretch of road the men of the 101st would come to call "Hell's Highway." The command post would remain at the site near Son for the next three days. The Jeds had not yet contacted the Dutch underground, but they gathered useful information for the division staff from local citizens.

The first Screaming Eagle had jumped a few minutes after one o'clock. Within thirty minutes, the division's D-Day lift of 6,769 paratroopers had made it safely to the ground. Gliders of the division's second lift arrived with an additional 252 men, but because only fifty-three of the expected seventy gliders completed the trip,[21] just a portion of team Daniel II's gear arrived. The team's spare radio set was not included.

Taylor's paratroopers then began pushing toward Eindhoven, five miles to the south, a town still untouched by the war. Because of reports from civilians of a strong German garrison in the city, though, the general chose to delay the final assault until morning.

On the northern route, planes and gliders carrying the British 1st Airborne Division and the U.S. 82nd Airborne Division passed over the Dutch coastal islands and began to encounter flak, sporadic at first but growing steadily heavier. Bomber crews who had often flown this route over the Scheldt estuary and coastal islands in the past had come to call it "flak alley," and for good reason. Few planes were hit, though, and the air armada continued over a large flooded area of southern Holland, where bomb-damaged dikes had given way.

Now men peering through the tiny windows of the C-47s could see the windmills and dikes and green fields below. They looked down upon small Dutch villages of red-tile-roofed buildings. They could also see the flak guns and even individual German soldiers with rifles firing up at them. Fighters and fighter-bombers dove on German antiaircraft positions or on enemy vehicles on the roads, firing rockets and wing-mounted machine guns. One or two C-47s could be seen going down, trailing flame or smoke.

Then the planes banked to the left, dropped to an altitude of four hundred feet, and made their approach to the drop area. Flak continued to increase as they approached the drop zone, rocking the C-47s. Because planes could be hit at any time, many jumpmasters shouted the "Stand up and hook up!" order earlier than they normally would. At times, small-arms or antiaircraft machine-gun fire ripped through a C-47 fuselage, and all aboard looked about to see if anyone had been hit.[22]

Nine miles west of the American drop zones, Generaloberst Kurt Student, commander of the First German Parachute Army, was sitting down to lunch at his headquarters in the Villa Bergen in Vught. On hearing the approaching rumble of the air armada, the general and his chief of staff, Oberst (Colonel) Reinhard, stepped outside and stared skyward in awe. As a mile-long column of C-47s paraded directly over Student's headquarters, the German paratroop commander gazed admiringly at the spectacle, then turned to Reinhard and said, "Oh, if ever I'd had such means at my disposal. Just once, to have this many planes."[23]

As the C-47s neared the drop zone, the fighter escort gained altitude and peeled away as the troop transports slowed to 110 miles per hour and leveled off at an altitude of four hundred feet. Men shuffled toward the rear of the aircraft, closer to the door, anxious to exit the flying target. In the open door stood the lead jumper, his left foot planted on the doorsill, his hands gripping the outer skin of the aircraft on either side of the door. When a small light near the door turned green, the jumpmaster screamed, "Go!" and the lead jumper stepped and pushed himself out the door and into the "prop blast." The static line, anchored to a cable inside the C-47, yanked the parachute pack open, releasing the parachute, and by the time the jumper had fallen another eighty-three feet, he had a full canopy overhead. Because the drop was made at such a low altitude, the men seemed to hit the ground almost immediately after their parachutes opened.

The 504th Parachute Infantry Regiment jumped to a drop zone in a meadow near the medieval fortress town of Grave, south of Nijmegen and fifty-seven miles behind German lines, with the objective of seizing the bridge over the Maas River located there, as well as two bridges over the Maas-Waal Canal that connected the Maas with the Waal River farther to the north. One company of the regiment's 2nd Battalion was dropped south of the Grave bridge over the Maas and the remainder of the battalion on a pasture north of the bridge, as Dutch cows stood idly by. Attacking the bridge from both ends, the American paratroopers were able to capture it intact in under three hours.[24] The long steel-girder bridge reminded paratroopers from New York of Hell's Gate Bridge back home.[25] By day's end, the 504th had also secured the town of Grave, making it the first Dutch town to be liberated by the Allies. At four in the afternoon, against stiff resistance, a battalion of the 504th captured a bridge over the Maas-Waal Canal at Heumen that would become the crossing point over the canal for the British ground column. The Germans demolished at least three other bridges over the canal before the Americans could seize them.

————

The 505th Parachute Infantry's first serial jumped shortly after one. On the ground below, Germans manning antiaircraft guns could be seen running for the cover of wooded areas as the sky above them filled with parachutes. The entire 505th and the accompanying division headquarters were on the drop zone within ten minutes, and all of the regiment's companies assembled and moved out to their assigned objectives within the hour.[26]

Troops of the 505th's 3rd Battalion were still on the drop zone when the 1st Battalion, along with the division headquarters and Jedburgh team Clarence, jumped at six minutes past one from an altitude of four hundred feet.[27] Men were still on the drop zone, crawling out of their parachute harnesses, as others were floating to earth above them. Drop Zone N lay about a mile and a half south of the town of Groesbeek and roughly a quarter of a mile west of a dark and hilly forested area called the Reichswald. General Gavin came down awkwardly, falling rearward and landing flat on his back. Years later, an X-ray would reveal that Gavin fractured his back on the jump.[28]

At once the men of the 505th, still struggling to get free of their parachute harnesses, came under small-arms fire from the nearby woods. Immediately, Gavin got to his feet, grabbed his rifle, and moved off toward the assembly point in a wooded area. Captain Bestebreurtje and Lieutenant Verhaeghe landed safely on the soft, sandy Dutch soil and quickly joined the general.

Once Gavin had his battle staff assembled, the small group headed for a farmhouse in the woods about a mile away, where Gavin planned to establish the division command post. The group set out down a sunken dirt road that ran through a thick pine forest. A small team of engineers accompanied the command group, and Gavin directed them to send a small element out on "point," to provide security for the remainder of the command group following behind. But the engineers moved slowly, wary of what lay ahead because of all the firing that had come from the woods. Gavin quickly realized that the group would make slow progress with the engineers in the lead. He ordered Captain Bestebreurtje to take the point, walking along the left side of the road. Gavin would follow about five yards behind on the right side of the road. The remainder of the group of staff personnel and engineers were told to keep up because they were going to move as quickly as possible.

After walking down the road at a quick pace for five or ten minutes at a level seven or eight feet below the banks on both sides, a German machine gun opened up. The gun was firing from a position directly above Gavin's head and was apparently shooting at Bestebreurtje. Gavin immediately began climbing the embankment to engage the Germans above him. As he reached the top, he saw a German running off through the woods but was unable to get a shot at him because of the trees. The general then looked toward the machine-gun position to his left and saw that the gunner was dead with a bullet through the forehead. No other Germans could be seen.

Gavin descended to the road to check on Bestebreurtje. When he approached the Dutch Jedburgh officer, the general asked how the captain was able to make such an accurate shot while under fire. Bestebreurtje explained that he had wheeled about as soon as he came under fire and immediately saw the gunner's white forehead between the machine gun and his helmet. The Dutchman had fired from the hip with his M1 carbine and hit the German square in the forehead.[29] Still excited at such a close call, the men continued to lead the command group to the farmhouse.

The group approached the outskirts of Groesbeek, where they intended to turn back into the woods on a paved road that led to their planned command post. Before continuing on the paved road, Bestebreurtje entered a house and found the telephone in operation. Using a code he had been provided during their briefings back in England, he began placing calls to Nijmegen and other towns in the area, gathering information and notifying the Dutch resistance of Jed team Clarence's arrival with the paratroopers. He was able to learn that the Arnhem landings had also taken place and that all seemed to be going well.[30] The captain rejoined Gavin and briefed him as the group continued toward the command post. Reaching the command post within half an hour, Gavin and his staff made radio contact with all three regiments of the 82nd and learned that everything was proceeding according to plan.

When Technical Sergeant Bud Beynon's turn came to jump, he made a strong exit. He, too, came down safely, got to his feet, turned the parachute harness quick-release knob on his chest, and punched it in; the harness fell to the ground. Beynon heard gunfire around the drop zone. Eager to locate his radios, he quickly found a corporal from the 82nd who volunteered to help him search for the package containing his radios. Once the fire quieted down somewhat, the two men made a dash for the woods. Enemy automatic weapons fire spoiled their plans, however, and the search was postponed until later. As Beynon feared, though, the packages were lost. Dropped too early during the approach, the packages landed in the Reichswald, the forest just across the nearby border in Germany.

Having had no luck in finding the radios, Beynon asked other paratroopers where General Gavin was. He wanted to link up with his teammates and knew that the two Jedburgh officers would most likely be with the division commander.

During his search for the radios, Beynon had encountered an English-speaking Dutch kid who appeared to be close to his own age. The young man explained that his name was Theo Smiet and that he was from Apeldoorn, a town seventeen miles north of Arnhem. He began tagging along with Beynon, telling the sergeant who among the local people could be trusted and who couldn't. Beynon wasn't sure at first if he could even trust "Smitty," as he began calling the kid. But the young man did indeed prove helpful. He knew the resistance people and the area, and he stayed with Beynon for the remainder of the mission.[31]

Germans in Groesbeek soon found themselves trapped between two battalions of the 505th, and many quickly surrendered. Men of the regiment entered the town within an hour of landing, while the division command post was set up about a thousand yards west of town.

As soon as Sergeant Beynon linked up with Bestebreurtje and Verhaeghe, the team set out to locate members of the Dutch resistance in Groesbeek. Within an hour, they contacted a group of around eighty men and began organizing and arming them at once, equipping several men with weapons taken from American and German soldiers who had been killed. When English-speaking resistance men were found and their reliability attested to, they were assigned to the regiments of the 82nd to act as guides and interpreters. While in Groesbeek, Lieutenant Verhaeghe captured three Germans single-handedly, the first enemy prisoners to be taken in the area.[32]

That evening, the Jeds set out in a jeep for Nijmegen to find Captain Bestebreurtje's uncle Piet. They found his house but saw no sign that anyone was home. As the three men approached the door to the house, Bestebreurtje told Beynon, who was armed with a submachine gun, to enter first. Beynon pushed through the door and moved from room to room, only to find the house empty. Then the men found a door that led to the cellar, where they found the uncle and his family. A spirited reunion followed, and the Jeds gained much information to take back to General Gavin, including enemy positions and information indicating that the Nijmegen bridge over the Maas would probably not be blown up by the Germans.[33]

Later that night, the Jeds drove down a tree-lined road on their way back to the division command post. Suddenly they ran into a German ambush, machine-gun fire raking the jeep. As the driver tried to turn the vehicle around, the engine stalled. A soldier riding with the Jeds was killed instantly. A bullet tore into Lieutenant Verhaeghe's right hip, and another hit him in the right leg above the knee. Bestebreurtje was also hit, though less seriously, in the left arm and the right hand.

The driver got the jeep started again and sped away back toward Groesbeek, where the wounded were treated at an aid station. Bestebreurtje asked to be patched up so that he could remain in the field, and his wounds were bandaged. The more seriously wounded Verhaeghe was found to have a shattered femur and would require evacuation. The Jedburgh team was suddenly reduced to two men with no radios. Sergeant Beynon felt that his job now included watching over his remaining officer.[34]

While at the aid station, Bestebreurtje learned that doctors wanted to amputate a finger, but he refused to allow it. When they were ready to evacuate him, he rolled under a tent flap and took off back to the division command post.

With Groesbeek and the wooded ridge east and south of town in the hands of American paratroopers, the 505th established a defensive perimeter and threw up roadblocks and strongpoints on all roads leading into town.

Planes of the 440th Troop Carrier Group, carrying the 508th Parachute Infantry, flew for two and a half hours, thirty minutes of that time over the rolling waters of the North Sea, crossing the Belgian coast and continuing to its target over Holland. Cruising at 140 miles an hour for eighty miles over German-held territory, they encountered scattered but fairly accurate flak and ground fire. British and American fighter protection fought off an attack by about thirty Luftwaffe planes. Paratroopers in the first serial jumped at around one-thirty northeast of Groesbeek, about four miles southeast of Nijmegen, on some of the highest ground in Holland. The drop zone was within two miles of the German border. The 508th's area of operations lay just to the south of Nijmegen. German crews of an antiaircraft artillery battalion positioned on the drop zone broke and ran at the sight of the hundreds of parachutes descending above them. The 508th's battalions assembled and began moving toward their objectives in slightly more than an hour.[35] A few minutes after the 508th dropped, the 440th Group's second serial dropped the 376th Parachute Field Artillery Battalion on Drop Zone N.

One of the regiment's battalions moved west to establish defensive positions to halt any approach of enemy forces down the highway from Nijmegen into the 82nd's perimeter. Another battalion marched off to secure the northern extent of the wooded ridgeline to the east of Nijmegen and capture the tiny village and resort hotel of Berg en Dal, four miles east of Nijmegen, which they accomplished by nightfall.

The 508th's remaining battalion, the 1st, had begun moving into the outskirts of Nijmegen soon after landing. Narrow cobblestone streets soon filled with Dutch people intent on welcoming the Americans; but the Germans meant to defend Nijmegen, and many civilians and paratroopers were killed when mortar rounds began falling in the area. Later that afternoon, General Gavin ordered Colonel Lindquist to send the battalion on through the city and to the bridge without delay.[36]

With members of the Dutch resistance serving as guides, scouts, and ammunition bearers, men of the 1st Battalion made their way to the center of the city, taking only sporadic small-arms fire. But when they reached a large traffic circle near the southern entrance to the bridge at around ten that night, they ran into trouble. While taking machine-gun fire from German positions in a nearby park, the Americans soon heard a convoy of vehicles down a side street; then came the sound of German troops dismounting from trucks.[37]

Unknown to the Allies, the tanks of SS-Obergruppenführer (SS Lieutenant General) Wilhelm Bittrich's II SS Panzer Corps, now including both the 9th and 10th SS Panzer Divisions, had been sitting under trees and camouflage netting in assembly areas north of the Neder Rijn, a few miles north and east of Arnhem.

Field Marshal Model, the commander of German Army Group B, was at his headquarters in a modest hotel in the town of Oosterbeek, west of Arnhem, at the time of the Allied airborne assault. He immediately recognized the importance of the Nijmegen bridge to the Allied operation and took steps to reinforce the few low-quality troops defending the bridge. Late that afternoon, he ordered an advance element of the 9th SS Panzer Division's reconnaissance battalion to Nijmegen. Bittrich ordered the 10th SS Panzer Division to move south to Nijmegen from their position northeast of Arnhem. Aware that British paratroopers had dropped to the west of Arnhem earlier that afternoon, Bittrich judged that they could be dealt with in time; the first priority, he sensed, was to defend the bridge at Nijmegen.[38]

The 9th SS Reconnaissance Battalion crossed the Arnhem bridge, en route to Nijmegen, prior to the arrival of British paratroopers in Arnhem. Somewhat later, after the arrival of British paratroopers at the north end of the bridge, elements of the 10th SS Panzer Division crossed to the south bank of the Neder Rijn by ferry from a point southeast of Arnhem. Men from at least one of these units reached Nijmegen in time to block the 508th's attempt at capturing the highway bridge on D-Day. Although the Americans fought desperately to take the bridge, General Gavin soon realized that this initial attempt had failed and ordered the companies of the 508th engaged in the fight to withdraw and reorganize.

The first 82nd Airborne Division units to jump had done so at one o'clock; the last regiment dropped twenty-eight minutes later. The division's landings met almost no immediate resistance, and little fighting took place as units assembled near the drop zones. All battalions had begun moving toward their assigned objectives within an hour of the jump, one battalion within twenty minutes.[39] All the division's initial objectives had been achieved by eight-thirty that evening.[40]

A total of 7,277 men of the 82nd jumped, and another 209 men landed in gliders, sustaining no more than 2 percent casualties in the process. Only one plane and two gliders failed to reach the drop and landing area out of 482 planes and 50 gliders that left England. Even the artillery fared well, with eight seventy-five-millimeter guns arriving undamaged.[41]

Near Groesbeek, the huge Horsa gliders carrying General Browning's airborne corps command group and Jedburgh team Edward landed at ten minutes after two following an uneventful flight. Enemy opposition near the drop zone was minimal. At once, the Jeds followed the planned route to their assembly point. There, they linked up with headquarters personnel and moved out in search of the corps command post established in the woods nearby.

The Jeds had been instructed to send a radio message to Special Force Headquarters, reporting the team's safe arrival, immediately upon landing in Holland. Sergeant Billingsley sent the message at eight that evening, also informing SFHQ that the team had not yet made contact with the resistance.

Contact was made, though, later that night, with a local group from Groesbeek numbering about three hundred. Although the Dutchmen were eager to help the Allied cause, no immediate task was given them.

Shortly after two that afternoon, following an artillery barrage, British XXX Corps, with its Guards Armored Division in the lead, launched its attack northward from the Belgian frontier toward Eindhoven. Almost immediately, the division ran into stiff resistance from five German battalions, two of them SS, not known to be in the area. By dark, the British force had fought their way forward and captured the village of Valkenswaard, about six miles south of Eindhoven.

Some sixty miles to the north, pathfinders of the British 1st Airborne Division jumped west of Arnhem just after one o'clock on Sunday afternoon. With orange and crimson strips of nylon weighted down by stones, the pathfinders marked the drop zone and landing zone for the main force. Gliders carrying the division's 1st Airlanding Brigade then arrived, skidding to a stop in the green, wide-open field laced with bright yellow sunflowers, between the villages of Wolfheze and Heelsum. Accompanying the brigade were a light artillery regiment as well as reconnaissance, antitank, and medical units. Following the 1st Airlanding

Brigade would be the 1st Parachute Brigade and the division reconnaissance squadron. The 1st Airlanding Brigade was to secure all drop zones and landing zones for the arrival of follow-on units scheduled to arrive in three successive lifts over the next few days.

Gliders carrying the 1st Airborne Reconnaissance Squadron slid to a halt at twenty minutes after one. Lieutenant Knottenbelt, the Dutch commando attached to Jedburgh team Claude, spent the remainder of the afternoon vetting civilians who were volunteering their services. He felt frustration at not knowing how he was supposed to tell who were actually members of the resistance and who were only pretenders. But his situation was helped when one man appeared to be acknowledged by all those present as a leader of the local resistance. With this man's help, Knottenbelt was able to identify resistance fighters and issue armbands to them.

Following the gliders onto the field near Wolfheze came Brigadier Gerald Lathbury's 1st Parachute Brigade, whose primary mission was to capture the highway bridge over the Neder Rijn, about eight miles to the west in Arnhem. An additional task assigned to the brigade was the seizure of an area of dominating high ground north of Arnhem to secure a bridgehead large enough to allow XXX Corps to quickly and safely cross to the north bank of the river. With the 1st Airlanding Brigade tied up in its job of securing the drop zones and landing zones, it would be unable to assist the 1st Parachute Brigade in the operation's main objective, the capture of the Arnhem bridge.

Planes carrying the parachute brigade and the remainder of Jedburgh team Claude had enjoyed an uneventful flight from England. They experienced calm skies and bright sunshine, the temperature inside the aircraft was comfortable, and the formation encountered very little flak. As they approached the drop area, the command "Action stations!" came when the red light next to the door came on. When the green light glared, the jumpmaster shouted, "Go!" to the lead jumper, and the plane emptied quickly as paratroopers followed one another closely through the exit.

The parachute drop went extremely well, and when Lieutenant Allan Todd jumped at about two that afternoon, there was little indication that things would not go as planned. Endless formations of C-47s passed overhead, disgorging more and more paratroopers, each soon sprouting a canopy in green-and-brown camouflage. Weapons containers, supply canisters, and bundles hung in idle suspension from parachutes of assorted colors, while Allied fighters buzzed in and out, protecting both the troop carriers and the men on the ground. Soon the vast drop zone was blanketed with parachutes. German opposition on the ground was almost nonexistent. Rather than sounds of battle, only the steady drone of C-47s could be heard as they continued passing overhead, leaving a trail of parachutes blossoming in the clear sky.

Small clusters of men walked from the drop zone in various directions, congealing into larger groups as they neared their particular unit's assembly area. Todd set out at once for the brigade headquarters assembly point in a nearby wooded area, arriving there just as half a dozen German prisoners were brought in. The enemy troops had apparently surrendered to the brigade medical officer, who had landed in a tree. So eager were the Germans to surrender that they helped the British officer out of the tree.[42]

Lieutenant Todd searched for Captain Jaap Groenewoud, his Jedburgh teammate who had jumped from the plane immediately in front of Todd's. He soon found his Dutch counterpart, and the two agreed to split up briefly to get some help from Dutch civilians as quickly as possible. Todd took a local civilian with him and immediately went in search of wagons or other vehicles to carry the supplies that had been dropped with the paratroopers. Meanwhile, Groenewoud went into Oosterbeek in search of men to help clear the drop zone and load the supply bundles and containers onto the wagons or other vehicles.

Not far away, next to a potato patch, Todd found a German truck manned by two enemy soldiers. He shot the Germans, killing both. As the local civilians were eager to help, Todd was able to enlist the aid of about thirty Dutchmen, and an hour after splitting up with Groenewoud, he returned to the drop zone with the German truck and three wagons. Groenewoud arrived shortly and organized the work parties.

By three-thirty, all division units were on the ground.[43] All 331 planes dropped their paratroopers on the correct drop zones, and all 319 gliders came to earth safely just where they were supposed to; not a single aircraft of any kind was lost.[44] The landings had been textbook perfect. But almost immediately after landing, the luck of the "Red Devils" changed. The 1st Airborne Division would quickly learn, as the 101st and 82nd had already learned, that something was terribly wrong with the intelligence they had been provided. Rather than the weak, demoralized, and fleeing enemy they had been told to expect, they found themselves engaging tough, confident, well-equipped German troops.

With enough planes to carry only about half the division to Holland on D-Day, and with the 1st Airlanding Brigade committed to guarding the drop and landing zones, only the 1st Parachute Brigade would be available to seize the division's objectives on the first day. Brigadier Lathbury had assigned to his 3rd Battalion the task of taking and holding the western part of the city of Arnhem. The 1st Battalion was to take up positions north of the city and serve as the brigade reserve. To Lieutenant Colonel John Frost's 2nd Battalion went the task of capturing the highway and railway bridges over the Neder Rijn. The division's 1st Airborne Reconnaissance Squadron, under the genial Major Freddie Gough (pronounced "Goff"), was to race ahead of 2nd Battalion in jeeps and seize the main objective, the highway bridge, and hold it until Frost's battalion arrived.

Once the glidermen had unloaded jeeps and guns from the Horsa and Hamilcar gliders, men began breaking out equipment from the man-size metal containers that had been dropped. It was hot, and sweat ran down the faces of paratroopers as they assembled into company- and battalion-size elements. While the airlanding brigade secured the landing zone for the second wave, scheduled to arrive the next morning, troops of the 1st Parachute Brigade set out for their assigned objectives.

Shortly after Gough's reconnaissance squadron left the drop zone, they came across a German staff car that had been shot up; a dead German general and his driver lay next to the vehicle. Dutch people came out to welcome them as they continued through the village of Wolfheze. Just as they approached the outskirts of Oosterbeek, a town five miles west of Arnhem, they saw many patients, all dressed in white, who had escaped from a nearby asylum that had been damaged during preliminary bombing that morning. Soon the British were met by hundreds of Dutch citizens in Oosterbeek, many of them waving flags and bunting. Then gunfire erupted, and the men dispersed and took shelter in the many gardens in the area.

The 1st Parachute Battalion moved out to the northeast to secure the high ground north of Arnhem, and the remaining two battalions set out on separate routes to the east, toward Arnhem. Almost immediately, the 1st Battalion ran into elements of the 9th SS Panzer Division a couple of miles northwest of Oosterbeek. The 3rd Parachute Battalion, moving toward Arnhem, also encountered the enemy just west of Oosterbeek. Both of these battalions would be held up in firefights at these locations for the rest of the day.

The 2nd Parachute Battalion had jumped at two that afternoon and was assembled and ready to move out within forty-five minutes.[45] Captain Groenewoud and Lieutenant Todd wanted to accompany the 2nd Battalion as it set out toward the bridge in Arnhem. Todd summoned Sergeant Scott and sent him, with a wagon, to collect the team's containers. He told Scott that once he had recovered the containers, he was to report to the supply officer at division headquarters and accompany that officer into the city to join Todd and Groenewoud. Todd also wrote out a message for Scott to send, time permitting, before moving into town. The two officers then departed with the advance unit headed for the main bridge.

Lieutenant Colonel Frost* received a message from brigade just after three instructing him to move out at once with his 2nd Parachute Battalion. He was to move as quickly as possible and was not to wait for stragglers. Frost ordered his A Company to lead the battalion on the march to the bridge. The company commander, Major Digby Tatham-Warter, was new to the battalion, but he was a smart and aggressive officer, and Frost was confident that he would push through to the objective without delay. The company struck out for the bridge at three-thirty, following a winding cobblestone road, with the remainder of the battalion following.

Taking the southernmost route toward Arnhem, a road that initially skirted the north bank of the Neder Rijn, the battalion made good progress. At one point, Brigadier Lathbury drove up in a jeep for a quick conference with Frost. Off to their left, the men could hear the fighting where 3rd Battalion was fully engaged. Lathbury told Frost to push on with all possible speed; brigade headquarters would follow immediately behind Frost's battalion. The battalion was briefly held up shortly after Lathbury departed; A Company apparently had run into the flank of the German force then battling 3rd Battalion. Tatham-Warter sidestepped his company slightly to the south, toward the river, and soon they were able to bypass the enemy and press on toward the bridge. As the battalion passed through the village of Heveadorp, with its neat houses and carefully tended gardens, Dutch citizens, many speaking English, welcomed the paratroopers and showered them with

---

* Lieutenant Colonel John Dutton Frost, a Sandhurst graduate, was born in 1912, the son of Brigadier General F. D. Frost of the Indian Army. He was one of the first parachutists in the British Army and had been with the 2nd Battalion from the unit's beginning.

fruit, flowers, and jugs of milk. To Frost, the "people seemed familiar rather than foreign."[46]

After leaving Heveadorp, Frost and his men continued through the town of Oosterbeek. There, Frost dispatched C Company to secure the railroad bridge that spanned the river just south of town. The British knew that bridges were best captured by seizing both ends at once, and Frost hoped to send a small force across the railroad bridge to attack the south end of the highway bridge while the remainder of his battalion secured the north end. He watched as C Company men prepared to cross the railway span, and it appeared as though they had captured the bridge intact. Just then a tremendous explosion rocked the bridge, and when the smoke had cleared, part of the bridge was gone, collapsed into the river. German engineers had blown it. Farther upstream, the men found a pontoon bridge that they thought could be used, but it was found to be disassembled and unusable.

Frost's remaining element, B Company, was engaged in a firefight with German forces on the outskirts of Arnhem. Radio communication with both B and C Companies broke down at this point, and C Company would not be heard from again. A Company, along with Frost's battalion headquarters, continued toward the main bridge.

Captain Groenewoud and Lieutenant Todd stopped briefly at one point so Groenewoud could place telephone calls to the pre-occupation mayor and to the chief of police in Arnhem. He learned that the German occupation *Bürgermeister* (*Burgemeester* in Dutch), or mayor, had already left town. The man had actually gone out to see what was happening when the British began jumping west of the city and was cut down by a British bullet. Todd and Groenewoud then caught up with Frost's column and proceeded with them into the city.

Soon the 2nd Battalion column reached an intersection with a street called Utrechtseweg. On the north side of that street, not far from the intersection, stood a large building that was St. Elizabeth Hospital. Groenewoud and Todd, accompanied by Frost's battalion medical officer and two orderlies, headed toward the hospital to arrange for the treatment of wounded while the main column continued on toward the highway bridge. There was a brief skirmish when a German guard outside the hospital opened fire on the five men, and Todd shot and killed the German. The men then entered the large brick building. Captain Groenewoud found the German doctor in charge of the hospital, and the two men came to an agreement. German casualties would be kept on one side of the hospital, British on the other. Having done all they could at the hospital, Groenewoud and Todd started off once again toward the Arnhem highway bridge.

As the Jeds walked down a street lined with three- and four-story brick buildings, an enemy sniper fired on the two men but missed, and Todd shot the man before he could try again. Before long, they caught up with the British column. Frost's battalion had been able to bypass much of the enemy, encountering only small pockets of Germans, and continue moving at a fairly good pace. Groenewoud and Todd caught up to Frost and his men just as A Company, up ahead, ran into some stiff resistance by patrols of armored cars and were pinned down for about thirty minutes.

Eventually, Tatham-Warter's men broke through and the battalion pressed on. At a local police station along the way, the men received some disturbing news. A helpful civilian there provided information about occupation government officials and about German troops in the area. Instead of the enemy garrison of old men and young boys that the British had been told to expect, they now learned that the 9th and 10th SS Panzer Divisions were located near Arnhem.[47] In fact, with elements of these two divisions and 425 German corporals at an SS school, there were some six thousand enemy troops in Arnhem on September 17.[48] Soon more enemy reinforcements would be arriving every day from throughout northern Holland and Germany.

Frost's small group now wound speedily through the back streets and alleyways of Arnhem until it reached the northern approach to the highway bridge. Tatham-Warter's company had reached the bridge at around eight o'clock and had taken up positions in buildings on both sides of the bridge, near the river, by the time Frost arrived at eight-thirty, just as it was getting dark.

When Groenewoud and Todd arrived at the bridge, they joined three British officers from 1st Parachute Brigade headquarters—Major Tony Hibbert, the brigade major, Captain Bernard Briggs, and Lieutenant Morley—on a reconnaissance to the eastern side of the highway to locate a suitable site for the headquarters.

When the reconnaissance party began their return to the western side of the bridge, they found themselves being cut off from the remainder of the British force by an advancing German column. A tank, two armored cars, and several trucks, as well as dismounted soldiers, were advancing up the road. When the approaching Germans neared the bridge, Todd and the others opened up with machine-gun and anti-

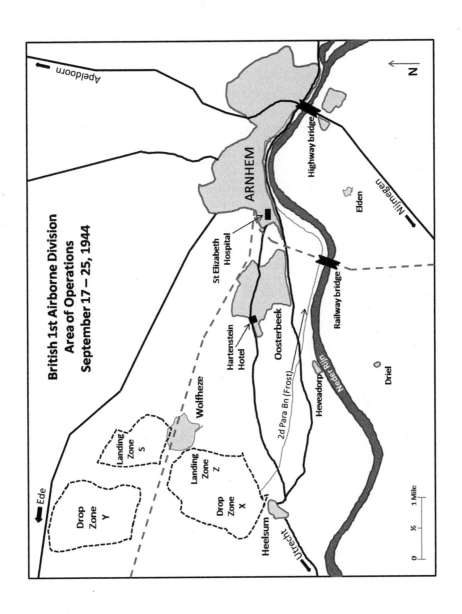

British 1st Airborne Division
Area of Operations
September 17 – 25, 1944

tank fire. The Germans lost one armored car and two trucks as a result, and the dismounted enemy hastily retreated. As soon as it seemed safe enough, Groenewoud, Todd, and the others scampered back across the highway to rejoin the British force on the west side.

The northern approach ramp to the bridge extended several blocks back into the city. A street called Eusebius Binnensingei ran along the western side of this raised road until, just a couple of blocks short of the river, it curved to the west and ran parallel with the river. Lining this curved section of the street were several two- and three-story brick houses and government office buildings. For his battalion command post, Frost chose a house on the corner overlooking the bridge, much to the displeasure of the owner, who retreated to the cellar as Frost's men began fortifying the building. The battalion headquarters company occupied a municipal waterworks building next door, where space behind the building could be used to park vehicles. Shortly afterward, the brigade headquarters arrived, without Brigadier Lathbury, and took over the attic of the waterworks building. Included in the brigade headquarters contingent were signalmen, engineers, and a much welcomed truck loaded with ammunition. Lieutenant Colonel Frost relocated to the brigade headquarters area in the waterworks building as the senior officer in command at the bridge.

Major Freddie Gough showed up at around nine with two jeeps from his reconnaissance squadron. Gough's jeep-mounted squadron had run into Germans shortly after leaving the drop zone earlier in the day. Several of his jeeps had been badly shot up, and he had withdrawn to the division headquarters, where most of the squadron remained, while Gough, a ruddy-faced, white-haired forty-three-year-old, took two jeeps and followed Frost's battalion on the southern route to the bridge. Gough sent some of his men to check out the Limburg Stirum school, a large red brick building near the bridge. Reaching the building, the men broke in through the locked door and searched the school. The main classroom on an upper floor featured several windows looking out to the west and a room with a good view of the bridge.

As the battalion and brigade headquarters were being set up and fighting positions established, A Company attempted to assault the southern end of the bridge. A platoon led by Lieutenant John Grayburn started across the bridge at eight forty-five but was met by heavy machine-gun fire from an armored vehicle parked on the bridge and from two twenty-millimeter guns in a pillbox. The platoon was ordered to withdraw after sustaining eight casualties, including Grayburn, who had been shot through the shoulder. In spite of his wound, the platoon leader skillfully directed the withdrawal and was the last man off the bridge. Grayburn was killed three nights later and was posthumously awarded the Victoria Cross, Britain's highest decoration for valor.

Another platoon, armed with a flamethrower and supported by mortars, tried approaching the bridge embankment from the side. The result was a brief but fierce firefight. When the shooting stopped, wrecked and burning vehicles stood on the bridge and a nearby building burned. Several fires burned brightly enough to illuminate the entire bridge as if it were day. Frost's men captured several Germans, raising the number of prisoners being held by the battalion to well over a hundred.[49]

Frost considered that his only hope for getting troops over to the southern end of the bridge now was to send them over by boat. He planned to have B Company and the brigade defense platoon cross the river if boats could be found. Radio communications with B Company and C Company had broken down, so Frost dispatched patrols to pass on his orders. But adequate boats could not be found, and the patrol sent to B Company was never seen again.

The brigade headquarters and two companies of the 2nd Battalion now occupied several buildings on the west side of the highway ramp leading to the bridge. Captain Groenewoud and Lieutenant Todd decided to remain with the brigade headquarters, which had co-located with part of the 2nd Battalion headquarters in the city waterworks building.

Todd helped the British establish defensive positions and outposts in and around the buildings. The brigade's radio operators tried repeatedly throughout the night to contact division headquarters and the brigade's other two battalions, but no response was heard. The British radios were incapable of reaching division headquarters back near the drop zone, let alone any Allied forces south of Arnhem. The small group of paratroopers at the north end of the bridge was out of contact with everyone. Todd and Groenewoud wondered about the whereabouts of Sergeant Scott.[50]

Based on the report of the patrol that had searched the school building on the eastern side of the highway, the building was occupied at around ten-thirty that night. Captain Briggs took about forty-five to fifty men and moved back across to the eastern side of the highway to occupy the school and three other buildings that were close to the bridge and provided good fields of fire. Elements of Frost's 2nd Battalion, along with the brigade headquarters and the recon squadron, now occupied buildings and fighting positions along both sides of the approach ramp. The 1st and 3rd Parachute Battalions were still held up by German panzer units on the western outskirts of Arnhem, and Lieutenant Colonel Frost learned that they would remain outside the city through- out the night. This delay only provided the Germans more time to move forces into the city. Frost's small force was surrounded, sealed in at the northern end of the bridge. Fires could already be seen burning in some parts of the city.

The long, ten-year-old bridge, with its tall, steel-arched superstruc- ture, was still intact. The British force at the bridge now included about 350 men of the 2nd Battalion and another 150 from brigade headquar- ters. They would have to hold the bridge until other units of the division broke through to reinforce them or until XXX Corps arrived. But the small British force held only the north end of the bridge, occupying a number of buildings within a perimeter about five hundred yards square. The southern end, the end that XXX Corps would be approach- ing, was still in German hands.

Lieutenant Colonel Frost knew that all he could do now was try to get some rest before the battle that was sure to come at dawn. If all went according to plan, he thought, the tanks of XXX Corps could arrive as early as noon the following day. His 2nd Battalion and brigade head- quarters troops would have to hold at least until then.[51]

As dusk settled over the city, Frost noticed a figure walking on the dark street outside his headquarters building. From the outline of the figure, the man appeared to be in some sort of uniform, and Frost thought it might be a member of the local resistance. He sent a para- trooper outside to determine the man's identity. The soldier returned a few minutes later.

"Well?" asked Frost.

"Oh, he's not resistance, sir," the paratrooper replied casually. "He says he's Panzer SS."[52]

Frost turned away to stifle a laugh.

The area around the bridge was quiet for the remainder of the night.

———

That evening, Lieutenant Knottenbelt and the sergeant who had piloted the glider the Dutch officer had flown in tried to contact Captain Groe- newoud and Lieutenant Todd. Knottenbelt knew the two officers had taken off toward the main bridge with the 2nd Battalion. Unable to contact Groenewoud and Todd, Knottenbelt returned to division headquarters on the Arnhem–Utrecht road. Along the way, he saw a German staff car with all occupants killed.

Farther to the south, Allied commanders received a message from the Dutch that accurately described the dangerous situation of the 1st Airborne Division at Arnhem.[53]

D-Day for Operation Market-Garden came to a close with the Allies having achieved remarkable success in the airborne phase of the operation. Only 2.8 percent of all transport aircraft and gliders taking part in the operation had been lost; planners had been prepared for losses of up to 30 percent.[54] In what proved to be the most successful airborne landings in the history of all three divisions involved, roughly twenty thousand American and British troops landed deep in enemy territory, almost completely according to schedule and precisely on their planned drop zones and landing zones and all in a span of an hour and twenty minutes. The decision to drop in daylight had been a wise one.

Fortunately for Field Marshal Model, the British had not known of his presence in Oosterbeek, and they missed an opportunity to capture the army group commander and his entire staff. Model and his headquarters were able to pack up and drive to General Bittrich's II SS Panzer Corps headquarters at Doetinchem, fifteen miles east of Arnhem.

Elsewhere, at Hitler's headquarters in East Prussia and at Field Marshal Rundstedt's Oberbefehlshaber (OB) West headquarters, reports trickled in of Allied parachute and glider landings in Holland, though the scope and size of the operation remained unclear.

But Germans in the immediate area of the drops quickly learned much about Market-Garden. Near General Student's First Parachute Army headquarters, German troops searched an American glider that had been shot down during the initial assault. On one of the bodies in the wreckage they found a copy of the Allied operation order. It was quickly delivered to General Student.

At nine on the morning of September 17, about forty miles northeast of Arnhem, Jedburgh team Dudley and the resistance men of their headquarters arrived at a farm that was to serve as their new command post. The small group had packed all of its equipment on a farm cart and begun their move earlier the previous night. Having successfully avoided German patrols and roadblocks throughout the night, the men saw the area surrounding their new headquarters subjected to a raid shortly after their arrival. But the Germans were only looking for bicycles to commandeer, and the group of Jeds and resistance men lost one bicycle but was otherwise not bothered.

That afternoon, the men rested in the barn and enjoyed a lunch that had been sent out to them by the farmer's wife. When the Jeds decoded messages they'd received from London, they were thrilled to learn of the Allied parachute drops farther to the south. The message informing the Jeds of the airborne operation instructed team Dudley to support the operation by keeping the roads in their area open and by seizing and guarding bridges that might be needed by the advancing forces of British XXX Corps should they make it that far.

But Majors Brinkgreve and Olmsted had another problem to deal with. All summer, young men of the Dutch resistance, listening on illegal radios to BBC news broadcasts and reading stories in *Der Fliegende Holländer* (*The Flying Dutchman*)—a paper regularly air-dropped to the citizens of the Netherlands by British and American bombers—marveled at the rapid advance of Allied forces across France. Now, with word quickly spreading of the parachute drops in southern Holland, the young men of the underground grew anxious to take an active part in the liberation of their country. Surely Allied forces would soon be sweeping through the Gelderland and Overijssel. The Jeds had to act quickly to contact as many resistance leaders as possible and convince them that it was too soon to strike. Premature uprisings, as some resistance groups in France had learned the hard way, could be disastrous. They would have to wait until Allied ground forces grew nearer. Some of the bolder young men, though, having grown restless after living a clandestine existence for four long years, attacked some German troops, and the enemy responded with terrible reprisals on their communities.

NINE

MONDAY, SEPTEMBER 18

The Second Day

German units that had been taken completely by surprise on September 17 began to react more effectively on Monday morning, with makeshift task forces thrown together to strike back at the paratroopers. To respond to the parachute landings near Eindhoven, Field Marshal Model gave General Student the 59th Infantry Division and the 107th Panzer Brigade, both of which had been passing through the area. Student's First Parachute Army constituted Germany's front line in Holland, with thirty-two battalions manning a front of seventy-five miles.

At ten that morning, fighting broke out once again on the St. Oedenrode drop zone, as small German elements attempted to penetrate the 101st Airborne's perimeter. They were held back but remained in the area for the next forty-eight hours.

At eleven, troops of the 101st made contact with lead elements of the Guards Armored Division at the village of Vieuw Acht. Thirty minutes later, a radio message from the main body of the Guards Armored informed the Americans that the British were heavily engaged in a fight five miles south of Eindhoven.[1]

By noon, the 101st had seized four bridges over the Dommel River, just in time for the approaching British ground force.

At twelve-thirty, two British armored cars entered Eindhoven from the northwest. They found a city of around 130,000 people that had grown from a turn-of-the-century backwoods village to an industrial center because of the Philips family's electronics firm and a large DAF automobile plant.

Paratroopers of the 101st were in Eindhoven by one that afternoon.[2] No more than a company of German troops had been in the city when the Americans attacked, not the regiment that had been expected. Throughout the afternoon, troops of the 506th Parachute Infantry continued clearing out small pockets of enemy troops scattered about the city, particularly in the southern outskirts in anticipation of the arrival of the main body of the Guards Armored Division. Meanwhile, the people of Eindhoven broke out the tricolor Dutch flag and celebrated in the streets, welcoming the Allied soldiers with kisses and fruit, and orange streamers and flags were unfurled from windows.

The Guards Armored continued to fight through stiff resistance but finally made contact with the 101st at seven that evening just south of Eindhoven.[3] When they reached the city, the British force, led by a column of Bren gun carriers, Sherman tanks, and motorcycles, pushed right on through. That night, the Royal Engineers began work to erect a temporary Bailey bridge in place of the destroyed Son bridge. At eleven, the Germans blew a concrete bridge over the Wilhelmina Canal that the 502nd Parachute Infantry had been fighting to secure.[4]

The Jeds of team Edward moved on Monday, along with the I Airborne Corps command post, to a wooded area. While searching through neighboring towns for vehicles to help move the corps headquarters, the Jeds met a resistance leader in Malden, a village on the road toward Nijmegen. They quickly arranged a conference with leaders of the Orde Dienst from Malden and the nearby villages of Heumen, Overasselt, and Mook.

Power lines buried underground in Holland often had telephone lines included with them. These lines were connected to telephone terminals in power stations, and this became a primary means for the resistance to pass information throughout the country. The Germans never caught on to it.[5] Through such telephone communications with resistance people in the center of Nijmegen, the Jeds were able to gather up-to-date information on enemy disposition and activity in that city, particularly the nature of the defenses on the railway and road

RIGHT: Major Henk Brinkgreve, Dutch officer on Jedburgh team Dudley, in a portrait painted by his brother. Brinkgreve was killed in action in Holland in March 1945. (*Elizabeth Olmsted*)

BELOW: Major John M. "Pappy" Olmsted, U.S. Army, of Jedburgh team Dudley, in Scotland in the spring of 1944. (*Amanda Todd*)

Sergeant John P. "Bunny" Austin of the British Army, radio operator on Jedburgh team Dudley, in a photograph taken by Dutch resistance for preparation of false identification papers. Austin was captured in Holland and was executed by the Germans in 1945.

LEFT: Captain Arie D. Bestebreurtje, Dutch officer on Jedburgh teams Clarence, Stanley, and Dicing, at war's end. *(The Bestebreurtje family)*

BELOW: First Lieutenant Harvey Allan Todd *(left)* and First Lieutenant George M. Verhaeghe, American officers on Jedburgh teams Claude and Clarence, respectively, in Scotland, May 1944. *(Amanda Todd)*

Technical Sergeant Willard W. "Bud" Beynon, U.S. Army, radio operator on Jedburgh teams Clarence and Stanley. *(Willard Beynon)*

A street scene at Camp Mackall, North Carolina, where John Olmsted and Allan Todd were recruited for the Jedburgh project. *(U.S. Army photograph)*

Wartime view of the mall area in Washington, D.C., showing the Main Navy and Munitions Buildings surrounding the reflecting pond. American Jedburgh officer candidates arriving in Washington first reported to the office of the adjutant general in the building along Constitution Avenue on the right in this photograph. Today the Vietnam Veterans Memorial sits in this area. *(National Archives)*

Aerial view of the clubhouse at the Congressional Country Club, outside Bethesda, Maryland, during World War II. The property became an OSS training area known as Area F. American Jedburgh volunteers underwent physical and psychological assessment and selection here. *(Congressional Country Club)*

HMS *Queen Mary*, the troopship that carried American Jedburgh radio operators from New York to England in December 1943. Her sister ship, HMS *Queen Elizabeth*, carried the officers a week earlier. *(National Archives)*

Main wing of Milton Hall, an estate near Peterborough, England, that became the Jedburgh training center. *(National Archives)*

Jeds on the confidence course at Milton Hall. *(National Archives)*

Jedburgh trainees scaling a wall on the obstacle course at Milton Hall. (*National Archives*)

Demolitions lecture at Milton Hall. (*National Archives*)

Jedburgh radio operators practice wireless Morse telegraphy communications at Milton Hall. *(National Archives)*

ABOVE: Jedburghs firing pistols under the guidance of instructors on the outdoor range at Milton Hall. *(National Archives)*

RIGHT: Dutch captain Arie Bestebreurtje training on a motorcycle at Milton Hall. *(National Archives)*

Exercise area in the rear courtyard at Milton Hall, including the boxing ring where Technical Sergeant Bud Beynon of Jedburgh team Clarence fought the training center's British sergeant major. *(National Archives)*

Dutch Jedburgh team members in Scotland for small-boat training. *Left to right:* Captain Arie Bestebreurtje (Dutch, team Clarence), First Lieutenant George Verhaeghe (U.S., team Clarence), Technical Sergeant Carl Scott (U.S., team Claude), Technical Sergeant Willard Beynon (U.S., team Clarence), and Captain Jaap Groenewoud (Dutch, team Claude). *(The Bestebreurtje family)*

Jedburgh team Clarence during training at Loch Moray, Scotland, in May 1944. *Left to right:* First Lieutenant George Verhaeghe (U.S.), radio operator Technical Sergeant Willard Beynon (U.S.), and Captain Arie Bestebreurtje (Dutch). (*Amanda Todd*)

Jedburgh team Claude during training at Loch Moray, Scotland, in May 1944. *Left to right:* Captain Jaap Groenewoud (Dutch), First Lieutenant Harvey Allan Todd (U.S.), and radio operator Technical Sergeant Carl Scott (U.S.). (*Amanda Todd*)

LEFT: British Field Marshal Bernard Law Montgomery (*left*), commander of the Twenty-first Army Group, who won approval of the plan for Operation Market-Garden from General Dwight D. Eisenhower (*right*), Supreme Commander, Allied Expeditionary Force. Photograph taken in Normandy, July 1944. (*U.S. Army Military History Institute*)

BELOW: Major John Olmsted (*center*), in a photograph taken at the end of the war, with two members of the Dutch resistance who worked closely with him in Holland: Cor Hilbrink (*left*), area leader of the KP, and Daan (*right*), Hilbrink's intelligence officer. (*Elizabeth Olmsted*)

Major John Olmsted's false identity papers, prepared for him by the Dutch underground. (*Elizabeth Olmsted*)

U.S. Army soldiers at Area H, the OSS packing station near Holme, England. The men are packing arms, ammunition, and other matériel into Type C containers such as those dropped with Jedburgh team Dudley for the Dutch resistance. *(National Archives)*

Brigadier General James M. Gavin, commander of the U.S. 82nd Airborne Division, prepares for the jump into Holland on September 17, 1944. *(U.S. Army photograph)*

Major General Maxwell D. Taylor, commander of the U.S. 101st Airborne Division, just prior to takeoff for Operation Market-Garden on the morning of September 17, 1944. (*U.S. Army photograph*)

A platoon leader in the 82nd Airborne Division briefs his men one last time at the airfield before departing for Holland. (*U.S. Army photograph*)

Paratroopers boarding two lines of C-47 transport planes at an airfield in England just prior to takeoff for Holland on September 17, 1944. *(National Archives)*

General Gavin's aircraft just prior to takeoff on September 17, 1944. The officer on the left is Lieutenant Colonel John Norton, Gavin's operations officer (G-3). Next to him is Lieutenant Hugo Olson, Gavin's aide. Captain Bestebreurtje and Lieutenant Verhaeghe of Jedburgh team Clarence were also on this aircraft, though out of view in this photograph. *(U.S. Army photograph)*

Parachutists of the 101st Airborne Division, with attached Jedburgh team Daniel II, land near Son in Holland on September 17, 1944. (*National Archives*)

The Jeds coordinated with Dutch citizens to provide support to the airborne divisions. Here a Dutch farmer near Son gives men of the 101st Airborne Division a ride to their assembly point on September 17, 1944. (*National Archives*)

bridge across the Waal. This critical information was promptly passed on to the corps staff.

———

For paratroopers of the 82nd Airborne, the new day began with a barrage of enemy mortar and artillery shells. Later in the day, there would even be reported sightings of German armor. Counterattacks hit the 508th's sector near Wyler during the morning, and the regiment had to fight to once more clear the drop zone of Germans so that it could be used as a landing zone for glider-borne troops expected later that day.

Because their radios had not been recovered, the Jeds of team Clarence had been unable to get a message through to team Edward to inform mission headquarters of the casualties the team had sustained in Sunday's ambush. Bestebreurtje and Beynon were finally able to provide a report to Jaap Staal and McCord Sollenberger when team Edward arranged a mass meeting of all resistance groups in the area at the Malden town hall. Though some discord among the different groups had surfaced at the earlier meeting, resistance leaders now settled on a division of roles, duties, and responsibilities. All agreed to focus their hostility on the Germans. The Jeds explained to the two hundred resistance members present what they could do to help the 82nd Airborne Division. They issued fifty orange armbands to the group leaders and instructed them to distribute the armbands to resistance members chosen to serve as guides, guards, and patrols for the units of the 82nd. Later, the Allies would add an official stamp to these armbands after enemy agents were found to use easily made copies to infiltrate resistance groups.[6]

General Gavin made a visit to Colonel Lindquist and the 508th Parachute Infantry at dawn on the eighteenth. After the meeting, Gavin headed back on the road toward Nijmegen. At a main road intersection just outside Nijmegen, he came upon Captain Bestebreurtje and hundreds of men of the Dutch resistance standing about in the street and on the lawn of the Hotel Sionshof on Groesbeeksweg, which Jed team Clarence had established as its headquarters. Many of the Dutchmen—Gavin later estimated that there were six hundred by the time he arrived—wore orange armbands.[7]

Bestebreurtje explained to Gavin that the resistance men had volunteered to fight alongside the Americans and were asking for weapons. The general warned the Dutchmen of the dangers involved in fighting the Germans in civilian clothes. If they were captured, they would certainly be killed.

Gavin then explained that there was one mission he needed the resistance to carry out and that it was of the utmost importance. He wanted the Dutch to save the Nijmegen bridge from demolition by the Germans. The task would involve cutting any wires leading to the bridge and then keeping the Germans away from the bridge. The resistance men assured Gavin that they would do their best; they would cut the wires, and their snipers would keep the Germans off the bridge until the Americans captured it.[8] Gavin later wrote that these men "proved to be among the bravest and most patriotic people we had liberated."[9]

Allied commanders soon found another job they could entrust to the Dutch resistance. As more and more Germans were taken prisoner, it became evident that using members of the resistance as guards would free more Allied soldiers to continue fighting. The 82nd had captured twenty-two hundred German prisoners, and with the aid of six Allied glider pilots, the resistance formed a guard force to watch over them. Some guards were Dutch boys, not yet fourteen years of age, armed with captured German weapons.[10]

During General Gavin's early morning meeting with Colonel Lindquist of the 508th, the two had made plans for another attempt at seizing the highway bridge over the Waal. They planned to send one company through the eastern outskirts of the city to assault the bridge from that direction. Moving out at seven forty-five, the company made good progress until it neared the traffic circle at the southern approach to the bridge. There and in the adjoining Hunner Park, German infantry equipped with twenty-millimeter and eighty-eight-millimeter antitank guns waited in dug-in positions. They opened fire when the Americans had approached to within a few blocks. Men of the 508th attacked and came within a block of the traffic circle before being stopped when they were hit with artillery fire from north of the river. With the remainder of his regiment already committed elsewhere, Lindquist had no reinforcements to send to the aid of the company engaged near the bridge. At two o'clock, the company was ordered to withdraw; the third attempt to seize the vital Nijmegen bridge had failed.

A German force of two understrength battalions entered the 82nd's area from the Reichswald on Monday morning and occupied landing zones where Gavin expected gliders of the second lift to be arriving shortly after noon. Colonel Lindquist committed forces to clearing and holding the northern of two landing zones. A company from the 505th attacked the small German force on the southern landing zone, clearing the enemy from the area half an hour before the first gliders were expected.

On the northern landing zone, a battalion from the 508th met stiffer resistance as the German troops there opened up with fire from small arms and sixteen twenty-millimeter antiaircraft guns. After an eight-mile forced march, the Americans charged the enemy on the run. In the face of such an aggressive assault, the Germans broke and ran just as the first gliders swooped onto the landing zone at ninety miles per hour. The U.S. battalion suffered only 11 casualties, while 50 Germans were killed and another 150 captured.[11]

A total of 450 gliders arrived on the two landing zones, delivering the remainder of General Gavin's artillery. Twenty minutes later, 135 B-24 bombers dropped resupply bundles on a drop zone south of Groesbeek.[12]

Men of the 505th Parachute Infantry west of Groesbeek scored an unusual coup before sunrise on September 18. During the night, a German troop train had departed Nijmegen and passed through Groesbeek, escaping to the east. Early Monday morning, a second train approached Groesbeek, attempting the same run. This time, 505th paratroopers stopped the train with a bazooka and raked it with small-arms fire. Most of the enemy troops aboard the train scattered into the surrounding woods, but the Americans pursued them and, after some small skirmishes, captured them.

Elements of the 82nd continued to solidify their position throughout the day, with a battalion of the 505th liberating the village of Mook on the important stretch of highway between Venlo and Nijmegen and a battalion of the 508th taking Beek and establishing roadblocks there on the highway to Nijmegen.

Neither General Gavin nor General Browning, the airborne corps commander, knew what the situation was in Arnhem. The only report received from Arnhem thus far was a cryptic telephone message that had been passed to the 505th by a resistance unit in the Nijmegen area at 10:40 A.M. Monday morning. The message was necessarily brief because the report was made over an open telephone line connecting power and waterworks stations in the region. As relayed to Gavin's headquarters by the 505th, the message was: "Dutch report Germans winning over British at Arnhem."[13]

Jedburgh team Edward, located at Browning's airborne corps

headquarters, radioed a message to Special Force Headquarters in London urgently asking for any news they might have on the situation in Arnhem. Browning had yet to hear anything from the 1st Airborne Division. Perhaps SFHQ could contact Jedburgh team Claude for the information and relay it to Edward.

———

The 1st Airborne Division had its hands full in Oosterbeek and Arnhem. Field Marshal Model ordered General Christiansen of the Armed Forces Command Netherlands to attack British forces in Arnhem from the north and northwest. For this purpose, Christiansen's operations and training deputy, Generalleutnant Hans von Tettau, took command of a hastily formed task force of regional defense and training battalions. This force, referred to as Division von Tettau, attacked the British 1st Airlanding Brigade defending the drop zones and landing zones. Meanwhile, Obergruppenführer Bittrich, II SS Panzer Corps commander, ordered his remaining units to clear the British from the northern end of the bridge at all cost. The bulk of the 9th SS Panzer Division and elements of the 10th SS Panzer Division were already in Arnhem or were about to enter the city from the east.

In the process of recovering and rebuilding after the mauling they had taken in Normandy, these units were divisions in name only. They had not yet been fully restored, and each was scarcely larger than a reinforced regiment. Both divisions were now often referred to by the Germans as *Kampfgruppen,* ad hoc formations thrown together from the remnants of several depleted regiments and divisions. The 9th SS Panzer Division, also known as Kampfgruppe Hohenstaufen, was under the command of Obersturmbannführer (SS Lieutenant Colonel) Walther Harzer. With around six thousand troops, the 9th was the stronger of the two divisions, with an armored infantry regiment, a battalion of artillery, a reconnaissance battalion, two assault gun batteries, a company of about twenty Mark V* Panther tanks, an antiaircraft bat-

---

* German tank models Panzerkampfwagen III (twenty tons with a fifty-millimeter gun), Panzerkampfwagen IV (twenty-three tons with a seventy-five-millimeter gun), Panzerkampfwagen V (known as the Panther, fifty tons with a seventy-five-millimeter gun), and Panzerkampfwagen VI (the Tiger, fifty-six tons with an eighty-eight-millimeter gun) were often referred to by the Allies simply as Mark III, Mark IV, Mark V, and Mark VI, respectively. The nicknames Panther and Tiger were also used.

talion, and an engineer battalion. (Normal strength for an SS panzer division was nine thousand men and 170 tanks.)

Thirty-eight-year-old Brigadeführer (SS Brigadier General) Heinz Harmel's 10th SS Panzer Division, also called Kampfgruppe Frundsberg, had around thirty-five hundred troops and almost no tanks, having lost most of its vehicles in the fierce fighting in Normandy and having not yet completed its refitting and rehabilitation. The division had an armored infantry regiment, an armored reconnaissance battalion, two artillery battalions, an engineer battalion, and an antiaircraft battalion.[14]

Of the two companies of Lieutenant Colonel Frost's battalion that had been held up in fighting Germans in the outskirts of Arnhem, one, B Company, succeeded in breaking through to join the small group at the north end of the highway bridge over the Neder Rijn at five on Monday morning. The company, which was short one platoon, took up positions in a building next to the river. A company commander from 3rd Battalion, Major Lewis, arrived with the remnants of his company, barely more than a platoon, and occupied a building on the east side of the bridge. Frost now had around six hundred men and a few six-pounder antitank guns with him at the bridge.[15]

By daybreak on Monday, the eighteenth, Frost's priority was to establish a defense strong enough to hold their position until reinforcements arrived. But, as yet unknown to him, there was little chance of any more units breaking through to the bridge to strengthen his position.

Frost's men did not have to wait long for action on that bright, clear morning, though it came in an unexpected fashion. Several truckloads of German soldiers drove slowly into the area immediately in front of the buildings occupied by 2nd Battalion. Frost noticed a look of trepidation on the faces of the Germans, as if they were hesitant to proceed any farther.[16] But it was too late. British small-arms fire cut the enemy to pieces, and the few Germans left alive were taken prisoner.

Next came an ambulance that approached and stopped just outside Frost's headquarters. Out scrambled several SS troops firing Schmeisser submachine guns from the hip. British fire quickly killed them all.[17]

"Suppose they'll send a hearse next," remarked one paratrooper.[18]

Captain Groenewoud had remained with Major Tony Hibbert and the brigade signal officer throughout the night, trying desperately to make contact with division headquarters. Groenewoud was eager to learn the whereabouts and status of Sergeant Scott.

Lieutenant Todd now occupied an observation post at a small window among the rafters in the attic of the two-story brick house in which Frost had located his command post. From his perch, Todd had a clear view of the bridge and both sides of the long concrete highway ramp leading up to the bridge from the north. He would be able to direct the antitank fire of the crews a floor below him. But he was also in a great position to act as a sniper, as he soon proved by shooting three Germans attempting to cross the road.

At midmorning, someone shouted, "Armored car coming across the bridge!"[19]

For a moment, upon hearing the alert, Frost thought the vehicle might be the vanguard of British XXX Corps. Others believed it to be an enemy unit withdrawing from the Nijmegen area. Soon enough, though, everyone realized that this was a deliberate counterattack aimed at destroying 2nd Battalion's position on the north end of the bridge. By now, an entire column of armored cars and other vehicles could be seen trailing behind the lead car.

The force crossing the bridge from the south was the 9th Panzer Reconnaissance Battalion of the 9th SS Panzer Division. This was the same unit that had moved to Nijmegen from Arnhem the day before to block attempts by the 82nd Airborne Division to capture the bridge over the Waal. Commanding the battalion, and leading the assault on the British force holding the north end of the Arnhem bridge, was SS-Hauptsturmführer (SS Captain) Viktor Gräbner, a man who only the day before had been awarded the Knight's Cross. A small but brave and flamboyant young man, well liked by all who knew him, Gräbner had earned a reputation as a man of action since transferring to the Waffen-SS from the regular army.

Gräbner's force included armored cars and infantry in half-track armored troop carriers, twenty-two vehicles in all. The first five vehicles, all large Puma wheeled armored cars, raced across the bridge with their cannon and machine guns firing to both sides of the northern bridge ramp. One car hit an antitank mine the British had placed on the road, stopping dead, a shambles from the explosion, one of its wheels cartwheeling wildly through the air. Following were several slow armored half-tracks. The British on both sides of the bridge ramp opened up with every weapon they had—rifles, machine guns, mortars, Bren guns, antitank guns, and Gammon bombs. Included were PIATs, the shoulder-fired "Projector, Infantry, Antitank," the British equivalent of the American bazooka that was so effective at short range.

The sluggish half-tracks, with their open troop compartments, were death traps for the German soldiers. British paratroopers in buildings next to the bridge tossed hand grenades into the vehicles. Automatic fire tore into the personnel carriers as men tried to escape from them, then British marksmen picked off the Germans as they tried to find cover among the bridge's superstructure.

More infantry came across the bridge on foot. The dismounted Germans were cut down by the heavy British fire. While Todd and the others with the brigade headquarters and much of 2nd Battalion were firing from the west side of the bridge ramp, a group of Royal Engineer troops led by Captain Eric Mackay fought from buildings on the east side of the ramp.

Two half-tracks, in an attempt to smash through the obstacle formed by destroyed vehicles, ended up breaking through the guardrail along the bridge's edge and falling to the street below. As vehicles were hit, Germans dismounted and tried to run for cover, but most were mowed down. Sometimes British tracers would ignite the fuel on the stalled German half-tracks, and they began burning, sending black smoke billowing into the sky.

At least nine half-tracks, around half a dozen troop-carrying trucks, and ten armored cars were destroyed. In all, an estimated seventy Germans were killed before the battle came to an end at around eleven. Captain Gräbner was among the dead.

Another attack came in the afternoon. This time, following a devastating artillery and mortar barrage, an infantry force supported by two Mark IV tanks hit the British-occupied buildings from the east and continued beneath the bridge to come under fire from British troops on both sides of the bridge. After an intense fight, both tanks were destroyed, one by an antitank gun and the other by a PIAT, and the infantry eventually withdrew.

With the battle at fever pitch, tracers flew in all directions and German antiaircraft guns fired at ground targets straight down the streets of Arnhem.[20] Buildings around the northern bridge ramp were burning. Often, the British Parachute Regiment's war cry, "Whoa, Mohammed!" adopted in North Africa in 1942, could be heard, perhaps to keep spirits high or as an indication of a triumphant encounter with an enemy vehicle. As fighting became a door-to-door affair, the cry aided in iden-tifying friend from foe.

As German infantrymen tried to slip past the damaged vehicles one at a time, Lieutenant Todd had a clear shot at them and picked off six Germans. Then, shortly before noon, a German marksman spotted Todd's position.

Todd was standing next to the small window when the German's bul-let smashed through the window and glanced off Todd's helmet about an inch above the rim. Glass splinters sprayed him and buried them-selves in his eyes and face. Major Gough and Captain Groenewoud, who had returned from the signal officer's location, carried the wounded Todd to the basement, where an aid station had been set up, and he was treated immediately by a British medical officer, Captain Wright. The doctor placed a clamp on a cut on Todd's forehead, just above the left eye, then worked carefully for thirty minutes to pick out shards of glass and clean and bandage the wounds. After washing out Todd's eyes, the doctor put a bandage over them, and Todd spent the remainder of the day resting there. He had much company, as the basements of all the buildings occupied by the British were filling fast with the dead and wounded.

When Jaap Groenewoud returned to check on Todd later in the day, he said that he and the signal officer had finally gotten through to division headquarters. The rest of the division, unfortunately, was being held up about two miles away and could not get through to the bridge. The brigade's 1st and 3rd Battalions were pinned down in the center of the city.

The battalion's position continued to be heavily mortared for most of the morning. After a time, the fighting died down, and the remainder of the day was fairly quiet.

The 1st and 3rd Battalions of the 1st Parachute Brigade, both of which had been held up in fighting near Oosterbeek, to the west, at-tempted to bypass enemy resistance to the south on Monday, hoping to break through to the bridge. On the outskirts of Arnhem, however, they ran into elements of one of the panzer divisions moving through town. The British forces were stopped cold, suffering heavy casualties. Gen-eral Urquhart even sent a battalion of the 1st Airlanding Brigade, then engaged in fighting off the assault by Division von Tettau, to reinforce the battalions of the parachute brigade, but they, too, failed to make any headway.

Lieutenant Knottenbelt had spent the day clearing drop zones with the help of local civilians. At around two in the afternoon, he organized some civilians to search the woods around the drop zones for supplies that might have dropped into the trees. Many containers were found and recovered.

At about four o'clock, Knottenbelt learned that reliable telephone communications existed between Arnhem and Oosterbeek. He found a telephone and was able to get a call through to Colonel Frost's command post at the bridge, speaking with Captain Killick, the division counterintelligence officer. He learned of the 2nd Battalion's situation and passed on the information to division headquarters. At six that evening, Knottenbelt moved with the division headquarters to the Hartenstein Hotel in Oosterbeek.

The rest of Urquhart's division arrived between three and four that afternoon. This lift, delayed in its departure from England because of fog, included the remainder of the 1st Airlanding Brigade and another parachute brigade. Of the newly arrived parachute brigade's three battalions, Urquhart sent one to secure the high ground north of Arnhem, dispatched another to assist the battalions attempting to push eastward toward the bridge, and kept the third in reserve.

General Urquhart, frustrated at the lack of radio communications, went forward to see what was happening with the battalions advancing toward the bridge. He soon caught up with the 3rd Battalion and found Brigadier Lathbury, the brigade commander, with the battalion. The two generals soon found themselves in the middle of a firefight. Lathbury was wounded in the leg and taken prisoner. Urquhart managed to avoid capture but soon was cut off and had to hide in an attic, surrounded by Germans on the streets below. It would be nearly forty hours before he could make his way back to division headquarters.

The British paratrooper who had replaced Todd at the observation position in the attic had been shot dead by a sniper. Major Hibbert would later report that when the fight was over, some eighty dead Germans were found around the British perimeter and that Todd had the highest individual score with his six confirmed killed. He had hit and wounded others as well.

Lying in the basement among the many wounded British soldiers on Monday evening, Todd removed the bandage from his head and found that his eyes had cleared and that he could see. Then he fell asleep.

Still nothing had been seen of the Guards Armored Division of XXX Corps.

In London, Special Force Headquarters sent a message to all Jedburgh teams in Holland on Monday, informing them of a planned mission to reinforce team Dudley. Britain's Special Air Service proposed dropping a reconnaissance party consisting of a Belgian and a Dutch sergeant about six miles northwest of Almelo. The SAS drop was to be made Monday night. Twenty-four canisters would also be dropped. Bomber Command, however, balked at flying any night missions during the non-moon period. Although No. 38 Group was willing to fly the mission, they were overcommitted at the time.

Majors Brinkgreve and Olmsted of team Dudley spent Monday hiding in a dense forest of young pines. Word had reached the Jeds that German occupation authorities nearby were conducting *razzias,* searches carried out to round up Dutchmen to be shipped off to forced labor camps. Sergeant Austin had narrowly evaded one of the search parties and made it to a new safe house. When a German squad approached the brush pile that concealed the two Jedburgh officers, they opened fire on the patrol. The Germans, misjudging the strength of the ambush they had just walked into, broke contact and went for help. As soon as they departed, Brinkgreve and Olmsted left the area.

Later that evening, the two officers relaxed and talked about the Allied airborne operation they had been asked to support. They kicked around ideas on what they might be able to do to help the advancing ground force, but as the discussion continued they began to express doubt that the Allied force would reach them anytime soon. Both men had received enough reports from the underground to have developed a sense of the strength of enemy forces in the area north of the Neder Rijn, and they also understood the risks involved for paratroopers operating so far behind enemy lines.[21]

TEN

TUESDAY, SEPTEMBER 19

The Third Day

On Tuesday, team Dudley observed an increasing flow of German troops and matériel headed in the direction of Arnhem. That afternoon, Cor Hilbrink and Johannes arrived on a motorcycle, both men wearing dark blue suits and looking like Gestapo plainclothesmen to Major Olmsted.[1] Brinkgreve held a meeting with Johannes, Cor, Evert, and several of Evert's RVV men. The Jeds were growing more and more skeptical of Evert's leadership ability, and they now decided to visit the KP headquarters of Johannes and Cor to see how well their organization operated. If they liked what they saw, they might decide to team up with them.

When Brinkgreve's meeting concluded, Cor and Johannes left on their motorcycle to return to their headquarters, promising to return later in the evening with a car to pick up the Jeds. The Dutchmen returned at around nine that evening in a sharp-looking 1940 Lincoln four-door sedan that had been loaned to the underground by a wealthy merchant for the duration of the war. In the dark, the automobile strongly resembled one of the cars commonly used by the Gestapo. With Cor and Johannes were a gunner named Kees and the driver, a man named Klaas. Brinkgreve and Olmsted got into the Lincoln and began their journey to KP headquarters.

Klaas stuck to back roads as much as possible, hoping to avoid German checkpoints, but for a stretch of about nine miles he had to use the main highway. There were several German convoys on the road, and the big Lincoln was delayed at times. But the Dutchmen and the Jeds inside were never challenged. German troops were hesitant to stop what appeared to be a Gestapo car, fearing the trouble they could find themselves in for doing so. The car and its occupants proceeded unmolested, even as they joined one of the troop convoys for a while, heading in the direction of Arnhem. Their greatest danger at that point came from an Allied fighter that strafed the column, hitting a few of the trucks. Like the German troops throughout the convoy, everyone in the car breathed easier when the fighter eventually flew away.

Soon the Lincoln reached the town of Enter, where the driver was to turn off the main highway onto a secondary road to proceed to the KP command post. Klaas drove through the town until he reached the corner where he was to turn. Suddenly a German sergeant on the street yelled, *"Halt!"*[2]

Drivers in the underground knew every location where the Germans routinely established roadblocks, and they always went out of their way to avoid them. But now they had stumbled upon a group of SS men who had set up a roadblock where there had never been one before. Klaas never hesitated; he calmly gunned the engine and drove straight for the gap in the barbed-wire barrier. At the same time, Johannes, Cor, and Kees opened fire on the Germans with their Stens as the driver crashed through the barrier opening. At least five of the SS men fell to the ground as the Lincoln sped off down the road in the dark with no headlights on. No one in the car had been hit during the brief gun battle. Pappy Olmsted had felt something hot on his back and thought for a moment that he had taken a ricochet, but it turned out to be nothing more than one of the many spent cartridges that had ejected from Cor's submachine gun. When the car had gone far enough to be out of immediate danger and everyone had reloaded their weapons, Johannes began to laugh. He explained that prior to encountering the roadblock, he had been wondering whether or not the safety was engaged on his Sten. Luckily, it was not.[3]

Finally, the big car pulled into a place called Villa Lidouenna, which served as KP headquarters. There, the Jeds were introduced to several men and women of the underground, including Johannes's wife and Cor's brother, father, and wife. Brinkgreve and Olmsted were pleased to find a very alert and efficient command post. It was the nerve center of a well-organized and efficient intelligence network. Outside, vigilant guards watched all approaches. The place was even equipped with electrical warning systems. A variety of automobiles and motorcycles sat ready and waiting nearby.

Soon the men were relaxing with a cup of ersatz coffee and recounting their adventure at the roadblock. After the women had gone off to bed, Cor broke out a bottle of fine French brandy and a bottle of cherry brandy. A third, stone bottle contained genuine Dutch Bols gin, which the locals drank straight or with bitters. For hours, the men drank and talked of how they would organize for the work that lay ahead. The Jeds shared their American and British tobacco with their Dutch friends, and all enjoyed the camaraderie and looked forward to a close partnership.[4]

British engineers finished erecting the Bailey bridge at Son, and tanks of the Guards Armored Division began crossing just before seven on the misty morning of September 19. The ground force was now more than thirty hours behind schedule and still had thirty-nine miles to go to reach Arnhem.

After a hard-fought three-day battle with elements of the German 59th Division, the 101st Airborne Division's 502nd Parachute Infantry Regiment captured the Best bridge at six that afternoon. British tanks gave the paratroopers the edge they needed when they joined the battle in the early afternoon. In the course of the battle, the British tankers and American paratroopers killed more than three hundred Germans and captured another fourteen hundred.[5]

More of the 101st Airborne arrived that afternoon when 428 gliders delivered 2,579 men, including two battalions of the 327th Glider Infantry.[6]

Most of the Guards Armored Division had passed through Son by four in the afternoon, and they continued on to the north. An hour later, some Dutch cyclists arrived near the 101st Airborne Division command post and reported that they had observed German tanks approaching the area. Two officers of the 101st, accompanied by Lieutenant Dubois of Jedburgh team Daniel II and a bazooka team, walked eastward along the Wilhelmina Canal to see if they could spot the tanks.[7] Suddenly, three or four Panther tanks broke out of a wooded area about three hundred yards ahead of the men. Dismounted infantry spread out alongside the tanks as they moved along the south bank of the canal toward Son and the bridge. The tanks were from the 107th Panzer Brigade, just arrived from Aachen to reinforce the First Parachute Army. When the lead tank came within a hundred yards of the bridge, it was knocked out by a British six-pounder gun.

It was dark when German shells began pounding the village, including the area around the division command post. Only a small security force and headquarters staff troops were available to defend the headquarters and the newly emplaced Bailey bridge. Jedburgh team Daniel II fought alongside the men of the division staff, while Lieutenant Dubois helped the bazooka team that was then engaging the tanks south of the canal. A Panther fired several rounds into the division command post, causing some casualties. General Taylor then arrived with reinforcements from a glider infantry battalion. With their only fifty-seven-millimeter antitank gun, the Americans knocked out one tank; a man with a bazooka got another. The enemy tanks eventually withdrew, and work began on improving defensive positions in case they returned. A single burning British truck sat in the center of the Bailey bridge, but Hell's Highway was once again open to traffic.[8]

At dusk, a different threat appeared at Eindhoven as 120 German bombers struck the city, leaving at least a thousand civilian casualties. Few Americans were in the city at the time and so avoided being hit, but some British units incurred casualties.[9]

That night, the 101st Airborne Division held defensive positions at Eindhoven, Son, St. Oedenrode, and Veghel.

―――――――

A reconnaissance unit of the Guards Armored Division linked up with elements of the 82nd Airborne Division's 504th Parachute Infantry in a sugar beet field near Grave at 8:20 on Tuesday morning.[10] Soon the long column of Guards Armored tanks, at least thirty-three hours behind schedule, appeared through the cold and foggy dawn and crossed the Maas River bridge at Grave.[11] Now the planned capture of the Nijmegen highway bridge took on a new level of urgency for the 82nd Airborne.

General Gavin met Lieutenant General Brian G. Horrocks, XXX Corps commander, early that afternoon and briefed the British ground force commander on the 82nd's plan for capturing the Nijmegen bridge.

Gavin was bringing up his reserve, the 2nd Battalion, 505th Parachute Infantry, from its position west of Groesbeek to seize the southern end of the bridge. He intended to send another force across the river by boat to take the north end of the bridge. Since no civilian boats could be found, Gavin accepted an offer by the British of thirty-three collapsible canvas assault boats belonging to an engineer unit in their column. The boats, Gavin was assured, could be brought forward by the following morning.

At midday, as a seemingly endless column of British tanks and trucks rumbled across the Grave bridge and up the road toward Nijmegen, 150 shiny B-24 bombers came in at low level and dropped supply canisters under brightly colored parachutes to the troops of the 82nd.[12]

Tanks and infantry of the British Guards Armored Division joined a battalion of the 505th in an attempt to seize the southern end of the railroad bridge over the Waal that day, but they were forced to turn back in the face of stiff German resistance. Likewise, a combined American-British tank and infantry assault on the southern end of the highway bridge resulted in the fourth failed attempt at that objective.[13] By nightfall, the 82nd Airborne Division intelligence staff revised its estimate of enemy strength in Nijmegen, now figuring that around five hundred crack SS troops held the highway bridge, supported by artillery and mortars positioned north of the river.[14]

Resistance leaders in the Nijmegen district met again with Jed teams Clarence and Edward on Tuesday as paratroopers of the 82nd fought through the city. Working from a command post set up in a large public building in Nijmegen, Captain Bestebreurtje organized resistance activity to support the assault on the Waal River bridge and to maintain some semblance of civil order within the city. Dutch patriots formed teams of firefighters and rescue parties. An aid station for treatment of the wounded was organized with women and elderly citizens serving as orderlies and nurses. Others served as sentries or guarded German prisoners or formed an ad hoc police force to patrol some parts of the city. And all the time resistance members provided Bestebreurtje with information about the German forces still within the city and the outlying areas. By the time the Jeds got their first message back to Special Force Headquarters on the nineteenth, they were reporting the use of a partially armed resistance force numbering eight hundred.[15]

Bad weather prevented Tuesday's scheduled arrival of the 325th

Glider Infantry Regiment. Commanders, with mounting casualties taking a toll on infantry strengths, now had to use 450 glider pilots as infantry replacements.[16]

Jed team Clarence made contact with the British 1st Airborne Division on Tuesday through telephone contacts with the resistance in Arnhem. Corps took advantage of this link to pass orders to the beleaguered airborne division; those at Arnhem passed intelligence back on the same line.

Meanwhile, the airborne corps headquarters relocated to a site just south of Nijmegen. That night, Sergeant Beynon took a car and set out to find the corps command post. After experiencing some trouble with the car, Beynon ended up on the wrong road. He was stopped by a platoon of 505th paratroopers as he approached a viaduct. The platoon informed him that a minefield lay ahead. Beynon had nearly driven right into it. Rather than try to go any farther on a very dark night, Beynon chose to spend the night with the soldiers in their position along the canal near Mook.

"I guess you've got another man," said Beynon. He asked a paratrooper where the platoon leader was. The 505th man said that their senior man had been killed. Noticing the technical sergeant stripes on Beynon's sleeve, the paratrooper pointed out that the Jed NCO was now the ranking man in the group.

"I guess you're in charge,"[17] he said.

Twice during the night the Germans attacked, trying to cross over the canal, but the platoon, with Beynon fighting alongside, turned back both attacks. Six members of the platoon were lost in the action.[18]

––––––––––

Elements of the 1st Airborne Division attempting to break through to the 2nd Battalion at the Arnhem bridge, around two hundred men from three battalions, failed to make any progress on Tuesday. That night, they slipped quietly back through German lines to the drop- and landing-zone area. There, they joined the remainder of the 1st Airlanding Brigade, whose perimeter was shrinking after combating German ground forces and being subjected to aerial bombardment and artillery and mortar shelling throughout the day.

Inclement weather prevented the division's reinforcements, the Polish 1st Independent Parachute Brigade, from arriving that day as scheduled. Leaden skies had closed over British airfields and remained all day, grounding the third airlift. From September 19 through the twenty-third, the ceiling remained at zero.[19]

General Urquhart's headquarters communications section had so far failed to establish radio contact with General Browning's corps headquarters near Nijmegen. Heavy vegetation and built-up urban areas prevented successful radio signal transmission.

To make matters even worse for the British, the few resupply drops that were able to get through from England dropped their loads of food and ammunition and medical supplies to areas that were now in the hands of the Germans.

Lieutenant Allan Todd's eyes were still sore when he woke on Tuesday morning as he lay with the other wounded in the basement of the building at the north end of the Arnhem bridge. He could soon hear that their position was once again under attack. The Germans had resumed probing attacks and mortaring from the east. Many officers had become casualties, and no one was manning the position he had established in the rafters of the building, so he left the basement and returned to his perch in the attic. His eyes were still sensitive, and they became watery from the sunlight. Almost immediately upon getting himself back into position, he shot and killed another three Germans. Todd remained in the attic position for the rest of the day.

Downstairs, Captain Groenewoud received disconcerting news from a local civilian. A column of some one hundred German armored vehicles were reportedly en route from Amsterdam to Arnhem. The brigade staff quickly tried to get confirmation from division headquarters, but they were unable to make contact.[20]

The 2nd Battalion was then threatened from another direction. At about ten in the morning, two German tanks—a twenty-three-ton Mark IV Panther, with its seventy-five-millimeter gun, and a Tiger, a fifty-six-ton behemoth armed with an eighty-eight-millimeter gun—approached the British positions from the north. Both tanks opened fire. Then a British antitank gun knocked out the Mark IV as it tried to reposition for a better shot. The Tiger, however, proved impervious to the same antitank fire. It slowly turned and drove away. A and B Companies, near the river, battled German armored and infantry assaults throughout the day.

Around noon, another attack by German infantry proved much more serious than previous ones. From his position, Allan Todd was able to shoot five more of the enemy before heavy machine-gun fire drove him away from the window. He took over another position where a Bren gunner had been killed. Firing from his new vantage point, Todd knocked out a twenty-millimeter antiaircraft gun. The gun, devastating when used in a ground role, had been set up about twenty yards down the street from Todd's position and had been firing from point-blank range into a neighboring house occupied by British soldiers. Both Lieutenant Colonel Frost and Major Gough complimented Todd on his shooting, but it was clear that the battalion's position was becoming increasingly desperate.[21]

Sporadic firefights continued in Arnhem throughout the day, and when the Germans began hitting the British positions with mortars and artillery, fires broke out in many buildings in the city.

There were already fifty casualties in Frost's building alone. Medical supplies were running low, and the medics were not equipped to handle such a casualty load. Attempts to telephone the hospital proved futile; the phone lines had been knocked out. To make matters still worse, many of the battalion's medics had also become casualties by now, and they were unable to care for the other wounded.

Captain Groenewoud was determined to get help for the wounded, both British and German. The Dutchman found a telephone and tried to call the hospital for an ambulance to pick up the most seriously wounded, hoping they could bring desperately needed bandages and medicine to aid the others as well. But the telephone line was dead.

Groenewoud ran to the basement, where the British soldiers had ushered the Dutch occupants of the building for safety. He asked the civilians where another telephone could be found. The locals told him there was another phone in a doctor's office two blocks down the street. The Dutch Jed rushed back upstairs and asked Lieutenant Todd to accompany him down the street to the doctor's office. Todd withdrew from his position, and they were off at once.

The two Jedburgh officers made a dash down the street. About a block away, they stopped next to the corner of a building and prepared to run across the street. Captain Groenewoud turned to say something to Todd, but just then Todd heard a shot from a sniper. Groenewoud never heard it; the bullet hit him square in the forehead, exiting from the back of his head and killing him instantly. Todd jumped into the nearest doorway for cover and found himself next to a Dutch civilian. The Dutchman knew enough English to understand what Todd was looking for, and he led the American to a telephone in the next building.

Together, the two men placed a call to the hospital, only to find that a battle was raging outside the hospital walls. To make matters worse, the Germans were taking control of the hospital for treatment of German wounded, allowing no more British to be brought in. Todd spoke with a British doctor who explained that he had attempted to send medical help to the men at the bridge, but the Germans had been too strong. Any ambulance or medics they sent out were fired on; two medics had already been killed. Moreover, German casualties were taking more and more space in the hospital, forcing all British casualties to be moved into a single room.

Todd returned to the brigade command post to report this information to Lieutenant Colonel Frost, but he found that Frost had been wounded during his absence, shrapnel having shattered bones in his leg and ankle, and Major Gough was now in command. Todd realized the seriousness of their situation—ammunition, food, and medical supplies were almost gone. They were out of contact even with other elements of the brigade, not to mention division headquarters. Furthermore, the signal officer reported that they had made contact with XXX Corps and had learned that the corps was tied down near Nijmegen.

Later that afternoon, two RAF planes flew over and dropped supply containers. The Germans met them with heavy fire, and one of the planes went down in flames, crashing into a church spire. The containers had been dropped too far away for the British troops to reach them. At some point that day, someone shouted the unit's war cry, "Whoa, Mohammed!" and others echoed the cry throughout the British perimeter at the bridge. It lifted spirits.

More German reinforcements began arriving that afternoon and evening. The 208th Assault Brigade, with its Sturmgeschütz III armored assault guns, arrived from Denmark and took up blocking positions between the British force at the bridge and the remainder of the division west of Arnhem. The first two tanks of a company of fourteen Tigers commanded by Hauptmann Hans Hummel arrived at the bridge. After trading a few shots with a British antitank crew, the two Tigers left the area for the time being.

Todd spent the remainder of the night back in his observation position in the attic. From time to time, Major Hibbert, in his camouflaged paratrooper smock, climbed up to the attic and was amazed to find Todd there most of the time; he wondered when the man ever slept.[22] It was quiet for much of the day, and then, at dusk, came yet another German assault. Major Tatham-Warter saw a Tiger tank drive down the street in front of the buildings occupied by 2nd Battalion and brigade headquarters, firing two or three rounds into each building at point-blank range.[23] Todd thought the British antitank gun crews were performing magnificently, knocking out six tanks—two Tigers and four Mark IVs.[24] When the artillery officer serving as forward observer was hit, Todd filled in for him, directing artillery fire from guns back at the division perimeter west of the city. He remained at his observation post throughout the night.

Frost's 2nd Battalion was now completely cut off from the rest of the division. Throughout the day on Tuesday, the 1st Parachute Brigade's other two battalions tried to break through to the small force at the bridge, 1st Battalion along a northern route and 3rd Battalion on a southern route along the riverbank. Every attempt at relief was futile, though, as fresh German SS infantry and armor troops that had been rushed into the city stopped the two battalions. That afternoon, General Urquhart came to the decision that Frost's force at the bridge would have to be abandoned to their own fate.[25] He now had to organize the remainder of the division into a perimeter defense at Oosterbeek.

Earlier that day, Lieutenant Knottenbelt, located with the 1st Airborne Division headquarters, heard of the increasingly grave situation in Arnhem and tried once again to get through to Frost's command post and Jed team Claude by telephone. He called the same number he had used earlier when he spoke with Captain Killick. This time, a German answered the phone.[26]

ELEVEN

WEDNESDAY, SEPTEMBER 20

The Fourth Day

On Wednesday morning, a courier reached Jedburgh team Dudley with news of an incident that the men found amusing. The courier, who lived near the site of the roadblock the Jeds and resistance leaders had rammed through in Enter, said that the men firing from the Lincoln had killed three Germans and wounded several others. Then, according to the Dutchman, a car looking very much like the Lincoln came along about fifteen to thirty minutes later and refused to stop. The SS troops still manning the roadblock—alert, frightened, and angered by the shooting of some of their comrades by Johannes and Cor—raked the second car with machine-gun fire and grenades. All of the car's occupants—an SS officer, a Gestapo plainclothesman, and the driver—were killed.[1]

Pappy Olmsted later recalled how the roadblock incident was evidence that a minor act by irregular forces, even an unplanned one, could have an impact on the tactical situation that was out of proportion to the action itself. Prior to the incident, the Germans had maintained six roadblocks in the village of Enter with a garrison force of eighty to one hundred men. As a result of the deadly incident with the Lincoln operated by the Dutch resistance, the Germans increased the garrison strength to some five hundred troops manning eighteen roadblocks.

These were five hundred men who could have been deployed on the front line facing Allied soldiers. All of this resulted from their car stumbling unexpectedly on an SS roadblock.[2]

The team spent all day Wednesday at their new quarters, a place near the village of Borne called the Villa Lidouenna. The villa lay just west of the railway connecting Almelo and Hengelo. While Henk Brinkgreve met with area resistance leaders throughout the day, Pappy Olmsted and Bunny Austin spent the day coding, decoding, and transmitting messages with the Jed radio. Several of the messages they sent to Special Force Headquarters in London provided map coordinates for new drop areas, fields that special operations aircraft could use to parachute arms and supplies to the Jeds and the resistance. Much of the incoming message traffic sought information from team Dudley on the situation in Arnhem and the status of team Claude. But the Jeds had no knowledge at all of the outcome of the airborne operation or the status of the other Dutch Jedburgh teams.

Brinkgreve and Olmsted decided to send a man to Arnhem to make contact with the Allies, learn what he could about the situation, and advise the paratroopers on what kind of support could be provided by the Overijssel resistance. They briefed Dolf, a Dutchman serving as a messenger in the KP, on what they needed, and the young man departed for Arnhem late Wednesday afternoon. The Jeds then radioed London that they had dispatched a messenger.

Dolf made it to Arnhem and was able to talk with Captain Jaap Staal, the Dutch officer on Jedburgh team Edward, in Nijmegen, on a telephone line controlled by the underground. Several weeks would pass, though, before Dolf could get back to Brinkgreve and Olmsted and tell them what he had learned.

———

Wednesday marked the fourth day of Operation Market-Garden. Near Nijmegen, the linkup of XXX Corps with the 82nd Airborne was completed. British I Airborne Corps headquarters moved its command post to the outskirts of Nijmegen at three on the afternoon of September 20.[3] Captain Staal's team established a Jedburgh command post at the St. Anna Hospital in Nijmegen, employing two Dutch resistance girls to help with the encoding and decoding of messages. Team Edward received the first report from team Daniel II, who reported little resistance activity in the 101st Airborne's area at Eindhoven. Team Clarence was also heard from that day, but no word had yet been received from team Claude with the 1st Airborne Division in Arnhem. Radio traffic soon became extremely heavy, so much so that Captain Sollenberger had to radio London, asking Special Force Headquarters operators to ease up. Corps continued to receive intelligence reports from the 1st Airborne Division over the underground telephone link, still the only form of communication established with Arnhem.

Tanks of the 107th Panzer Brigade returned again on the misty morning of September 20 to hit the infantry battalion guarding the Son bridge. The Germans came close to recapturing the bridge until ten British tanks arrived and knocked out four German tanks, forcing the remaining enemy tanks to pull back.[4]

The 82nd, too, came under attack that morning when two understrength battalions of German paratroopers, with tank support, attacked from the Reichswald. A battalion of the 505th Parachute Infantry, holding the area that took the brunt of the attack, was stretched thin and outnumbered. By three in the afternoon the Germans had taken the village of Mook, and only after bitter fighting did the Americans, supported by six British tanks from the Guards Armored Division, take back the village, with nearly two dozen men killed and more than double that wounded and missing.[5]

In Nijmegen, tanks of the British Guards Armored Division joined an element of the 505th in an assault on the south end of the highway bridge over the Waal. Movement of infantry through the streets on foot was impossible in the face of strong dug-in fighting positions the Germans manned near the bridge. Paratroopers advanced toward the bridge from building to building by blasting holes through adjoining walls.

At around three on the afternoon of the twentieth, the 82nd Airborne Division's 504th Parachute Infantry Regiment set out to cross the Waal with the objective of seizing the north ends of both the railway bridge and the highway bridge at Nijmegen. Three hundred to four hundred yards wide, the Waal was a deep river with a strong current. Tasked with the initial assault crossing was the 504th's 3rd Battalion under Major Julian A. Cook. Using the only boats available—flimsy nineteen-foot canvas rowboats with reinforced plywood bottoms—the paratroopers prepared to cross the river about a mile downstream from the railroad bridge. Only twenty-six boats were available for the first wave of the assault, carrying about 260 men. Each boat also carried three engineers to paddle on the return trip to the south bank to pick up the next wave.[6]

Fifteen minutes prior to beginning the crossing, Allied artillery pounded the northern shore. British tanks on the south bank laid a smoke screen to hinder the Germans' view of the river, but the screen was quickly dissipated by the wind and proved ineffective. The paratroopers were in full view of the enemy on the opposite bank and on the bridge from the time they carried the flimsy boats to the bank and embarked. Once in the boats and under way, the men were under heavy direct fire by Germans on the north bank during the entire crossing. Some four hundred to six hundred Germans fired every weapon they had at the oncoming boats—eighty-eight-millimeter and twenty-millimeter guns, artillery and mortars, machine guns and rifles. Enemy fire came both from the far bank and from Germans positioned among the girders of the railroad bridge. British tanks and American mortars provided supporting fire, engaging the enemy on the north bank as best they could.

Paratroopers fought the strong current as they paddled furiously with wooden oars and rifle butts. Artillery and mortar rounds created huge geysers of water, and enemy machine-gun bullets pelted the surface of the river the way hail does in a fierce storm. Many men were hit and slumped in their boats or fell overboard. In Major Cook's boat, the regimental chaplain heard a thud next to him when an enemy shell blew the head off the man sitting shoulder to shoulder with him. Cook, meanwhile, continued to row furiously, repeating aloud: "Hail Mary, Mother of God, pray for us . . ."[7] Sometimes entire boats were sunk or drifted aimlessly downriver when all aboard were killed. Those who survived the ordeal crawled ashore on the north bank, exhausted and soaked, many of them vomiting. Half of the paratroopers in the first wave were killed or wounded, and only thirteen of the twenty-six boats were able to begin the return trip to the south bank to pick up the second wave.[8]

From his viewpoint on the river's south bank, a British officer remarked, "I went through the terrible fighting when the Germans invaded the Lowlands and France, the war in North Africa, and the experience at Dunkirk," but the officer confessed that he had "never observed such a display of courage as I've seen today."[9]

Those who made it to the north bank on the first lift were then faced with the task of crossing eight hundred yards of wide-open grassy flatlands to assault German machine-gun positions on a dike. In what seemed like a certain suicide effort, the paratroopers charged across the open area through grazing machine-gun fire. As they reached the dike, the men used grenades to knock out machine-gun nests; they shot or bayoneted Germans in their foxholes. Then they formed a hasty defense to await more boatloads of paratroopers.

The engineers paddling back to the south bank continued to take fire from the Germans, and only eleven of the remaining thirteen boats completed the return trip. With those boats, six more crossings delivered the remainder of Major Cook's battalion and the 1st Battalion to the north bank.[10]

Meanwhile, a battalion of the 505th Parachute Infantry, supported by British tanks, finally captured the southern end of the bridge at around seven that evening. A few tanks pulled onto the bridge and sprayed the steel girders of the great arch structure with machine guns. As it was getting dark, paratroopers of the 504th near the north end of the bridge saw tanks approaching from the south end of the bridge and were elated to know that the British armored column had arrived and soon would be on its way to Arnhem. Now the tanks had less than fifteen miles to go to reach the British paratroopers fighting to hold the north end of the bridge at Arnhem. Three of the American paratroopers stepped onto the bridge at ten minutes past seven, just as the first tanks arrived at the north end.[11]

After hard fighting, the 82nd Airborne had, at last, secured both the railroad and highway bridges over the Waal. The division lost around 200 men in the assault that resulted in the capture of the highway bridge. In Major Cook's battalion alone, 28 men were killed, 78 were wounded, and 1 man remained missing.[12] As a testament to the intensity of the struggle, 267 dead German soldiers lay on the railroad bridge, 80 of them lodged among its girders. An untold number had dropped into the river below.[13]

Suddenly, a German eighty-eight farther up the road to the north fired and knocked out the lead British tank sitting at the north end of the bridge. The next four tanks spread out off the road and remained in position. Then, to the astonishment of the Americans, the British tank crews got out of their tanks and began brewing tea. The 504th had just performed one of the most heroic feats of the war, paying a heavy price in blood to seize the Nijmegen bridge, thereby allowing British XXX Corps to cross the Waal and continue their rush to relieve the desperate situation of the British 1st Airborne at Arnhem. American soldiers, feeling a kinship with the brave British paratroopers at Arnhem, screamed at the tankers in disbelief.

"Why are you stopping?" asked one of the American company commanders of the British captain in command of the tanks.

"I can't proceed," came the reply. "That gun will knock out my tanks."

"We'll go with you. We can knock out that gun."

"I can't go on without orders."

Incredulous, the American said, "You mean to tell me you're going to sit here on your ass while your own British paratroopers are being cut to shreds—and all because of one gun?"

"I can't go without orders."

"You yellow-bellied son of a bitch. I've just sacrificed half of my company in the face of dozens of guns, and you won't move because of *one* gun."[14]

When the American captain then threatened to blow the British captain's head off if he didn't get the tanks moving, the tank commander sank into his turret and closed the hatch. Soon the American battalion commander, Major Julian Cook, arrived and had a similar argument with the tank commander. Within an hour, the commander of the 504th, Colonel Reuben Tucker, arrived and did likewise.

Men of the 504th expanded their perimeter on the north bank and settled in for the night. For some, the bitterness, frustration, and anger they felt that night would remain with them for the rest of their lives.[15] It would be another twenty-four hours before the British tanks pushed on toward Arnhem.[16]

————

Special Force Headquarters sent a message on Wednesday informing Jedburgh team Edward that a radio set was to be dropped for team Clarence later that day. London also relayed a message from team Dudley, which was reportedly attempting to send a messenger to "Allied Headquarters" in Arnhem. Dudley reported, "ALL MEN 17 TO 45 ORDERED TO REPORT FOR DIGGING ALONG RIVER IJSSEL NEAR OLST AND WYNE,* NORTH OF APELDOORN AND SOUTH OF ZWOLFE. GERMANS RAPIDLY INCREASING EAST OF THE IJSSEL. WAAL LINE BEING FORTIFIED. HO CHRIS-

* Probably Wijhe.

TIANSEN REPORTED SOON IN DENIKAMP."[17] The London base station still reported no contact with team Claude.

––––––––

Prince Bernhard announced on September 20 that he would exercise his command of the Dutch resistance through the leadership of the OD-RVV-KP coalition. Nine local resistance groups were now actively participating in Operation Market, and team Edward reported to Special Force Headquarters that I Airborne Corps was "delighted" with the tactical information provided by these groups; such information was unobtainable from any other source.[18]

––––––––

In Oosterbeek that day, Lieutenant Knottenbelt gathered together all of the Dutch civilians he had recruited. There was nothing more they could do for now, he explained, and their continued presence at the British headquarters only put them in danger from the constant shelling. He encouraged them to return to their homes, but many insisted on staying. He relented and kept a few on.

That afternoon, Knottenbelt found Sergeant Scott searching the area around the drop zone for his radio. Scott had been searching for two days, even though there continued to be a considerable amount of sniper activity in the area. He never did find the set. Lieutenant Knottenbelt realized that the situation was becoming more desperate by the hour, and he wondered how Captain Groenewoud and Lieutenant Todd were getting along with 1st Brigade. Later that evening, an attempt to reach the troops on the north end of the bridge with a jeep and a carrier loaded with ammunition, food, and water failed to get through.

Ammunition was critically short at the bridge as German troops continued to draw nearer, pressing again from the east in the morning. Shots had to be deliberate. An enemy machine gunner located on a second-story balcony across the street repeatedly sprayed the windows of the building Allan Todd was in, keeping him and the others in the upstairs observation post pinned down. Finally, Todd crawled out onto the roof of the house with a Bren gun. Positioning himself along the gutter, he fired on the German machine-gun position, killing two of the three enemy soldiers there and silencing the gun. But his action drew considerable sniper fire in return, and a German bullet smashed into the stock of Todd's Bren gun. Somehow, he made it back into the building. By firing at Todd, the enemy snipers revealed their positions, and British troops killed many of them.

Todd and the others were fully aware of the danger they were in. Captain Briggs had returned from the east side of the highway with four men, the remainder of his group having been killed or captured and the building they had occupied burned. Those still alive were now in two buildings, completely surrounded by Germans and continuing to take heavy casualties. There was no relief or help of any kind in sight.

Mortars continued to hammer the British positions throughout the day on Wednesday. Tiger tanks began taking point-blank shots at the buildings with their deadly eighty-eight-millimeter guns. Two German tanks drove up onto the bridge and began firing their eighty-eights at the school on the east side of the road, with direct hits killing and wounding many inside and setting the roof on fire. British soldiers abandoned the building, using doors to carry the wounded.

Todd was back at his top-floor observation post at four-thirty that afternoon when an explosion nearby knocked him unconscious. The floor of the room opened up and Todd fell through, landing on the ground floor, still unconscious. The explosion might have been a direct hit by a mortar or it might have been a high-explosive round from a German tank's main gun. Major Hibbert later reported that the building took three direct hits from a 105-millimeter gun and two from an 81-millimeter mortar. The roof had been blown off, and the remainder of the building was in a shambles.

When Todd regained consciousness, he found that he had caught a piece of shrapnel in the first finger of his left hand. Another, more serious wound was just above his left knee. His back also hurt, and he had an excruciating headache, unable to hear anything out of his left ear because the eardrum had burst.

Todd could see that the building was now on fire. Dead and seriously injured men lay everywhere. Other men were scrambling to get out of the building. All the overworked medical officer could do for Todd was to quickly dress the hand wound. Todd applied his own field dressing to the leg wound, although it continued to bleed as he began fighting fires with the others. Todd was amazed at how the medical officer had held up, working day and night with the wounded.

It was clear by now that the end was near. The British perimeter had been reduced to no more than about a hundred yards square. Todd had only two rounds remaining in his carbine and two grenades. Those manning the antitank gun were down to their last few rounds of ammunition. No more rockets remained for the PIATs. Machine-gun ammunition, too, was completely gone. Now the Germans took a new approach, deciding that using phosphorous shells rather than high-explosive shells in their tanks was more effective. Burning buildings proved easier than blowing them apart.

By nightfall, the building holding the remaining British troops, the waterworks building where the brigade headquarters had been established, was burning out of control, and Major Gough ordered his men to move the wounded—now numbering more than 250 British and German soldiers—outside. Then he told those who were able to move, about 120 men, that they were free to attempt to break out in small groups. Most of the men broke up into groups of ten, and Todd, one of the few remaining officers, took charge of one group and led the men out the back of the building. They followed a brick wall until they came to a burned-out school building about four hundred yards north of the waterworks building. From the school, Todd and the others saw Germans enter the building they had just left, and they witnessed the capture of their wounded comrades who had not been able to escape. The men were comforted, at least, to see that the wounded were taken prisoner rather than shot.

The battle at the bridge had come to an end. Since first arriving at the bridge on the seventeenth, eighty-one British soldiers were killed or would later die from their wounds.[19]

Major Hibbert arrived and told Todd to get the remaining men organized into small sections. Ammunition was almost gone and the men were exhausted, having had no sleep in over twenty-four hours. Hibbert then ordered the sections of men to try to make it back to the division position west of Arnhem. Realizing then that the Germans were beginning a search for the others, Todd's group left the school and continued down a side street. Hibbert watched as Todd and the others crept off into the darkness. It was the last he would see of the American. Todd's small group was in no shape to put up much of a fight if they ran into trouble. Todd still had only two rounds in his carbine and one grenade. He had given his forty-five to a man who had no weapon. Personally, the American had taken a tremendous amount of physical punishment over the past four days, and he was bone-weary from lack of sleep. Now the instinct for survival provided the necessary adrenaline to keep going; training took over to guide his actions.

Following an alley to a wide street, the group saw that the Germans were close behind them. Todd and the others raced to a building across the street. Just as they reached the curb on the far side of the street, a machine gun in a nearby doorway opened up on the group. Todd was knocked off his feet, and he felt a stinging sensation in his side and was sure he had been hit. As he came down next to the curb, he spotted the machine gun's location. From his prone position, he tossed his only remaining hand grenade and knocked out the machine gun.

Knowing he could not remain where he lay, Todd struggled to his feet and ran around the corner of the building just as another machine gun farther down the street began firing in his direction. Trying to distance himself from the Germans, he ran through the wreckage of three burned-out buildings and crawled over a brick wall into a small courtyard. Still he could hear his pursuers closing in. Todd quickly looked around and saw no way out. His only means of evading capture was to hide, so he climbed a nearby tree.

Before long, a group of German soldiers passed beneath the tree. They did not look up. Soon Todd heard a German voice shout in English, "Lay down your arms, pick up your wounded, and come over here."[20] Todd realized this meant the remainder of his group had been captured. Then came the rain.

As night settled in under a moonless sky, the streets of Arnhem grew quiet. Occasionally, Todd could hear voices or intermittent gunfire. Fearing capture or worse if he left the tree, he decided to remain there, miserable as it was with the rain, until morning. He no longer felt the stinging in his side, so he examined the area for wounds. None were to be found; a machine-gun bullet had lodged itself in an empty magazine in his carbine pouch. Sitting in his tree perch in the rain, surrounded by the enemy, Allan Todd felt very lucky.[21]

TWELVE

THURSDAY, SEPTEMBER 21

The Fifth Day

Only a small British armor contingent began the northward drive to Arnhem from Nijmegen on Thursday, September 21. Not three miles north of Nijmegen, elements of II SS Panzer Corps held a tough strongpoint. An SS battalion and an infantry battalion were supported by eleven tanks, two batteries of eighty-eight-millimeter guns, and twenty smaller, twenty-millimeter antiaircraft guns.[1] The British tanks were stopped cold, unable to deploy off the narrow two-lane elevated road because of the soggy bottomland along both sides of the highway. What the armored force needed was infantry to help clear the enemy strongpoint so the tanks could proceed. But they would have to wait. The British 43rd Infantry Division was on its way, but it had taken the division three days to cover the sixty miles from the Dutch-Belgian border over the crowded highway. They arrived in Nijmegen after dark on Thursday but would be unable to attack until the following day.

By two that afternoon, the skies over England had cleared enough to allow 110 planes carrying Major General Sosabowski's Polish 1st Independent Parachute Brigade to lift off and head toward Holland. Plans now called for the Poles to jump to an area near the village of Driel on the south bank of the Neder Rijn. After dark they were to use the

Heveadorp ferry to cross to the north bank, where they would then reinforce the tenuous perimeter being held by British paratroopers.

But the sky over Holland was still overcast, and only 53 of the 110 planes were able to reach the Driel area and drop their loads of paratroopers. Major General Sosabowski reached the combat zone with just 750 men, only to learn that the Germans had recaptured the northern terminus of the ferry from the British. They then sank the ferryboat.

The enemy had also pressed their attacks on the bulk of the 1st Airborne Division at Oosterbeek, reducing the British perimeter to an area of one and a half miles by less than half a mile. The British hospital had been captured on Wednesday. Late that afternoon, the division made radio contact with an artillery regiment of XXX Corps.

———

Again, at around eight on the morning of September 21, German tanks attacked the paratroopers of the 101st Airborne at Son. Approaching from the east, the enemy this time succeeded in cutting the road and destroying a number of British vehicles before being turned back.

Reports from the Dutch people of German force movements east and west of the road held by the 101st Airborne Division indicated that the enemy was planning a converging attack to cut the road somewhere near Veghel and Uden. These reports were accurate. The 107th Panzer Brigade, an element of the 10th SS Panzer Division, and an infantry battalion from the 180th Division, all supported by an artillery battalion and operating under the control of Kampfgruppe (Battle Group) Walther, were to attack from the east while three infantry battalions and four Panther tanks of the 59th Division, supported by artillery, would attack from the west.[2]

On Thursday afternoon, Major Wilson of Jedburgh team Daniel II went to I Airborne Corps headquarters in Nijmegen to pay a visit to team Edward. Wilson found the road completely open from Son to Nijmegen, but on the return trip he encountered small bodies of German troops near Uden, about halfway between Nijmegen and Son. He succeeded in making it back to Son, but with considerable difficulty.

That same day, possibly as a result of Major Wilson's visit, Captain Sollenberger of team Edward went to see the intelligence officer, or G-2, of the 101st Airborne. The two men agreed that team Daniel II's work would conclude once British XII Corps and VIII Corps, operating on the flanks of XXX Corps, passed through the 101st.

Taking advantage of telephone contacts with underground cells in the cities of Amsterdam, Utrecht, Rotterdam, The Hague, Arnhem, Elst, Geertruidenberg, and Zwolle, Jedburgh team Edward set up an information collection center in the power station at Nijmegen. Among the earliest messages received was a report from Elst that included an eyewitness account of the Polish 1st Independent Parachute Brigade's landing and the Germans' reaction. Advancing British forces made good use of the intelligence source, and the Jeds eventually turned over the operation of the information center to XXX Corps.

In a message to Special Force Headquarters in London, team Edward reported that it had arranged for some 250 local workers to help build an airfield near Malden. The Jeds also reported that they still had no contact with team Claude.[3]

North of Arnhem, team Dudley continued to work toward building a coalition of the three main resistance organizations. On Thursday, the Jeds met with several KP leaders from throughout the area. Attendees included a man named Gerard from Zwolle, another named Jules from Hengelo, and, from Almelo, a man called Dirk. All three men agreed to place themselves and their groups under the command of Colonel Guizinga, an Orde Dienst leader from Zwolle who had served in the Dutch East Indies as a colonel in the Royal Netherlands Army. Guizinga, with no men or arms under his control at the time, gladly agreed to work with the Jeds. Another meeting, scheduled for the twenty-fourth, was to be attended by the leaders of all three resistance organizations in Overijssel Province. Evert, however, the man the Jedburghs had grown skeptical of during their first few days in Holland, said he would be "too busy" to attend.[4]

When dawn broke on Thursday morning in Arnhem, Allan Todd could clearly see the bridge from his tree perch. He hoped desperately that he would soon see XXX Corps clearing the wreckage from the bridge and coming to his rescue.[5] With the light of day, he looked around to take stock of his situation. No more than fifty feet from his tree stood a building that appeared to serve as a headquarters of some sort. All day long, Germans moved in and out of the building and around the area. Todd was almost afraid to breathe, fearing that someone might hear him.[6]

Weariness also took its toll on him. He had slept little since the battle at the Arnhem bridge began. To keep from falling from the tree if he fell asleep, he tied his belt around one arm and a tree limb. At one point during the day, two German soldiers approached and sat down under the tree. They remained there, talking, for about half an hour. When they had gone, Todd descended from the tree, feeling nearly paralyzed. Still there was no sign of XXX Corps.

Miserably wet, tired, lonely, and hungry, Todd almost didn't care if he was captured.[7] Finding a space under a bush next to the headquarters building, Todd crawled in and fell asleep.

Any British paratroopers still at the Arnhem bridge, wounded or otherwise, were now in German hands, as was the bridge itself.

———

That night, team Daniel II moved with the 101st Division's command post to St. Oedenrode. Here at last the Jeds of Major Wilson's team made contact with the Dutch resistance, an eight-man contingent of the KP. Allied troops now noticed another group in the area. Armed with an assortment of German and American weapons, young men wearing armbands bearing the letters "PAN" roamed the streets, taking advantage of the chaos to pillage the neighborhood. Seemingly leaderless and undisciplined, the group never interfered with British or American forces but nevertheless caused trouble for local civil authorities.[8] This is not reflective of the tremendously helpful members of PAN who worked with paratroopers of both the 82nd and 101st Airborne Divisions.

THIRTEEN

FRIDAY, SEPTEMBER 22

The Sixth Day

The slow progress of British VIII and XII Corps on the flanks of XXX Corps made the 101st Airborne's task of keeping Hell's Highway open much more difficult. On September 22, D plus 5, the 506th Parachute Infantry fought to defend Uden. Other Screaming Eagles engaged Kampfgruppe Walther, supported by tanks of the 107th Panzer Brigade, in Veghel. Although the American paratroopers fought hard, the Germans succeeded in cutting the main road between Veghel and Uden, then proceeded down the highway toward Veghel. Lieutenant Dubois of Jedburgh team Daniel II, who was in Uden to help organize the KP in that town at the time, was now cut off from the 101st Airborne.

At that same time, another German battle group, Kampfgruppe Huber, was assaulting Veghel from the west but was soon driven back by troops of the U.S. 327th Glider Infantry. In addition to the glidermen, battalions from the 501st and 506th Parachute Infantry Regiments, supported by artillery and two squadrons of British tanks, defended Veghel. Though the village was held, miles of British armored vehicles and supply trucks were backed up. The highway to Uden had to be reopened.[1]

Team Edward contacted Captain Strutt of No. 1 Special Force Detachment* at Second British Army headquarters on Friday. The civil affairs officer on the British I Airborne Corps staff had requested that team Edward arrange for an armed resistance force of three hundred to four hundred men to be used in "mopping up" operations. The task of organizing this group fell to Jedburgh team Clarence. Before work had proceeded very far, though, the XXX Corps headquarters staff objected, pointing out that corps policy prohibited the arming of large groups of Dutch resistance.

It was now D plus 5, and team Edward, as the Jedburgh mission headquarters, had still not heard from team Claude. By now they were aware that there was German armor in Arnhem. Some members of team Edward even tried to go to Arnhem in an attempt to reach team Claude. With considerable difficulty, they managed to reach the south bank of the Neder Rijn but were unable to cross. The entire area was under tremendous fire, and contact with the 1st Parachute Brigade of the 1st Airborne Division, the brigade to which team Claude had been attached, was impossible.

Lieutenant General Horrocks, the XXX Corps commander, still held out hope that part of his force could reach Arnhem in time to save the beleaguered 1st Airborne Division. On September 22, he ordered the British 43rd Infantry Division "to take all risks to effect relief today."[2] But the 43rd, not even halfway to Arnhem yet, was unable to fight through a reinforced German defensive screen.

Because the paratroopers north of the Neder Rijn had not received a scheduled air resupply drop that day due to bad weather, and because the surrounded force was desperately short of ammunition, food, and other supplies, a different method was tried. Several amphibious vehicles known as DUKWs were loaded with the needed supplies. A battalion of infantry then climbed aboard the DUKWs and the column proceeded on back roads, reaching Driel late in the day. It was hoped that the Polish paratroopers could cross the river in the DUKWs, deliv-

* Special Force Headquarters' field army staff element attached to Second British Army headquarters.

ering the much needed supplies and providing reinforcements to the British force. Deep mud along the riverbank, though, prevented the use of the DUKWs. Some fifty Polish troops, employing makeshift rafts, were still able to cross the river to the north bank that night.[3]

In Arnhem, Allan Todd spent all day Friday under the bush next to the German headquarters, with Germans often passing within a few feet of him. During the day, it again began to rain. Todd crawled out from under the bush and sought shelter in the evening, finding an abandoned machine shop in a burned-out building about a hundred yards away. The tin-roofed shop appeared to belong to a plumber. Inside, Todd discovered a bushel of pears. Tonight, at least, he would have food and a roof over his head. Famished, he ate half a dozen pears, then lay down on the shop's workbench and slept.

Jedburgh team Dudley was living comfortably at the Villa Lidouenna, which the men found to be a smoothly functioning headquarters. Security was enhanced by a system of electrical warning devices and a twenty-four-hour guard force. The Dutch used an efficient network of motorcycle- and bicycle-mounted couriers. Some couriers even wore German uniforms when necessary to get messages through. Information on German troop locations and activities was often obtained from local priests who served as intelligence collectors while moving around the area on their parish rounds.

Late on Friday, September 22, Johannes, one of the Dutchmen working with team Dudley, departed for Almelo on a motorbike to visit a comrade who had been wounded several days earlier during a sabotage attack. Occupation authorities had forbidden the use of civilian motorbikes on the roads. Upon his arrival in Almelo, SS men stopped Johannes and took him into custody. He was placed in a cell to await questioning by an SS captain, but the SS men failed to search him. Later, the SS captain arrived and began his interrogation. Alone with the captain, Johannes pulled out a pistol and shot the German in the chest. He then jumped out of a window and ran.

After running a short way down the alley, Johannes decided to go back for his motorbike. When he reached the bike, he kick-started it and tore off just as the Germans opened fire with automatic pistols.

None of the pistol shots hit him, but two blocks away he was struck in the leg by a bullet from a submachine gun fired by an SS man at a road-block. Severely wounded and unable to continue, Johannes was recaptured. He was taken to a German hospital, where the bullet was removed, then returned to the waiting Gestapo, who proceeded to interrogate and torture the Dutchman into the night.

Meanwhile, the Jeds at Villa Lidouenna heard of the incident soon after the shooting. Knowing that the Germans would likely succeed, through torture, in getting Johannes to talk, they decided to quickly abandon the headquarters. Because they would have to walk right down the main road, the Jeds and other men of the headquarters carried only what could be concealed under their overcoats, as well as the B-2 radio, which was built into a suitcase, and the Jed radio. The group split into smaller parties, each proceeding to a different safe house. Brinkgreve, Olmsted, Austin, and a brother of Cor Hilbrink's took the radios with them and found shelter for the night at a nearby farm.

Later that night, they made an attempt to rescue Johannes, but he was held in a building that was heavily guarded by SD and SS. Moreover, German paratroops maintained a strong garrison force in the town. The recovery of Johannes was impossible.[4]

FOURTEEN

SATURDAY, SEPTEMBER 23

The Seventh Day

I n England, scattered showers fell from low-hanging clouds. Just before one on Saturday afternoon, a break in the clouds allowed ninety-six planes of the 440th Troop Carrier Group, each towing a CG-4A glider, to take off with reinforcements for the 82nd Airborne Division.[1] They were part of the final serials of the two American airborne divisions. Elsewhere, British Typhoons and American P-47s were able to strike German positions along Hell's Highway and around the perimeter of isolated Red Devils at Oosterbeek.

British forces at Driel, on the south bank of the Neder Rijn, were now in continuous radio contact with the surrounded paratroopers north of the river. British troops and equipment continued to build up around Driel, though hopes of expanding the 1st Airborne's perimeter into a bridgehead on the north bank were dwindling. That night, a limited amount of supplies and another 150 Polish paratroopers were delivered by assault boats to the Red Devils across the river. Later that evening, Lieutenant General Miles Dempsey, the Second British Army commander, authorized the withdrawal of the remainder of the 1st Airborne Division if nothing else could be done.[2]

On Saturday morning, still with no sign of XXX Corps, First Lieutenant Allan Todd assessed his situation. He had little chance of further evading capture, and he was in need of medical care. His left ear still ached, and a runny, waxy substance drained from it. He had lost the field dressing from his knee wound while crawling along a hedge, and he thought it looked infected. Each morning, his eyes were stuck together. He had only pears to eat, and his canteen was nearly empty. Todd decided to ration himself to a few pears and a swallow or two of water each day and to remain hidden until he was found, either by XXX Corps or by the Germans.[3]

Saturday proved to be a costly day for the resistance men working with team Dudley farther to the north. That morning, Daan, the KP intelligence officer, and several other resistance members returned to the old headquarters at Lidouenna to pick up gear and documents that had been left behind when the post was so hastily vacated. Majors Brinkgreve and Olmsted and Sergeant Austin were with a group of men who followed about thirty minutes behind the first element. At the Lidouenna command post, men from the lead element had just finished loading everything in the cars when several truckloads of SD men arrived. Unknown to the resistance, the building had been under surveillance, and when Daan's group arrived, reinforcements were immediately called for. The Germans quickly raided the house.[4]

As the follow-on group approached, they heard trucks arriving at the headquarters ahead and almost simultaneously heard a fierce volume of gunfire from the villa. Within minutes, three of the twelve resistance men in Daan's group and several Germans had been killed.

Looking for information, the SD then tortured Cor Hilbrink's father all afternoon until he died of bayonet wounds later that evening. Two girls who had accompanied the men were beaten but were then allowed to leave. Knowing that they would be followed, the girls refrained from contacting anyone in the resistance for several months. The remaining men in Daan's group were able to escape.

Jedburgh team Dudley was forced to return to the farm where they had stayed the previous night. Because of the action at the villa, the men knew that the Germans would be conducting searches throughout the area. The farmer had created an arms storage area in a hay shed that could be accessed only by crawling under an adjoining woodpile and proceeding along a tunnel that came up in the barn. Now the farmer urged the Jeds to take shelter in the hidden armory. Not thrilled at the prospect of being so confined, the men crawled in and soon found themselves sharing a cramped space with some thirty containers full of plastic explosives, ammunition, grenades, and incendiaries.

Armed only with pistols, the men remained hidden in the arms store, in total darkness, for thirty or forty minutes. Bunny Austin began a spell of sneezing and couldn't stop. Majors Brinkgreve and Olmsted, their nerves already on edge, were sure that Austin's sneezing would give them away.

Soon two of the resistance men, Toon and Klaas, arrived with news that the Germans were searching every farm but were still several farms away from where the Jeds were hiding. The Jeds decided to take their chance on bicycle and left at once. Toon led them to a farm that only he among the resistance knew about.

The day was overcast and gloomy, with intermittent rain showers. As the four men pedaled farther away from the area where the deadly raid had taken place, they found the German sentries along the road to be less vigilant, seldom even stopping the men to check their identity cards.

Eventually the Jeds and Toon arrived at the new farm, and the Jeds spent the remainder of the day lying on a bed of moldy hay in a seemingly deserted barn and wondering what they were doing in Holland.

That night, the Jeds witnessed something unforgettable. It began with the growing drone of scores of bombers passing directly overhead. Then came the distant rumble of bombs impacting. Through holes in the tile roof of the old barn, the men watched the drama unfold as the Allied bombing raid hit a target just across the border in Germany. They saw planes hit by very effective antiaircraft gunnery, and they were speechless as they watched bombers go down in flames, some of them seemingly thoroughly burned before crashing to earth. A sickeningly helpless feeling came over the men, but they knew that at least some of the bomber crews, if they were able to bail out, might be rescued by the Dutch underground and passed through the remarkably efficient escape and evasion network operated by the resistance, enabling them to return to England.[5]

Jedburgh team Edward's mission was considered to be completed now that XXX Corps had arrived in strength. Resistance in the area was well organized and needed no further arms or other supplies. With the approval of I Airborne Corps headquarters, Captain Mills, one of the team's British officers, radioed London and asked that he be ordered back to London. His message informed Special Force Headquarters that Captain Staal, the Dutch team leader, wished to be sent to northern Holland on another Jedburgh mission. Captain Sollenberger, the American officer, in a message to London later that day, suggested that team Edward be allowed to remain together and be given another mission as a team. But Sollenberger didn't consider the current mission complete until he had made contact with the men of team Claude. He hoped to do just that before the night was over.

Moving as far forward as possible, team Edward spent the night near Driel, on the south bank of the Lower Rhine. Thinking that Claude's wireless set might be the problem, the men brought a set, but crossing to the north bank proved impossible. They knew that Lieutenant Knottenbelt had been slightly wounded, and unconfirmed reports told of the remainder of team Claude being wiped out. It was becoming more difficult to harbor much hope for Groenewoud, Todd, and Scott.

On Saturday, St. Oedenrode came under heavy shelling. Another German attack developed, this time from the west by a force of parachute troops supported by a few tanks and some artillery. The defenders of St. Oedenrode were able to turn back the attack at the edge of town.

Germans had cut the highway between Uden and Veghel, causing a halt to the long line of British vehicles on the road leading from Eindhoven to Nijmegen. At eight-thirty that morning, the German 6th Parachute Regiment counterattacked to recapture the town of Veghel but were stopped short of that goal. At the same time, the town was attacked by another enemy force, Kampfgruppe Walther, from the east. But by noon, the advance of British VIII Corps on XXX Corps' right flank forced the Germans to pull back. Screaming Eagles of the 101st had fought fiercely against German tanks and infantry until, at last, the enemy withdrew toward Erp. At one in the afternoon, two battalions of the 506th Parachute Infantry capitalized on the shift of initiative in their favor and struck the small German force still blocking the stretch of Hell's Highway between Veghel and Uden. After advancing about a mile, the American paratroopers linked up with British tankers driving southward from Uden. The highway to Nijmegen was once again open.

The remaining elements of both the 101st and 82nd Airborne Divisions arrived by glider on Saturday, September 23. With his 325th Glider Infantry Regiment now on the ground, General Gavin was able to expand the division perimeter somewhat to further secure the area near the bridge at Nijmegen.

FIFTEEN

SUNDAY, SEPTEMBER 24

The Eighth Day

On the twenty-fourth, German forces struck Hell's Highway once again, cutting the road between Veghel and St. Oedenrode. Paratroopers of the 101st joined with British tanks again to fight back and reopen the road. British tanks and supply trucks roared along the highway the rest of the day while the paratroopers formed a defensive line along both sides of the road.

Lieutenant Dubois was reunited with the other members of team Daniel II on Sunday when the division command post moved to Veghel, the road between St. Oedenrode and Veghel having just been reopened. In Veghel, the Jeds found a group of the Orde Dienst resistance organization and a well-organized KP contingent that had begun with fifteen members but was now growing stronger with increased recruiting as liberation seemed imminent. The KP and the Orde Dienst were efficient and worked well together, and they were soon to be of service to General Taylor.

A factory in Veghel had been used by the Allies as a makeshift holding area for some four hundred German prisoners of war. At the direction of General Taylor, Major Wilson of team Daniel II organized a prison guard detachment from the local KP men. Once the road back to

St. Oedenrode was considered secure, the resistance guards escorted the prisoners to that town, where the Allies could better hold them.

Lieutenant Dubois returned to Uden on September 24 to try to resolve a heated dispute between the KP and the Orde Dienst in that town. Although he was able to get the groups to cooperate, they were of little use to the Allies at this point. The Jeds also witnessed the unwelcome development of renegade individuals with German or American weapons, similar to the PAN gangs in St. Oedenrode. Fortunately, the ever-effective, cooperative KP of Veghel quickly subdued these people and confiscated their arms. Even amid the shelling that Veghel was undergoing at this time, the KP energetically collected all American arms once they were no longer needed by the resistance and, in accordance with General Taylor's orders, returned them to the division.

The Jeds of Daniel II were short on rations by this time, and captured German rations made up much of their daily fare. Food was in short supply throughout the town, but the Orde Dienst was doing a commendable job of distributing what little there was.[1]

In a final attempt to gain a bridgehead north of the Neder Rijn, General Horrocks ordered the remainder of the Polish paratroopers to be ferried across the river on the night of September 24. Most of the Poles were delivered successfully to the north bank, though many were lost to machine-gun fire when the Germans discovered the crossing operation. Two companies—four hundred men—of the British 43rd Division attempted to cross in assault boats not far away but failed to reach the British perimeter. Only about seventy-five of the four hundred made it back across to the south bank of the river.[2]

What remained of the British 1st Airborne Division north of the river continued to fight back incessant German attacks from within a steadily contracting perimeter. By now, the thumb-shaped perimeter was about one thousand yards wide at its base on the riverbank. It extended northward from the river for about fifteen hundred yards to the Oosterbeek area. The nearly encircled paratroopers suffered from a shortage of food, water, and ammunition, and they were continually subjected to mortar, artillery, and tank fire. Casualties continued to mount, overwhelming the division's small medical staff. German troops had begun referring to the British position as "the Cauldron."

Major Brinkgreve, Major Olmsted, and Sergeant Austin talked at length on Sunday morning as they lay on the old hay pile in the barn Toon had taken them to. They discussed what they might be able to accomplish in Holland, and they wondered aloud if they would ever get out of the country alive.[3]

At noon the farmer's son arrived, carrying a large basket filled with black bread, wild honey, cheese, and milk. As the hungry Jeds ate, a steady roar suddenly came from overhead. The men ran outside to see the sky filled with planes again, but this time the planes were low-flying German fighters, the most the men had ever seen at one time. That evening, on the Berlin radio broadcast, the Jeds heard of the great German victory at Arnhem.

Cor Hilbrink arrived during the evening, along with Toon and Daan. Hilbrink, who was well known to all resistance leaders in the area, had assumed command after Johannes's capture. For security reasons, the headquarters had to keep on the move, and they now decided to relocate to another farm about six miles to the east. The bicycle convoy began at dusk, hoping to reach their destination before curfew, which allowed no one on the roads from eight in the evening to four in the morning. Because the group was short one bicycle, Bunny Austin was required to ride perched uncomfortably on the back of Daan's bike.

When the group arrived at the new farm at ten minutes to eight, several young men of the resistance met the newcomers and ushered them to a group of straw stacks, where they hid the bikes. As homegrown cigarettes were passed around and everyone began smoking, the greeters explained that there were three Germans inside. This was puzzling news, as the farm was reputed to be one of the most secure sites in the Dutch underground. The Jeds quickly learned that the Germans were an anti-Nazi family—father, mother, and eighteen-year-old son—who had lived in Holland for several years. Now they were fugitives, the boy having deserted the Wehrmacht shortly after being conscripted and the parents, considered disloyal Herrenvolk, the subject of a search by the Germans. Although the farmer assured the men that the German family was no threat, the Jeds, with Toon and Klaas, remained outside for half an hour. As they waited, Olmsted and Austin broadened their limited Dutch vocabulary as Toon and Klaas, neither of whom spoke much English, taught them the Dutch words for various farm animals, tools, and implements. After a thirty-minute wait, the Jeds and the two Dutchmen finally joined the others in the farmhouse.

Cor Hilbrink introduced everyone to the farm family, identifying Olmsted and Austin as Allied airmen shot down during one of the recent bombing raids.

Throughout the stay of the headquarters group at this farm, the host family carried on its daily life with no hint of the critical role they played in the underground war, though frequent and unannounced spot checks by Germans left a constant undercurrent of fear.

The highlight of each day came when it was time for the radio news broadcasts. Under Nazi occupation regulations, it was forbidden to own or to listen to radios, but BBC broadcasts from England had a large and devoted audience throughout occupied Europe. When the time for the scheduled broadcasts approached, Heinz, the German deserter, set up the radio. Whatever work was under way on the farm came to a halt as everyone congregated at the house to listen to the broadcast while two men remained on guard outside to warn of any German night patrol or raid. At eight-fifteen every night came a program called *Radio Oranje,* intended especially for Dutch listeners. The following program, at eight-thirty, was of particular interest to the Jeds. *Radio Belgique,* targeted to the people of occupied Belgium, also served as the vehicle for Special Force Headquarters to transmit messages confirming or rescinding drops of arms and supplies for the resistance.

The Jeds initiated these airdrop arrangements by signaling London with their own radio. The messages included in the *Radio Belgique* program served as a last-minute means of letting the Jeds know whether a drop was scheduled for that night, how many planes there would be, and at what time they would arrive over the drop zone.

When confirmation of a drop was received, a carefully choreographed process began. The Jeds set up the field and ensured that the reception committee—resistance members or sympathizers who stood by to quickly load the supply canisters onto hay wagons, remove them to a designated hiding place, and dispose of the parachutes—was organized and in place. When the planes approached, the Jeds flashed the planned recognition signal. Upon receiving and recognizing the signal, the plane made its pass over the drop zone and emptied its load of a dozen containers.

Life at the farm settled into a routine. Henk Brinkgreve, Cor Hilbrink, and Daan, directing resistance activity for the entire area, held almost endless conferences and saw to administrative details. Brink-greve worked at making new contacts and seeing to the organization of the various underground elements. Pappy Olmsted worked at collecting and recording intelligence data, while Bunny Austin kept them in radio contact with SFHQ. At the beginning of their stay, Olmsted and Austin coded and decoded all messages that were transmitted and received, but they eventually trained some of the Dutch boys to use the code-books, freeing Olmsted to concentrate on the intelligence work.

At Olmsted's suggestion, the men prepared a small pamphlet that provided instructions to each of the many small resistance groups on the types of information the Jeds needed and how it should be obtained. The effort soon paid off; within a week, Olmsted began to receive a steady flow of information.

The men ate well and were accepted into the traditionally conserva-tive and very private home life of a Dutch farm family, where the men were serious and hardworking, the women kept a comfortable home, and children were raised to be polite and respectful.

In the evenings, after dinner and after the news broadcasts, everyone gathered with the family in the living room to talk and sing as two of the Dutch boys accompanied with the harmonica and accordion. Olmsted marveled at the number of popular American songs the Dutch people knew—"Home on the Range," "Springtime in the Rockies," and "Ra-mona," for example—and how the Dutch could sing them in accent-free English. But the accent quickly returned when the singing stopped and conversation began.[4]

SIXTEEN

WITHDRAWAL

The Last Day

Near Eindhoven, American and British forces attacked from three directions at eight-thirty on Monday morning, September 25, but the Germans still held a small stretch of Hell's Highway at nightfall. Even those stretches of highway the Allies gained could not yet be used. Before withdrawing, the Germans had mined the highway, and engineers were unable to clear the mines and open the road to traffic again until midday on the twenty-sixth. From that time on, the 101st successfully fought off several German attempts to cut the road again.

North of the Neder Rijn, in Oosterbeek, Lieutenant Knottenbelt, who had remained with the British 1st Airborne Division headquarters, took part in the fierce house-to-house fighting that continued for days following the airborne assault of the seventeenth. He had moved to a position in a house on the northern perimeter on the twenty-first, only to be shelled out of the building the following day. He had then joined a platoon of parachutists and assisted in its defense of some houses on the eastern perimeter. The British paratroopers surrounded in Oosterbeek had been taking a terrible pounding for a week now as their perimeter continued to shrink. Most of the trees in Oosterbeek had been stripped of all foliage. Two smells dominated the area—that of cordite from all the expended ammunition and that of the many bodies that littered the area.[1]

At nine-thirty on the morning of the twenty-fifth, General Horrocks and General Browning concluded that nothing more could be done but try to save as much of the 1st Airborne Division as possible. They agreed to withdraw the division's survivors from the north bank of the Neder Rijn and Montgomery approved, issuing the order for the withdrawal to take place that night.[2] Medical officers and nursing orderlies of the division were to remain behind with the roughly two thousand wounded, all of them soon to become prisoners of war.[3]

At seven that evening, Knottenbelt was ordered to accompany the division headquarters as it crossed to the south bank. He went to the basement of the Hartenstein Hotel and burned all the secret documents in his possession, then joined other members of the headquarters staff to the river to make the crossing.[4]

At dusk, weary men of the 1st Airborne prepared for their move to link up with their rescuers at the river's edge, evading notice by the Germans along the way. To move as quietly as possible, the men wrapped scraps of clothing around their boots. They were unable to take any wounded with them. Shortly before ten, the Red Devils, organized in boatload groups of fourteen men, began making their way through a heavy rain to the riverbank. In addition to the rain and darkness, the movement was masked by a continuous protective barrage along the British perimeter by XXX Corps artillery.

Knottenbelt reached the south bank at two o'clock on Tuesday morning. Boats manned by Canadians shuttled men throughout the night, but an estimated three hundred still remained north of the river when dawn arrived. Some of those stranded on the north bank attempted to swim to the south bank, but most were captured.

In the misty early morning light, on the south bank, British Sergeant Major Jimmy Sharp was determined to gather the remnants of 2nd Parachute Battalion from among the recovered 1st Airborne troops. Standing in a field beside a small peach tree, he shouted, "Fall in, 2nd Battalion."[5] Seventeen weary men answered the call and fell into formation in front of the sergeant major.

"Is this the lot?"[6] asked Sharp. With watery eyes, the sergeant major realized that the seventeen men standing before him were all that remained of the 509 members of 2nd Battalion who had jumped into Holland on September 17.[7] Not far away, answering the roll call for 3rd Battalion were one officer and thirty-six enlisted men.[8]

Of the roughly 9,000 Allied troops who had fought north of the Rhine since September 17, only 2,398 British and Polish men were safely withdrawn to the south bank. Of the senior commanders of the 1st Airborne Division, only the commanding general, Urquhart, and one of the brigadiers, Hicks, returned. Only one battalion commander was saved. The balance of the division's recovered force included 125 officers, 400 glider pilots, and 1,700 enlisted men. German casualties during the battle numbered about 3,300, a third of them killed.[9]

With the retrieval of the remaining soldiers of the 1st Airborne Division on September 25 came the realization that team Claude was not among the survivors. Team Edward reported Groenewoud, Todd, and Scott missing in a report to London the following day. They added that Knottenbelt was last seen on the north bank the previous night and that they would check to see if he had arrived at Nijmegen. Sergeant Scott, team Claude's radio operator, was last seen, wounded, on the twenty-second.[10] It was later determined that he was killed during the fighting at Oosterbeek.

———

Team Daniel II was at Veghel when they were contacted by team Edward on Monday evening. If the 101st consented, said team Edward, the Jeds were to wrap up their work and return to Brussels. Major Wilson was having great success at the time in collecting information from the local population for the 101st, but he was not happy with the performance of Lieutenant Dubois, who had not been trained as a Jed.[11] At any rate, the division approved of the team's withdrawal, and Wilson and his men left in a captured car for Brussels on September 26. After nearly crossing the German lines near Turnhout, the team finally reported to No. 3 Special Force Detachment at Twenty-first Army Group headquarters in Brussels that evening. They were welcomed back by an SOE officer, Lieutenant Colonel M. A. W. Rowlandson, who then directed Wilson and Dubois to make a personal report to Prince Bernhard. The team departed for England at six the following afternoon, arriving at Greenham airfield at eight and proceeding to London by train.

———

On Tuesday, the men of team Edward searched in vain for the Jeds of team Claude among the withdrawing British 1st Airborne Division. They found only the wounded Lieutenant Knottenbelt; the rest were missing.

With their work finished, the men of Edward believed that they had contributed something to the operation, if only organizing resistance groups to perform tasks that allowed Allied soldiers to fight where they were most needed. Of course, they had provided much in the way of valuable and timely intelligence. But it was too late to do any more.

Team Edward left Nijmegen on September 27 and reported to No. 1 Special Force Detachment at Second British Army headquarters. The team was flown out of Brussels and back to England the next day.

The 82nd Airborne Division had formed a defensive line southeast of Nijmegen and would hold that area—repelling German counterattacks and patrolling into enemy territory to capture prisoners for information—until they were relieved by Canadian troops in the middle of November.

Jedburgh team Clarence was to remain with the 82nd Airborne Division for the time being. As team Edward prepared to leave, Lieutenant Willmott left the team's B-2 radio set with Sergeant Beynon of team Clarence. The B-2 had taken a beating but still worked perfectly; all Jedburgh sets that had been issued to the sub-missions, including Beynon's, had been lost on landing. Beynon continued to use the B-2 transmitter with a Jedburgh receiver. Since the B-2 transmitter, unlike the Jedburgh set, operated off the main power source in any building, this eliminated the need for the hand-cranked generator that was required when transmitting with the Jed set. Captain Bestebreurtje, with his arm in a sling because of his wounds, was unable to crank the generator, and Beynon did not trust his equipment to the resistance men.[12]

Operation Market-Garden had been a costly failure. Losses among the British airborne force, from D-Day on September 17 through the 1st Airborne Division's withdrawal to the south bank of the Neder Rijn on September 25, were 7,212 men killed, wounded, or missing. American casualties, though much lower than the British, were still high, with the 82nd Airborne Division losing 1,432 men (killed, wounded, or missing) and the 101st Airborne Division 2,110. Another 378 men of the Polish 1st Independent Parachute Brigade were lost. When transport aircraft, glider pilot, and XXX British Corps casualties are added, the total number of casualties for the operation comes to nearly 12,000 men. Of these, just under 1,000 were killed, nearly 3,000 wounded, and more than 8,000 missing, most of those having been captured. Matériel losses included 144 transport aircraft and 70 tanks.[13]

Although the Allied divisions participating in Market-Garden fought gallantly and accomplished much—gaining bridgeheads over five significant water obstacles to drive more than sixty miles into enemy territory—the final and most important objective of the operation, gaining a foothold across the Rhine and thus positioning Twenty-first Army Group to encircle the Ruhr industrial area from the north, was not realized. For that reason alone, the operation was considered a failure. Neither did the battle result in the anticipated isolation of the enemy's Fifteenth Army or the collapse of the overall German defense in the west, as some had dared to hope.

Lack of enough aircraft to carry all three airborne divisions on the initial drop resulted in a plan to deliver these forces over a three-day period, something that could happen only if the weather cooperated, which it did not. This meant that only a fraction of each division was available to seize initial objectives. Moreover, not even all of those forces dropped in the first lift were available for such operations, because as much as half of them were required to secure the drop zones and landing zones needed by the follow-on lifts.

Market-Garden was an ambitious plan, but it came at a time when just such a bold and imaginative plan was needed. In a 1966 interview with biographer Merle Miller, Eisenhower said, "I not only approved Market-Garden, I insisted upon it. What we needed was a bridgehead over the Rhine. If that could be accomplished I was quite willing to sit on all other operations."[14] But the retired five-star general and former president also pointed out the weakness of Montgomery's single-thrust argument. "What this action proved," Eisenhower said, "was that the idea of 'one full-blooded thrust' to Berlin was silly."[15]

Unfortunately, the plan was based on faulty intelligence or, perhaps more accurately, on the faulty use of the intelligence available. There is no doubt that Montgomery's and Browning's misjudgment of the combat effectiveness of II SS Panzer Corps and other very capable enemy forces in the vicinity of Arnhem, or failure to even take seriously reports of their presence from the Dutch underground, doomed the mission from the start. Underestimating some very capable German commanders and forcing the British airborne division to drop so far from the

Arnhem bridge, again because of faulty intelligence and poor terrain analysis, only made success more improbable. The fact that the twenty thousand vehicles of British XXX Corps were confined largely to one two-lane road, so narrow and elevated in places that it resembled a causeway, was another major shortcoming. The Market-Garden plan contained many moving parts, necessarily requiring the successful accomplishment of each part in succession. If any one part failed, the entire operation was bound to fail.

Then there was the overemphasis on the part of the air force to avoid losses of aircraft and crews by keeping away from areas known to be heavily defended by antiaircraft artillery. This resulted in airborne units being dropped much too far from their objectives and prohibited the dropping of paratroopers at both ends of important bridge objectives such as Nijmegen and Arnhem. Disapproving General Gavin's request, for example, to drop troops near the northern end of the Nijmegen bridge necessitated the heroic but costly river crossing in flimsy canvas rowboats by elements of the 82nd Airborne Division's 504th Parachute Infantry Regiment.

In his 1958 memoirs, Montgomery accepted blame for the 1st Airborne Division being dropped so far from the bridge, writing that he should have ordered at least one parachute brigade to be dropped in the immediate vicinity of the bridge. He also wrote that his command was fully aware of the presence of the II SS Panzer Corps in the Arnhem area, but that "we were wrong in supposing that it could not fight effectively; its battle state was far beyond our expectation."[16] Concluding his brief account of the battle, Montgomery wrote: "I remain Market-Garden's unrepentant advocate."[17]

Montgomery's headquarters, as well as SHAEF, was indeed aware of the presence of the 9th and 10th SS Panzer Divisions in the Arnhem vicinity, but according to retired Major General John Frost in his 1980 memoir, they did not share that information with XXX Corps and the 1st Airborne Division.[18]

SEVENTEEN

PRISONER OF WAR

Lieutenant Allan Todd, having remained hidden in the burned-out machine shop, living off pears and half a canteen of water, was unaware that the withdrawal of the 1st Airborne Division from Arnhem was under way. He could hear Germans going through buildings down the street, apparently conducting a house-to-house search, and he knew he had to get farther away. That night, he began moving from one burned-out structure to the next. Many of the buildings were still smoldering, and when he thought some Germans had heard him, he hid in the corner of one building, standing for nearly an hour on hot ashes, burning one boot so badly that blisters formed on the foot. Still, he managed to evade his pursuers for another day.

It had been exactly one week since Todd and the 2nd Battalion survivors had been forced to abandon the building near the bridge where they had fought so hard. At around noon on Wednesday, September 27, he heard German soldiers approaching the building he had taken refuge in. He quickly hid behind a sheet of tin leaning against one wall. The Germans entered the building and began searching it. Whether they were searching every building in the area for survivors of the battle or simply on a looting spree, the soldiers kept poking around until one of them looked behind the tin. The Germans were startled at the sight of

Todd, and one of them pulled out a pistol and directed the American outside, where they marched him off down the street.

They halted in front of the headquarters building Todd had seen a few days earlier. He was ushered inside, and soon an officer appeared and interrogated him briefly, asking routine questions such as "Are there any more men in this vicinity?" and "Where have you been hiding since September 20?"[1] A German soldier searched him but found nothing. Fortunately, he had already buried his code pads and the cash he had carried into Holland for the Dutch resistance. But he still had a thirty-two-caliber pistol rolled in a handkerchief in his hip pocket; the German searching him missed it.

Next came an interview with the major who was the military commandant of Arnhem and commander of a panzer unit. When the major learned that Todd was an officer, he released the guards and Todd found himself alone with the German, who treated him well. The major poured Todd a drink. Then he asked the American when he had last eaten. Todd replied that he hadn't had a meal in ten days, so the major ordered dinner for him.

The German officer then directed his orderly to show Todd upstairs to the major's quarters, where he was left alone to shave and clean up, using the German's razor, soap, and brush. Standing by himself in the bathroom, Todd thought of the gun in his pocket and decided that it was now a liability. It probably wasn't going to do him any good and would certainly cause him much trouble if the Germans found it on him. He pulled the gun from his pocket and buried it in the wastebasket.

When Todd returned downstairs, his dinner was ready. He sat down and ate, and when he had finished, much to his surprise, the Germans gave him a Nestlé chocolate bar and a package of Camel cigarettes. Then, over a bottle of wine, the German officer began discussing the Battle of Arnhem, showing Todd a map indicating where landings had taken place and filling him in on what had happened at each location. The major accurately recited how the 82nd Airborne Division had jumped at Nijmegen, the 101st near Eindhoven. He told Todd that the British armored column had been stopped at the Waal River, well south of Arnhem.

As the two men sipped their wine, the discussion changed course. The major asked Todd where home was, and Todd said that he was from Illinois. Surprisingly, the German said he had attended the University of Wisconsin at Madison before the war, returning to Germany in 1939. In fact, he said, his brother was still in Chicago. The two men chatted a while longer about the States. Then the German asked Todd why America had gone to war against Germany, but Todd refused to respond. The major did not appear upset by his prisoner's reticence; Todd got the impression that the German simply wanted the company of another officer. He even shared with Todd his belief that Germany had no chance of winning the war. At around five, the major ordered another small meal of eggs and toast.

After the two men had eaten and had some coffee, the German informed Todd that he would be picked up at about six o'clock and taken to a transit camp.

A motorcycle arrived, and Lieutenant Todd was put into a sidecar. He was taken to a house on the outskirts of the city, where he joined a group of about twenty enlisted British prisoners who had been captured about a week earlier. The British officers had already been sent on to a regular prisoner of war camp. Todd learned that the Germans had been using the British men to collect and bury the dead.

Todd was searched again. This time a German soldier took his cigarette lighter, a pen and pencil, and his personal watch, but he was allowed to keep an army watch. Then a German doctor washed out his eyes and dressed his wounds. Todd and the others slept on the floor that night, knowing they would be shipped out to Germany in the morning.[2]

That same afternoon, the Jeds of team Dudley received a grim reminder of the dangers inherent in clandestine warfare. Johannes's torn and battered body was found by the side of a road near the farm where the Jeds were staying. A sign on his chest proclaiming "This was a Terrorist" served as a warning to members of the Dutch resistance and to those, such as the Jeds, who helped them.[3]

On Thursday, September 28, Captain Arie Bestebreurtje requested that he and Sergeant Bud Beynon be allowed to return to London to be refitted for another mission. The Dutch captain had by then developed a reputation in the 82nd for his coolness under fire, and General Gavin approved the request, adding that he hoped they would return to continue their work. What remained of Jedburgh team Clarence returned to England on the first day of October.

———

At around ten o'clock Thursday morning, a truck picked up Lieutenant Todd and the other prisoners and carried them to a warehouse next to a railroad siding in the quaint old walled town of Zutphen, eighteen miles northeast of Arnhem on the banks of the IJssel. Todd soon realized that his treatment as a prisoner of war was taking a turn for the worse. It was cold and damp in the warehouse, yet the prisoners were given neither blankets nor food, and the wounded were provided no medical care.

American bombers had struck the rail yard two days before their arrival, and the warehouse had been damaged in the attack. One prisoner had been wounded and still had a bullet lodged in his back. Todd asked the Germans for medical care for the man and blankets to keep him warm. The Germans told him no help was available, nor was there any food. Some loose straw was scattered over the damp concrete floor for the men to lie on. It proved to be a long, cold, miserable night without much sleep. They were to remain in the warehouse until October 2, living on a small portion of sugar beet soup and a slice of bread each day.

It might have comforted Todd somewhat to know that Jedburgh team Dudley was not too many miles away.

EIGHTEEN

TODD'S JOURNEY BEGINS

Jedburgh team Dudley and the Dutch underground leaders working with them gathered representatives from all three major resistance groups—the KP, the RVV, and Orde Dienst—for a conference on Sunday, October 1. The site of the meeting was a farm about six miles from the one where the Jeds were staying. At the gathering, Major Olmsted met a man named Gerard who would be joining the Jeds at their headquarters. Gerard was the leader of the KP in Zwolle and the Northeast Polder, an area of farmland reclaimed from the Zuiderzee in 1932.

Delegates at the conference agreed to the selection of an elderly Dutch officer named Colonel Houtz to be the senior military leader for the underground in the local area. Houtz, who had returned to Holland to retire after serving in the Dutch East India Army, had joined the underground when the Germans interned all Dutch officers after invading the country in 1940. Regardless of his age, he was eager to become more involved, and the Jeds saw the status that came with Houtz's rank as a recently retired regular officer as a major asset. The colonel was pleased with the appointment and seemed confident in the abilities of Henk Brinkgreve, Pappy Olmsted, Cor Hilbrink, Daan, and Gerard.[1]

When the conference concluded, the two Jedburgh officers, along with Cor and Gerard, rode their bicycles through intermittent rain showers back to their farm headquarters. The Dutch weather in these first days of October was uncomfortably cold, and with the rain adding to the misery of sentry duty, German roadblocks were not well manned. The small group made it back to the farm without being stopped.

Back in the farmhouse that night, the Jeds joined their host family in the living room for an evening of fun. The men challenged one another in Indian wrestling or in contests to see who could do the most push-ups. One of the children threw an apple core at one of the men, and soon everyone, including the old grandparents, were chucking apple cores around. Then the grandmother put a stop to the nonsense and supervised a general cleaning of the room.

Most evenings at the farm were much quieter, with the Dutch family retiring early and the Jeds spending their time working or reading if they were not out on operations or receiving airdrops. Major Olmsted enjoyed reading selections of poetry and prose from a book titled *The Knapsack* that had been given to him by a friend back in England. The little volume was a collection of short stories and poems that included selections from Homer, Shakespeare, Donne, Milton, Yeats, and Eliot. The book became one of Olmsted's closest friends during his time in Holland, and he would be reading it through for the second time before he left the country. He had also brought a small New Testament with him, and he and Sergeant Austin both enjoyed reading from it.[2]

On the second of October, Allan Todd and the British prisoners were again transferred by truck, this time farther north to a small, temporary prisoner of war camp run by the Luftwaffe in the manufacturing town of Deventer, on the meandering IJssel River. This camp was a welcome change, with the men being fed a good thick soup and bread and later a Dutch stew. More food came when the men had a supper of meat with bread, jam, butter, and ersatz coffee. The prisoners stuffed themselves. Those who needed it received medical care, and when it came time to turn in, each man had a bunk with a straw mattress and a blanket.

The good treatment continued the next morning with a hearty breakfast. Surprisingly, the Germans did not interrogate the prisoners. Lieutenant Todd and the others were simply photographed and asked to provide their names, ranks, and serial numbers. That afternoon, the guards allowed the men thirty minutes outside for exercise. Todd then spent a couple of days in a Luftwaffe hospital before rejoining the group for another transfer. On October 5, the guards put the men on a train bound for a prisoner of war interrogation center at Oberursel, a small German town near Frankfurt am Main.

Todd was apprehensive about being moved to a camp in Germany, where he was sure he would be interrogated by experts. He knew that it was no more than about forty miles to Allied lines. If he could escape, he might be able to make it safely back to friendly territory. As the train rolled along that evening under a full moon, he was able to find an opening, and he leaped from the train.

Todd hit the ground and rolled. When he came to a stop, he looked up to see that he was surrounded by German soldiers. He realized at once that the game was up. Using what little German he spoke, Todd explained that he was a prisoner of war and was attempting to escape. The Germans, a crew from an antiaircraft artillery battery, laughed at his misfortune. One of the soldiers, a man who had lived in the States and spoke English well, explained that if Todd had jumped a hundred yards in either direction, he might well have escaped.

The Germans seemed friendly and shared some of their food with Todd as they questioned him about how things were back at his home and how the war was going. He learned that most of the men were farmers who served on duty with the battery a few hours each day. They were aware that Germany was losing the war and wondered how much longer the war could last. In the morning, the Germans put Todd in a truck and drove him through a long valley to a small railway station, where he was put back on the same train he had jumped from. The guards on the train seemed glad to see the American; they would not have to report that a prisoner of war had escaped from them.[3]

Back in Nijmegen, Captain Bestebreurtje and Sergeant Beynon of team Clarence returned on October 3 after a brief two-day stay in London. With them was Captain Peter Vickery of the British Army, joining the team as a replacement for the wounded Lieutenant Verhaeghe. Team Clarence had been given a new mission and a new name. They were now called team Stanley,* and their mission was to train Dutch

---

* Records often refer to the follow-on mission of Jedburgh team Clarence as team Stanley II because another Jedburgh team code-named Stanley had already deployed to France.

resistance volunteers in liberated areas to serve as infantrymen under Allied commanders and to continue to smuggle arms to resistance elements behind German lines. The team would answer directly to Prince Bernhard.[4]

Bestebreurtje worked with the largest group of volunteers and placed Captain Vickery in charge of the resistance in an area west of Nijmegen, between the Maas and the Waal. Arms arrived from Prince Bernhard's headquarters, and Vickery armed 150 men of the Orde Dienst. During the first three or four weeks that Vickery was in Holland, the Germans conducted several night raids into his area, apparently for no other purpose than to burn and loot. The first such raid had come at Leeuwen, where the Germans burned forty-two houses. Several towns were heavily shelled and mortared, leaving many casualties, with the town of Wamel being very badly damaged. Vickery was wounded slightly by mortar shrapnel during an October 19 attack, but he remained on the job. The Dutch had already begun to form uniformed army units, known as *Stoottroepen,* from volunteers among members of the resistance in areas of the country already liberated. Near the end of October, Company No. 1 of the Regiment Stoottroepen Prins Bernhard arrived to stiffen the resistance, taking over Leeuwen and Wamel. The Orde Dienst maintained responsibility for other towns in the area.

Captain Vickery also placed agents across the Waal River, infiltrating them by canoe. Soon he began arming men on the opposite bank, sending about thirty Sten submachine guns and ammunition across for them. He maintained telephone contact with three Dutch intelligence men in Tiel, a large town just across the Waal from Wamel. These sources passed information to Vickery about German troop movements, headquarters locations, and artillery positions. The British officer then relayed the information by runner back to British artillery batteries. On one occasion, the British were able to shell a railway bridge northwest of Tiel, rendering it unusable by the Germans for two weeks.[5]

The British 8th Armored Brigade arrived in the area and took over a defensive sector with a twenty-five-mile front. The brigade commander, Brigadier Prior-Palmer, requested as many of the newly trained Dutchmen as the Jeds could get, telling Captain Vickery to use them to establish strongpoints along a four-mile stretch of the dike from Dreumel to Leeuwen. Vickery used a group of 140 men of the Orde Dienst, under Dr. van Hocher, and 165 men of the Regiment Stoottroepen Prins Bernhard, placing six to eight men at each strongpoint. Most of the men were armed with Sten submachine guns or rifles, but Vickery tried to put a Bren light machine gun at each position.

Prior-Palmer knew Vickery, who had served under him at Sandhurst, and he took a keen interest in the Dutch volunteers and made a point of inspecting the men and their fighting positions. While the Regiment Stoottroepen came better equipped and uniformed, the Orde Dienst men wore civilian clothing. Prior-Palmer saw to it that the resistance fighters were equipped with maps and map boards, binoculars, and mortars. The British Army provided rations for Vickery's men, and local civilians were able to augment this with some vegetables. Meat became available only when shellfire killed a cow or a pig.

Vickery initiated a training program to further improve their defensive capability, conducting a two-day course in mortar gunnery for two dozen men, installing telephone communications between posts, and implementing a plan for the use of Very signal pistols. He taught men how to prepare shell reports and how to draw up range cards so that they could cover their assigned areas to the front at night. British forces provided fire support, and an army medical officer looked after the wounded Dutchmen. Vickery also trained some of the Dutch in first aid and set up an aid station in a wing of the local hospital.

German patrols probed their defensive line nearly every night, and brief skirmishes resulted in a few casualties on both sides.

Bud Beynon returned to London on November 3. At the end of November, Brigadier Prior-Palmer's brigade was relieved by the Canadian 7th Armored Brigade, whose commander, Brigadier Bingham, inspected Captain Vickery's Dutchmen and was impressed with their readiness and efficiency. Vickery remained with these men until he was recalled to England on January 25, 1945.

NINETEEN

DULAG LUFT

Majors Brinkgreve and Olmsted and Sergeant Austin had become well-known in the area surrounding the farm that served as headquarters for Jedburgh team Dudley and the resistance leaders working with them. Many people had come to know them and had learned where they were staying. Couriers and others arrived for one reason or another every day. To make matters worse, the Germans had begun to use the surrounding area to train units preparing for combat. Battalions of enemy paratroopers and SS troops were settling in the area for training, and their maneuvers filled the days and nights, making the work of the Jeds and the resistance much more difficult. Often the unexpected arrival of German troops forced the men to cancel airdrop operations.

By October 5, the Jeds decided that for the sake of security, the time had come to move, to find another safe location for their command post. They opted to relocate to a spot some ten to twenty miles farther to the north, on the Dutch-German border, where they would be nearer some of the fields they used as drop areas. Because of the distance involved and the fact that the move would be made on bicycles with bad tires, they planned to divide the trip into two segments. They set out at dusk on the first leg, allowing a ride of two to three hours to be completed prior to the eight o'clock curfew. Everything went smoothly, and they reached the farm that was to be their layover site without incident. They were resting—chatting and listening to the radio—when a breathless courier arrived with news of trouble ahead at their destination. Several resistance men had been killed in an attack on one of the new drop zones, and a stock of supplies on the field had been seized.

But it hadn't been the Germans who had attacked the field. It was a group of Dutch collaborators known as the Landwacht. They were part of the pro-German NSB, or National Socialist Movement, a Fascist organization of black-shirted Dutch Nazis, thugs led by the vain Anton Mussert. These traitors were ruthless in their actions against loyal Dutchmen of the resistance. Now the Jeds and their small headquarters group were stuck; they couldn't continue on to the field, which was surely being watched, and they chose not to return to the old farm for fear that they had been compromised in that area. Their only option was to lie low for a few days right where they were.[1]

On October 6, the train carrying Lieutenant Allan Todd and other Allied prisoners of war pulled to a stop in front of a two-story, half-timbered building. They were at the train station in the large town of Oberursel, eight miles northwest of Frankfurt. From the station, the men were taken to a prisoner of war compound located on a level stretch of ground not far from town.

Two twelve-foot-high fences surrounded the five-hundred-acre camp, and barbed-wire entanglement and a trench occupied the ten-foot space between the fences. Trained dogs patrolled the perimeter, and machine-gun emplacements were scattered throughout the area beyond the fence. To prevent Allied bombing of the camp, the letters "POW" were spelled out with large white stones on a grassy area. The same letters were painted in white on the roofs of most of the camp's buildings.

To the Germans, the camp was known as Auswertestelle West (Western Evaluation Center). It was a *Durchgangslager,* or transient prisoner of war camp, run by the Luftwaffe, Germany's air force. This was the gateway to the German prisoner of war camp system, a place where Allied prisoners underwent their initial interrogation before being assigned to a permanent camp. It was more commonly known by its abbreviated name, Dulag Luft. From here, officers would be shipped off to an *Offizierlager,* or Oflag; enlisted men to a *Stammlager,* or Stalag.

Upon arrival, each new prisoner was photographed and finger-printed. He was asked to give his name, rank, and serial number. Then he was given a Red Cross form to fill out, providing his home address so that the Red Cross could notify his family of his status. Todd gave his parents' address so that they and Mandy could learn of his situation.[2]

One of Dulag Luft's principal functions was that of an interrogation center, where the Germans would extract as much information as they could from each prisoner before sending him on to a permanent camp. Interrogators took full advantage of the depression, the anxiety, the vulnerability experienced by prisoners in the early days of captivity. They used every trick to pry out of the captives time-sensitive information about their unit, its current strength and location, the morale of the men, or the names of commanders and other key officers. Under the terms of the Geneva Conventions, prisoners were required to give only their name, rank, and service number. But trained interrogators used many techniques, from psychological interviewing techniques to threats of physical violence, to extract more information. Physical searches of the prisoners might uncover valuable documents or even something as simple as a matchbook or theater stub that could reveal where the man had been based and thereby suggesting what unit he was assigned to.

One method used by the Germans at Dulag Luft was to modify the standard Red Cross form that every prisoner filled out during processing. After filling in the required data—name, rank, and service number—the form went on to ask a series of questions about the prisoner's unit. Most Allied prisoners were wise to the ploy, but a few did fill in more information than was necessary. Another favorite tactic was to accuse a prisoner of being a spy rather than a serviceman. The interrogator made sure that the prisoner knew what happened to spies and implied that the man would be turned over to the Gestapo. Some prisoners argued heatedly to establish their true status as uniformed combatants and, in the process, provided the interrogators with information about their units.

The Dulag Luft staff were skilled at identifying prisoners who were likely to be good subjects for interrogation. Men who showed signs of nervousness or who appeared frightened during initial questioning, for example, were handled roughly and subjected to increasingly stressful interrogation sessions. Threats of torture were made. The Germans also quickly learned which prisoners would answer questions in exchange for cigarettes or food. Every aspect of the confinement at Dulag Luft and the methods used by the staff of interrogators had one goal—to break down a prisoner's power to resist. No mail was allowed. No Red Cross food or clothing packages. No work or recreation of any kind. It was a place where harsh treatment was used deliberately to lower morale. And because men were more likely to talk if subjected to the loneliness of solitary confinement, all prisoners at the Dulag Luft interrogation center were confined separately to instill or reinforce a sense of isolation and helplessness.

The Dulag Luft camp had grown in staff and prisoner population over the past two years, and by 1944 it had a staff of three hundred and employed at least sixty interrogators. These men—all officers or enlisted men of the Luftwaffe—were well educated, spoke English fluently, and were trained in the art of extracting information from their subjects. They were adept at engaging prisoners in idle conversation, often getting the men to reveal scraps of information through offhand remarks that might seem unimportant. But when many such scraps of seemingly trivial information were combined, much could be learned. Interrogators usually specialized in a particular Allied unit. Most of the prisoners passing through the camp were Allied airmen, and an interrogator might focus his efforts on Eighth U.S. Air Force bomber crewmen or on fighter pilots of the British RAF.

Twenty-nine thousand Allied prisoners would pass through the camp at Oberursel in 1944 alone. Every one of them spent, on average, one to two weeks locked alone in a cell with no one to talk to and nothing to read. The cell block was a long, one-story building with four wings branching off one side. Prisoners referred to the building as "the cooler." Individual prisoner cells—some two hundred in all—lay along both sides of a central corridor. Each room measured ten to twelve feet by five feet, had a window, and was furnished with a cot, a small table, and a chair. A prisoner's daily food ration consisted of four slices of black bread with jam (two slices in the morning and two at night) and at midday a bowl of watery soup made from sugar beets.

Todd's first interrogation session at the new camp came on the second day. He was taken to the camp's white cinder-block administration building and led down a long corridor to room 47, an interrogation room.

Many of the questions were routine, but the German officer elicited little response from Todd. Whereas prisoners who appeared likely to talk were treated roughly, the Germans showed more respect to men who

were resolute in their refusal to answer questions. The strong, uncoop-
erative prisoners were treated with much more care, although they were
often confined to long stretches in even more isolated solitary confinement cells.

When Lieutenant Todd refused to answer a question regarding his
duties with the British, the German let it go for a while. He switched
topics and began scolding Todd on U.S. politics and foreign policy, expressing the view that America should not be fighting Germany. Rather,
the United States should be allying with Germany in the fight against
the Russians. When Todd showed no interest in discussing such nonsense, the interrogator returned to the question of what Todd was doing
with the British airborne division. Again, Todd refused to answer, and
the German ordered that he be placed in solitary confinement for a
week.

For the next seven days, Allan Todd lived in a dark, damp basement
cell below the main cell block, kept alive on a daily ration of two thin
slices of bread and a bowl of turnip soup with the vegetables strained
off. He slept on the only furnishing, a wooden shelf made for the purpose, and he wondered how he was able to avoid catching pneumonia.
The small cell and everything in it was alive with lice.[3]

———————

Henk Brinkgreve and Pappy Olmsted and their small group had chosen
to remain for a few days at the midpoint of their journey northward, but
their extended stay was more than their hosts had bargained for. The
family who lived at the farm where they were staying had expected the
resistance men to stay one night, at most, before continuing their move.
Now it became clear that the men's presence made the family very nervous. Unlike those who had hosted the Jeds until now, these people
were filled with fear that the Germans would find the men and their
beautiful farm would be destroyed. Olmsted sensed that if the family
knew he was American and Bunny Austin British, they would have
turned them in. Perhaps the only thing that prevented the family from
reporting the group to the Germans was the fear that the underground
would retaliate against them.

There was reason for the family's concerns: The Germans had expanded and stepped up the frequency of searches in the area, intent on
locating resistance fighters and those who supported them. To allay

some of the family's fear, and to somewhat decrease the risk to their own small group, Olmsted and Austin snuck their radio out to a nearby wooded area. Before long, though, the Jeds and their resistance staff decided that they could no longer afford to isolate themselves at this site. Resistance leaders throughout the area had lost contact with them. The men decided that it was necessary, after all, to return to the farm where they had originally established a command post.

For the journey back to the old farm, the group had one less serviceable bicycle than they had riders. Pappy Olmsted was forced to ride on the back of Cor Hilbrink's bike, and the experience was enough to make Olmsted and Austin insist that in the future no moves be made unless each person had a good bicycle of his own.

When the little group arrived back at the farm they had hated to leave, the family greeted them as long-lost relatives, treating them as though they had been gone and dearly missed for years. Olmsted and the others were touched by the honest expression of care and concern and camaraderie by these simple country people. This family's outlook on the war, on the German occupiers, and on the bold and risky efforts of the underground were in stark contrast with that of the family whose farm the group had just left. These people were by no means naïve; they were fully aware of the risks they were taking and of the terrible price to be paid if the Gestapo learned of their support to the resistance. All male members of the family would be shot, probably after being tortured for information. Women and children would be shipped out to concentration camps, and the farm buildings would be burned to the ground. It was the unwavering patriotism and selfless support of citizens such as these that kept the resistance alive. Olmsted couldn't help but wonder how many of his own people would risk so much under similar conditions.[4]

Operating from this solid base, the Jeds and their underground network began to function smoothly and effectively again. A well-established network of agents and informers provided a steady stream of target sightings, which the Jeds reported to London and which Special Force Headquarters passed on to the air force, who attacked and destroyed them. On one occasion, they were even able to report the location of General Christiansen's headquarters. Unfortunately, the commander of all German rear-area forces in the Netherlands was not present at the time.

Sergeant Austin learned of another underground support network when he befriended an English-speaking Catholic priest who had been aiding downed Allied airmen. Many clergymen, the Jeds learned, had been supporting the Allied effort and the resistance by hiding British and American fliers, members of the underground, and striking railway workers. Some had even smuggled arms and other clandestine warfare matériel to those who needed them by carrying the contraband under their robes. Then the bishop of Utrecht issued an edict forbidding such activities for fear that, if discovered, the Germans would take over all church properties, including monasteries and hospitals.[5]

Life in occupied Holland was hard, and only farm families had enough to eat. Particularly hard hit were the railway workers, who had been on strike since the first day of September. Jedburgh team Dudley helped as best they could, requesting 150,000 guilders from London to be distributed to the railwaymen's families. A family of four, the workers calculated, could live on one hundred guilders, about thirty-eight dollars, a month.

As comfortable as the Jeds had grown living and working at this farm, they knew that their safety and security were at risk by remaining at one location for very long. The best way to avoid being discovered by the Gestapo was to keep constantly on the move. By the middle of October, the men had decided to pack up once again and move on; this time they would travel westward.

Major Olmsted and Sergeant Austin spent a sunny October morning preparing for the journey. They thoroughly examined the bicycles, which appeared to be in generally good condition, needing only some minor tire repair. As the men worked, Olmsted was aware of onlooking chickens and cows and pigs, and he thought of how their habits and noises were the same the world over, and they reminded him of home.[6]

The two men then went to a small wooded patch near a main road. Sitting still and silent among the pines, they counted German trucks and other vehicles for a couple of hours, getting a sense of the pattern of traffic in the area. Only the occasional P-47 or Spitfire passing overhead disturbed the bright blue calm, bringing the war back. Not far away, many men were killing and being killed.

On their ride back to the farm, the men enjoyed the journey through the woods, the trees awash in autumn colors. Olmsted felt as though he were a child on a beautiful afternoon stroll through the forest.[7] At one

point, the men neared a recently emplaced Luftwaffe outpost, and although they often enjoyed seeing how many Germans would let them
pass with little regard, on this occasion they took a detour, bypassing the
enemy station. They arrived at their destination just as the sun settled in
deep vermilion behind a long row of poplars lining a dike. Dark clouds
crept across the coral twilight sky, and in less than half an hour a heavy
rain began.[8]

TWENTY

THE INSUFFERABLE LORD HAW HAW

Team Dudley's command group set out on bicycles on their journey westward, carrying with them their personal weapons, radios, maps, and intelligence data. The men reached Zenderen, a small town on the highway running north from Hengelo to Almelo, at dusk, which made it easier for the group to pass through the town and cross the highway. After passing through town, the men cycled on into the night along narrow, winding sand paths. They used the lights on their bikes until curfew, after which they continued in total darkness, each rider following the cyclist in front of him by sound and by the occasional glimpse of the white tip of the bicycle's fender.

After hours of cycling, the men reached their destination, an attractive farm not far off the highway. A boy escorted the men to the barn, where they hid the bicycles and equipment and prepared their sleeping area. Then they entered the farmhouse. It was a typical Dutch country home, with a spotlessly clean tile fireplace, walls adorned with pictures, and racks filled with lovely hand-painted blue-and-white Delft dishes. Inside the house, the men set up their little radio receiver to pick up the BBC, both for the family's enjoyment and to hear the coded messages that the station included in their broadcasts at the behest of the government. These "personal messages" were directed to clandestine teams and agents operating in the field throughout occupied Europe. Jedburgh team Dudley needed to listen for any messages addressed to them that might inform them of scheduled supply and arms drops to be made on their designated fields. Later, the group retired to the barn. German military traffic on the highway nearby was fairly heavy throughout the night, but none of the vehicles stopped at the farm, and the Jeds and resistance men slept well.

The farm where the Jeds now ran their command post proved ideal in many respects, although it lay only about half a mile outside Enter, the village where the team had earlier shot their way through a roadblock. Life at the farm appeared normal, and German occupation authorities had so far seen nothing to make them suspect underground activities there. The farmer and his family always appeared to live within the restrictions of occupation regulations, and they responded punctually to every request by the Germans for milk or eggs. The place was appealing from a security standpoint as well, secluded by patches of woods and bordered along each side by large canals.

One night shortly after their arrival, the farmer's wife fed the men a supper of black bread and jam, boiled potatoes, and hot milk. Henk, Cor, Gerard, and Daan had arrived, and though darkness had fallen, the men gathered in a room where they could work by the light of a carbide lamp. Shutters on all the windows were closed in accordance with blackout regulations. While Major Olmsted worked on his records of German troop movements and supply dump locations, Sergeant Austin tinkered with his radio transmitter.

Soon the men were startled by the sound of bicycles approaching on the rough lane leading to the farmhouse. It was around eight-thirty. Hurriedly dousing the light, the men grabbed weapons and grenades and waited for some indication of who the visitors were. The men remained as still as possible, listening as the bicycles pulled up in front of the house and stopped. Then came a knock at the door. They heard the woman of the house open the door and ask a few questions, then the new arrivals were allowed to enter. Olmsted and Austin were introduced to the two girls who would be working as couriers at the new headquarters.

The Jeds had heard of the girls from the resistance men earlier and had been told that the couriers would be joining them at the farm. When they hadn't found the girls at the farm upon their arrival, the men assumed that they had been delayed by the heavy rain shower, and they didn't expect them until morning.

Ank, a sturdy blonde, headed a group of several girls working as couriers in the area, planning their routes and arranging for accommodations. She was devoted to her work in the resistance and was absolutely fearless in carrying it out. The second girl, Riek, had darker hair and a slighter build but was no less capable or dedicated. And her skill as a typist was to prove invaluable to the Jeds and the resistance leaders in the administrative chores that are an unavoidable part of running a guerrilla command post. Unfortunately, the girls, soaked to the skin, had arrived at the chilly house unexpectedly after supper, and there was little food left for them.

Work picked up as the headquarters staff continued to grow. Another girl arrived the morning after the Jeds' arrival at the farm. Marie, the sister of a local resistance leader, would serve as cook, preparing food that arrived daily, along with extra ration coupons, all arranged by her brother. Families throughout the area donated food items to the men of the underground, even though most of them had no idea where the resistance elements were located. She prepared the meals on a laundry stove in an old shed, but she was an excellent cook and the food was always well prepared. Soon Marie was feeding a full-time staff of twelve,* and the grateful men and women of the headquarters ate well.

The men spent many hours at the tedious work of locating fields or other open areas in the countryside for receiving parachute drops of arms and ammunition, explosives, and other supplies from England. Referred to as "dropping grounds" or "drop zones," such areas had to meet certain specifications to qualify. Team Dudley had already been receiving drops at several fields, and the parachutes delivered more than just arms and other equipment. A recent special drop brought the Jeds a bundle of cash, one hundred thousand guilders to be used to pay striking railroad workers.

But before identified dropping grounds could be reported to London for use in a parachute drop, property owners, usually farmers, had to be sold on the idea, convinced that it was the proper thing to do for Holland. That job went to a young man named Coos. As a result, he was often absent from the headquarters, scouring the countryside on his bicycle, continually searching for suitable drop locations.

Major Olmsted's job of collecting and documenting information from various intelligence sources became increasingly demanding.

---

* Brinkgreve, Olmsted, Austin, Cor, Daan, Gerard, Toon, Klaas, Coos, Marie, Ank, and Riek.

Much information surfaced during the many meetings arranged by Major Brinkgreve, Cor, Gerard, and Daan. More and more reports flowed in, enough to fill ten to fifteen typewritten pages each day.[1] Particularly important and time-sensitive information had to be radioed to London, and Sergeant Austin's work picked up as well.

Relations with the Dutch underground continued to grow stronger, and the Jeds were pleased to see the various factions cooperating so well. Colonel Houtz, who commanded the resistance of the Overijssel and the Northeast Polder, visited the new headquarters often and seemed pleased with the work of the Jeds. He never shied from taking necessary risks and always carried maps with him, carefully hidden inside his heavy underwear and stockings.

One man, though, continued to be a nuisance. He led a group of fewer than five hundred resistance fighters but claimed to be in command of the entire Overijssel, and he was a constant bother to Henk Brinkgreve.

The girls spoke English very well, and Bunny Austin enjoyed talking with them in his off-hours.[2] Austin spent many days by himself, as the officers were busy with their work. For hours on end, he would listen to broadcasts by the BBC and the American Forces Network on his receiving set. From time to time, he inadvertently picked up Radio Hamburg or other German stations, which at least offered excellent music, appealing especially to Wagner enthusiasts.

For amusement, Austin tuned in to German propaganda broadcasts. He particularly enjoyed listening to the character known as Lord Haw Haw, which was the nickname of a British expatriate who had become Nazi Germany's most well-known propaganda broadcaster. In reality, Lord Haw Haw was a thirty-eight-year-old Fascist politician by the name of William Joyce, a man who seemed to have been out of place his entire life. Born in America, he was raised in Ireland, where as a teenager he helped British forces by informing on IRA rebels, even though he was Catholic. Later, in England, he became a prominent member of the British Union of Fascists and fled the country in 1939 to avoid arrest. He became a citizen of his new home, Nazi Germany, the following year.*

---

* William Joyce, or Lord Haw Haw, made his final broadcast for the Germans on April 30, 1945, a day before British forces seized Radio Hamburg's studios. After his capture and arrest by British forces at Flensburg, near the Danish border, Joyce was returned to England, where he was tried for treason, convicted, and hanged at Wandsworth Prison on January 3, 1946.

Joyce's radio program, *Germany Calling,* reached British audiences from the Radio Hamburg station. Its purpose was to undermine the morale of Allied troops in the British Isles, as well as the civilian population. In a taunting and sarcastic voice, Lord Haw Haw ridiculed Allied leaders, mocked Allied military forces, and urged his listeners to accept defeat and make peace with Germany. But his broadcasts had an unintended effect on Allied listeners, who were amused by his menacing tone and entertained by his sometimes informative accounts of the war's progress.

Bunny Austin, like thousands of others, listened intently when Lord Haw Haw opened his program by announcing, in his odd nasal drawl, "Jairmany calling, Jairmany calling . . ."[3] What followed often indicated how the war was going for Germany. If Allied forces were successful, he complained bitterly of their underhanded tactics. But when the Allies suffered a setback, Haw Haw's tone became chiding, even condescending, as if scolding the Allied troops for being naughty. And after the defeat of the British 1st Airborne Division at Arnhem, his gloating broadcasts became almost unbearable.

Sergeant Austin also found amusement in some unintended consequences of radio transmissions made by himself or by another nearby Allied agent. If Austin transmitted with his Jedburgh set as a German formation of tanks or self-propelled guns passed by outside, chaos resulted as his transmissions jammed the German unit's internal radio signals. At times, he similarly interfered with radio traffic at a Gestapo office in Rijssen, a large town less than six miles to the northwest, where a German operator could be heard complaining about the clicking noise made by Austin's set as he tapped out his messages in Morse code. Apparently, there was an Allied intelligence agent operating not far away, and whenever he transmitted over his radio, the larger and more powerful British B-2 set, he completely disrupted German radio communications in the area. Austin enjoyed listening as the German radio operators scrambled to reestablish contact with one another.[4]

Henk Brinkgreve, Pappy Olmsted, and Bunny Austin grew more comfortable working with the resistance people who took such great care of them. At about this time, the Jeds received new forged identification documents from the Dutch underground.

A month had passed since the battle at Arnhem, and German forces in the area north of that city had resumed a routine training schedule. New SS and parachute units in the area consisted largely of recently conscripted youth, many of them former members of the Hitler Jugend (Hitler Youth) organization, with leadership and training provided by a small corps of seasoned veterans. The units had new weapons and other equipment, although well below authorized numbers; armored and artillery units might have less than half their authorized number of tanks or guns. The men of team Dudley grew somewhat discouraged as they watched these units train, knowing that the Allies had suffered a major setback at Arnhem and that the liberation of central Holland would be a long time in coming. All the Jeds could do was continue their work in the hope that it would contribute to that eventual liberation.

Major Olmsted did his part by continuing to gather intelligence reports on the enemy units, their strength and composition, their training and preparations. Then he began to receive several detailed reports from underground sources of German defense plans for a northern extension of the Siegfried line, as the string of fortifications along Germany's western border was called. The plans described a network of defensive positions centered on the beautiful old fortified town of Zwolle, with its star-shaped moat and bastions dating from medieval days. Included in the plans were the locations of every fighting position in the city, every command post, every troop barracks, and every large weapon. Every trench was shown, as well as every artillery or antiaircraft gun, antitank weapon, machine gun, tank trap, and barbed-wire entanglement. Olmsted was elated and eager to relay the information to England.[5]

On their last afternoon at the farm, Henk and Pappy took some inactive grenades out to a pasture to teach some of the young men from the local underground cell how to use them. For instruction purposes, they had removed the detonator from a British Mills 36 grenade, the British Army's standard fragmentation hand grenade. The boys had used grenades in action before but had complained to the Jeds of sore arms after a skirmish in which they had thrown several. Even the big strong Dutch farm kids couldn't throw a grenade as far as the Jeds, so the Jeds taught the young Dutchmen the best throwing technique.

Bunny and Ank, the courier, had gone ahead to the new area several days earlier. The new farm was about twenty miles farther west. For security reasons, they were instructed to stay at farms other than the one that was to serve as the new headquarters.

TWENTY-ONE

SOLITARY CONFINEMENT

At the Oberursel prisoner of war camp, Allan Todd had served his week in solitary confinement. He also had undergone a second round of questioning. On Sunday, October 15, 1944, he was taken back before the interrogation officer for a third time. Once again, the German demanded to know what Todd's duties had been with the British, explaining that he simply needed to confirm the American's status as a prisoner of war rather than a spy. Todd's name, alleged the German, had been found on some documents captured in France the previous winter.

Though Todd could not be certain of what the Germans did know, he held his ground, laughing it off, accusing the German of bluffing. He continued to refuse to explain his connection with the British paratroopers. Furious, the German officer pounded the desk and informed Todd that he would soon be visited by a "special investigator." The American was returned to his solitary cell, but he did not sleep that night. Thoughts of his luck having run out kept him awake.[1]

A Luftwaffe colonel made an inspection through the facility on the seventeenth, and found Todd in solitary confinement. He asked Todd why he was there. When Todd explained that he had been in solitary for nearly nine days for not answering the question about his duties, the colonel had him moved upstairs to a regular cell. The German also saw to it that Todd received medical attention for his ear and eyes and was given a bowl of turnip soup. Then the colonel gave Todd a cigarette and informed him that he would be interrogated again that afternoon and would probably be shipped out to a permanent camp later that night.

At about five that afternoon, Todd was taken before another interrogator, a Luftwaffe officer. He answered routine questions at first, and then, again, he refused to answer the "duties with the British" question. Surprisingly, this time the German suggested that they simply put "liaison officer" on the form. They needed some answer, the interrogator explained, or he would never be allowed to move on to a permanent camp. Todd agreed.

At eight o'clock that night, he and a number of others who had just gone through interrogation were taken to a building where they were allowed to mingle and talk. All of the men had come from several days in solitary confinement, staring at four bare walls with no one to talk to. Now they chatted until dawn.

The following morning, October 18, Todd and the small group of other prisoners boarded a train that took them about thirty miles north to another compound, a branch of the Dulag Luft camp. Located about two miles northwest of the town of Wetzlar, it was a transit camp—a place where prisoners were further processed before being shipped off to permanent camps. An American prisoner, a colonel, more or less oversaw the care given to prisoners passing through the camp. The dining hall at Dulag Luft–Wetzlar was clean and tidily kept. There were tables sufficient for all the men to sit and eat. Drawings and pinup girls adorned the walls. A good meal of bread, butter, and cheese was given the prisoners upon their arrival at nine o'clock that night. Here they found decent one-story wooden barracks with hot showers, a good bed, and good medical treatment from an American doctor, himself a prisoner of war. They went through delousing and then received a Red Cross issue of cigarettes and clean U.S. Army clothing and toilet articles—shaving kit, tooth powder and toothbrush, socks, underwear, towels, and a greatcoat, which would be needed for the winter ahead.[2]

After two days at the Wetzlar transit camp, all air force officer prisoners were moved to a Luftwaffe camp, and army personnel, including Lieutenant Todd, were taken to a camp called Stalag XII-A, at the medieval town of Limburg in the valley of the winding Lahn River, some fifty miles northwest of Frankfurt. Before departing Wetzlar, Todd and the other prisoners were each issued a full Red Cross food parcel.

From the Limburg rail station, on the southern edge of the town of twisting streets and half-timbered houses, above which towered the seven spires of a thirteenth-century Romanesque cathedral, Todd and the other prisoners marched four miles to the prison camp. When they arrived at the camp, they passed through a tall wooden gate with a large spread-winged Nazi eagle emblazoned on a panel overhead. In his talons the eagle gripped a swastika, and on either side of the eagle was the huge designation XII-A. The camp was in horrible condition, and there was an immediate and unwelcome change in the way the prisoners were treated. Here the Germans' attitude toward the prisoners was clear by the rough treatment, the confiscation of prisoners' watches and other personal items, and the austerity of concrete floors and no bunks, simply straw mats or loose straw on the floor. There was little in the way of food, and what they did get was barely edible—moldy bread and worm-infested soup.

The building was very cold. Enlisted prisoners in the British-American compound were housed in four large tents, with around seven hundred men crowded into each. The tents were devoid of any furniture, and there were no lights. Prisoners slept side by side, covering every inch of the cobblestone surface, with no blankets and only a scattering of straw to provide some degree of comfort. A terrible stench issued forth from the overused stone toilets. For drinking water, the men had to stand in line at a pipe where the water was turned on for one hour three times a day. The entire camp was overcrowded in the weeks following the Market-Garden operation; it has been estimated that the prisoner population of Stalag XII-A might have risen to over twenty thousand.

Morning roll call came at six, after which each prisoner received a cup of ersatz coffee. Meals at this camp left much to be desired. Breakfast typically consisted of bread (rationed at one-fifth of a small loaf per man) with a bit of margarine that was usually augmented with a filler of some kind. From time to time, a bit of cheese or sausage meat or jam was available. The two remaining meals of the day consisted solely of a watered-down soup.

Red Cross parcels never made their way to the prisoners of Stalag XII-A, and those who arrived from Wetzlar with their parcels tucked under their arms had to keep them with them at all times. Many had items pilfered from their parcels while at Limburg, and the unluckiest had their entire parcel stolen. There was almost nothing in the way of medical care. But there was a Dr. (Captain) Wolfe on the staff of a hospital in Limburg who also served as the prison camp doctor. He treated Todd's ear, washed out his eyes, and put a clean dressing on his arm.

Occasionally the prisoners saw the camp commandant, over six feet tall and with a scar on his face, strolling about the camp, accompanied by his huge, raven-black German shepherd.

Fortunately for the captives—at least for the Americans and British—Limburg was another transit camp, an army camp similar in purpose to that of the air force camp Todd had just left at Wetzlar, so they would not be staying long. The same was not true for Russian prisoners, though, or for a large group of Indian prisoners captured in North Africa. These groups were kept in a separate area of the camp, and for them Stalag XII-A would be home for the rest of the war. And as bad as conditions were for the prisoners taken on the Western Front, they were even worse for the Russians, who were treated little better than animals.

Todd and the other new arrivals would be interrogated and documented and moved on. It was a stopover required of all army prisoners captured on the Western Front, and because of this it was always crowded. With such a transient population, the men were unable to organize themselves as they would in the permanent camps. Someone did enlighten the new prisoners on a few rules to be followed at Limburg, though, if they wanted to stay alive. The main rule was never to go near the tall barbed-wire fence that surrounded the camp. Anyone touching the fence would be shot.

On Allan Todd's second day at the new camp, he was taken to a place about two miles away called "the castle" for interrogation. He was locked in a cell that was a step up from those he had seen so far. The cell was heated, and the three blankets provided ensured that he would not be cold. An open window made it possible for prisoners to talk to one another, which at least helped to reduce the boredom somewhat. Todd was told that he would be interrogated within the next couple of days and then would be shipped out to a permanent camp.[3]

On October 22, Todd's second day at the facility, he was taken before a Luftwaffe colonel for interrogation. Todd accepted a cup of coffee and a cigarette from the colonel, who proceeded to ask some rather routine questions. When asked about his reason for being in Arnhem, Todd explained that he was a liaison officer with the 1st Airborne Division. This time, the German accepted Todd's answer. Since elements of two American airborne divisions were so near Arnhem, the German officer reasoned, it would only make sense for them to have exchanged liaison officers to effect better coordination.[4]

But the interrogator continued to dig for more details. Which airborne division was Todd with, he asked, the 82nd or the 101st? Todd remained silent. The German said that it was simply a routine question, and if Todd chose not to answer, he would assume that the American belonged to the 82nd, since they were the nearest of the two to Arnhem. Now the officer tried a new approach. He said that Todd would somehow have to prove that he was from the 82nd Airborne. It was absolutely necessary that all prisoners be properly identified to ensure they were not agents of the underground posing as soldiers.

Then something happened that unnerved Allan Todd. The interrogator produced a roster of officers of the 82nd. Included on the list were names from the commanding general down to company commanders. The German recited where each regiment of the division had landed in Holland and even identified those officers who had been killed in the fighting around Nijmegen. To prove that he had served as the 82nd's liaison officer to the British 1st Airborne Division, Todd was asked to identify some of the 82nd's officers. Todd scanned the list the German provided and pointed out a few names as men he had known. The German, who claimed to have complete descriptions of all officers on the list, asked Todd to describe the officers he claimed to know, but Todd refused. If Todd could give accurate descriptions of just two of the officers, the German promised, this part of the interrogation would be completed. Fortunately, Todd did, in fact, know some of the 82nd's officers, and he described them for the German. After checking Todd's descriptions with his own information, the interrogator seemed satisfied. Then the German showed Todd some cards he had been holding, and Todd could see that each card contained the name of an officer from the 82nd and included a physical description of the man.[5]

Curious as to how the Germans had gotten such information, Todd asked and was stunned when the German officer smiled and told him that he had been in one of the 82nd Airborne Division regimental command posts just a week ago. He explained to Todd that he was a fluent Dutch and English speaker and that he had been able to pass himself off as a Dutch patriot volunteering to assist the Allies. The officer spoke English without an accent, and when Todd asked him about it, the German said that he had worked for an oil company in the United States for twelve years. He went on to explain that he had traveled to Germany for a visit in 1939, was drafted into the German army, and was not allowed to return to the United States. To Todd, it was a familiar story; American soldiers had often heard variations of it from captured Germans. Then the German began to casually name a few of the officers he had met while passing himself off as a Dutchman with the 82nd. Allan Todd nearly fell out of his chair when the German mentioned Arie Bestebreurtje. Luckily, Bestebreurtje was believed by the German to be nothing more than a Dutch interpreter serving with the Americans.[6]

The interrogation now took a different direction as the German asked about General Ridgway. The interrogator said he was aware that Ridgway was no longer with the 82nd. He wanted to know where the general had gone, but Todd, who really didn't know the answer to that himself, was unable to provide the information. Todd was then returned to his cell.

The next day's questioning picked up where they had left off. Again the German asked Todd where General Ridgway had been transferred to, and again Todd had no answer. Now the American was subjected to an hour-long lecture on the supremacy of National Socialism and on the greatness of the Führer. Then it was back to the cell again.

Tuesday, October 24, brought one final round of interrogation. After another brief and fruitless quest for information on General Ridgway, the German once again resorted to lecturing Todd on the politics of the war. America should not be fighting with Russia, ranted the officer; she should be standing alongside Germany in their defense of Europe against the Bolshevists, whose goal was to conquer all of Europe and then attack the United States. When the session drew to a close, the German informed Todd that he was to depart the next day for a permanent prisoner of war camp. On the following day, Allan Todd returned to the camp at Limburg to prepare for the move.

TWENTY-TWO

STOLEN PLANS
TO BE DELIVERED

At the same time that Allan Todd was undergoing his final interrogation at "the castle," the Jeds of team Dudley prepared for the final leg of their westward journey. They felt fortunate to be leaving, at last, as the farm family who had been keeping them had been growing increasingly nervous by their presence. The family's obvious uneasiness whenever German soldiers were about caused the Jeds some tense moments; they were certain the family's behavior would give them away.

Among the small headquarters group traveling with the Jeds, only a local Dutchman by the name of Jaap knew the best route to the new area, so he served as guide. Everyone mounted his or her bicycle on a cold and rainy October afternoon, and Jaap, the girl named Ank, and Gerard started down the road. Next came three men who served as lookouts, or outriders, following the first group by about two hundred yards. If anything went wrong up ahead, the lookouts would alert those following behind. Major Pappy Olmsted, Major Henk Brinkgreve, and Klaas formed the next group. Finally, trailing about three hundred yards behind Olmsted's party, came the last threesome consisting of Marie, Riek, and Daan.

Each cyclist was dressed in common Dutch clothing and had a small bag packed with personal items, blankets, and wooden shoes tied to the bike frame. They all appeared to be refugees from Arnhem or some other bombed-out city. Brinkgreve carried the resistance organizations' administrative records in his pack. Tucked away in Olmsted's bag were all the maps and intelligence reports associated with his work.

The dispersion of the headquarters group into widely separated groups of three was for the sake of security and survival. If the lead group ran into trouble, the following parties could make a break for it. Anyone who was detained or otherwise engaged by the Germans was to be left behind. The others could not risk capture by trying to help him or her. Because of the importance and sensitivity of the documents several of the men were carrying, it was essential that as many get through as possible.

Every man carried a Colt forty-five-caliber automatic pistol, which the Dutch called the *groote* Colt (great Colt), and a hand grenade. Pappy Olmsted was comforted by the thought of the big pistol in his coat pocket, but the bulge formed by the gun seemed enormous whenever the group passed through a German roadblock or checkpoint.[1]

The group had cycled about three miles when they passed by a rifle range where German recruits were firing. The road they were traveling on passed about a hundred yards to the rear of the firing line, so that the soldiers were shooting in the opposite direction at targets posted in front of a backdrop of large sand dunes. Troops stood idly in line behind each firing position, waiting for their turn to shoot. Each small group of cyclists continued past the firing range, then turned right onto a trail that ran along the west side of the range. A thousand yards down that trail, they turned right again onto a primary road that ran behind the sand dunes at the end of the range. The road was a busy one and there were many cyclists on it, and the Jeds and their resistance friends pedaled on for several minutes.

Suddenly Olmsted, Brinkgreve, and Klaas saw Jaap, Ank, and Gerard, up ahead, quickly turn off the road to the left and into the pine woods. Three SS men immediately raced to the spot on bicycles from the opposite direction, reaching the area where the men had turned off just as Olmsted, Brinkgreve, and Klaas were passing by. Olmsted was certain the Germans would notice the bulges in their pockets where they carried their forty-fives and grenades, but the SS men were too intent on following the three cyclists who had left the road. The Germans also turned off, following the path into the woods taken by the outriders. Soon voices yelling *"Halt!"* came from the woods, and as Olmsted,

Brinkgreve, and Klaas continued down the road, they heard several shots being fired.[2]

The men felt terrible at the thought of leaving their comrades to battle the Germans on their own, but they could not risk losing the plans and intelligence documents they carried. On they pedaled until they passed by the sentry box from which the Germans had come. Apparently it was a newly established sentry post, and Jaap, unfamiliar with it, had panicked at the sight of the SS men. Now, with the Germans all in pursuit of the three cyclists in the woods, the sentry box was left unattended and the other groups passed freely by. Olmsted's group came upon a farmer, and the men asked for directions to a place near their destination. The farmer gladly led the cyclists down some back trails until they came to a highway that would take the men where they wanted to go.

Standing beside the road, Olmsted, Brinkgreve, and Klaas took out their pipes, filled the bowls, and lit them. Then they began pedaling down the road, smoking and appearing as carefree as possible. Several hours later they were in an area that Klaas was familiar with, and shortly after that they arrived at their new village.

Soon the men found the house where they were to report, the home of a policeman who was the head of the underground in the area. Still feeling bad about the loss of their three friends, Olmsted, Brinkgreve, and Klaas walked up to the front door. Before they could knock, the door burst open and out rushed Ank, Gerard, and all the others to give the three newcomers a warm reception. Olmsted, Brinkgreve, and Klaas learned that the others had all followed a more direct route, beating them to the village.

The three who had ridden off into the woods had survived their encounter with the SS men. Two of the resistance members, Ank and Gerard, had stopped when the Germans fired at them, and Gerard had been able to get rid of his grenade before they arrived. The SS men caught up with them and asked for their papers. Ank and Gerard produced their false papers. Fortunately, they passed scrutiny. The Germans then searched Ank, but they missed the pistol that she had tucked away beneath her sweater. Then they quickly searched Gerard and made him open his suitcase. When he did so, there on top of everything else lay a pair of British Army socks that Gerard had gotten from an airdrop of supplies the previous week. Immediately the SS men became excited, sure that they had nabbed members of the underground. But Gerard convincingly explained that he was a refugee from Arnhem and that he had traded food to British paratroopers for the socks. The Germans bought the story. After admonishing the two cyclists for fleeing into the woods, they let them go, but they kept the socks.

When Ank and Gerard arrived at the house, they found that all the others had already arrived, except for Olmsted, Brinkgreve, and Klaas. Everyone feared the three men had been picked up.

After briefly celebrating their reunion, everyone sat down to a cup of tea with some biscuits and rye bread.

At around seven-thirty in the evening, they began departing by twos and threes for their new safe house. Before too long, they were together again in their new quarters, a new, modernly furnished house where they found the rooms to be very cold. The men lit a carbide lamp and built a fire in the fireplace. As with most farm homes in the Netherlands, the house and barn were attached, and the hayloft above the barn was to be the sleeping area of the Jeds and the resistance men. A blanket for each man, provided by the local underground, added to the men's comfort as they stretched out to sleep on a bed of barley straw.

The girls were to be quartered at a nearby farm, and since it was well after the eight o'clock curfew, Henk Brinkgreve and Daan accompanied them to the farm.

Early the next morning, the girls returned and everyone enjoyed a breakfast of bread and cheese and coffee. The men quickly found that their new home was ideally suited to serve as their command post. The house was centrally located in the area in which they would now be operating, and it was not too far from the village.

Soon Henk Brinkgreve, Cor Hilbrink, Gerard, and Daan were meeting regularly with local resistance leaders. Every day, Pappy Olmsted received around thirty typed pages of information on German troop emplacements, supply and ammunition dumps, and detailed plans of several military installations.[3] Bunny Austin, too, kept busy with the increased radio activity resulting from the work of the others. Time passed quickly for everyone.

Olmsted labored for days preparing map overlays of several large enemy defensive systems. Colonel Houtz was pleased with the amount of information Olmsted was gathering to keep the situation map up-to-date, and he wanted to find a way to get this information to Allied

commanders. The Jeds radioed Special Force Headquarters requesting
to be picked up by a small aircraft to take the information to London,
where they could discuss many things with the staff at Prince Bernhard's headquarters that they were unable to discuss over the radio because of the amount of airtime it would require. Also, a trip to London
would allow them to relax for a while before returning to the field. But
SFHQ did not agree to the pickup operation, and the men were very disappointed.[4]

One day, an interesting Dutchman named Johan came to one of
Brinkgreve's meetings. He was from Deventer, an attractive manufacturing town on the IJssel River. Brinkgreve had met Johan earlier, had
talked with him and judged him to be trustworthy. Major Olmsted heard
that Johan was to bring some very complete and detailed German defense plans, so he accompanied Brinkgreve on the seven-mile journey to
the meeting. It was a brisk day, and the trip seemed much longer because the two men wore only threadbare overcoats and had no gloves.

At the meeting, the Jedburgh officers were not disappointed. Johan
had not been exaggerating; he produced not only German plans for the
fortification of Deventer and the defense of the IJssel line, but also a
typed seventeen-page paper describing in detail how the enemy planned
to deploy all troops in the area in the event of an Allied attack from western Holland. A Dutch servant on the local German commander's staff
had stolen the plan, page by page, from the officer's headquarters.

On November 1, Major Brinkgreve attended another meeting where
he heard about plans for a group of American and British paratroopers
and airmen, stranded and in hiding north of the Neder Rijn since the
withdrawal of the 1st Airborne Division, to attempt a crossing to friendly
territory on the southern bank of the river. The attempt was to be made
soon. Brinkgreve recognized this as the best opportunity to get the German defense plans into the hands of Allied commanders who could
make use of them. With the approval of the local resistance commander,
a good friend of Henk's, Major Olmsted's name was included in a list
that was radioed to London. When and if the crossing took place, the
list would be used to vet those who arrived safely on the southern bank.
Henk Brinkgreve never considered going himself; he fully realized that
he was the glue holding the Overijssel underground together. Bunny
Austin, of course, would have to remain in Holland to continue operating the team's radio.

Pappy Olmsted would make the hazardous journey to link up with the group of Allied evaders and join them in the perilous crossing. At once, he began arranging for someone to assume his duties at the headquarters. He had been building a card index cataloging German troop strength and disposition, as well as identification of units, in some two hundred towns and villages in the area. Now Olmsted hurried to train one of the young Dutchmen to take over the job.

TWENTY-THREE

OFLAG 64

Until now, Lieutenant Allan Todd had been in transit camps, temporary holding facilities where prisoners were kept for interrogation and processing while awaiting transportation to a permanent camp. His time for moving on to a permanent camp came on Sunday, November 5, 1944, when he was among a group of prisoners who were marched to the Limburg railway station. There the Germans crammed the prisoners into the boxcars of a train bound for a camp at Schubin,* Poland, about 170 miles northwest of Warsaw.

In Todd's boxcar, he and about two dozen other prisoners crowded into a space occupying roughly a third of the car, with barbed wire laced across the width of the car to keep them in place. Four German guards made themselves as comfortable as possible in the remaining two-thirds of the car, their end plus the area adjacent to the door. The boxcar was cold and there were no blankets, not even straw on the floor to provide the meager level of comfort that might be afforded animals. With many of the men suffering from dysentery, a bucket that served as a latrine proved insufficient. The trip lasted five days, and for the first two days

* Schubin was the German spelling, Szubin the Polish. Most of the towns in German-occupied Poland had been given German names; Schubin had been renamed Altburgund.

the men went without food. On the third day, the guards provided a loaf of bread to be shared by ten prisoners and a two-pound can of meat for every twenty prisoners. Only once during the long journey were the men allowed off the train to relieve themselves.[1]

On Friday morning, the train rolled to a stop in northern Poland. The sign on the water tower at the tiny station indicated that they were outside a town called Altburgund. Below that name on the sign, in smaller lettering, was the name Schubin, the German spelling of the Polish name for the town, Szubin. All signs in Poland were now in German, towns and streets having been given German names.

The half-starved men, many racked by dysentery, climbed down from the boxcars. Two men had died during the trip. It took some time for the German guards to get all of the men unloaded and formed up, and then they marched the prisoners for more than a mile toward a small town that lay on a sloping hillside. They stopped just outside the town at the main gate of a camp called Kriegsgefangenen Offizierlager (Prisoner of War Camp for Officers) 64.* As with other prisoner of war camps of the Third Reich, the place was normally referred to by the abbreviated term Oflag 64.

The Germans housed the many thousands of Allied prisoners of war in more than fifty such camps spread throughout Germany and Poland. Oflag 64 lay amid hilly farm country in a part of northwestern Poland that had been alternately part of Germany or Poland for centuries.

The main entrance to the camp, which lay on the western edge of the market town of Schubin, was on the north side of Adolf Hitler Strasse, the cobblestone road that led into town and was its main thoroughfare. The gate into the camp was about eight feet wide and constructed of metal beams.

Just inside the compound, to the right of the main gate, stood a large, three-story white stone building, once a Polish manor house. Nearby was a wooden latrine building capable of accommodating as many as fifty men at a time. To the left of the entrance were three long, single-story

---

* Most German prisoner of war camps were identified by Roman numerals according to the military district (*Wehrkreis*) of Germany in which they were located. Capital letters were added to the numbers of additional camps opened in the same district. The second camp for enlisted prisoners built in Wehrkreis IV, for example, was named Stalag IV-B. The camp known as Oflag 64 carried an Arabic number because it was opened in 1939 and predated the initiation of the Roman numeral system.

red brick prisoner barracks. Directly ahead and to the left of the main gate was another three-story building, a brick structure with a sidewalk and flower beds in front. This building, the prisoners learned, housed the hospital with its thirty to thirty-five beds, the showers, the chaplain's quarters, the barbershop, and some classrooms. Behind that building, to the north, lay a long brick greenhouse.

The entire camp, an area three hundred by two hundred yards, was enclosed by double barbed-wire fencing, about eight to ten feet in height, supported by wooden poles. Filling the ten-foot space between the two barbed-wire fences was a tangled web of rusted, barbed concertina wire. At intervals around the perimeter of the camp stood thirty-foot-high guard towers; a smaller one stood near the camp entrance. Known by the prisoners as "goon boxes," they were equipped with swivel-mounted floodlights and were manned by guards armed with machine guns. At night, guards on foot patrolled the area between each guard tower, and lights illuminated not only the perimeter fence, but the entire compound.

Across the street from the main gate were the administration building and the barracks that housed the German guard company, a one-hundred-man force from the 813th Grenadier Regiment. Just to the west of the camp stood an imposing Protestant church; a large Catholic church lay to the east.

The camp commandant of Oflag 64 was Oberst (Colonel) Wilhelm Schneider, a portly Prussian at least sixty years of age, who was in his forty-third year of service in the German army. Described by one prisoner as resembling "an old Berkshire boar with his flattened nose,"[2] he was a military professional—strong and officious, strict when he had to be, but fair. He clearly was not a member of the Nazi Party, prohibiting anyone under his command from using the Nazi salute. Unlike Schneider, the camp's security officer, Hauptmann (Captain) Zimmerman, was a committed Nazi and a crude bully.

The compound of Oflag 64 had once housed a school for girls, the campus having been converted to a prisoner of war camp early in the war to house Polish prisoners. The camp was then used to hold French, and later British, officer POWs. Beginning in June 1943, as Germany began taking in many American prisoners from North Africa, the camp was designated exclusively for American ground combat officers. Some had been captured in North Africa in the early days of 1943; others had been captured later—in Sicily or Italy or France. As the war dragged on through 1944, the prisoner population grew. When Lieutenant Allan Todd and others captured in Arnhem arrived at the camp, the ten-acre compound was home to around a thousand men.[3]

The American prisoners at Oflag 64 were well organized, and discipline was maintained through a staff of U.S. officers. The senior American officer, or SAO, was fifty-two-year-old West Pointer Colonel Paul R. Goode. "Pop" Goode had been leader of the prisoners for only about a month, having taken over from the previous SAO in October.

The gruff, pipe-smoking Colonel Goode, a tough thirty-year veteran and Boston native who had starred in football, boxing, and track at the academy and had gone on to command four different infantry regiments, continued to provide the same style of leadership. He had been captured while commanding the 175th Infantry Regiment of the 29th Infantry Division during the hedgerow fighting in Normandy just a week after D-Day. Under Goode's leadership, every prisoner at Oflag 64 was to be clean-shaven, uniforms were to be kept as presentable as possible under the conditions, and each man was encouraged to take a daily walk for an hour around the perimeter of the camp on a path just inside the wire enclosure. Goode expected the prisoners to remember their status as officers and to present themselves appropriately to their German captors at all times.

Headquarters for Colonel Goode and his prisoner staff was in the three-story white building with the russet-tiled roof located just inside and to the right of the main gate. Referred to by the prisoners as "the White House" or "the Big House," the building also housed the kitchen, the mess hall, and the German camp headquarters. Goode's staff included two other full colonels and a handful of lieutenant colonels. His S-3, or operations officer, was a handsome, soft-spoken thirty-eight-year-old West Point graduate who had been captured while serving as executive officer of the 1st Armored Division's 1st Armored Regiment in Tunisia in February 1943. He was Lieutenant Colonel John K. Waters, and he was the son-in-law of Lieutenant General George S. Patton, Jr., commander of the Third U.S. Army in France.*

Lieutenant Allan Todd and the other new arrivals at Oflag 64 were marched to the administration building, outside the barbed wire and

---

* Born in 1906, Waters was the son of a Baltimore banker. He married Patton's daughter Beatrice ("Little B") on June 27, 1934. Waters retired as a four-star general in 1966, commanding U.S. Army, Pacific, and died on January 9, 1989.

across the street from the arched gateway to the camp, for processing. Each man had to give his name, rank, and serial number. Once they were officially registered as prisoners of war, their names were added to the roster for roll calls and were provided to the Prisoner of War Information Bureau of the International Committee of the Red Cross in Switzerland. The bureau ensured that each prisoner's government and family were notified of the captured man's status. Next, the men were photographed, fingerprinted, and given numbers. Within a week, they were issued brown cardboard prisoner of war identification cards with their photographs on them, and they were instructed to keep the cards with them at all times. They were now full-fledged *Kriegsgefangenen* (prisoners of war). But Allied prisoners of war used an abbreviated form of that term when referring to themselves. They called themselves "kriegies," and those who had been captured in North Africa or Sicily, early in the war, were known as "old kriegies." Their hosts—the German guards and administrators who ran the camp—were "goons" in prisoner jargon. Todd and the others were now permanent residents.

After the administrative processing was completed, the men were turned over to the prisoners in the camp for billeting arrangements. Lieutenant Colonel Waters assigned each new prisoner to a barracks and to a numbered wooden bunk, measuring about two and a half by six feet, complete with a mattress filled with straw or wood shavings or sand laid over seven supporting boards. Each single-story barracks building measured 120 feet by 40 feet and was built of brick with a cold floor of stone or concrete. The building was divided into two large sleeping areas with a washroom, accessible from either end, in the center. The taps in the washroom offered only very cold water.

The barracks were numbered 1 through 9, with letter designations for the two sleeping areas. The bunk rooms in Building 2, for example, were designated Barracks 2A and 2B. Barracks 1A had been converted into a theater or auditorium. The other half of that building, Barracks 1B, served as a crude recreation room. Lower-numbered barracks stood in the southwest corner of the camp. Barracks 6 through 9 were located on a higher area in the northwest corner, with the main latrine and athletic field, where roll call formations were held, between the two areas. To the east of the northern set of barracks stood a large barn.

By the winter of 1944–45, Oflag 64 was bursting at the seams with prisoners. Each barracks bunk area, measuring forty feet by twenty feet, housed forty to fifty prisoners; the entire barracks building held up to a hundred men. Bunk rooms were further divided into fifteen-foot-square cubicles, formed by arrangement of the triple-deck bunks and lockers, with each cubicle sleeping as many as twenty to twenty-five officers. Some smaller cubicles held only eight or nine men. A small, rough wooden table stood beneath each of the single twenty-five-watt light bulbs hanging from the ceiling. A coal-burning porcelain stove provided so little heat that the men had to take turns huddling around it, and they joked that it required a certain number of bodies crowded around to keep the stove warm. The weather in this part of Poland, so close to the Baltic, was growing cold in mid-November, and snow was beginning to fall. Soon the indoor temperature would seldom rise above forty degrees, and at night it dropped below freezing. Men had to sleep with their uniforms on for the added warmth.

One barracks was reserved for the enlisted men held at the camp as orderlies.

The daily routine of prison camp life usually began when the men were rousted from the barracks at six a.m. for morning *Appell,* the German term for roll call. All prisoners assembled in formation on the parade ground. The guards made a count of the prisoners, and then the commandant, Oberst Schneider, might briefly address the men. If they were lucky, the count went quickly; if not, they could stand in the cold, perhaps even in rain, for anywhere from thirty minutes to two hours or more. Breakfast followed and rarely consisted of anything more than hot water, perhaps with some ground and parched grain mixed in to create ersatz coffee. Lunch would be either a few small potatoes or some soup made of barley or cabbage. There was a second *Appell* late in the day. The evening meal would be cabbage soup and, if the men were lucky, perhaps a bit of horsemeat. Each man received a loaf of hard, black pumpernickel bread, about five inches in length, once a week, and everyone received a daily ration of roughly an ounce of sugar processed from sugar beets. Such a meager diet did little to restore the loss of strength and body weight Allan Todd and the other prisoners had suffered during their journey to Oflag 64. Todd's weight had dropped from 205 to 165 since parachuting into Holland on September 17.

That afternoon, showers, delousing, and an issue of new clothes and toilet articles went a long way toward making Todd and the others feel human again. Each man also received a haircut and three blue German army blankets to take back to their bunks. Todd's morale was furthered improved when each new man was issued a third of a Red Cross food

parcel in accordance with a standing practice in the camp for welcoming new prisoners. As he settled in that night, Todd felt relieved that the
long train journey and the uncertainty of their destination were now in
the past.[4]

The day after their arrival, Todd and the other new kriegies were
given an opportunity to write to their families back home. The Germans
provided form letters for them to complete, and they included instructions on what to write. Todd wrote to Mandy and to his parents.

Most of the prisoners were assigned to some form of work in the
camp to keep them busy. Allan Todd went to work in the post office,
where he helped censor the prisoners' mail. The Germans provided each
prisoner two form letters and two postcards each month for correspondence with families back home. The Germans censored all outgoing
mail, so the men were never able to write more than brief messages that
provided little information.

On the third floor of the White House was a six-thousand-volume
library to serve the men, and even more important information was
available in the attic. British prisoners had given the Americans the
components of a small radio receiver, and the Americans had smuggled
the kit into camp. Two prisoners assembled the radio and got it to work.
Now they used it in the attic, accessed by stairwells at either end of the
building that could be entered from the outside, to receive news on the
war's progress by picking up BBC news broadcasts. When not in use,
the radio was disassembled and stored in two cans of the type commonly found in Red Cross parcels. They remained undetected through
numerous searches by camp guards.

As their most reliable source of war news, the radio came to be
called "the Bird," and the prisoners established a routine for getting the
news out to all POWs without tipping off the Germans. At around two
each afternoon, an officer skilled in shorthand recorded the BBC news
broadcast almost verbatim. This was then read to men selected from
each barracks. At night, in each barracks building, men would pass the
word that "the Bird was going to sing," and they would gather together
to hear the latest news. A man was posted at the door to watch for "fer-
rets," as the prisoners called the solitary German security NCOs who
roamed about the camped looking for any suspicious activity. The man
with the news shared it with his barracks mates, often reading from the
notes he had taken earlier. If a German sentry on his rounds of the camp

came too near the barracks building, the door guard gave the alert and the group quickly dispersed.

Such news dissemination could be difficult in cases where the presence of a German "stooge" might be suspected. The Germans were known to introduce "plants," or stooges, among the prisoners from time to time to learn if the POWs were getting any information illicitly from the outside. These men were Germans who spoke English without an accent and were very knowledgeable about life in the United States. They wore American uniforms and claimed to be from well-known units of the United States Army. To guard against these spies, every new prisoner arriving at Oflag 64 had to be vetted by someone already in the camp. Almost always, someone in the camp would know of the new man either from civilian life or, more often, by having served in the same unit in the army. If no one knew the man personally, careful questioning could verify that the man actually knew other people within the unit he claimed to be from. It usually did not take long for a new man to be "cleared," at which time all news from the outside was shared with him.

Representatives of the International Committee of the Red Cross and the YMCA War Prisoners Aid program visited the camp from time to time to see for themselves the status of the prisoners' health and welfare and to report any violations of prisoner of war treatment under the provisions of the Geneva Conventions.

Athletics and other activities were organized on a continuing basis in the camp to help occupy the prisoners' time. Sports equipment, musical instruments, and other items for the recreation and amusement of the prisoners were provided by the YMCA and had been delivered through a Swedish intermediary. Books for the camp library, too, came from the YMCA and from the United States government. Red Cross parcels provided the men with additional items of clothing and food.

Religious services were routinely held in the camp's small chapel by the four Protestant and two Catholic chaplains who were among the prisoners held at Oflag 64.

Sports activities were conducted year-round, with the winter program being organized by a prisoner who had been a ski coach at the University of Montana before the war.[5]

Other prisoners organized a theater group that presented three-act plays, many based on Broadway shows such as *You Can't Take It with You* and *The Man Who Came to Dinner*. Productions were complete with costumes, settings, and lighting. Performances took place on a prisoner-built stage—the YMCA and the Germans provided the lumber—in a converted barracks called the Oflag Little Theater. Tickets were in such high demand that they often had to be rationed among the various barracks buildings. One-act productions being staged during the last week in November included *Pot Luck* and *In the Zone*. Just a week before Todd arrived at the camp, the musical *Full Swing* completed a six-day run.

Concerts were staged by a group of twenty prisoner musicians known as Bob Rankin's Orchestra, and not an empty seat was to be found at the group's performances. As testament to the band's talent, several German officers were regularly in attendance. Rankin, a trumpeter and first-class jazz musician, had been an orchestra leader before the war. The group, which included trumpets, trombones, tenor saxophones, alto saxophones, baritone saxophones, drums, and a piano, began a three-day "Swingland" show on November 9. A baritone recital was scheduled for the following week. The orchestra charged a cigarette for admission. Prisoners could also join the thirty-voice Glee Club chorus, which staged minstrel shows and oratorios. They could even enroll for piano lessons. For men who enjoyed music but had no talent to perform, several hand-wound record players were available, along with an ample supply of current records.

With books on a wide variety of subjects available at the camp library, prisoners formed study groups, which collectively came to be known at various times as "Schubin Prep" or "Schubin College" or "Altburgund Academy." Some preferred to call it the "Kriegy Kollege of Diabolical Knowledge."[6] Ten prisoner professors taught a wide variety of classes to some sixty students. In mid-November, ten men were enrolled in beginner's German, although the subject was sometimes banned from the curriculum because of its possible use in the event of escape. A dozen prisoner students met five times a week for two-hour classes in law presented by a team of four captive lawyers. Other subjects covered at the "college" at various times included economics, social science, physics, geology, mathematics, algebra, geometry, literature, speech, journalism, salesmanship, Spanish, primary and advanced French, Italian, and English.[7] A lecture series was held in the Little Theater on Wednesday evenings.

The prisoners even published a monthly camp newspaper, the *Oflag Item,* with the Germans arranging for the printing by a guard named

Willi Kricks, a German who had settled in Schubin before the war and ran a printing shop and bookbindery in town. Kricks became friendly not only with the newspaper staff, but also with the prisoners who worked at repairing damaged books at the camp library, and had even provided the prisoners with a large book press and trimmer. Typically four to eight pages in length, the *Item* carried entertaining stories of home taken from prisoners' letters, humorous stories and poems, cartoons, reports of camp sporting events, reviews of theater productions and schedules of upcoming events, biographical sketches of prisoners, editorials and commentaries, and even a literary supplement offering short stories written by prisoners. Photographs from home provided material for contests for the best-looking sweethearts or cutest babies.

The prisoners were kept abreast of war news and news from the home front by a daily news sheet, called the *Daily Bulletin,* which the *Item* staff prepared in hand-lettered form and posted on the White House bulletin board. In a play on the slogan *Freiheit und Brot* (Freedom and Bread), found on the Nazi Party newspaper *Völkischer Beobachter,* the *Daily Bulletin* featured the slogan *Freiheit und Weissbrot* (Freedom and White Bread) carefully camouflaged in scrolls and flourishes.[8] News items about the war were taken from German newspapers and radio broadcasts, though the staff edited and modified the stories as much as possible without alerting the Germans as to their source, based on information gleaned from BBC broadcasts received on the camp's secret radio. Stories from the home front usually came from newly arrived prisoners. A separate box provided announcements of upcoming activities within the camp.

A map posted to the bulletin board showed the progress of ongoing operations. Of course, the map could only show what the prisoners learned from German sources. But toward the end of the war, as Soviet forces approached the camp from the east, the prisoners boldly began to indicate the true progress of Allied forces on the map, based on information received from BBC broadcasts over their secret radio. In time, even the German guards could be seen consulting the map for updates.[9]

Most meals were served in the big dining room in the White House, although breakfast, seldom consisting of anything more than ersatz coffee, was carried to the barracks and served to the men there. Lunch often consisted of soup prepared from barley or oatmeal and perhaps with a little meat stock or dried vegetables. An evening meal could consist of boiled potatoes and a small cut of sour black bread that the prisoners called "goon bread." At times, a man could find pockets of sawdust in it, and it never seemed to spoil.

In late 1943, a year before Todd's arrival at the camp, each prisoner received a Red Cross food parcel about once every eight to ten days. Designed to supplement camp rations and provide sufficient nutrition for a man for one week, each eleven-pound parcel contained a tin of meat, a can of powdered milk, a chocolate bar, instant coffee, and cigarettes. At times when Red Cross parcels routinely arrived at the camp, the cooks removed the meat servings from all parcels so that these could be pooled and served at evening meals in the mess hall. The remainder of the parcels were then issued to the prisoners. Men often collected food items from the parcels and "bashed"—a term used to refer to an eating orgy that included attempts at mixing various items to replicate familiar dishes back home.

The men made use of the Red Cross parcel packaging materials, letting nothing go to waste. Small tin containers, such as those that contained milk, were fashioned into cups. The most common brand of milk in the parcels was Klim (milk spelled backward), so the cups the men made from the cans were known as "Klim tins."

As isolated as the prisoners at Oflag 64 were, though, they had found a way to continue to contribute to the Allied war effort. Observant prisoners were able to gather information that would be helpful to the Allies. The men established a system for delivering such information by encoding messages and integrating them into letters to their loved ones back home. Without their families being aware of it, such letters were intercepted and reviewed by military authorities, and the encoded information was extracted and decoded before the letter continued on to its destination. One of the officers directing this intelligence-gathering enterprise was Lieutenant Colonel Waters.[10]

Todd soon became acquainted with Colonel Goode, whom he considered a good and fair leader, but Todd also noted that the colonel "knew how to handle the Germans."[11] Goode's stern appearance and authoritative presence contributed to his success as the SAO.

The one subject that was constantly on the mind of every prisoner was food. The men were preoccupied with it to the point that they seldom thought of anything else. They talked of favorite dishes, of home-cooked meals, of fondly remembered restaurant menus, of recipes, and of how certain foods should be prepared.

There had been no Red Cross parcels since October 10—the Germans claimed they had been held up because of the battles in France or because the trains carrying the parcels had been bombed—and there would be none, other than the portions from existing stocks issued to new arrivals, until December 3, some three weeks after Todd's arrival.

The new prisoners soon found that, largely because of the efforts of "Pop" Goode and his energetic staff, life as a prisoner of war in Oflag 64 wasn't as bad as it might have been. But no matter how much Goode and his staff did to ease the suffering and isolation of prison life by providing work and other diversions, there was one constant reminder of their condition—hunger. Emaciated men—eyes staring vacantly from gaunt faces, gums receding from poorly maintained teeth, discolored fingernails—dreamed of such simple fare as hot oatmeal and candy. Hunger and boredom defined the life of the prisoner of war.

Quite simply, the men were slowly but steadily starving to death. Meals provided by the Germans were skimpy and of very poor quality, usually consisting only of potatoes or a weak soup made from sugar beets. The food was almost always worm-infested, many of the potatoes were rotten, and the cabbage used in soups was often rehydrated after years in storage. What kept the prisoners alive were the Red Cross parcels, which were issued one per man per week when they were available. Before long, Allan Todd was seventy pounds below his normal weight, and he continued to grow thinner every day.

Some of the one-story barracks buildings that housed the prisoners had been constructed with a clear crawl space between the floor of the building and the ground and were supposedly escape-proof. As in other German prison camps, the Allied prisoners at Oflag 64 had formed an escape committee to oversee all planned escape attempts. All escape plans were to be put before the committee for coordination and for approval by Colonel Goode.

The most elaborate escape plan had been approved by Colonel Goode's predecessor as senior American officer, Colonel Thomas Drake, during the previous winter. It called for a tunnel to be dug, extending from beneath Barracks 2 on the western end of the camp, under the perimeter fence, to a spot well beyond the enclosure. Work began immediately and progressed without being detected until something happened in the spring of 1944 that brought the enterprise to a halt.[12]

On the night of March 24–25, 1944, seventy-six Allied prisoners of war escaped from Stalag Luft III, near the town of Sagan, in the forests of Silesia southeast of Berlin, by tunneling beyond the camp's perimeter fence. The "Great Escape," as it would forever be known, resulted in the shooting execution of fifty of the seventy-three recaptured prisoners. Only three men successfully made their way to freedom. At prisoner of war camps throughout Germany and Poland, those who were caught attempting to escape were now taken into custody by the Gestapo, and the brutality with which these men were treated grew worse as the war progressed. Soon a posting by the Germans on the Oflag 64 bulletin board warned that anyone escaping from the camp would be shot upon recapture. Colonel Drake, Goode's predecessor, had then ordered all tunneling at Oflag 64 to cease, considering it to be too risky.[13]

The camp was becoming crowded, with all barracks filled to capacity, and with the onset of winter, morale in the camp was plummeting. The mess hall was serving each meal at two sittings, and the *Appell* formations now filled the athletic field.

Allan Todd settled into the grim life and monotonous routine of a prisoner of war—rising each morning at seven-forty, *Appell* at eight, then a breakfast of hot water or ersatz coffee, noon meal of soup served in two sittings in the mess hall, the first man for each table ladling out the soup servings for the eight men seated at his table, perhaps hot water again in midafternoon, afternoon *Appell,* and the evening meal. At roll call time, the guards would yell, *"Appell!"* and the men would fall out of the barracks and head to the recreation field. There they would form into fifty-man platoons, with the men standing five ranks deep to make the count easier for the Germans. There were now nearly thirty platoons. The Germans called the formation to attention and then put the men at parade rest as they made their count. Then the prisoners were told to stand in the rest position while the tallies were verified. Sometimes discrepancies resulted in an *Appell* that was long and cold. Men who had grown feeble from the poor diet might faint while standing in formation. When the Germans were satisfied, they called the formation to attention again and dismissed the men.

While the men were free to roam about the camp during the day, they had to be inside the barracks after lights out. Guards with police dogs patrolled throughout the camp after dark.

From time to time, Gestapo men would arrive at the camp to search the barracks and the men's belongings, often confiscating items of clothing for no reason. Red Cross shipments earlier in the year had provided enough clothing for each prisoner to have two winter uniforms and an overcoat, along with field jackets, underwear, shoes, and socks. But in

November, the Germans stipulated that each prisoner was limited to one uniform. Anything in excess of that was confiscated. Although the prisoners failed to see a reason for these thefts, the Allies would later learn that American uniforms confiscated from POWs were used in out-fitting German troops masquerading as U.S. soldiers to infiltrate Allied lines during the German Ardennes offensive in mid-December 1944.

TWENTY-FOUR

GOODBYE TO BUNNY AND HENK

As Allan Todd was experiencing his first days as a prisoner at Oflag 64, the men of Jedburgh team Dudley were busier than ever. But they took time out from their work to join their Dutch friends in the celebration of two events. First, everyone cheered the news of President Roosevelt's reelection. Then came Gerard's birthday on Saturday, November 11.

Gerard had been gathering and saving food for his birthday party for several weeks, and he had managed to accumulate an impressive variety and quantity of delicacies and beverages that had become difficult to come by during the occupation. When the day finally arrived, Gerard's friends enjoyed a birthday celebration that none of them would soon forget. Friends in the underground, coming from miles around, began arriving on Friday night in hopes of getting an early start with the partying the next day.

As it turned out, everyone slept late on Saturday morning, but then they were up and everyone pitched in to help prepare breakfast, with a table set for sixteen people and adorned with colorful fall flowers. Some of the food had been saved from rationed goods, but there were also items that were difficult for Dutch citizens to come by, undoubtedly acquired on the black market with underground money and coupons. The money had come from England; the coupons were stolen during a raid on the *Reichskommissar*'s office. For two hours, Gerard and his guests talked and feasted on ham, bacon, eggs, coffee, tea, and milk. Three kinds of bread were served as well as both brown and white sugar. Finally, at around noon, everyone finished eating. One of Gerard's friends was a wine and tobacco merchant, and as late in the war as November 1944, he was able to provide some excellent cigars for the occasion. As the girls cleaned up, the men sat and smoked and talked of their plans for the future.

Sergeant Austin had come to the party, and since he was staying at a different farm and didn't get to see much of the officers, he and Pappy Olmsted talked for a long while. Bunny was unhappy being isolated from his Jedburgh teammates, living with a group of resistance men who spoke little or no English. Each day, he would go out to send and receive radio messages, and a small army of Dutchmen accompanied him as guards. Austin's elementary French allowed for some rudimentary communication with those who were capable in that language. Recently three new men, a Pole and two Belgians, had arrived at the farm where he was staying. The men claimed to be deserters from the German army.

The real party began at around six, when everyone gathered for a dinner of beef, pork, and potatoes, all served on a beautifully decorated and candlelit table. Then came an attractive pudding decorated like a birthday cake, complete with candles. When everyone had finished eating and the dishes were done, there was accordion and harmonica music and singing. Gerard and his friends surprised everyone with the variety of beverages they pulled out of hiding—Dutch Bols gin, Beste genever, and cherry and apricot brandy. There was a rich yellowish eggnoglike drink called *advocaat,* a creamy liqueur made from eggs, sugar, and brandy. As a special treat for Bunny Austin, there was British Army rum recovered from a downed RAF bomber. At the close of a day that had given everyone the opportunity to laugh again and forget the war for a moment, the group toasted Gerard and retired for the night.[1]

Sunday, November 12, was a cloudy and dreary day. Gerard's friends had all left by four or five that afternoon, and the Jeds went back to work. Bunny Austin was among the guests who had to depart. When Pappy Olmsted said goodbye to him that afternoon, he had no way of knowing that it was the last time he would ever see Austin.

Olmsted had finished updating the intelligence notes and copying the overlays that he planned to take with him on his trip to friendly territory. All that remained was to complete the daily situation reports. Henk Brinkgreve talked with Olmsted about tasks that the American could take care of while in London. It was expected that Pappy would stay in England for about ten days and then return to Holland with a re-supply airdrop.

Brinkgreve and Gerard also were preparing for a trip. The two planned to start the following day on bicycle to Zwolle, where they would meet a wine dealer from a town west of Zwolle who was one of the very few Dutch civilians allowed to operate a car in occupied Holland. This man was to drive Brinkgreve and Gerard to the western part of Holland, where the two men would meet with underground contacts in the area. The trip would also give Brinkgreve an opportunity to visit his parents.

But traveling with the wine merchant was a risky venture. By all appearances, the man was a collaborator of the first order. Because of this, he was despised by his own countrymen; even his unhappy wife was now shunned by her former friends. What she didn't know, and what most of the Dutch people didn't know, was that he was, in fact, a very active supporter of the Dutch resistance. The man had cultivated many important and useful friends among the German occupation authorities, supplying them with wines and liquors, dining with them, and going shooting with them. Through these connections, he obtained papers that allowed him to travel freely anywhere in Holland, even exempting him and anyone in his car from scrutiny at German roadblocks or other control points. The thorough raids and searches known as *razzias,* though, were a different matter. No vehicles, including German army or SD cars, were exempt from inspection during a *razzia.*

The wine dealer had secretly served his country and the Allies. On one occasion, he had bribed a German officer to prevent the planned demolition of a twenty-mile dike on the Zuiderzee, an act that would have resulted in the flooding of thousands of acres of productive and fertile farmland. Furthermore, many downed Allied airmen owed their lives to this man, as he had helped transport them to safe areas in occupied Holland.

The wine dealer also was to provide transportation for Major Olmsted on the first leg of his journey, taking him in his car as far as Ede, a town west of Arnhem, where the American would go to a safe house and await further instructions.

Major Brinkgreve and Gerard departed, as planned, on Monday,

Brinkgreve happily anticipating the hot bath he had been promised would be available to him in Zwolle. It would be his first since August.

Major Olmsted remained at the farm, awaiting a courier who was to arrive on Tuesday with instructions for him on where he was to meet the wine merchant's car, how he should be dressed, and the phrase to use as his bona fides for gaining entrance to the safe house in Ede.

On Tuesday, November 14, Olmsted finished up what work he could and explained to Cor Hilbrink and Daan how to maintain his card index file. During the day, the courier arrived as expected with Olmsted's instructions. The rendezvous with the wine dealer's car, a black 1940 Chevrolet, was to take place near the village of Raalte, at a railroad crossing over the highway to Zwolle. He was to be there no later than eight on Thursday morning and was to be accompanied by another person who was to wear a light-colored raincoat and was to position himself three hundred yards beyond the railroad crossing in the direction of Zwolle. This would serve as an indication to the driver that Olmsted was in position up ahead and that the car should be prepared to stop and pick him up. Olmsted decided that Toon would be the one to accompany him.

On Wednesday evening, Olmsted sat down with Toon and Ank and finalized plans for the ride to the pickup point the next morning. They all agreed that both men should be armed with pistols and grenades. Ank surprised the two men by insisting that she go with them and carry Olmsted's small black suitcase, which would be packed with intelligence documents. If they were stopped along the way by a two- or three-man German patrol, she argued, she would have a better chance of getting away, allowing the two armed men to deal with the Germans without having to worry about the suitcase. Olmsted was not in favor of her going, but Ank argued effectively that she had been working as a full member of the team and should share the risks involved. They all agreed that she would go.

Olmsted awoke to a very cold and cloudy morning on Thursday, the sixteenth. He had been told that after being picked up by the car, he might have to ride on the fender as a lookout to guard against air attacks, a precaution that was now being followed by all cars traveling in Holland. The threat of air attack came more from Allied planes than German, as British and American fighters made a practice of strafing everything that moved on the roads. The Germans had established camouflaged parking spaces every couple of hundred yards along every road, along with foxholes about every twenty-five feet for personnel to dive into during strafing attacks. Riding the fender on a bitterly cold day such as this was not something to look forward to. Olmsted bundled up in long underwear, wool pants, and an overcoat.

He joined Ank and Toon for a cup of hot tea and some bread, and then the three said goodbye to the others at the farm and set out on their bicycles at seven-fifteen. Many Dutchmen were on the road, cycling carefully over the intermittent patches of ice as they went about their daily routine. As Olmsted and Ank and Toon pedaled down the busy road, they met several truckloads of German troops on their way to relieve others who manned the many checkpoints throughout the area. Every time they passed a German vehicle, Olmsted imagined that the enemy could almost hear the papers in his briefcase beckoning them to stop and search the three cyclists.[2]

But they were not stopped, and they arrived at the rendezvous point at around seven forty-five. Toon proceeded on ahead to take up his position. To avoid appearing as though they were waiting for someone, they all began going through the motions of repairing bicycle tires, something that had become a common sight along the roads of Holland. Time seemed to drag by as they waited for the eight o'clock arrival of the car, but when the time came, no car was in sight. Olmsted decided they would wait another ten or fifteen minutes. Toon and Olmsted each kept a hand on the pistol in his pocket in case something went wrong.

At twenty minutes past eight, the three were just preparing to leave when they spotted a car approaching in the distance. As the black car drew closer, Olmsted recognized it as a 1940 Chevy, just the type they had been told to expect. Since the car was traveling alone and speedily, he thought that it surely must be the wine merchant. Then he noticed that the car began to slow after passing Toon. Olmsted turned to Ank, shook her hand, and grabbed the briefcase.

When the car rolled to a stop, a well-dressed man jumped out, startling Olmsted when he said, "So long, Pappy. Best of luck."[3] Olmsted had not immediately recognized Henk Brinkgreve, all clean and shaved and dressed in a new suit. The two friends shook hands warmly.

As the two men reviewed the bona fides phrase that Olmsted was to use at the safe house in Ede, Toon rode up on his bicycle and shook hands with both Jedburgh officers. Then Olmsted climbed into the car, relinquishing his pistol to Brinkgreve. The wine dealer had agreed to transport Olmsted under the condition that he be unarmed and that in the event they were stopped and questioned by the Germans, the wine dealer would turn the American over to the Germans, claiming that he had infiltrated the underground and had captured Olmsted. Although this would be a tough break for·Olmsted, it would allow the wine dealer to continue dealing with the Germans. Olmsted said goodbye to Henk Brinkgreve, wanting to say more than time allowed and unaware of the fact that he would never see the Dutchman again.[4]

The wine dealer got the car turned around, and they started down the road and soon were in Zwolle. The town was heavily defended, and the streets were crowded with Germans, about four for every Dutchman, Olmsted figured, more than he had ever seen in one place. Army trucks, artillery pieces, and horse-drawn wagons were everywhere. Bridges spanning the town's many canals were blocked by barbed-wire entanglements. Whenever the car came to a checkpoint, the wine merchant's papers worked like magic and they proceeded through town without difficulty, getting only cursory glances from German guards along the way. Olmsted took the opportunity to make a mental note of all the gun positions and other defensive measures as they motored along.

Eventually, the car left Zwolle behind and proceeded nine miles west along the IJssel to Kampen, a large medieval town spread along the river's southwest bank. There, they approached a large bridge where the car was well known to the guards, and they were waved through. Soon they arrived at a business address and pulled into a yard as an iron gate closed behind them.

With no gasoline available for use by civilians in occupied Holland, those few cars and trucks that were on the road were fueled by charcoal burners. Some men in the yard loaded the car's burner with new charcoal and threw in several extra bags for the trip. Olmsted remained in the car while this was being done, and several of the men in the yard came to the window of the car and wished him luck. A young man and a girl brought tea and cookies out to him.

As soon as the refueling was finished, the wine dealer got the car under way again. As the car passed German troop concentrations and gun emplacements, Pappy Olmsted noted with satisfaction the accuracy of the underground reports he had compiled and used to update his situation maps. He grew concerned, though, as the car neared the villages of Wezep and Epe, north of Apeldoorn. For it was here that the renegade Grüne Polizei (Green Police) and the Dutch SS troops were quartered.

The multinational Grüne Polizei were the thugs the Gestapo used to do their dirty work, and the Dutch people despised them. Equally hated by the loyal people of the Netherlands were the Dutch SS. Olmsted could feel an almost palpable tension in the two villages as the car passed slowly through them.

Traffic became heavy as the car approached Apeldoorn, a beautiful garden city seventeen miles north of Arnhem that was the site of a German headquarters. The charm of the place, with many homes built among the woods that grew right to the city's outskirts, even encroaching into the city itself, was spoiled by the omnipresent field gray of the Wehrmacht and the incongruous artillery emplacements. Even Het Loo, the sprawling seventeenth-century summer palace of the royal House of Orange-Nassau, with its fabulous gardens, so elegant that it was sometimes called "the Versailles of the Netherlands," was occupied by the Germans. The car passed through the city, stopped only briefly for cursory checks, and then the wine dealer drove on toward Ede.

Along the route to Ede, the car entered the village of Otterlo. Turning sharply to the right at a corner, the men saw that the street ahead was jammed with villagers. A combined force of SS, SD, and Grüne Polizei were herding several Dutchmen wearing white armbands into a group, prodding them with bayonets. Women and children cried as the men were taken away from them.

The air lookout, riding on the fender of the wine merchant's car and dressed in black leather, had enough of the appearance of an SD man that when he quickly threw up his right arm in the Nazi salute and shouted, "Heil Hitler,"[5] the villagers parted and let the car proceed. The Germans, their attention fully occupied by the men wearing the white armbands, paid little heed to the car and its occupants. As quickly as possible, the wine dealer drove through the village until they made another turn to get back on the main road.

The air lookout spotted an SS captain and once again gave the Nazi salute. The captain returned the salute but then shouted, "Halt!"[6]

Without hesitation, the wine dealer pressed the accelerator to the floor and sped off. Apparently assuming that the car had already been checked when it entered the village, the SS captain made no further attempt to stop them. Visibly shaken by the close call, the wine dealer passed around cigars to everyone to relieve the tension.

Shortly after noon, the car arrived at Ede, northwest of Arnhem. Once again the men found a town crowded with Germans, Ede being the hub of all the enemy's artillery currently engaging the Allied troops south of the Rhine. Just as the wine dealer's car crossed a set of railroad tracks at the edge of town, one of the tires went flat. For a quarter of an hour the men worked to change the tire, all the time answering questions from prying Germans and feeling the hatred of the Dutch civilians, who naturally assumed that anyone having a car on the road must be a collaborator. As soon as the tire was changed, the men piled back in the car and the wine dealer sped off.

Soon the car pulled up near the safe house, and Olmsted got out with his small suitcase. The men in the car wished him well and drove off. All around Olmsted the streets were filled with Germans and Dutch; he suddenly felt more alone than he had ever been in his life. Sixty miles separated him and his nearest friends, and he had a suitcase full of very compromising documents. His Dutch language skills were rudimentary at best, and the forged papers in his pocket were the only protection he had against arrest.

He approached the building at the address he had memorized, and his heart was doing backflips as he walked up to the front door. The entrance had been destroyed at some point and was boarded over. Olmsted knocked on it several times, but he heard no response from within the house. Several men, he noticed, were walking around to the back of the building, so he decided to follow suit. At the rear door he knocked again, and this time the door was opened by a young maid. In the very best Dutch he could muster, Olmsted recited the line he had memorized that was to serve as his bona fides, but the girl gave no indication of understanding what he meant by it. He tried a second time, and still there was no sign of comprehension. In fact, the girl was new at the house and not yet aware of everything that went on there.

Suddenly, several bursts of submachine-gun fire broke the stillness from somewhere nearby, and Olmsted ducked into the kitchen without waiting for an invitation. Then the Dutch boy who had been riding as air lookout on the wine dealer's car showed up and quickly explained to the girl who Olmsted was and why he was there. The girl took the major to meet the head of the household, a man who spoke English fluently. At last, Olmsted began to relax as the two men chatted over a cup of hot tea, and he took off his wooden shoes and warmed them by the small peat fire.

Just then, a young man entered the house and excitedly related what the shooting down the street had been all about. He explained that a woman and her two small daughters had gone downtown to receive their food ration. The little girls had made some disrespectful noise toward a pair of passing SS men, and the Germans had wheeled around and shot all three without hesitation. Then the SS troops ordered that the three bodies be left on the street for twenty-four hours as a warning to others.

While he was at the house in Ede, Major Olmsted met a man known as Pete von Arnhem. Pete already had done much work for the Allies in Arnhem, and now he was organizing the escape party that Olmsted would be joining. He briefly described to Olmsted how he planned to get the group of evaders across the river, and then he left to round up the remainder of the party. Olmsted watched as the remarkable man sped away on his motorbike dressed as a Red Cross worker.

All Pappy Olmsted could do now was wait for further instructions. While looking around the house, he found a collection of several books in English and he read for a while. In the middle of the day, he explored the house further, going into a small room at the front of the house that contained a radio workshop. As he was looking around the room, he suddenly noticed a shadow fall over the table. Olmsted looked up at the window for the source of the shadow and discovered a curious SS man who had parked his bicycle next to the house and walked around to a side door and knocked. When the door was opened, the SS man entered the living room and talked to the residents for fifteen or twenty minutes and then left. As the man was leaving, Olmsted thought he detected a gesture, a slight flip of the hand in the American's direction. Could it have been a signal to some unseen cohorts?[7] But the man of the house explained to Olmsted that the SS man was a young Dutchman who was not a true Nazi. In fact, the boy stopped by the house every week or so, and often he left some food or chocolate.

Shortly another visitor arrived, the wife of a Dutchman who had come earlier to pick up some underground newspapers. When the lady had heard from her husband that an American was at the house, she couldn't resist coming to see him. She had studied for several years in English schools and looked forward to any opportunity to speak the language again. Olmsted enjoyed talking with the woman, but he was concerned that so many people seemed to be aware of his presence. How long could it be before the Germans learned of it?

But then a uniformed nurse arrived with instructions for Olmsted. He was to accompany the nurse, who would guide him out of town and into the countryside, where he was to spend the night. He would then join the escape party the next day.

In order to travel through the towns and countryside to the place where he was to link up with the escape party, Olmsted had to adopt a disguise. He was to appear as a Dutch farmer traveling on bicycle, attired in an old pair of blue overalls and wooden shoes. He had grown a heavy beard by now, and in his mouth he held an old pipe.

Olmsted tied his satchel full of documents onto the back of an old bicycle that had no tires. Bikes without tires were not that unusual in occupied Holland and it provided some measure of security because the Germans weren't interested in confiscating tireless bicycles.

When they were ready to depart, the nurse led the way and Olmsted trailed behind at a distance of fifty to a hundred feet. At one point in their otherwise uneventful journey, as the two cycled slowly through a town, German troops joked about the old farmer on his beat-up, tireless bicycle, unaware of the treasure of documents in Olmsted's briefcase.

Once or twice along the route, Olmsted was stopped at roadblocks, where German soldiers demanded his identity card and asked him a few questions. Each time, the Germans were satisfied that he was the harmless old farmer he appeared to be and allowed him to pass through. On the main road that ran from Ede to Utrecht, they cycled past a long column of horse-drawn supply wagons, and then, a couple of miles west of Ede, they met a column of eighteen Mark V tanks headed in the direction of Arnhem. These quite likely were en route to an area southeast of Arnhem where the Germans were secretly marshaling the large armored force that would launch their Ardennes offensive, which would break through Allied lines in mid-December to start what would become known as the Battle of the Bulge.

Olmsted followed the nurse as she crossed a road and entered a farmyard about four miles west of Ede. The two were welcomed into a beautiful and well-kept farmhouse that had just been built in 1941. Olmsted was taken upstairs, where he was introduced to a Dutchman named Martin Dubois* who had jumped into Holland for the Market-Garden operation, had then returned to England, and had now been dropped back into Holland a second time with the mission of organizing

---

* Probably Abraham Dubois, a Dutchman who had parachuted into Holland with Jedburgh team Daniel II and the 101st Airborne Division.

and supervising the crossing of the large group of evaders that Olmsted was about to join. He had hoped to return to England immediately upon completion of that mission in order to keep a date with a blonde in London, but a radio message had just arrived from Special Force Headquarters directing him to remain in the Veluwe area, the area of Gelderland north of the Rhine, to assist a British officer who was working there. Dubois shared British cigarettes, chocolate, and rum with Olmsted as the two men discussed the current situation in Overijssel and Veluwe. Later, Olmsted ate supper with Dubois and a young man from a news-gathering agency known as Group Albrecht.

A column of twenty large German self-propelled guns passed by the house on the highway to Arnhem that evening, and the men sent reports of the movement to SFHQ in London and to Group Albrecht.

Later, the men listened to radio broadcasts of the BBC and the American Forces Network. At around eleven that night, they went to bed, Dubois and his friend from Group Albrecht sleeping in a second-floor room while Olmsted, because his Dutch would put everyone at risk in the event of a late night check by occupation authorities, spent a cold night on the floor of a small office on the top floor of the house. The office was illuminated with fluorescent lamps and contained all the equipment necessary to publish an underground newspaper, as well as a handsome Philips radio. Despite the chill in the room and the hard floor, Olmsted slept soundly.

On Friday, November 17, Olmsted and the two Dutchmen continued discussing the planned escape. In the afternoon, they were startled when several SS men arrived at the farm, but the Germans were only in search of milk and eggs. At around three, a man called Bill, a member of the local underground organization, arrived to guide Olmsted and Dubois to the rendezvous area. The three men said goodbye to the farmer and his family and set out on bicycles in a cold drizzle. Because of the miserable weather, they passed through roadblocks without being stopped.

As the three men neared the rendezvous area, they turned off the main road and followed several sandy paths until they arrived on the outskirts of the village of Lunteren, three miles northwest of Ede. Leaving the bikes, the men walked on through several small fields until they reached the rear of a small barnlike structure. Bill approached the shed alone while Olmsted and Dubois waited. Soon Bill gave the signal for the other two men to come forward.

When the three men entered the shed, they stared into the muzzles of several forty-fives and Sten submachine guns. The small building, roughly fourteen feet by thirty-five feet, held around fifty people, mostly British paratroopers and British and American airmen. Several Dutchmen were also present. Sten guns covered every crack and knothole, ready to open fire on any luckless German who might happen by.

The rescue operation that Olmsted had become a part of was known by British planners south of the Neder Rijn as Operation Pegasus II. An earlier rescue, Operation Pegasus, conducted in the same area on the night of October 22, had resulted in the successful retrieval of more than 150 Allied paratroopers, airmen, and others.[8]

Major Hugh Maguire of the 1st Airborne Division, who was in command of the group of evaders, recognized Dubois and indicated to the others in the barn that the three men were friends. Maguire was puzzled by Olmsted's presence, though, mistaking the American for the Dutch farmer he appeared to be and unsure why he was joining the group. A short time later, after Maguire had walked away, a British sergeant major from the 1st Airborne Division approached Olmsted and began speaking in very broken, elementary-level Dutch. He, too, had been taken in by the American's disguise. When Olmsted answered him in colloquial American English, the sergeant major appeared to be especially confused. The two men chatted briefly, and then the sergeant major attempted to take Olmsted's satchel; when the "Dutch farmer" refused to surrender it, the sergeant major went to report this suspicious activity to Major Maguire. The major came back and began to question Olmsted in the corner of the room, while all around curious British and American troops eyed Olmsted with suspicion. Eventually, Dubois helped convince the major that Olmsted was an American, just as Olmsted's U.S. Army identification card, which he was still carrying, indicated.

Several young men from the Dutch underground arrived to serve as guides for the group. In exchange for their service, they wanted weapons and rations. They also wished to have some of the British battle-dress uniforms that had been air-dropped for use by the evasion party.

Rain poured down as the men in the shed waited. Those not on guard at one of the openings sat around or slept. After dark, someone delivered hot soup. For the trip, each person received a ration of ten ounces of black bread, a chocolate bar, and five or six pieces of hard candy. This was to last the men three days, as the group expected to reach friendly territory by early Sunday morning.

Olmsted was given the task of preparing a roster of all those who had so far joined the group of evaders. Enjoying the opportunity to visit briefly with each of the men, especially when he could speak to most of them in his own language, he noted that the party included British, Canadian, and American airmen, even a Polish Spitfire pilot. There were a couple of American paratroopers and around forty British airborne troops stranded after the battle at Arnhem. The group was rounded out with a handful of Dutchmen.

At one point, Olmsted and Major Maguire chatted about the fight at Arnhem. Pappy was dumbfounded to learn that Allied planners had chosen to drop airborne forces in areas with such a large concentration of German troops, especially since he knew that the underground had diligently reported these pockets of enemy strength to the Allied intelligence staffs. Olmsted's own Jedburgh team, inserted only a week prior to the Market-Garden operation, had radioed reports on German strength and activities back to London. After Olmsted expressed his disbelief at length, Maguire asked the American if he knew who he was. Olmsted said that he did not. Maguire said, "I am the intelligence officer of the British 1st Airborne Division."[9]

At last, the time came for final preparations for moving out. The group had grown considerably larger since Olmsted's arrival, and the men were now formed into groups of fifteen to twenty, each with a designated leader. Group leaders gathered and went over the plans for the night's march, including the order in which the groups would proceed and actions to be taken if they encountered the enemy. Instructions even included what the men should do in the event of capture.

TWENTY-FIVE

PAPPY'S RETURN

Major Olmsted and 118 others had been standing in the driving rain for forty-five minutes in the early morning darkness of Saturday, November 18, 1944. They were awaiting the arrival of a group of about thirty more people who were to join them. When the group had not arrived by three in the morning, Olmsted and the others decided to set out for the Allied lines without them.

Everyone formed into a single file with their guide and Major Maguire in the lead. Next came Colonel Graeme Warrack, the ADMS (assistant director of medical services) of the British 1st Airborne Division, and his small group of medics. As ADMS, the thirty-one-year-old Warrack was the senior medical officer in the division, equal to a division surgeon in the United States Army. He had been wounded by mortar shrapnel during the fighting near the Tafelberg Hotel. Major Olmsted followed, carrying a gunnysack over his shoulder containing, among other items, a pair of wooden shoes he hoped to take as a souvenir of Holland. Then came a group of airmen and, bringing up the rear, a makeshift platoon of British paratroopers, led by Major John Coke, an officer of the KOSB* who had been captured, had his boots

* The King's Own Scottish Borderers Regiment.

stolen by the Germans, and had escaped and walked fifteen miles on bare feet. He had, of course, been stranded north of the Rhine when the 1st Airborne Division had withdrawn to the south bank and had been lucky to be found by the underground. Just forty-seven weapons were available for the entire group of evaders. Five Sten gunners accompanied those at the head of the column, two weapons each went to the British and American air force groups, and the British soldiers at the rear of the column carried the remainder. The column started out.

The night was so dark, the men had to hold hands or otherwise hold on to the man ahead to keep from becoming separated. But the darkness and the rainy weather proved a blessing as the column skirted several German artillery positions. They were able to sneak by unnoticed, and when they had to cross large highways, they encountered no traffic.

At eight in the morning, the men found a sheltered spot, a clearing that was slightly elevated from the surrounding woods, where they planned to hide out during the day. This was the rest area that had been reconnoitered by the underground earlier, and it was ideal for the purpose, being relatively secure and defendable except against a force of considerable size, and a small pond of freshwater was nearby. The guides from the underground distributed bread and jam and some chocolate from supplies they had received by parachute sometime earlier.

They would cross the river on Saturday night. The leaders posted guards around the perimeter of the rest area, and the men ate some of their rations and spent much of the day sleeping, cold and wet as they were. The American paratroopers proved to be a colorful and entertaining pair and soon were accepted as buddies by their British airborne cousins.

Major Olmsted felt fortunate to have spent so much time traveling around by bicycle over the past several weeks, for he was in much better condition than those in the group who had escaped from prisoner of war camps or slipped away from hospitals. Some of those men, having had little exercise for weeks or months, were in bad shape for the march.

Later in the afternoon, the men rehearsed movement techniques and reaction drills, agreeing on the best formation to use for the remainder of the trip, practicing the actions they would take when crossing highways or when the column was held up for some reason and what procedures they would follow once they reached the river. Major Olmsted and several other officers grew concerned that the commander of the column concentrated too many of the weapons in the rear portion of the formation. With 119 men in the column, communicating from front to rear would be a problem under the best of conditions. The officers feared that if the front of the column ran into trouble, the column would quickly disintegrate. They approached the commander and suggested a more even dispersal of the weapons, but the commander refused to change his plan.

Several of the men carried Benzedrine tablets that were used to maintain alertness when having to go long periods without sleep, and the medics in the group wanted to make sure no one took more than was needed. They collected all the Benzedrine, planning to issue one tablet per man at the halfway point in the journey.

A single map was carried by the group. Included on the map were the names of significant farms in the area, but the farm names had been blacked out, a cautionary measure to ensure that anyone in the group who was captured would be unable to tell interrogators where he had been. The group leaders gathered around the map to study the route they planned to take to the river. Major Maguire announced that the distance to be covered to reach the river was roughly six to nine miles. But Olmsted and some of the other officers judged that, given the meandering nature of the route, the distance must be closer to twenty-two miles. They confronted Maguire about the discrepancy, but Maguire told the officers that if he had told the men how far it actually was to the Rhine, many of them would have given up. Olmsted and a few of the other officers, knowing that the men would not be fooled and believing that they had a right to know the true distance, went around and shared the true distance with all subordinate leaders.[1]

That evening, Dubois arrived along with several members of the Dutch underground to join the group, though Dubois himself would remain behind. He was anxious that everything was all right and somewhat bitter about not being able to accompany the group.

Major Olmsted carried about twenty letters from men who had to remain in Holland, too sick or too far away to join the evaders. The underground had also given him some microfilm to carry out with him.

Darkness was just approaching as the long column slowly moved out at around six that evening. For the first hour or two, everything went smoothly. They were drawing close to a busy, hard-surfaced road when someone in the column discharged a single round from a Sten gun. Everyone hit the ground and remained motionless, frozen to the surface.

Each group—the British, the Dutch, and the Americans—blamed one of the others for the accidental firing.

After waiting until they were confident that no Germans had been alerted by the mishap, the men stood and moved on toward the highway. Although there was fairly heavy traffic on the road, everyone in the column made it safely across. Shortly afterward, the column halted while they awaited the arrival of a group of thirty more men who had failed to show up the night before. After a short time the group arrived, and Olmsted saw that it included several Dutchmen, among whom were a doctor and a nurse. The nurse was in uniform and wore a dark coat and had an ebony coif perched on her head. Olmsted recognized her as the nurse who had guided him to the rendezvous. Colonel Warrack gave the woman a piece of chocolate and told her to follow directly behind him and in front of Major Olmsted.[2]

The Dutchmen serving as guides for the column, now numbering about 150 people, disagreed on the best trail to follow, and soon the single-file column disintegrated somewhat into smaller clusters. At this point, the leaders had decided that they would take the guides with them across the river because of the difficulty they would have in making it safely back to their homes. On they marched, rarely talking among themselves and then only softly.

At times Major Olmsted drew alongside Colonel Warrack, who by now was holding the nurse by the hand to keep her from becoming separated. The two men talked of how lucky the group had been, remaining undetected thus far. Warrack guessed that they should be at the Rhine in another hour or two, but Olmsted didn't see how this was possible. They had still not reached some main highways and railways that needed to be crossed, and the river lay another five or six miles beyond.

Suddenly, a long stream of crimson tracer fire rose into the sky to the south. It was the signal from the Bofors guns marking the spot of the crossing, and the guides picked up the pace.[3]

Sometime around ten that night, the men heard something off to their left. It was the sound of someone walking through the woods. At first, Olmsted thought the major had decided to put out some guards to provide protection along the flanks of the column.[4] But when a brief patch of moonlight provided a glimpse of the man walking alongside the column, it was clear he wore a helmet, and no one in the march column was wearing a helmet. It was a German sentry, and by now he had seen or heard the column of evaders.

"Halt!" ordered the sentry.[5]

As one, the entire column froze in place. Silence. A few men could be heard slinking off the trail into the underbrush. Then Olmsted heard boughs breaking and branches cracking underfoot as nearly everyone in the column broke and ran off into the woods, a dense forest of young pines no more than ten or fifteen feet in height. The trees grew so close together that moving between them in daylight would have been difficult, but now a hundred men stampeded through the area.

Colonel Warrack, too weak to make a run for it, and Major Olmsted, saddled with his bulky pack, dropped to the side of the road. "Keep still, for Christ's sake," cautioned Warrack.[6] They cursed the nitwits who had broken ranks and caused so many others to panic and run off.

Soon Major Coke arrived from the head of the column. "What is all this bloody noise about?" he asked.

"They've taken fright and gone into the woods," whispered Warrack.

"Get them out quick," Coke directed. "We must go on. That sentry will give the alarm."[7]

Surely the sentry knew this was not a German patrol he had encountered. But rather than fire at the scattering men, he moved off, apparently to return to his guard station and call in an alert to his headquarters.

This was a break for the evaders, and the leaders took full advantage of it. Crawling around, they were able to reassemble some thirty-five to forty men, including the five armed men from the head of the march column and the medical group. Most of the remainder were Dutchmen. The column got under way again. They could still hear their comrades struggling in the woods to put more distance between themselves and the sentry. Now the men could also hear German trucks and half-tracks starting their engines and beginning to move about the area. The column moved several hundred yards before halting. Then they sent a patrol back to the area where the men had scattered into the woods, hoping to locate some of them and bring them back. Later, the patrol returned to report that no one had been found, but they had lost one member of the patrol when he had been shot by a sentry.

The remaining column of evaders now hid behind a small dike as a German machine-gun crew arrived and set up their gun position less than a hundred feet away. Screened by the dike, the men pulled out, unseen and unheard by the Germans.

Moving slowly through the dark Dutch countryside, the column continued for ten minutes before the guides halted the men as they approached a large road. It was the highway running between Ede and Arnhem. About thirty yards to their left, the road was blocked by a barricade. At least two guards could be seen, and Olmsted was certain the guides would have the column of men retrace their steps for a ways and then move farther down the road to find a spot to cross. But the guides whispered back word that they would proceed with the crossing here.

As the guides moved up to the road, everyone followed, placing total confidence in the guides and not wanting to be left behind. The men stepped carefully onto the broad white road, moving cautiously, but bunched up rather than moving separately. Hobnailed British boots scraped loudly as they struck the pavement.

"*Halt!*"[8]

A sentry fired his rifle, and soon there followed a burst from a submachine gun. Sten guns returned the fire. Then a light flashed on and found the group of men bunched together in the middle of the road.

Olmsted and most of the others raced the rest of the way across the road, dove down the four-foot embankment, and scampered off into the woods. The two sentries ran to the point where the men had left the road and began firing their submachine guns into the woods. But the Germans fired from the hip, and their bullets passed over the heads of the evaders, now some three or four feet below the level of the road. Bits of leaves and tree limbs, shattered by the Germans' fire, rained down on Olmsted as he rushed deeper into the forest. Then he came across Colonel Warrack.

Olmsted asked the surgeon, "Why in heck don't they shoot lower? The bullets are all going over our heads."

"I'm darn glad they aren't," Warrack responded. "Who are we to complain?"[9]

At this point, the British surgeon decided to remain behind. "Doc," as Olmsted had begun calling him, had spent weeks hiding amid straw piles after escaping from the Germans, and he was not strong enough to run any farther. He also told Olmsted that he thought he should stay to tend to the wounded. Olmsted departed to make his way to the Rhine. Colonel Warrack successfully evaded capture, eventually linking up with the Dutch underground, who hid him and cared for him until he could reach Allied lines the following spring.

Major Olmsted crawled on through the woods, across the damp ground, rain dripping from the trees overhead, until he linked up with several other members of the scattered group. The men took a chance and started across an open field, but they had not gone fifty yards before a German sentry fired a flare pistol. Most of the men hit the ground at the sound of the familiar dull pop of the gun. Others, unfamiliar with the sound, were still standing when the bright flare burst high above them. Well-trained men in such a situation would freeze, the lack of motion making their detection less likely, but some of the less experienced men panicked at their exposure. Making matters worse, they now sprinted toward Olmsted and the others who were lying motionless on the ground. Their unfortunate action drew fire from the Germans, and one or two of the men were hit.

But the Germans failed to keep the area illuminated, firing a flare only periodically. In the intervening seconds of darkness, Olmsted and the other men hustled farther away from the sentries. Random small-arms fire from the Germans continued to follow them, and on one near miss, Olmsted's satchel full of intelligence documents was shot away. Because the accuracy and amount of enemy fire were increasing, the bag had to be left behind. The documents and maps in the satchel represented weeks of intense and high-risk work on the part of Pappy Olmsted and the underground members who helped him, and now it was lost.

Two other men from the group joined Olmsted as they set out in what they hoped was a southerly direction. Flares continued to illuminate the area from time to time, forcing the men to hit the ground each time they heard the distinctive popping sound.

Eventually, the three men came to a thick stand of scrub pines, so dense that the only way a person could penetrate the growth was by crawling. Such an area of nearly impenetrable vegetation, while almost impossible to move through, was ideal for concealment, and the men advanced slowly through the undergrowth.

The men thought they saw tracer rounds in the night sky, and they wondered if it could be the Bofors gun that they had been told would fire twenty rounds northward over the river every half hour until the crossing took place. But heavy patrolling in the area by the Germans prevented them from going any farther that night. The men decided to remain hidden in the dense brush until daylight.

Sunday morning, November 19, began cold and dreary. Although the men slept well under the circumstances, they were disappointed that the crossing had not gone as planned.[10] In the daylight, Olmsted learned that one of the men with him was Corporal Hal Cook, a British para-trooper. The other was a Royal Air Force flight sergeant called Mac. When Cook saw Olmsted's face, he said, "My God, you're the last guy I expected to see this morning!"[11]

Olmsted asked what he meant, and Cook explained that he and his buddy had been tasked with keeping an eye on Olmsted. Apparently, the commander of the escape group was not convinced that Olmsted was who he claimed to be, and he had given the two men the mission of watching for any act on his part that might indicate that he was a dou-ble agent.* If Olmsted did anything questionable, the men were to shoot him. Olmsted showed Cook his United States Army identification card. The British paratrooper accepted that the mysterious man was, in fact, an American officer, and the two men got along well. Mac, the flight sergeant, complained of his sore feet after running out of his shoes during the night's excitement.

During the day, the men heard heavy firing off to the north, where a small group of paratroopers from the escape party was engaged in a fight for their lives; by late afternoon, the group was nearly wiped out.

As a result of this action, most of the Germans in the area were drawn toward the skirmish. This unplanned diversion provided an op-portunity for Olmsted, Cook, and Mac to attempt to move closer to the Neder Rijn. At around four that afternoon, the three men, equipped with the silk map and tiny compass from Mac's escape kit, crawled off in the direction they thought would take them toward the river. Inching their way through countryside that was unfamiliar to them, the men were not sure how far they were from the river, and they had no way of knowing what a small area the Allies held south of the river. Whenever they did reach the river, it had to be in just the right spot.

They left not a minute too soon, as shouts from German soldiers be-hind them indicated that the enemy was now searching the woods the men had been hiding in.

Shortly the men came to an asphalt trail running through the woods. With the German search party slowly advancing toward them, spread out at six-foot intervals and now only fifty yards away, the three evaders decided to take a chance and sprint across the path and deep into the

---

* Major Olmsted later learned that when the British officer finally returned to Lon-don at war's end, he filed a report in which he described Olmsted as "a mysteri-ous guy that calls himself an American major with the special forces."

woods on the other side. Cook checked to the left for any sign of German patrols or approaching vehicles, while Olmsted looked to the right. Both men indicated that the way was clear. All three quickly got to their feet and dashed across the trail and kept on through the woods on the south side of the path until exhaustion overcame them. In the early evening, several scarlet flares shot into the area to their rear. The men waited and rested until about seven-thirty, when darkness had fallen, and then they started off again, still having eaten nothing, nerves keyed up from the uncertainty of what lay ahead. Now the men moved more quickly but avoided the heavily patrolled paths.

Soon they came upon a long stretch of clearing in the woods, through which ran the railroad to Arnhem, the dual set of tracks mounted on a twenty-to-thirty-foot-high embankment. Patrols could be seen watching over the railway. Crawling at an agonizingly slow pace, Olmsted led the way, inching his way up and over the embankment. While crossing one of the tracks, he reached forward, exploring the area immediately ahead with his hand, and froze when his fingers touched a thin slack wire that he found was attached to a booby trap. Aware of the device and careful to alert the others to it, he guided the other two men safely over the tracks. Then Olmsted slowly began his descent down the slope on the south side of the embankment. Mac followed him, and Cook went last. A sentry box stood about a hundred yards down the track, close enough that the three men would be in full view of an alert guard, but the cold and the rain kept the sentry sheltered inside the box. Still, the slightest noise might alert him, so the men moved at a snail's pace, stopping at the least sign of trouble. Mac, following closely behind Olmsted, accidentally brushed the American's shoe with his hand. Olmsted froze, thinking it was a signal, and Cook, in the rear, was sure that Olmsted had seen something. After lying still for about twenty minutes, the three men continued their slow advance down the slope. By the time they reached the wood line at the bottom of the southern embankment, an hour and a half had passed since the men had started up the opposite side.

Soon after entering the thick woods, the men discovered that they were in the middle of a vast supply dump, sheltered from aerial view by the forest. Workers in the area were busy, and the sentries were generally inactive and inattentive, so the men had no trouble continuing a mile or two, unmolested, until they had put the dump behind them.

Farther on, the men entered another wooded area, but here the

Germans had put the thick stand of trees to another use. All underbrush had been cleared from the forest floor as far as the men could see, and every tree had been stripped of branches to a height of ten feet. Just as the men began speculating on the strange sight, German voices shouted commands to fire.

Certain that the orders were meant to direct fire at them, the three men dived to the ground. But rather than hearing the crack of small-arms fire, the men were stunned by a volley of discharges from a battery of self-propelled eighty-eights. Two more volleys quickly followed before the big guns pulled out and left for another firing position. At once, the men understood that the battery's hasty departure was a defensive measure. Allied counterbattery fire would soon be slamming into the woods where they lay. The men sprang up and ran and were relieved when the first Allied volley overshot the area. Before the next volley arrived, they were out of danger and moving to the south.

Yet another obstacle lay ahead, as the men exited the woods and encountered a labyrinth of trenches laced with barbed wire. Unarmed and weary, the men worked their way through the system, never sure that the trenches were completely unoccupied.[12]

At around two in the morning on Monday, November 20, the men came upon a deserted village and concluded that it must be the one they had been directed to skirt to the left during their briefing. The men moved to the edge of town, where they ran into an eight-foot-high woven-wire fence topped by an angled bank of three strands of barbed wire. They began searching for an opening through the fence, but then a door opened in a nearby house and a beam of light scanned the area. Then came the sound of the door closing, and the men heard several people approaching on the road.

Somehow Olmsted, Mac, and Cook scrambled over the fence and dropped to the ground on the opposite side. Mac landed on a glass-covered garden plot, noisily shattering the glass, but no fire came from the road at the edge of town.

The evaders pushed on for a short time until they came to a field. Exhaustion overcame the men, so they lay down in the early morning darkness to rest. They had eaten nothing for days. Cook tried munching some leaves but quickly gave up in disgust. He then began digging and soon discovered that they were in a turnip field, so the men sat and ate a few raw old turnips.

As soon as the men felt revived enough to move on, they marched on through the night, evading patrols, stumbling through more trenches and more wire, largely unaware of the resulting cuts and tears because of the numbing cold.

Just when they were sure they would never reach the Neder Rijn, the men spotted red tracer fire from a Bofors gun directly ahead of them. Could it be the Bofors gun that was to signal their crossing site? It seemed impossible to the men that they would have arrived at exactly the right spot. On they struggled, through more wire, until they reached a thick tree line. Beyond the stand of trees, visible through gaps in the woods, the men saw water. They had, it seemed, reached the north bank of the Neder Rijn.

The men filtered through the trees until they came to a sharp drop-off, where the bank, covered with oaks and thick brush, sloped steeply to the water's edge sixty feet below. Olmsted started down the bank, followed by Cook and Mac. Descending slowly in the dark, Olmsted had inched his way well down the slope when he took a step and suddenly broke through a thin surface, falling until he hit the ground. Mac and Cook also fell and landed on Olmsted. The men discovered that they had broken through a covering of camouflage netting above what had been a gun position. The position appeared to have been only recently abandoned—the familiar scent of cordite still lingered in the air—and no one seemed to be in the area. The three weary men walked along the shoreline to a small bridge, where they sat down and looked into the darkness, across what they assumed to be the wide Lower Rhine, wondering if anyone on the southern bank would see their signal.[13]

Luck had been with the three weary men sitting on the north bank of the Neder Rijn when they had, by chance, fallen in together during the hectic scramble for safety a couple of days earlier. Hal Cook had been designated a signalman during the planning leading up to the evasion operation. He therefore carried a red flashlight for that purpose. As a security measure, though, the signalmen had not been given the letter of the alphabet that was to be flashed in Morse code to the rescuers on the south bank of the river. Likewise, those who were told the correct letter were not given the physical means of transmitting the signal. This way, if a lone signalman was captured, he would be unable to signal, under duress, in the hands of the Germans, who would then lie in ambush awaiting the rescue boats. Pappy Olmsted, as it turned out, was one of those who knew the correct letter to be flashed. If either Cook or Olmsted had been absent from the trio, no signal could have been sent.

Cook began signaling with the flashlight, but no response was detected from the opposite bank. Discouraged at the failure to make contact with anyone and growing anxious as daylight approached, Cook walked off to explore further to ensure that they were in the right place. Olmsted and Mac struck out in different directions, remaining close enough to hear each other. Quickly the men discovered that they had been sitting not on the bank of the Neder Rijn, but on the bank of one of a network of lateral canals. The river was another three hundred yards to the south.

Carefully, the men began working their way toward the river, and as dawn approached, they grew fearful of being shot from either side of the river. Olmsted discovered the wreckage of an old boat. Again the men attempted to get the attention of someone on the southern bank with their flashlight signal, but still to no avail. As they explored the area for shelter from the cold and rain, they met a Polish Spitfire pilot called Toots, who described how he had failed in an attempt to paddle across the river on a board that morning. Dejected, the four men found a spot to try to get some rest, although the disagreeable weather ensured that they would not be comfortable. Hungry, soaked, and chilled to the bone, Olmsted searched every pocket for stray crumbs and found none. Then he lay down, with a cushion he found in the wrecked boat, and slept until five in the afternoon.

It was growing dark again, the men having slept through most of the day, and still there was no sign that anyone on the opposite bank knew they were there. The men decided to try a more bold approach. They walked to the water's edge and began waving and yelling and whistling.

Immediately, someone on the south bank shouted, "Take it easy. We'll be over after dark."[14]

When the 101st Airborne Division's operation at Eindhoven came to an end, the division had been moved to an area between the Waal and the Neder Rijn that the paratroopers called "the Island." Arnhem was to the north and Nijmegen to the south. Many times the Germans attacked in an attempt to dislodge the Americans from the area.[15] On this night, an element of the division prepared to conduct an operation to rescue Allied servicemen stranded on the north bank of the Neder Rijn.

At last the four evaders on the north bank of the river had contacted someone who might come to their rescue. After waiting two interminably long hours in the icy rain, the men grew excited as the opening salvo of an Allied artillery barrage began, obviously to cover the imminent crossing operation. An assault boat could be heard launching. The engine stalled briefly, then came to life again. Soon the men on the north bank saw a small boat emerge from the dusk, the engine chugging as the craft approached and came to a halt at the shore immediately in front of them.

Olmsted heard the challenge—"Red"—repeated twice. Then came the unmistakable click of an M1 carbine taken off safety. Through parched lips, Olmsted whispered the response: "Beret."[16]

Aboard the small craft, which was operated by Canadian engineers, were several American paratroopers armed with carbines and tommy guns. A lieutenant among them ordered, "Hands above your heads and come slow single file."[17]

After the previous days and nights of hunger and wet cold, the four bone-weary evaders responded with an alacrity unusual to the young lieutenant. The men, elated, half-sick, half-starved, spoke not a word but kept their hands above their heads.

Soldiers helped the evaders into an assault boat. Then, still under the cover of the British artillery barrage, the boat drew away from the shore and slowly chugged its way to the south bank of the Neder Rijn. Once ashore, paratroopers escorted the four evaders, hands still raised above their heads, to a forward battalion command post located in the ruins of a house. They went down the stairs to the dingy basement, past a small group of GIs heating K-rations and coffee over a radiant coke fire. Pappy Olmsted thought it looked pretty good.[18]

The men were led into a brightly lit room furnished with a field table and a few benches. Chocolate bars and a bottle of rum sat mockingly on the table. Mac, the British air force sergeant, took a seat at one of the benches, eager to get off his feet after walking for several days without shoes, having lost them in the dash to safety from a German roadblock. Toots, the Polish Spitfire pilot, sat on another bench while Hal Cook, the British paratrooper, and Olmsted eyed the chocolate and rum. But the men were quickly escorted into an adjoining room, where a very bright light shone on them as a British intelligence officer began asking them many questions. It was the beginning of what promised to be a lengthy interrogation.

Just then an American officer, a lieutenant from the 101st, entered the room, took one look at the four scruffy interrogation subjects, and said, "I'm a —— if that isn't Captain Olmsted."[19]

Blinded by the light, Olmsted was unable at first to recognize the man behind the voice. When the officer stepped forward, Olmsted saw that it was a man he had gone through jump school with back at Fort Benning. They had joined the same regiment in the summer of 1942. Now, two years later, the lieutenant had led the rescue party that had brought Olmsted and the others in the assault boat across to friendly territory. He personally vouched for Major Olmsted, and together, the two American officers succeeded in convincing the British officer that the remaining three evaders were Allied servicemen as well, just as they claimed to be, and not cleverly disguised enemy infiltrators.

The next stop for Olmsted, Cook, Mac, and Toots was to be a Canadian army hospital in Nijmegen. While awaiting a truck to take them there, the men enjoyed the chocolate and rum and caught up on news of the war, especially the recent Market-Garden operation. When the truck finally arrived, the men were bundled in blankets, put in the back, and warned against smoking.

In Nijmegen, the truck delivered the men to a large Dutch school building that had been converted to a military hospital by the Germans and was now administered by the Canadian army. Inside, the men enjoyed a bath after having gone months without one. Mac was afraid to look at his feet, and he asked an orderly to remove what was left of his tattered socks. Surprisingly, after crossing twelve miles of Dutch countryside without shoes, struggling through trenches and barbed-wire entanglements, and breaking through a glass-covered growing plot, his feet bore only one cut and a few scratches. Still, he refrained from putting his feet in the hot bathwater.

Later, the men were sitting comfortably in their beds when an attractive Canadian nurse arrived and said, "We have three of your buddies here who arrived two nights ago. They'll be in to see you in a minute."[20]

Soon the door opened, and three men in long white hospital gowns entered. They turned out to be two Dutchmen and a Royal Air Force sergeant who had been a crewmate of Mac's. Of the approximately 150 members of the Pegasus II evasion party, only these 7 had reached the relative safety of Allied territory on the south bank of the Neder

Rijn.* The men sat and smoked Players cigarettes, each group sharing its experiences with the other, and soon the nurse brought tea and biscuits.

Although a doctor had given the nurse strict orders that the men were to have nothing more to eat than the tea and biscuits—a precaution felt necessary because they had not been eating regularly— Olmsted persuaded the nurse to bring him some real food. She went to the kitchen and returned with a meal of stew, potatoes, bread, and raisin pie. Olmsted ate it all, then crawled between clean sheets and slept for the next twelve hours.

On awakening, Olmsted and the others learned that they were isolated from other patients in the hospital and forbidden to communicate with them. A nurse brought the men hot water and soap and razors and told them to quickly shave and get cleaned up; they were to have visitors.

Shortly, several intelligence officers and an artillery officer from the 101st Airborne arrived and began another detailed interrogation. After answering the questions as best they could, Cook and Olmsted eagerly volunteered to accompany 101st Airborne patrols back to the northern side of the river, but medical officers refused to allow it. The intelligence officers then decided that Major Olmsted would be flown to London for further debriefing. Several days later, all seven men were taken to Eindhoven, where they boarded an RAF transport plane that took them to England.

In London, the men went their separate ways, and Olmsted immediately ran into difficulty trying to get a room. It was late in the day, after normal business hours, and Olmsted's appearance made his claim to be an American officer unconvincing. His battle-dress uniform was torn and muddy, he wore British Army boots that were too large and unmatched, and he had no cap. Such was the lot of a special forces operator returning from the field. He was taken to a place where repatriated escapers and evaders were processed. There he received a new uniform, and arrangements were made for his formal debriefing. Pappy's ordeal was over.

* In his 1963 book, *Travel by Dark* (London: Harvill Press), Graeme Warrack, the British medical officer who had been in Olmsted's group during the attempt, described (p. 165) the seven successful evaders as "the American major [Olmsted], a Pole, two guides, and three others." Most of those who began the journey, Warrack reported, were recaptured. John Coke was killed.

The same could not be said for one of Pappy's teammates on Jedburgh team Dudley. Sergeant John "Bunny" Austin had been in a safe house in Luttenberg, Overijssel, for four days when German troops began searching houses in the neighborhood on November 18, 1944. When German soldiers entered the safe house, they found Austin's radio and codebook, two Colt forty-five-caliber automatic pistols, and three hand grenades. They immediately arrested Austin and the resistance man serving as his lookout and imprisoned them in the town of Zwolle.[21]

TWENTY-SIX

MISSING IN ACTION

One evening in early November 1944, a telegram arrived at the house at 1057 South 21st Street in Decatur, Illinois, the home of Arville Todd, Lieutenant Allan Todd's father. From the War Department in Washington, the cable read:

> THE SECRETARY OF WAR DESIRES ME TO EXPRESS HIS DEEP RE-GRET THAT YOUR SON FIRST LIEUTENANT HARVEY A. TODD HAS BEEN REPORTED MISSING IN ACTION SINCE SEVENTEEN SEP-TEMBER IN FRANCE. IF FURTHER DETAILS OR OTHER INFORMA-TION ARE RECEIVED YOU WILL BE PROMPTLY NOTIFIED.[1]

Mr. Todd was probably unaware at the time of the cable's error in citing France, rather than the Netherlands, as the location where his son had been last seen. Early notification to the next of kin of service members reported to be missing in action was one of the first steps taken by the Casualty Branch of the War Department's Office of the Adjutant General. Following such notification, every effort was made by the branch to determine the whereabouts and status of the missing soldier. The second War Department cable arrived on the morning of November 24 and notified Mr. Todd:

REPORT JUST RECEIVED THROUGH THE INTERNATIONAL RED
CROSS STATES THAT YOUR SON FIRST LIEUTENANT HARVEY A.
TODD IS A PRISONER OF WAR OF THE GERMAN GOVERNMENT.
LETTER OF INFORMATION FOLLOWS FROM PROVOST MARSHAL
GENERAL.[2]

Not long afterward, Arville Todd, grief-stricken at the news of his
son, and still under the impression that Allan had been captured in
France, sat down and composed the following poem:

Missing in Action

> *Old Top, they say you're missing,*
> *That's what we just have heard,*
> *In action over yonder*
> *So comes the cruel word,*
> *In battle's action, missing,*
> *Beyond the rolling sea*
> *But Oh, my prayers are fervent*
> *That you'll come back to me.*
>
> *In vision once I saw you*
> *There in the land of France*
> *Surrounded by the Nazi;*
> *It seemed you had no chance;*
> *Few buddies still were with you,*
> *Your plane had failed to land,*
> *Or else you were prevented*
> *From meeting it as planned.*
>
> *The Nazi had an inkling*
> *That you were there about,*
> *And though his searching parties*
> *Had scoured the land throughout,*
> *In force he failed to find you*
> *Though some, by two or one,*
> *Did stumble on your hiding,*
> *Their life's last race was run.*

Then, in a shaded vineyard
From 'neath the plumaged vine
You watched the Nazi marching
In never ending line;
'Twas there a patriot saw you
And later did provide
Some help and information
And places where to hide.

My heart is numb and heavy,
My mind is dull and slow,
But God is in His Heaven,
Just that, I surely know;
He watches o'er His children
And in His own good way
Will see them not forsaken;
To Him I humbly pray.

My prayer, that He'll be with you,
To strengthen soul and heart,
Bring comfort with His presence
And from you not depart;
That He will find us humble,
And if His will it be
At last to bring you safely
Through war's wild storms to me.[3]

Meanwhile, the American prisoners of war held at Oflag 64 in northern Poland experienced a cold and isolated Thanksgiving. On the eve of the holiday, the Germans issued each man a Red Cross food parcel, the first in several weeks. In preparation for a traditional holiday feast, at least as well as could be prepared under the circumstances, each prisoner donated an item from his parcel to the mess hall crew. Potato rations were cut back on the day before the holiday, and through black market purchase, the cooks also arranged for several cans of peas. From the Red Cross came an extra supply of canned meat in the form of Spam and Prem.

When the prisoners arrived at the mess hall at the appointed hour on

Thanksgiving Day, they were delighted to find the large dining room decked out in harvesttime decorations crafted by the kitchen crew. After a prayer led by the chaplain, the men sat down to tables adorned with centerpieces and place settings, and unusually large servings of food were delivered to each table. For once, the men ate until they were full, and then they shared cigarettes and enjoyed the morale-boosting camaraderie, however brief, and lost themselves in thoughts of home and family.[4]

As autumn turned to winter, the weather in northern Poland worsened. Days were gray and overcast, the sun hid behind gloomy clouds, and frequent rains soon turned to snow. Schubin would have a white Christmas.

The holiday season did not promise to be a happy time for Allan Todd; Christmas in captivity never is. The nearest thing to a Christmas present he received was a Red Cross Christmas parcel issued on December 19. Red Cross parcels had become scarce—it was later learned that the Germans had been withholding them—and the prisoners had eaten the last of their Red Cross food several days earlier. With the bitter cold weather and lack of food, the weak men had little energy to do anything but lie on their bunks day after day. But the arrival of the Christmas Red Cross packages proved to be a tonic, raising their spirits. The men decided to save the Red Cross parcels and pool the food for a Christmas feast.[5]

Colonel Goode arranged with Oberst Schneider to allow a prisoner to go into Schubin to buy a Christmas tree for each prisoner barracks. When the trees were delivered, the men of each barracks set to work decorating them. Tin cans from Red Cross parcels were fashioned into a variety of ornaments, and small scraps of paper were strung together to be wound around the trees.

On Christmas Eve, the men put together a meal of soup and sandwiches, potatoes with gravy, and cabbage provided by the camp kitchen. Allan Todd got one turkey sandwich, four cheese sandwiches, and two jam sandwiches. The feast was topped off with fruit bars, cherry pie, and coffee, and the camp Glee Club sang carols as the men ate.[6] At nine that evening, the Catholic chaplain served Communion in the dining hall; a Protestant service was held in the theater at midnight. Oberst Schneider had relaxed the normal lights-out schedule to accommodate the services.

On Christmas Day, the prisoners enjoyed a dinner much like the one served at Thanksgiving. Bob Rankin's Orchestra put on a musical program with six performances at the Little Theater, the shows running continuously throughout the afternoon and evening because of the theater's limited capacity.[7] Hits such as "White Christmas" proved as appropriate as they were popular, for more than two feet of snow had accumulated outside. Several German guards attended the performances and enjoyed them, applauding and thanking the orchestra afterward.[8]

But Christmas was a particularly unhappy time for the prisoners, a period of almost unbearable despair and agonizing depression. The Germans played Christmas music over the public address system, which went to speakers in every barracks, and the men longed for home and thought about their families. Sagging morale was not helped by the war news coming from "the Bird," as no great progress was evident on any front. The prisoners had learned of the massive German offensive in the Ardennes that had begun on December 16. American and British forces were still fighting to contain the attack in Belgium in what came to be known as the Battle of the Bulge. It seemed the war would never end.

No doubt feeling stronger and in better spirits as a result of the Christmas dining, Todd tried to escape from camp on Christmas night. Several prisoners, according to Todd's later account, had planned the escape. As expected, when the time arrived, many of the guards had been drinking all day and were less vigilant than usual. But the extra food received that day made some of the escape plotters less eager to break out, and in the end, only Todd and two others made the attempt. Unfortunately, the Germans were alert enough to stop the escape. For his part in the attempt, Todd was placed in solitary confinement.[9]

Todd was taken to the administrative building across the street from the main gate on December 28. He was to have been tried by court-martial that day, but Colonel Goode succeeded in having the trial postponed until January 3 so that a Swiss representative could be present to ensure a fair trial.[10]

———

While Todd awaited his trial, the Oflag 64 theater group performed their production of the hit Broadway comedy *Room Service* on New Year's Eve. Many of the prisoners played cards and bashed what food parcels they had, and they hoped that the new year would see an end to the war. Some walked about outside under the full moon as the Germans delayed the lights-out call until one in the morning.

During these final days of December, the prisoners learned of the tragic outcome of an incident that had occurred in the camp the previous July, four months before Allan Todd's arrival. In late July, a German sergeant had entered the camp and proceeded to Colonel Goode's office in the White House. Goode was out at the time, and the sergeant found two prisoners, Lieutenant Colonel Schaefer and First Lieutenant Schmidt, in the colonel's office. The sergeant carried several placards printed with a statement defaming citizens of the United States and Great Britain, labeling the people of those countries thieves and liars and murderers and describing them as subhuman. He told the two American officers that he had orders to post the placards throughout the camp.

Lieutenant Colonel Schaefer objected, telling the sergeant that such action was in violation of the Geneva Conventions. Schaefer then instructed Lieutenant Schmidt to stand in the doorway and block the sergeant's exit. Schmidt did so and did not move out of the doorway until Schaefer told him to do so after the German sergeant touched the lieutenant.

The result of this seemingly minor altercation was that Schaefer and Schmidt were brought before a German court-martial and both were sentenced to death. Schaefer was shipped to another camp following the trial, and the men at Oflag 64 never saw him again. Schmidt was placed in solitary confinement at Oflag 64 while he awaited execution.[11]

On January 3, 1945, according to Todd's journal, he was taken out of solitary only long enough to be tried. A German colonel presided over the trial. Todd stood at attention as the charges were read, the German colonel rose and read a typed order: "We, the high court of the German Third Reich, find you guilty of crimes against the Third Reich. Punishment for these crimes is death by a firing squad. Execution will be tomorrow morning, January 4, at five a.m. on this post."[12]

Colonel Goode, who was ordered to witness the execution, intervened, standing and declaring, "You cannot do this! This officer cannot be executed for thirty days. According to the Geneva Convention, we have thirty days to appeal."[13] The German colonel agreed to the appeal and postponed the execution for thirty days from December 28, the originally scheduled trial date. Todd was returned to solitary, where he would remain, under constant guard, for the next twenty-four days.[14]

TWENTY-SEVEN

THE LONG MARCH

Prisoners at Oflag 64 followed news of the fighting around Bastogne in Belgium on their clandestine radio known as "the Bird," but soon news of another attack brought hope to the men confined at the frozen camp in northern Poland.

On January 12, 1945, the Soviet Union, America and Britain's ally to the east, launched its winter offensive on a 750-mile front, with nearly three million troops, from positions more than a hundred miles east of Schubin. Red Army tanks and infantry attacked from bridgeheads on the Vistula River seized the previous summer. Marshal Georgi Zhukov, commanding the First Belorussian Front, waited two days for better weather before launching his attack through a heavy mist on the morning of the fourteenth. Within three days his forces had encircled and entered Warsaw, the Polish capital, only to find it largely abandoned by the Germans. Soviet armored forces took advantage of the good road network in western Poland to advance up to thirty miles a day, while infantry units made eighteen to twenty miles.[1] One element of Zhukov's command, the 2nd Guards Tank Army, drove hard to the northwest, directly toward the Polish town of Schubin.

Word of the Soviet offensive soon reached the German staff at Oflag 64. As the Soviet juggernaut moved into East Prussia and western

Poland, Adolf Hitler Strasse, the cobblestone street paralleling the perimeter fence of Oflag 64, became crowded with German civilians moving westward. Around the clock, prisoners heard their wagons crunch by on the snow-packed road. News of the Red Army's progress drove the Germans to a decision to relocate the prisoners of Oflag 64 to a camp at Hammelburg, Germany.

As Soviet forces drew nearer, it became a stressful time for guards and prisoners alike. For the prisoners, rumors about their fate proliferated. Of course, they looked forward to being liberated by the Russians, but would the Germans allow that to happen? And just how friendly would their Soviet allies be? No one really knew.

On the cold and blustery evening of January 19, many prisoners took shelter in the Little Theater to enjoy an entertaining variety show. Next morning, the camp staff made an announcement, informing the POWs of the impending move, though no mention was made of their destination. The prisoners were told that the camp was to be evacuated in twenty-four hours, at which time they would be marched about five miles to a town called Exin to board a train for movement farther away from the danger of the front lines. They were to have all personal items packed and be prepared to leave on short notice.

According to U.S. Army records, the prisoner population at Oflag 64 that morning included 1,459 officers, 2 warrant officers, and 136 enlisted men.[2] Those who were medically unable to march were instructed to make preparations to be evacuated as soon as transportation could be arranged.

With soaring spirits, the men spent the rest of the day rigging makeshift backpacks from old clothing and packing up their possessions. Older kriegies had the most to pack—bundles of letters, accumulated clothing, and toilet articles. Added to this was a Red Cross food parcel that the Germans now issued to each man.

All day long, the prisoners watched a ragged column of civilian refugees from the east trudge by on the highway just outside camp. The exodus had begun about a week earlier with only a few horse carts. Mostly they were German families who had settled in occupied Poland, and now they fled in fear of the advancing Russians. They had terrifying stories to tell of what was happening in East Prussia, where Soviet troops were taking their revenge on German civilians. With each passing day, more and more people and vehicles crowded the road. Wagons loaded down with furniture and other belongings were often pulled by handsome teams of draft horses. Some people had smaller carts pulled by a single horse. Others simply pulled sleds or pushed wheelbarrows or baby carriages. Day and night, the procession continued. Now the most popular phrase uttered by prisoners throughout the camp was, "Come on, Russkies!"[3]

That afternoon, two POWs went for a walk on the snow-packed exercise path around the camp perimeter. One of the men commented, "Them Russkies better get the lead out of their ass or we'll all be gone."

"At the rate they're going," replied the other officer, "they could be here today. Sixty miles away yesterday, I heard forty-two this morning."[4]

As the two men passed a guard tower, they noticed one of the guards staring off toward the eastern horizon. One of the prisoners yelled up at the guard, "Russkie comin'—ya!"[5] The guard looked down at the Americans and laughed.

On a gray and bitterly cold Sunday morning, January 21, several devout POWs attended a brief mass. Then all prisoners deemed fit to march, totaling around fifteen hundred, fell out to the camp assembly area for roll call.[6] They formed up in platoons, in five ranks, as they normally did during *Appell* to facilitate a quick count by the Germans. Even Lieutenants Schmidt and Todd were released from solitary confinement and, though still awaiting execution, were permitted to rejoin their platoons for the march.

This was no normal *Appell;* it was a final head count, and it took an unusually long time to complete. Some ten to twenty men had gotten permission from Colonel Goode to hide out in a tunnel that had been dug below the White House, hoping to escape once the column had departed camp. The Germans, unable to come up with the proper count of prisoners, searched the camp but could not find the missing men. The temperature hovered around ten degrees below zero, and six inches of snow covered the ground. As cold as it was, though, the prisoners welcomed any delay that might increase their chances of being liberated by the Russians. Rumors that morning had the Russians only twenty-three miles from the camp.[7] Some of the men shuffled about in formation, moving from one platoon to another to make the count more difficult for the Germans and thus further delay their departure.

At ten o'clock, after a fruitless search for the missing men, Oberst Schneider decided the movement could be delayed no longer. He called the men to attention and addressed them briefly through an interpreter, reminding the prisoners that they were officers and that he expected them to act like it when they left the camp. He further expressed his concern about getting the prisoners out of harm's way, apparently certain that the Russians represented a danger to Germans and POWs alike.

Guards barked commands, and the prisoners began shuffling in a long column of platoons, five abreast, through the main gate and out of camp, past the evil barbed wire, now glazed in ice, that they had longed for many months to put behind them. Colonel Goode led the formation with a set of bagpipes that had arrived in a YMCA package tucked under his arm. He was unable to play the pipes, but concealed inside was "the Bird," the camp's secret radio. Close by were the members of his staff. Also at the head of the column was Lieutenant Todd, kept under special guard while awaiting his scheduled January 27 execution. Then came the prisoner of war platoons in numerical order. Trailing behind the procession was an old truck, chugging along under the scant power of a wood-burning engine, carrying supplies and extra guards to relieve those marching alongside the prisoners. A sense of excitement was evident throughout the POW column, even though the men had no idea of their ultimate destination. They were going someplace new.

Oberst Schneider and Hauptmann Menner climbed into a small car and followed after the procession of marching men, weaving through groups of prisoners and refugees to get to the head of the column.

Hospital patients and other prisoners who were unable to march, along with doctors and orderlies to look after them, a total of ninety-one men, remained in camp until transportation could be arranged. As the stay-behinds watched their fellow prisoners march off into the distance, the Germans turned over the keys to the camp to Father Stanley Brach, the American chaplain. Father Brach had been the 1st Armored Division chaplain in North Africa and had been captured while attending to wounded soldiers and administering last rites. Now he held mass for the prisoners left behind, encouraging the men to remain confident and praying for their friends who were marching through freezing weather to an unknown destination. That night, the Americans remaining at Oflag 64 heard muffled explosions off to the east.

Once the column turned onto Adolf Hitler Strasse, the formation narrowed from five to four abreast and shortly disintegrated further into two single files as the prisoners competed for space on the flanks of the endless refugee caravan. Stretched out in a mile-long column, the disheveled prisoners, bundled up in every rag they owned and with blanket rolls coiled around their shoulders, were nearly indistinguishable from the refugees. With their heads wrapped in towels or blankets or sweaters against the penetrating cold and swirling snow, the men shuffled along, leaning forward into the wind. Snow three feet deep lined the road, and in places there were drifts twice that high. Below freezing temperatures would persist for the next ten days. Any efforts to maintain platoon groups were soon abandoned, and the march formation became further disorganized.

German guards, nearly all in their forties and fifties, had a hard enough time just keeping up and showed little interest in enforcing march discipline. While they had been eating much better than the prisoners, they were generally older, having been assigned as prisoner of war camp guards in lieu of frontline duty because of their age. It was primarily for this reason that the column of prisoners was given frequent rest breaks.

One platoon commandeered an abandoned one-horse wagon along the road, piled their few belongings on the wagon, and took turns pulling or pushing it along the road. Others found small sleds to use in hauling their packs. As the march continued, men struggled with their packs, and heavier articles were tossed to the side of the road. Only blankets and food were considered essential.

The column pushed on for several miles due west to the town of Exin* and continued for a mile or two into the open countryside beyond the town. There was no train to board, as the prisoners had been told back at Oflag 64. In midafternoon, the POWs as well as several of the refugee wagons entered a quadrangle formed by buildings on a large dairy farm. Guards divided the prisoners into groups and put each group in one of the large barns for the night. Some of the men shared stalls with cows or calves, others bedded down in a heated barn that was nearly full of sheep. Unconditioned to such marching after many months in confinement, the prisoners suffered from sore feet and aching, cramping muscles.[8]

The plight of the men from Oflag 64 would only worsen in the days and weeks ahead. Men who had endured the boredom and loneliness of

---

* Kcynia is the Polish name of the town the Germans called Exin and is the name identifying the town on maps today. Throughout this chapter, I refer to towns in Poland by the German name that was in use at the time. Polish names for those towns are shown at the beginning of the notes for this chapter in the back of the book.

lengthy confinement in a foreign land now faced a new challenge—that of surviving a forced march of unknown duration in the harshest winter weather Europe had witnessed in decades. Days became a routine of trudging for hours through snow and slush and biting cold wind. Watery soup for breakfast, ersatz coffee or cabbage soup at midday, and perhaps a piece of bread at day's end. Prisoners paired off into two-man buddy teams, walking together and eating together.

Most days concluded with the men crowding into barns along the route of march until every loft and stable was filled to capacity. At night the men removed their shoes, placing one in an armpit and the other in their crotch to allow body heat to warm and dry them. It was one small measure they could take to help prevent trench foot. Buddies who had marched together all day now shared the warmth of a double layer of blankets.

When a loft filled to capacity with POWs, the sleeping men left a narrow "aisle" for others to get to the ladder and make their way outside to relieve themselves during the night. In the darkness, it could take a man an hour to complete the trip outside and back again, and often those sleeping next to the aisle were stepped on. One night, a man could be heard to complain, "I don't mind you stepping on my face, but DON'T STAND THERE."[9]

Early on the morning after their halt near Exin, guards began another ritual that would become a routine way of beginning each day. Germans came through the barns shouting, *"Raus!"* and *"Schnell!"* and jabbing fixed bayonets randomly into the hay and straw in search of prisoners trying to hide. Some of the guards fired their submachine guns into the larger piles of hay. All prisoners were hustled out of the barns and into formation as quickly as possible. Outside, the fields were cloaked in a glistening blanket of frost as far as a man could see. The Germans allowed medical personnel among the prisoners to hold sick call to determine if any of the men were physically unable to continue marching. When they had completed their quick exams, the doctors identified some men to be formed into a slow-marching group and another 171 who were simply unable to continue at all. These men were left at Wegheim, the next town to the west of Exin, to await transportation.[10] A few other prisoners succeeded in hiding in the barns or other buildings to remain behind.

Platoons formed up at around eight-thirty, and by nine they were marching again, traveling in a northwesterly direction through the vast

Dutch people welcome paratroopers of the 101st Airborne Division's 506th Parachute Infantry Regiment. *(National Archives)*

Members of the Dutch resistance near Eindhoven provide information to men of the 101st Airborne Division. *(U.S. Army photograph)*

C-47 Skytrain troop carriers
(called Dakotas by the British)
just prior to discharging paratroopers of the 82nd Airborne
Division's 508th Parachute Infantry Regiment over Drop Zone
T in Holland on September 17,
1944. (*U.S. Army photograph*)

Serial A-7 of the 82nd Airborne Division's 505th Parachute Infantry, with the division command group and Jedburgh team Clarence, jumps over Drop Zone N near
Groesbeek, Holland, on September 17, 1944. (*National Archives*)

Captain Arie Bestebreurtje
of Jedburgh team Clarence
(*second from right*) chats
with other officers of the
82nd Airborne Division
command group shortly
after parachuting into
Holland. General Gavin
returns an officer's salute
behind Bestebreurtje.
(*U.S. Army photograph*)

Coordination between British forces and Brigadier General James M. Gavin *(center, facing front)*, U.S. 82nd Airborne Division commander. Captain Arie Bestebreurtje of Jedburgh team Clarence stands immediately to Gavin's right, facing camera. *(The Bestebreurtje family)*

Lieutenant General Frederick A. M. Browning, British I Airborne Corps commander *(left)*, confers with Brigadier General Gavin near Malden to discuss plans for capturing the Nijmegen railway and highway bridges. *(U.S. Army photograph)*

The bridge over the Maas River at Grave, Holland. With nine spans stretching 650 yards, it was said to be the longest bridge in Europe in September 1944, when it was captured, under fire, by paratroopers of the 504th Parachute Infantry Regiment, 82nd Airborne Division, on the first day of Operation Market-Garden. *(U.S. Army photograph)*

Montgomery's opposition: Generalfeldmarschall (Field Marshal) Walter Model (*left*), commander of German Army Group B, positioned on the northernmost part of the West Wall, and Generaloberst (General) Kurt Student (*right*), commander of the German First Parachute Army. (*Department of Defense*)

Nijmegen highway bridge over the Waal River. (*National Archives*)

Brigadier General Gavin (*right*), 82nd Airborne Division commander, briefs General Miles C. Dempsey, commander of Second British Army, during Operation Market-Garden. (*National Archives*)

Citizens of Nijmegen welcome paratroopers of the 2nd Battalion, 505th Parachute Infantry, as they enter the city's outskirts on September 19, 1944. (*U.S. Army photograph*)

RIGHT: A German Waffen-SS panzer-grenadier lies dead on the Nijmegen bridge. (*U.S. Army photograph*)

BELOW: Sherman tank of British XXX Corps passes two dead Germans on the Nijmegen highway bridge. (*U.S. Army photograph*)

Sherman tanks of the 2nd Irish Guards cross the Nijmegen highway bridge. (*National Archives*)

German commanders who battled the Allies at Nijmegen and Arnhem. *Left to right:* Obergruppenführer (SS Lieutenant General) Wilhelm Bittrich, commander, II SS Panzer Corps; Obersturmbannführer (SS Lieutenant Colonel) Walther Harzer, commander, 9th SS Panzer Division; and Brigadeführer (SS Brigadier General) Heinz Harmel, commander, 10th SS Panzer Division. (*Captured German photographs*)

The first stick of paratroopers from the 2nd Battalion, First Parachute Brigade, British First Airborne Division, drifts toward earth at Drop Zone X near Wolfheze, west of Arnhem, on September 17, 1944. Horsa gliders litter the field after the First Airlanding Brigade arrived earlier to secure the drop zone. Jedburgh team Claude jumped on the same spot thirteen minutes later, but joined 2nd Battalion in their fight to hold the north end of the Arnhem bridge. (*National Archives*)

St. Elizabeth Hospital on Utrechtseweg in Arnhem. Captain Groenewoud and Lieutenant Todd of Jedburgh team Claude stopped here en route from the drop zone to the Arnhem bridge on September 17, 1944. After a brief skirmish with German troops outside the hospital, the two men entered the building and persuaded the German medical officer in charge to agree to make room for Allied casualties. In this photograph, taken a few days later, Dutch Red Cross personnel are transferring casualties to other hospitals as the battle continues. (*Bundesarchiv*)

Aerial view of the Arnhem bridge over the Neder Rijn on September 18, 1944, showing debris from an attack by the 9th SS Reconnaissance Battalion. The German battalion commander, SS-Hauptsturmführer (SS Captain) Viktor Gräbner, was killed in the action, a day after being awarded the Knight's Cross. Lieutenant Todd's fighting position was in an attic window of a building at the extreme top center of the photograph. (*Imperial War Museum MH2061*)

German crew of a Sturmgeschütz III assault gun of the 208th Assault Brigade takes a break on an Arnhem street during the fighting. This is part of the force that battled elements of the British First Airborne Division attempting to reach the Arnhem Bridge, where Lieutenant Colonel Frost's heavily outnumbered and outgunned battalion and the officers of Jedburgh team Claude were cut off and fighting to hold their position. *(Bundesarchiv)*

View from about a half mile east of the Arnhem bridge on Wednesday morning, September 20, shows smoke billowing skyward from the burning buildings on the north end of the bridge, where British troops and Lieutenant Todd of Jedburgh team Claude were surrounded and fighting desperately. *(Bundesarchiv)*

ABOVE: Ruins of the waterworks building, on the western side of the approach ramp to the northern end of the Arnhem bridge. The headquarters of 1st Parachute Brigade operated from this building throughout the battle at the bridge. This is the building where Lieutenant Todd fought from a position at an attic window. *(Amanda Todd)*

RIGHT: One of the destroyed buildings in Arnhem, Holland, where troops of the British First Airborne Division, along with Captain Groenewoud and Lieutenant Todd of Jedburgh team Claude, fought September 18–20, 1944. *(Amanda Todd)*

Auswertestelle-West, the POW interrogation center at Oberursel, Germany, in 1944. Also known as Dulag Luft, this is where Lieutenant Allan Todd was held in solitary confinement October 6–18, 1944, undergoing a series of interrogations. *(After the Battle publications)*

The cooler (solitary confinement cell block) at the Dulag Luft POW interrogation center at Oberursel, Germany. *(After the Battle publications)*

Aerial view of the prisoner of war transit camp at Wetzlar, Germany, where Lieutenant Allan Todd was a prisoner October 18–20, 1944, while awaiting assignment to a permanent POW camp.

Main gate to prisoner of war camp Oflag XII-A at Limburg, Germany, fifty miles northwest of Frankfurt, where Lieutenant Allan Todd was held October 20 through November 5, 1944, undergoing further interrogation.

Perimeter fence at prisoner of war camp Oflag 64, at Schubin, Poland, where Lieutenant Todd was confined from November 1944 through January 1945. This photograph was taken on January 23, 1945, two days after the camp's evacuation, by Robert Keith, who escaped from the column of prisoners marching toward Germany and returned to the vacated camp to await the arrival of the Red army. Brick prisoner barracks buildings can be seen on the left, part of the town of Schubin on the right.

Leaders of the prisoners held in Oflag 64, the German POW camp for U.S. ground force officers at Schubin, Poland. *Left to right:* Lieutenant Colonel John K. Waters (son-in-law of General George S. Patton), senior officer Colonel Paul R. "Pop" Goode, an unidentified visiting YMCA representative, Lieutenant Colonel Schaefer, and Colonel George Millet.

First Lieutenant Harvey Allan Todd's prisoner of war identification card, issued at Oflag 64, Schubin, Poland, in November 1944.
(Amanda Todd)

Contents of a typical American Red Cross food parcel issued to U.S. POWs. The packaged parcel measured 10 inches square by 4½ inches deep and weighed 11 pounds to be in accordance with German postal regulations. (*American Red Cross*)

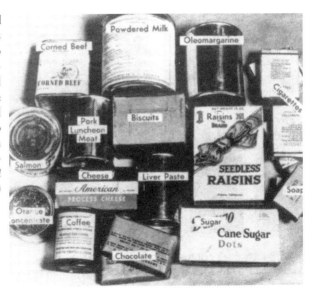

Prisoner of war camp Oflag XIII-B at Hammelburg, Germany. This photograph, taken in 1937, shows the camp as a German army training garrison before the war.

Captain Abraham Baum, the officer from the U.S. 4th Armored Division who led the doomed raid to rescue American POWs from Oflag XIII-B at Hammelburg, Germany. Among the prisoners who were briefly liberated before being recaptured was Lieutenant Allan Todd of Jedburgh team Claude. (*U.S. Army photograph*)

A 14th Armored Division tank smashing the fence at Hammelburg on April 6, 1945, when the camp was finally liberated, just one week after the Germans marched Lieutenant Todd and around 1,650 other U.S. POWs out of the camp. The prisoners in the photograph are Serbian. *(National Archives)*

ABOVE: Major General William Donovan, director of OSS, presenting Lieutenant Todd with the Distinguished Service Cross and the Purple Heart in Washington, D.C., 1945. *(Amanda Todd)*

LEFT: Newly promoted Captain Harvey Allan Todd, U.S. Army, sole survivor of Jedburgh team Claude, at war's end.

LEFT: Major John M. "Pappy" Olmsted, U.S. Army, sole survivor of Jedburgh team Dudley, at war's end. (*Elizabeth Olmsted*)

BELOW: John Olmsted in 1985 visiting a former wartime hiding place, a barn in Holland used as a safe house by the Dutch underground in 1944. (*Elizabeth Olmsted*)

Prince Bernhard of the Netherlands (*left*), after awarding the Dutch Resistance Cross to Willard "Bud" Beynon of Jedburgh team Clarence (*right*), in Washington, D.C., in 1982. (*Willard Beynon*)

ABOVE: Three survivors and best of friends at the Jedburgh reunion in Washington, D.C., May 1988. *Left to right:* Harvey Allan Todd, George Verhaeghe, and John Olmsted. *(Amanda Todd)*

RIGHT: The Rev. Dr. Arie Bestebreurtje, Jedburgh team Clarence veteran, and his wife, Gertrude, in Louisville in 1966. *(The Bestebreurtje family)*

Jedburghs with the president and first lady on the south lawn of the White House, Washington, D.C., May 1988. Harvey Allan Todd *(in wheelchair)* shakes hands with President Ronald Reagan. Both Reagan and Todd played varsity football at Eureka College in Illinois (Reagan class of 1932, Todd class of 1939). Amanda Todd is between Allan Todd and the president. Nancy Reagan looks on to the right of the president. *(Amanda Todd)*

Pomeranian countryside. Here the land was mostly flat plain with occasional small hills. But it was new territory for the prisoners, and the ever-changing scenery caused a certain excitement among the men. Monday proved to be another very cold day with intermittent snowfall. Again the prisoners shared the crowded road with a train of refugees that stretched for miles through the countryside. The brisk air filled with the creaking of wagon wheels, the crunching of weary feet and hooves and wheels on the hard-packed snow, and a trail of steam rose from the labored breathing of man and beast.

Dead horses littered the roadside as the march column again disintegrated into a disorganized mob. Prisoners shuffled along as guards yelled from time to time, and German refugees sometimes taunted the Americans. Men stopped and started more or less at will, taking short breaks alongside the road and then falling back in farther to the rear of the column. At times, when a prisoner could not keep up and fell back, guards would go back for him and the other prisoners would soon hear rifle shots.

Rumors that the Russians were getting close spread through the column, and the sound of small-arms fire not more than a mile or so in the distance seemed to bear this out. German guards grew visibly uneasy.

As the column wound its way northward, it reached a place where German soldiers were preparing a defensive line, digging zigzagging trenches in the snow-covered ground and laying long stretches of barbed wire. The POWs passed through the line and continued a few miles farther until, suddenly, they heard the rattle of machine-gun fire back in the direction of the hillside defensive line the German troops had been preparing, possibly evidence of a Soviet patrol in the area.

On the weary American officers trudged, crossing a heavily guarded bridge over the Bomberg Canal, until the column turned off the main road at around four in the afternoon. The day's march had covered some fifteen miles or more by the time the men entered the small village of Eichfelde, nothing more than a few brick houses and barns. Once again, groups of men were billeted in several small barns. Guards issued the customary four- or five-inch-long loaves of black bread and a little margarine, each loaf to be divided among six men, and as the prisoners ate they could again hear small-arms fire not far away.[11]

Prisoners who stepped outdoors to relieve themselves early on the morning of January 23 were puzzled to find no German guards about. Word soon spread that the guards had pulled out at four in the morning, no doubt because of the imminent arrival of Russian forces, and the POWs expected to be liberated within hours. One German officer, a captain, had remained with the column to prevent any confrontation with other German troops who might find the prisoners. The Americans kept repeating, "Come on, Russians!" At seven-thirty that morning, the men received hot water and soup. Colonel Goode and the other leaders among the prisoners established "command posts" and told the men to remain where they were; the safest thing would be to remain in place and wait for the Russians to overrun them. Small-arms fire continued to crackle off to the east.

Most of the prisoners naturally turned their attention to a search for food. Some men caught a hog and butchered it with hopes of having a pork supper. Polish women brought cherry preserves to share with the prisoners. Some of the men had other food scraps that they had saved, and the women helped cook for them over the fires they were huddled around. The Poles told the prisoners that the Russians were only about three miles away. Men sang as they listened to the approaching rumble of artillery.

Colonel Goode told Lieutenant Todd that when Oberst Schneider had departed, he had taken the briefcase containing Todd's execution order with him. The colonel told Todd to try not to worry about the pending execution; he had an idea.

Before long a new guard force arrived, a company of Latvian SS troops with German shepherd dogs. Germany's Waffen-SS included two divisions formed with Latvian volunteers. This new guard force likely came from one of these, the 15th Waffen-SS Division, also known as the Latvian Legion, which had been rebuilding and training nearby since September 1944. The division had been ordered into action the previous day and was fighting in the area around Danzig, not far to the east.[12] The SS men soon had the prisoners surrounded in an open, bowl-like depression in the middle of a wooded area. They informed the prisoners that they would move out again at three or four that afternoon.

Perhaps seeing it as their last chance to break away and reach the oncoming Russians, some of the American officers took off running toward the tree line and were shot down.

It was snowing again—a gentle, quiet snowfall—as the column began marching at half-past three that afternoon. A truck full of German troops camouflaged in white uniforms passed the POWs on a road that snaked through dense forest. Often the woods came right to the roadside, but the presence of the dogs deterred men from leaving the column. The prisoners marched another four miles through the snow until they reached a tiny village, where the men were served soup and then were put into the haylofts of huge dairy barns in a fenced-in compound on the southern end of a long lake.

On Wednesday morning, January 24, the men woke to another bitter cold day. They pulled frozen shoes onto their stiff and swollen feet and lined up for pea soup, kicking their feet together to keep them from freezing as they waited for what they hoped would be an equitable share. After breakfast, they shuffled loosely into platoons for the march. At nine, the disheveled prisoners moved out, marching northward, and soon the procession was strung out for nearly a mile.

As the column passed through villages, Polish inhabitants peered from windows and lined the streets to watch. Once the people learned that the men marching through their town were American prisoners, they came out of their houses to wave and cheer, welcoming the men warmly, almost as though they were liberators. Bolder civilians approached the column and gave the men bread and cheese or a cup of ersatz coffee. At great risk to themselves, some Poles pulled prisoners into their homes, hugging and kissing them and repeating, *"Amerikanisch, Amerikanisch."*[13] Women fed the men or gave them bread before releasing them back to the march formation. Grateful American officers paid for this kindness with the only thing they had to offer—cigarettes. While the column was halted in a village called Wirnitz, some of the men ducked into buildings to hide out until the column moved on and left them behind. For those brave souls, a whole new adventure in escape and evasion lay ahead.

Standing in the center of town during the halt, some of the POWs eyed an old man carrying two loaves of bread. Half-starved prisoners began yelling, *"Zigaretten für Brot!"* hoping to obtain the bread in exchange for cigarettes. Just then, one enterprising prisoner, noticing the tattered clothes the old man was wearing, stepped forward and gestured a different proposal. He offered to swap his uniform pants for the two loaves of bread, and the old-timer agreed. The prisoner promptly began removing his pants, hopping around on one foot in his long underwear as the town's citizens and the other prisoners roared with approving laughter. Then the clever but trouserless officer stood in the cold street until he found another prisoner who traded him a pair of pants for half a loaf of bread. Another prisoner received the remaining half loaf for a second pair of pants, leaving the crafty trader with two pairs of pants and one full loaf of bread.[14]

But the SS men soon took offense at the display of Polish geniality and tried to keep the townspeople at bay. One SS officer strutted about making threatening gestures with a "potato masher" hand grenade. He bullied his way through a group of refugees, even shoving a small child from a sled. Then more guards arrived, and the prisoners recognized them as the old Schubin guard force. Seventeen officers who had succeeded in escaping from the column along the way had been recaptured and now rejoined the column. Rumors quickly spread that the Germans were threatening to shoot the recaptured men.

Guards hustled the Americans back into march formation, and the column moved off to a group of barns that would provide shelter for the night. There to greet the Americans was Oberst Schneider, who now gathered the prisoners in a large crowd and addressed them, pleading with the men not to try leaving the march column. "Be gentlemen," he said, "don't try to escape."[15] When he finished his speech, the men broke into groups for billeting in the barns.

Thursday began with a breakfast of cold oatmeal, a minuscule loaf of bread for each five men, and a small serving of margarine. It was after nine when the column, better organized now with the larger guard force, marched off to the northwest. Throughout the day, faint sounds of battle reached the men from somewhere off to the south. Marshal Zhukov's main force reached the town of Poznań that day, some 40 miles southwest of Schubin and 140 miles from Berlin.[16]

Over the next few days, a heavy snowfall made walking more difficult. As they reached the large town of Jastrow at the end of one day's march, some men saw a sign that read BERLIN 271 KM (about 168 miles).[17] Evening mealtimes usually found the men standing in line in the freezing cold for as long as two hours awaiting their half-tin serving of anemic soup. In addition to illness and malnourishment, trench foot and frostbite claimed many victims. In an effort to avoid these painful and debilitating conditions, men tried to dry their wet feet at night after walking through deep snow all day.[18] Allan Todd's wounds had been treated by an American doctor in Oflag 64, but now he had developed a bad case of trench foot on the foot that had been burned back in Arnhem.

January 27 came and went without the execution of Lieutenant Harvey Allan Todd. At one point during Oberst Schneider's absence, the German captain who had been left in charge of the column told Colonel

Goode that as much as he regretted doing so, he would be required to see that Todd's execution was carried out at five on the morning of the twenty-seventh. Before departing, Oberst Schneider had left instructions that it had to be done. But Colonel Goode came to Todd's rescue. He asked the captain to show him the official orders for the execution. Because Schneider had taken his briefcase with him, the captain could not produce the order. Goode convinced the German officer that he could not legally carry out the execution without written authorization. The captain, a university professor in Vienna before the war—a draftee and not a professional military man—appeared relieved at having been provided an excuse for not seeing the execution through. Todd was placed under special guard for the remainder of the march, but his morale had been given a lift. No further mention of the execution was made, even after Oberst Schneider rejoined the column. Todd became friends with the German captain and with Schneider's sergeant major.[19]

Setting out again early on the morning of the twenty-eighth, the column of weary prisoners continued marching in a northwesterly direction, trudging through numbing cold as they crossed a flat and barren, snow-covered plain. Soon a very fine snow, driven by a fierce wind, reduced visibility to the point that the men had to move in single file. They wrapped towels around their heads, covering their faces except for a narrow slit to see through, but still faces and hands froze. Even Oberst Schneider suffered along on foot, having been relieved of his car by an officer who outranked him. At night, the men tried to sleep in unheated buildings as the blizzard howled across the desolate, tundralike landscape outside.

The blizzard that hit the area that weekend proved a blessing to the German army, for it dumped enough snow to immobilize Zhukov's tanks and infantry. Then, as the weather warmed over the following days, the snow melted just enough to leave the Soviet forces bogged down in mud.[20]

Shuffling along on roads drifted over with snow, the POWs continued marching through biting cold and windblown snow until they reached a large and recently vacated German garrison called Westhofen Barracks. Nearby, the men entered the deserted Oflag II-D, once a camp for French and Polish POWs, where they spent a comparatively comfortable night in bunks, warmed by charcoal fires. At every night's halt along the march route, prisoners too ill or weak to continue had been left behind to await rail transportation. Now only some eight hundred men remained of the roughly fifteen hundred who had marched out of the Schubin camp one week earlier.[21]

Fearing the approach of Russian forces, guards got the POW column moving again the next day. At one point, marching through knee-deep snow, the column passed a frozen corpse sitting upright against a fence-post. Roadways became congested with wagons and small groups of German soldiers dressed in white, and as the day wore on, road conditions became progressively worse. On the last day of January, the prisoners crossed the prewar German-Polish border and what appeared to be another thinly held defensive line. Then the snowstorm abated, the sun shone, and the men's feet were soon soaked from snow melting inside their shoes.

———

Soviet forces of Marshal Georgi Zhukov's First Belorussian Front, spearheading the Red Army's drive toward Berlin, had reached the bank of the Oder River by the first of February and were preparing to cross. They were now only forty to fifty miles east of the German capital. In all, some 180 Soviet divisions faced a depleted 80 German divisions in Poland. In the sector where Zhukov's armies had broken through the German lines to begin their assault on the Reich, the Soviets had nine thousand tanks and nine thousand planes and enjoyed a staggering four-to-one supremacy in artillery.[22]

———

When they reached a point roughly fifty miles from Berlin, the POWs were given a day of rest. Seizing a chance to make a good trade, some of the men brokered deals with SS troops stationed nearby, swapping cigarettes for bread or meat or cheese. An irate woman complained to a German officer that POWs had stolen three of her hens, and she produced the heads and feet of the chickens to back up her complaint. Oberst Schneider, certain that the allegation was true but unable to single out the chicken thieves, angrily scolded all the prisoners. Lieutenant Todd noted in his cryptic diary that it was the third Sunday since leaving Oflag 64.

Over the next few days, the prisoners filed through cobblestoned villages undergoing evacuation, townspeople hurriedly loading their most prized belongings onto wagons while German troops worked at building hasty roadblocks and fighting positions in preparation for the approach-

ing Russians. By February 9, the POW column was within a few miles
of the Baltic Sea coast.

———

Word of the evacuation of Oflag 64 reached the Pentagon in Washington in a message dispatched on February 9, 1945, by General John R.
Deane, head of the United States Military Liaison Office in Moscow.
Three of the American prisoners marching from Oflag 64 had managed
to slip away from the column and escape to the east. With the help of
the Soviet army, the three men made it all the way to Moscow, where
they reported the camp's evacuation to Deane. News of the POW movement was forwarded to General Eisenhower's headquarters in France,
and the supreme commander informed General Patton that his son-in-
law, Lieutenant Colonel John Waters, was probably still alive and
marching with the column from Oflag 64. Intelligence reports indicated
that the men were likely destined for Oflag XIII-B, a camp for American
officers just outside Hammelburg, Germany.

———

On Saturday, February 10, the column of American prisoners completed
a ten-mile march to the northwest, through the town of Fritzow. Then it
moved northward through a thick, ground-hugging fog to the coast,
where the men got their first glimpse of the Baltic Sea. Turning to the
west, the column marched along the coast, passing through villages of
well-kept cottages and countryside that appeared to have been a scenic
tourist destination in peacetime. Beyond the resort community, the column came to the town of Dievenow and then crossed a wooden bridge
to a naval air base, where the men marched on a two-lane concrete highway that doubled as a landing strip.

   In the afternoon, the sky cleared and seaplanes soared overhead.
There seemed to be a flight school on the base. Platoons of German soldiers marched to and from training; groups of young people, too, sang as
they marched by in formation. On the combination road and airstrip,
camouflaged seaplanes sat along the edge of a tree line.

———

Marshal Zhukov's armies, meanwhile, still stood on the east bank of the
Oder, almost due south of the POW column's location. The Red Army's
rapid advance across Poland had stretched supply lines to their limit.

For the time being, the Soviets would remain in positions on the Oder while reconstituting and building up logistical stores for the next offensive that would take them to Berlin.

Small-scale operations continued to mop up remaining German forces in bypassed areas and along the Pomeranian coast of the Baltic, where Soviet forces had brushed aside the paper-thin German Army Group Vistula, now under the inept command of Reichsführer-SS Heinrich Himmler, and were overwhelming the scattered infantry units that constituted Generalfeldmarschall Ferdinand Schörner's Army Group Central.

A thousand miles to the southeast, at Livadia Palace in the Crimean coastal town of Yalta, Soviet leader Joseph Stalin, British Prime Minister Winston Churchill, and President Franklin Roosevelt of the United States—"the Big Three"—were, on February 11, just concluding a conference. Among the points agreed upon was the establishment of the Oder River as the new eastern border for postwar Germany.[23]

———

The POWs from Oflag 64 marched again at noon on Sunday, February 11, crossing a bridge to the large, mostly forested island of Wolin. Stands of tall trees, intermixed with marshy areas, reminded some of the Americans of Camp Blanding, Florida.

For several days the men had been subsisting on soup, and the watery diet, served to the prisoners in their unclean KLIM tins, caused many to come down with diarrhea and dysentery. Men leaving the column to run off into the woods, dropping their trousers, became a common sight. The column proceeded ten miles southwest along the coast—through the resort town of Leimbrink, with its trim little blue-shuttered cottages and neat, conically shaped wood piles. Then on to another village, where the men crowded into two barns for the night. Lieutenant Todd noted in his journal that this was their fourth Sunday on the move.[24]

The next day meant another fifteen punishing miles westward along the coast, through an old seafront health resort overlooking the cliffs along the coast, to a German naval base at the port of Swinemünde. Occupying two large islands in the middle of the estuary at the mouth of the Oder, straight north of Berlin, Swinemünde was home to German destroyers and other naval ships. Many men had collapsed during the day's demanding march, and nine were sent to a hospital.[25] When the march had begun that morning, the Latvian SS unit that had been augmenting the column's guard force remained on the east bank of the Oder. The column's regular guards seemed relieved to now have a major water obstacle between them and the oncoming Russians.[26]

On Tuesday morning, Colonel Goode announced that the prisoners, thus far, had marched 235 miles in twenty-three days, and he angrily scolded Oberst Schneider about the poor diet the men were receiving.

For the next few days, the prisoners slogged on through raw weather, intermittent rain, and snow flurries, with more than a hundred men being left along the way with medical ailments.[27] On Friday, two officers created some excitement during the morning's march when they slipped away from the column in an escape attempt, but both men were recaptured that afternoon.

Ahead of the POWs now lay the sprawling lake country of rural Mecklenburg, a flat and featureless land of old Junker estates and scattered forests. Twenty miles to the north stood the great German rocket facility at Peenemünde, on the Baltic coast, where German scientists produced the V-2 long-distance rockets that had inflicted considerable damage on London and Antwerp in 1944.

Covering around six to twelve miles a day, the prisoners continued to march through miles of vast snow-covered potato fields and pastures, groves of poplars and alders, and colorful, modern-looking towns. In some places, the ruins of burned and shattered houses offered evidence of recent bombings. At the end of one day's march, the men were billeted in a barn next to a school for a youth organization of some kind. That evening, several youngsters from the school came over and chatted with the prisoners. Speaking fairly good English, the kids boasted of Nazi superdom.

Whenever time allowed during rest breaks, those in charge of the secret radio, "the Bird," took the opportunity to get it assembled and operating, and platoon representatives gathered quietly to receive the latest war news. One platoon's man returned a short while later to share the news with his comrades: "Today the Russians liberated seven thousand British POWs, twelve thousand Serbs, one thousand Americans, and everyone else but us God damn fools."[28] Lieutenant Todd noted in his diary that February 25 was their sixth Sunday on the road.

Soon the prisoners were plodding along in nice weather through rolling Mecklenburg farmland. At a town called Siggelkow, where the column stopped for the night, fires smoldered in the street as air-raid sirens wailed through the night. Guards informed the men that they would remain in place until transportation arrived to take them to a prisoner of war camp near Hammelburg.

For five days the POWs sat at Siggelkow, huddled around campfires, bashing on Red Cross food parcels. Since leaving Schubin, the men had walked 362 miles.[29] Fewer than five hundred prisoners remained from the roughly fifteen hundred who had marched out the gate of Oflag 64 thirty-nine days earlier.[30] Rain fell on Thursday afternoon as the Germans passed out postcards for the prisoners, telling them they could write to their parents or wives.

Every day now, new German jet fighters screamed overhead, the first jet aircraft any of the Americans had ever seen. One afternoon, the men lay about in the sun, watching an air raid off in the distance.

Guards woke the prisoners at four-thirty on Tuesday morning, March 6, 1945. The men formed up and marched a few miles to a large rail yard at Parchim, arriving at the *Bahnhof,* or train station, at six. The Germans issued each man half a loaf of bread and some margarine, and the men ate as they waited to board a train for a scheduled ten o'clock departure. When time came to board, three dozen prisoners and four guards crowded into each of thirteen boxcars. These were what were widely known as "forty-by-eight" cars, indicating that they were capable of carrying forty men or eight horses. On the roof of each car were painted the letters "U.S. POW" in hopes of warning off any Allied air attacks.

At eleven-twenty, the train slowly pulled away from Parchim Bahnhof and rolled westward through the town of Ludwigslust, then south through Grabow. By two that afternoon, it was passing through Wittenberg, nestled between the Elbe and a range of large wooded hills. All of these towns had been bombed, and large barrage balloons lingered over the gabled buildings of Wittenberg. The train finally came to a halt for the night at Osterburg at six-fifteen.

Under way again early the next morning, the train rolled through several bombed-out towns where fires still smoldered—Magdeburg, on the west bank of the Elbe, on to the industrial town of Halle, on the banks of the Saale, near Leipzig, then southwest to Naumburg. At four-thirty in the afternoon, the train rolled through the recently bombed city of Weimar, on the Ilm River, and at six-fifteen it pulled to a stop in Erfurt, whose churches and bell towers and old half-timbered houses remained undamaged.

On Thursday morning, the train snaked through the cool, moist forests of the Thüringer Wald. On either side of the tracks, low hills were densely wooded with fir, beech, spruce, and oak. From time to time, the forest broke as the train passed through narrow, beautiful valleys and meadows with orchards and small fields, and at noon it arrived at the spa town of Bad Kissingen. After a layover until late in the afternoon, the train continued through Grummenthal, Bad Neustadt, and Ebenhausen until it finally arrived at the wine town of Hammelburg at seven that evening. The prisoners remained confined in the crowded, unheated boxcars until morning.

———

Back in the Netherlands, with Major John Olmsted having returned to England and with Sergeant John Austin in captivity, Major Henk Brinkgreve carried on the mission of Jedburgh team Dudley by himself. On March 5, he sat in the kitchen of a safe house in the village of Losser in the Overijssel. Suddenly a resistance girl rushed into the room in a panic, screaming that German soldiers were approaching. She then ran from the house. Brinkgreve got out of the house just as SS men arrived. As he crawled away from the house on the ground, trying to remain out of sight, a German officer spotted him. The German raised his Luger, carefully aimed the pistol at the man on the ground some forty to fifty yards away, and fired. The bullet struck Brinkgreve in the head, killing him.[31]

TWENTY-EIGHT

PATTON'S HAMMELBURG RAID

At seven-thirty on Friday morning, March 9, Lieutenant Todd and the 489 other prisoners—423 officers and 67 enlisted men in all[1]—left the boxcars, stretched, formed up, and marched. Leaving the rail yard and the town, they crossed a river and trudged two and a half miles up a long, steep slope to the crest of a hill overlooking a scenic valley.

There, sprawled out in a depression atop the hill, stood the prisoner of war camp known as Oflag XIII-B. Forty-eight days after leaving Oflag 64, the surviving lice-infested men showed the effects of their ordeal. They had traveled 362 miles on foot, been given just enough food to keep them alive, and ridden an additional 340 miles by train, packed in crowded boxcars. Illness and freezing weather accounted for most of the men lost along the way, including the hundreds of sick prisoners who had been loaded onto boxcars and shipped to other camps. Still others had frozen to death or were shot.

It was nine-thirty when the group of POWs from Oflag 64 finished hiking up the long winding trail to the top of the hill and arrived at the gate to the camp. The large compound was secured by a ten-foot-high barbed-wire perimeter fence and twelve machine-gun-equipped guard towers. Surrounding the camp were fields, some of them dotted with haystacks. Oberst Schneider assembled the men just outside the gate and spoke to them for the last time, explaining that he would be assigned to other duties because the commandant at Oflag XIII-B was a general officer and thus outranked him. He sincerely wished the men well and expressed a hope that the war would soon be over.

The Hammelburg camp had been built in 1918 as a German army training site. Since its conversion to a prisoner of war camp, the facility had held Russians, Poles, Frenchmen, and Dutch. When the men from Oflag 64 arrived, the camp already housed more than seven hundred American officers and, in a separate compound, some three thousand to five thousand Serbian officers of the Yugoslav army who had been captured in 1941. A camp for enlisted personnel, Stalag XIII-C, was a mile away on the other side of a hill.

Generalleutnant (Major General) Günther von Goeckel, a tall and proper Prussian officer, was commandant of Oflag XIII-B. A regular officer who had been shot in the chest in World War I and had since been relegated to staff jobs, von Goeckel had taken command of the camp in August 1944.

Prisoners inside the compound were impressed at the sight of the Oflag 64 men marching through the gate and into the camp. As rough as they looked after their grueling walk from northern Poland, the men held their heads high. Guards ushered the newcomers into a large riding hall, where General von Goeckel introduced himself and briefly addressed them.

German soldiers then began individually searching the men and delousing them. From time to time, as the searching and delousing continued through the night, prisoners who had completed the processing were marched in groups of thirty to their assigned barracks. Bunk rooms in the barracks were about fifty feet square and furnished with the customary double- and triple-decked bunks, along with a few tables and chairs. Standing in the center of the room was a brick chimney and a stove. Each of the new prisoners received an issue of two blankets and mess gear. Blackout curtains, the men were told, were to be put up before dark every night, and lights were to be out by ten.

Todd and the others were dismayed at the disheveled appearance and the apathy of the hundreds of officers who made up the prisoner population at the time of their arrival. Many were from the U.S. 28th and 106th Infantry Divisions and had been captured in the opening days of the Battle of the Bulge, quickly overrun by the unexpected German assault through the Ardennes. The camp was in disgraceful condition, and the prisoners were filthy and unshaven, seemingly just biding their time until war's end. Nothing existed in the way of organized athletics or other activities. Only the regularly scheduled church services provided some semblance of order.

Disgusted at what he saw, Colonel Goode immediately took steps to turn things around. Because he outranked any officers held at the camp prior to his arrival, Goode assumed duties as the senior American officer. As soon as he was settled in, he sent runners to find the senior commanders in the American compound and tell them "to get their tails over here as fast as they can run!"[2]

When the four commanders arrived, Goode scolded them for being derelict in their duties as senior officers and made it clear that he wanted the camp brought up to his standards immediately. Work got under way at once, improvements noted with every passing day, and within a week the transformation was complete. The compound now resembled a military camp, and it ran with a new level of efficiency. The unfortunate veterans of the Battle of the Bulge, undisciplined and bereft of unit pride prior to Goode's arrival, now walked about camp clean-shaven and with neat haircuts, wearing clean uniforms and shined boots.

Amanda Todd, at home in Illinois, received a letter from Major Tony Hibbert of the British 1st Airborne Division in March 1945. A survivor of the battle at the Arnhem bridge, Hibbert had been captured at the close of the battle and later managed to escape. He provided details of Allan's actions during the battle and expressed hope that Amanda would soon hear good news about her husband. Arville Todd, Allan's father, received a similar letter. Hibbert wrote that he was sure the family already knew that Todd was missing in action. Apparently, the British officer was not aware that Todd was a prisoner of war.[3]

Todd and others fell into the routine of camp life, recovering from their journey, playing cards, washing clothes, and attending lectures given by fellow prisoners. *Appell* was held at eight in the morning and again at five in the afternoon. Food at the Hammelburg prison camp was even worse than what the American officers had experienced at Schubin, and there were no American Red Cross food parcels. Soups were even more watered down and came in two nauseating varieties. "Purple Passion" got its tint from the chips of sugar beet used to make it, while "Green Hornet" soup was prepared with green grass. Both soups were tasteless; neither was nourishing. Cooks prepared the meals in a central kitchen, and prisoners then carried the food in eight-gallon pots to be served in the barracks. To round out their meager diet, each man received about a tenth of a loaf of bread per day.[4]

Colonel Goode saw to it that a bulletin board was installed, just like the one they had at Oflag 64, and before long camp life in Oflag XIII-B began to resemble that at the Schubin camp. Classes, lectures, and other activities appeared regularly on the daily schedule and provided a variety of diversions for the men. These proved of great value in raising the morale of men for whom the greatest enemy was boredom. A typical day's eclectic agenda of classes and other activities, posted on the bulletin board at about this time, read:

0900	Irrigation of Crops
1000	How to Make Ice Cream
1100	Economic Geography
1300	Child Psychology
1400	Roller Coasters
1500	Glee Club
1600	Catholic Mass

Bring Your Own Chairs[5]

From war news received through "the Bird," prisoners were aware of Allied progress in the west. They knew that American forces were drawing near, and they probably had learned of the capture of the bridge over the Rhine at Remagen by U.S. forces on March 7. One afternoon, they cheered as an American fighter buzzed the camp.

In mid-March, the POWs began hearing rumors that the Germans were preparing to march the prisoners farther south. In January, at Schubin, it had been Russian forces approaching from the east that caused the prisoners to be moved; now American forces approaching from the west seemed to be having the same result. On Palm Sunday, March 25, the latest rumor reached the American prisoners from the Yugoslav compound. It was news of an American force approaching the camp, but few of the American prisoners gave the rumor much credence. They were unaware of a battle then raging near the town of Aschaffenburg, some sixty miles to the west on the Main River.[6]

Lieutenant General George S. Patton was in a jubilant mood as he sat down to write to his wife, Beatrice, from his Luxembourg headquarters on the evening of March 23. The previous night, an advance element of his Third Army had crossed the Rhine, and he would put the entire 4th Armored Division across the next day. Brimming with confidence, Patton wrote, "We are headed for John's place, and may get there before he is moved."[7] He was, of course, referring to their son-in-law, Lieutenant Colonel John Waters, now among the prisoners held at the Hammelburg POW camp.

On the twenty-fourth, Patton called the commander of his XII Corps, Major General Manton Eddy, with orders to prepare at once a task force for a very important, albeit risky, operation. Eddy was dismayed when he heard Patton's concept. The Third Army commander wanted Eddy to send an armored task force sixty miles behind enemy lines to liberate hundreds of American prisoners of war from a camp near Hammelburg.[8]

At two in the afternoon of the following day, Major Alexander Stiller, a former Texas Ranger serving as one of Patton's aides, arrived at General Eddy's headquarters in Undenheim, Germany, with orders for the Hammelburg operation. Eddy reluctantly assigned the mission to the 4th Armored Division. That evening, Patton again wrote to Beatrice, this time informing his wife: "Hope to send an expedition tomorrow to get John."[9]

General Eddy called Patton at four-thirty the next morning and argued for cancellation of the Hammelburg operation. Patton refused to call it off, but he agreed to Eddy's suggestion to commit only a small task force to the mission rather than an entire brigade-size combat command. Eddy then called Brigadier General William Hoge, commander of the 4th Armored Division, and relayed Patton's approval of the smaller force.

Patton, in his polished helmet bearing three shiny stars, waist-length Eisenhower jacket, and tailored jodhpurs, arrived by plane at Eddy's headquarters at ten o'clock. Since the corps commander was away at the time, he and Major Stiller proceeded directly to General Hoge's command post, arriving there at eleven.

An hour later, Patton, Hoge, and Stiller arrived at the headquarters of Lieutenant Colonel Creighton Abrams, the brilliant and energetic commander of the 4th Armored Division's Combat Command B. Abrams's command had been at the head of the 4th Armored's march clear across France, spearheading Patton's drive eastward. Combat Command B had also led the attack into the flank of the Fifth Panzer Army to relieve the encircled 101st Airborne Division at Bastogne during the Battle of the Bulge. It had now been just two days since the 4th Armored had jumped the Rhine, and the division had raced more than twenty-five miles since then to reach the Main River. The day before Patton's arrival, Combat Command B captured a railroad bridge south of Aschaffenburg, on the hilly bank of the Rhine some twenty-five miles southeast of Frankfurt, and its 37th Tank Battalion and 10th Armored Infantry Battalion were engaged in battle to secure a bridgehead on the far side.[10]

Patton ordered Abrams to organize a task force to carry out the Hammelburg rescue operation. When Abrams expressed a desire to conduct the raid with his entire command, Patton dismissed the idea and insisted on a smaller force of about three hundred men and fifty vehicles.[11] Abrams decided to give the mission to the 10th Armored Infantry Battalion, whose commander, Lieutenant Colonel Harold Cohen, unable to lead the mission himself because of a painful hemorrhoid condition, assigned the mission to twenty-four-year-old Captain Abraham J. Baum, a member of his staff.

Abe Baum had grown up in the Bronx, where his Jewish father was a blouse cutter in New York's garment district. Baum had enlisted in the army in 1941 and had gone on to earn a commission. As an armored infantry officer, he had already received two Purple Hearts serving with the 4th Armored Division.[12]

By one-thirty, Baum was at Abrams's command post, where he received orders for the Hammelburg operation. Then Patton pulled aside the six-foot-two Baum and whispered to him, "Listen, Abe—it is Abe, isn't it? I thought so. You pull this off and I'll see to it that you get the Congressional Medal of Honor."

"I have my orders, sir," said Baum. "You don't have to bribe me."[13]

General Patton soon departed, leaving Major Stiller behind to give details of the mission to Abrams, Cohen, and Baum. But Stiller had little information to share. He could say only that there were approximately three hundred American officers (there were, in fact, more than a thousand) held at the camp and that General Patton wanted them rescued. Although the camp was known to be in the vicinity of Hammelburg, Stiller could not even provide its exact location. Then, to the astonishment of Abrams, Cohen, and Baum, Stiller declared that he would be going along on the raid.*

When the task force had finally been assembled at five that afternoon, it included 293 weary men (they had slept one night in the past four) in fifty-three vehicles—ten M4 Sherman medium tanks of Company C, 37th Tank Battalion; a reconnaissance platoon of six light M5A1 Stuart tanks, armed with 37-millimeter guns, from Company D of the 37th; twenty-seven half-tracks carrying the men of Company A, 10th Armored Infantry Battalion; a platoon of three Sherman-mounted 105-millimeter mobile assault guns; half a dozen jeeps; and a medic vehicle known as a Weasel.

At eight-thirty, the guns of three artillery battalions roared as their shells pounded the town of Schweinheim for thirty minutes. At nine, tanks and armored infantry of the 4th Armored Division attacked the town in an attempt to breach the German line and make a hole for Task Force Baum to scoot through and begin its move toward Hammelburg. The Germans responded with Panzerfausts, their version of the bazooka infantry antitank weapon. One Panzerfaust rocket-propelled, shape-charged warhead soon knocked out the lead tank. Fierce fighting ensued, and eventually the Americans withdrew to their original positions, but not until they had held an opening long enough for Baum's task force to break through and disappear into enemy territory. As the task force sped on into the warm and moonless night, the temporary opening in the German lines quickly closed behind them.

The task force rolled through the countryside beyond Schweinheim, into the swarthy Spessart region. Passing through small villages and hilly oak forests all day, the column fought several skirmishes with small German forces encountered along the way.

In an attempt to prevent his column's movement from being reported, Baum ordered his tanks to knock down telephone poles on the

---

* According to historian John Toland in his book *The Last 100 Days* (New York: Random House, 1966), pp. 287–88, Major Stiller had by this time already informed Abrams and Hoge that Patton's son-in-law, Lieutenant Colonel John Waters, was believed to be among the prisoners at the Hammelburg camp.

side of the road, after which his infantry cut the wires strung along the ground. But he was too late. Reports of his column's activities had reached Seventh German Army headquarters an hour earlier. Within fifteen minutes, the commander of the Hammelburg Training Area received a message alerting him that an American armored force had broken through and was rapidly approaching his area.

The task force ran into its first real trouble shortly before seven at Gemünden, where two smaller rivers—the Sinn and the Saale—feed into the Main. The Americans had covered thirty-two miles in the dark of night and were more than halfway to Hammelburg. At the break of dawn, Captain Baum ordered a small tank and infantry force into the town to capture a bridge over the Saale. Even though they had the advantage of surprise, the force ran into stiff German resistance just short of the bridge. Panzerfausts knocked out three Shermans, and the infantry platoon was captured almost to a man.

Baum, who later estimated that sixty-five to seventy Panzerfausts were fired at the column during the firefight, was standing with the tank and infantry company commanders next to a Sherman when one of the antitank rockets exploded on impact nearby. The blast knocked Baum off his feet; shrapnel struck him in the knee and the right hand, opening wounds to the bone in both places. With his pant leg becoming soaked with blood, Baum shouted, "Let's get the hell out of here!"[14]

In all, Baum lost the three medium tanks that had been destroyed and a few half-tracks and a jeep that had been captured. Three men were killed, and eighteen, including a company commander and a platoon leader, were wounded. Thirty-seven men had been captured. Three German soldiers and a few civilians were also killed in the engagement. In a final act of defiance, German engineers blew the bridge, cutting the road to Hammelburg, just as two of Baum's men were running across it.

Baum ordered the remainder of his force to withdraw. When the interrogation of a prisoner revealed that the task force was in the middle of a marshaling area for two enemy divisions, the Americans backed out of town and headed north, along the west bank of the Sinn, until they found a small bridge still intact and crossed the river. Baum's job was suddenly much tougher; the Germans were now on the alert. As news of the American task force spread through the German command, units were ordered into action to block its advance.

With Allied armies approaching the Hammelburg area, the Germans had already decided to evacuate Oflag XIII-B. At ten-fifteen on the morning of March 27, the prisoners were told they would be leaving the camp early the following morning. Medics held a sick call to identify those unable to march.[15]

———

That afternoon, Baum's task force encountered two German tanks near the village of Obereschenbach, a mile and a half outside Hammelburg, where the Americans escaped after a brief skirmish with neither side suffering losses. A degree of luck had been with Baum and his men, but the captain felt sure they would soon be in a tough tank battle.[16]

After skirting around the town of Hammelburg, the American column reached the village of Pfaffenhausen, midway between Hammelburg and the prisoner of war camp. Here the task force once again encountered German tanks. Baum's six remaining Shermans and his assault guns fought hard, destroying three of the enemy tanks. Several German ammunition trucks exploded when hit by American high-explosive rounds.

When Task Force Baum reached an intersection at the approach to the Saale River bridge, near Oflag XIII-B, at three that afternoon, German tank destroyers fired on the column from across the river. Baum lost five half-tracks, one carrying gasoline and another loaded with 105-millimeter ammunition. The Germans lost three half-tracks.

The American column turned off the highway and began climbing the hill toward the camp. An estimated two companies of German infantry, dug in on the high ground, opened up on Baum's force as soon as it appeared over a ridge. For two and a half hours, the Americans fought to clear out the German infantry so the task force could continue on its mission.

The American light tank platoon, an assault gun, an infantry platoon, and most of the half-tracks moved on toward the camp, still under fire from German tank destroyers. The only two remaining assault guns silenced German machine guns that were firing on the American tanks and infantry advancing up the ridge.

———

At Oflag XIII-B, the Germans issued each man a quarter loaf of bread with a little margarine, jam, and sugar, just three hours after serving a noon meal of pea soup. Rations may have been increased, albeit only slightly, to prepare the prisoners for the evacuation march. Speculation among the POWs on their destination centered around Berchtesgaden, the Bavarian town high in the mountains near the Austrian border that had become famous as the site of Hitler's Alpine retreat.

Throughout the camp, men were busy packing for the next day's evacuation when, at around half-past three, they suddenly heard the firing of tank guns from the direction of Hammelburg and the ridgeline west of the camp. Colonel Goode and several others ran to the fence to see what was happening as German guards hastily manned prepared fighting positions just outside the camp. As the tank battle grew nearer, the men began to hear rifle and machine-gun fire, the thump of mortars, and the unmistakable sound of Panzerfaust antitank rockets. It was clear that the camp itself was under attack, and by three forty-five, the prisoners spotted the first American tanks.[17]

Several men ran for the camp kitchen and began breaking open stored food supplies. At three-fifty, the camp's sirens screamed a series of short alarm blasts. Guards ordered all prisoners to their barracks and told them to stay there, but they allowed Father Paul Cavanaugh, the Jesuit priest who had been the 106th Division's chaplain at the time of his capture, to hold his regularly scheduled four o'clock mass.

Cavanaugh's service got under way with around one hundred men in attendance. The priest, in his vestments, tried to conceal his fear as he stood behind the small wooden table that served as an altar. Shells from Task Force Baum's guns exploded nearby as the men inside awaited general absolution and Communion. During the gospel, an explosion shook plaster from the walls and sent everyone in the room sprawling on the floor. Cavanaugh, who had taken shelter beneath the altar, stood and tried to calm the prisoners in the room.

"If anything happens," said the priest to the roomful of frightened men kneeling before him, "just stretch out on the floor. I'll give you general absolution now."[18] After making the sign of the cross, Father Cavanaugh continued, "Men, be calm. I am going to shorten this mass as much as possible so that everyone may get to Holy Communion."[19] Then he prayed, "Graciously accept, O Lord, this offering of our subjection to You. Give us peace today. Save us from eternal damnation and number us in the flock of Your chosen ones, through Christ our Lord."[20] The priest sped through the remainder of the service and quickly served Communion.

Captain Baum ordered what was left of his task force—barely half of what he had started with—to make a direct assault on the camp shortly

after four. Many of his wounded GIs lay in the vehicles. The seriously
wounded had been left, with the dead, along the road to Hammelburg.

Dusk was already approaching as Baum's small force neared the
camp. Before them, his men saw the vast compound, with its double-
barbed-wire-fence perimeter and guard towers. By four-thirty, the task
force's guns were firing on the camp guards.

Baum watched as one of his infantrymen was cut down by machine-
gun fire coming from the compound. The wounded man rose to his
knees and returned fire at the machine gun until German bullets
knocked him down again. Even the medics showed uncommon gal-
lantry by risking their lives, caring for the wounded while under fire;
both aid men assigned to the tank platoon earned Silver Stars that day.

Lieutenant Colonel John Waters viewed some of the action from a
ground-floor window in the building that served as Colonel Goode's
headquarters. He watched as American tanks approached the camp,
their guns firing into the barracks area that housed the Serbian prisoners. General von Goeckel entered the building at around five-thirty and
asked the Americans to go out and make contact with the attackers and
get them to stop shooting. The Americans, he said, were firing into the
Serb barracks, apparently mistaking the prisoners for Germans because
of their uniforms.

"Okay," said Waters, "I'll go out."[21]

Von Goeckel informed Goode that he was surrendering the camp,
then he and a group of guards departed and left the camp area.

Not far away, fierce fighting continued between Baum's men and the
guards just outside the camp. Beyond, smoke billowed from the site of
Baum's earlier skirmish with the tank destroyers. A barracks building
burned in the Yugoslav compound. Colonel Goode, concerned for the
safety of the prisoners, encouraged them to return to their barracks until
the shooting stopped.

At six-fifteen, during a lull in the shooting, Lieutenant Colonel Waters quickly assembled a group of four officers. He walked out the main
gate with a German captain at his side and two other American officers
a step behind, one carrying a white sheet tied to a pole and the other
carrying an American flag.

Baum's main force was just appearing over the ridge, where the German camp guards were dug in on the high ground. Waters intended to
skirt around the area of the heaviest fighting and approach the American
force from the side. The small group advanced until they reached a barn

several hundred yards from the camp's gate. Then Waters saw a soldier in camouflage uniform running toward them.

When the soldier was about fifty yards away, Waters, unsure whether the soldier was American or German, shouted, *"Amerikanisch!"*[22]

Halting, the soldier, who turned out to be German, raised his rifle, steadied it on a fence, and fired. With the impact of a blow by a baseball bat, the bullet tore into Waters's right upper thigh and exited through his left buttock. He fell to the ground, severely wounded. The others picked him up and carried him back into the compound and straight to the Serbian hospital, where he was treated.

Darkness engulfed the camp as all lights in the compound went out just as the tanks of Task Force Baum, never hesitating, approached the perimeter fence. In a field just outside the compound, a haystack burst into flame as a Sherman tank raced up the hill and crashed through the camp's double row of barbed wire. Others followed, crushing the fence as they broke through. Baum's force quickly overcame the light resistance offered by the remaining guard force, many of whom had chosen to run off. By about six-thirty, the assault was over. Several men dismounted from the tanks and half-tracks and began running through the camp, yelling to the men inside the barracks that they were being liberated.

Prisoners inside the barracks had taken to the floor when the firefight outside grew closer and tracers began tearing through the camp. Now, as the shooting stopped, men emptied from the barracks and cheered as they saw the white star of the United States Army emblazoned on the turrets of the tanks that had crashed through the fence. Bedlam reigned throughout the compound as Oflag XIII-B erupted in jubilation, men shouting for joy and celebrating their long-awaited freedom.

Crowds of men in a wide variety of uniforms rushed toward the tanks and half-tracks at the camp's perimeter, trampled over the crumpled fence, and swarmed around their liberators. Confusion mixed with celebration overcame the POWs as they engulfed the tanks. Wildly cheering prisoners climbed onto vehicles, hugging and kissing and thanking the men of the 4th Armored Division. Baum's tankers and infantrymen literally had to push the POWs away.

Captain Baum and Colonel Goode got the situation under control at around eight-thirty. Baum's force consolidated on a hill just outside camp and prepared to take prisoners aboard for the return trip to

American lines. Later, when the prisoners were directed to assemble at the vehicles, it was clear that there were too few tanks and half-tracks to carry everyone.

As hungry prisoners munched on K-rations found in the vehicles, Baum's men explained that they were only a rescue party of two companies and that the main Allied lines were still fifty or sixty miles back. Odds were against their safe return to friendly lines.[23] The task force would carry as many prisoners as possible, but there was insufficient room in the vehicles to carry all of the American POWs.

Priority would be given to those healthy enough to make the return journey and help man the guns to fight through any German forces encountered en route. Someone suggested taking all armor officers among the POWs; they would be better suited to replace tank crewmen who had been killed or wounded. Prisoners judged to be too feeble or too sick to make the trip were encouraged to return to their barracks. Those who dared to try were told that they could set out on their own. But the task force had to get under way quickly if it was to have any chance of getting back to friendly lines. News of the precarious nature of their liberation was a blow to the morale of hundreds of men who believed they had finally been freed. Many of the POWs unfit for travel gathered together and returned to camp under a white flag.

First Lieutenant Allan Todd, a man accustomed to taking chances, thought it worth the risk. He climbed onto a tank, crawled through the hatch, and assumed the position of the number two gunner, who had been killed. In all, an estimated seven hundred prisoners boarded the remaining tanks and half-tracks until the vehicles could hold no more.[24] Some prisoners, unable to find a spot aboard the vehicles, decided to walk alongside the column. The rest returned to camp.

At ten-thirty, Lieutenant William Nutto moved out into the dark down a dirt road with a scout element of four medium tanks and three half-tracks, all crowded with freed POWs. Nutto sought a route through the military training area to Reichsstrasse 27, but within half an hour his small force encountered a roadblock between Hundsfeld and Bonnland. Captain Baum ordered a detour to the north.

Thirty minutes later, another roadblock near Zinkelsberg forced Nutto to withdraw toward the Schnieselt-Holz forest. He then turned his scouting party toward a group of buildings called the Reussenberg farm. At the same time, Baum's main column left Camp Hammelburg, en route to the Reussenberg farm by a more direct route, where Baum planned to receive Lieutenant Nutto's report.

Todd was in the lead tank of Baum's force as it moved out.[25] As the tank approached a village shortly after getting under way, it came to a sudden halt when the road ahead was blocked. Todd saw the flash of a Panzerfaust fired from the side of the road ahead. He instinctively turned his machine gun in the direction of the flash and fired. Suddenly the tank shook in the explosion as the Panzerfaust projectile hit. Todd was stunned by the impact of the rocket. Once he recovered, he saw that the tank commander and the number one gunner, as well as two men riding on the outside of the tank, were dead. The driver, like Todd, was dazed but still alive.

The night was moist and chilly, and a full moon only occasionally broke through the heavy cloud cover. With the lack of moonlight, it was too dark for Todd to tell if he had hit the Germans with his machine-gun fire, but he was sure the enemy would soon open up on them again. Other Panzerfaust rockets flashed through the night up and down the column, hitting several tanks and half-tracks. American and German machine-gun fire, marked by red and yellow tracer rounds, filled the air. Enemy machine-gun bullets pelted the hull and turret of the tank Todd was in. A Panzerfaust knocked out another tank in the column, and the rest of the tanks dispersed and disappeared.

Another hit from a Panzerfaust rocket would likely set Todd's tank on fire; he knew he had to get out and get away from the vehicle as quickly as he could. He exited through the hatch, jumped to the ground, and crawled over a nearby rise. Machine-gun fire continued to rake the area. Unarmed and on his own, Todd could only watch as the last of the surviving American tanks and half-tracks departed the ambush site.

Germans searched in the dark throughout the area for POWs. A patrol found the dejected Todd around midnight and escorted him back to camp. Upon his return to Oflag XIII-B, a camp doctor removed a piece of shrapnel from Todd's back and another small piece from one leg and then bandaged both wounds. The concussion from the Panzerfaust blast had left Todd with a terrific headache and caused his damaged ear to begin draining again. He learned that several other men had been killed or wounded in the same ambush where he was hit.[26]

One recaptured prisoner, being escorted back to camp by German soldiers, walked in the ruts made earlier by the treads of one of the tanks that broke through the fence. As he passed a German guard he knew, the guard said, "Get some sleep, fellows—you've had a tough night."[27] Shortly after midnight, a company of German officer cadets arrived at Oflag XIII-B to reinforce the camp guards, then in the process of reoccupying the camp. More German troops arrived throughout the early morning hours of March 28.

After the skirmish that cost Todd his newfound freedom, Baum struck out to the southwest with the surviving vehicles of his task force. The group crossed a small bridge, then ran into two more roadblocks at the next village. Panzerfausts again flared through the darkness, and Baum lost another Sherman. The diminishing column of survivors once again broke away and drove to Höllrich, the next village to the north, but an ambush there knocked out another Sherman; Baum lost a tank commander and several infantrymen.

Realizing the desperate situation he was in, Baum backed the column out of the area and drove to a hill a mile east of Höllrich, reassembling the remnants of his force there at around three-thirty in the morning. His task force was now down to around thirty vehicles, and only a third of the men he had started with were still capable of fighting.[28]

At four o'clock, Colonel Goode gathered the remaining men of the task force and the liberated POWs still with the column and spoke to them. He explained the grim situation they were in, but he said there was still a slight chance for some of the men to get away. Goode told the assembled men that he felt responsible for the prisoners and that he wanted to see as many of them as possible get home alive. He gave the men three options: They could take off across country toward the Allied lines on their own, they could remain with Baum's force as they tried to fight their way back, or they could return to camp with him. At four forty-five, the colonel and many of the POWs walked back to Oflag XIII-B.

Those prisoners choosing to remain with Baum's force grabbed weapons from the wounded infantrymen and took the place of men who had been killed or severely wounded during the drive to the camp. All told, Baum counted about 110 men in his small force. At five-thirty, he had the men consolidate all the remaining gasoline, siphoning fuel from eight of the half-tracks and putting it into the remaining tanks, a command vehicle, and a couple of half-tracks carrying the wounded. Then the men set fire to the emptied half-tracks.

Baum then sent his last radio message to his battalion command post back near Aschaffenburg. He reported that the mission had been accomplished and that the task force was on its way back. As dawn approached, all seriously wounded men were placed in a nearby stone building on which a large red cross was marked. They would be left behind and, hopefully, be tended to by the Germans.

At nine, Baum gathered the officers at his jeep for a quick briefing. During the return drive, he explained, they would have to cross back over some streams, and they might not have time to look for a bridge. There were only a couple of half-tracks left, and Baum now ordered that, if necessary, these vehicles were to be emptied and driven into a stream to serve as makeshift bridging equipment. The tanks would crawl over the half-tracks to the far bank and continue their drive toward friendly territory. The officers were well aware that the enemy had them surrounded, and they puzzled over why the Germans didn't attack. Baum then ordered all vehicles into march formation and climbed into his jeep.

Just as Baum's jeep was about to pull out, a devastating volley of artillery and cannon fire from German tank destroyers pounded the column of American tanks. The guns had opened up on signal, and Baum had never seen anything like it. The stunned Americans could provide no resistance. German infantry and armored vehicles, including Tiger tanks, approached from all directions, skillfully keeping up the fire as they maneuvered, closing in on the surrounded task force. Professionally, Baum couldn't help but admire the precisely coordinated combined arms assault.

The Americans struggled valiantly to move into fighting positions and return fire, but soon all of the task force's vehicles were knocked out, burning fiercely as Baum's infantry was being torn apart. German shells pounded the building with the big red cross that contained the seriously wounded. The entire task force was destroyed within twenty-five minutes.

It was around ten when Baum and the other Americans who could still move ran into the woods and gathered together. Every time they approached the clearing to see how near the Germans were, they were met by a storm of rifle fire. Officers ordered the men to break away in groups of four and attempt to find their way back to American lines.

German troops swarmed the area, bringing in dogs to track down survivors. They found the wounded who had been left in the building with the red cross, which by now had been nearly destroyed, and evacuated the men to the Oflag XIII-B hospital.

Baum's small group of survivors evaded capture throughout the day. But by nightfall most of the men, including Major Stiller and Captain Baum, the latter wounded in the process, were captured and marched back to the prison camp. Upon their arrival at Oflag XIII-B, Baum and about thirty-five other wounded men were taken to the Serbian hospital.

In a German radio news broadcast at eight on the evening of March 29, 1945, the broadcaster boasted of a German victory over American tanks near Hammelburg. In the village of Nesselroden, troops of the 4th Armored Division, having crossed the Main and moved northward, read of the failed American raid in German newspapers.[29] On April 5, the division's 10th Armored Infantry Battalion officially reported 206 soldiers of Task Force Baum as missing in action. The next day, the 4th Armored Division reported the same status for all men of the task force.[30]

Later, in a press conference, Patton denied having known, prior to the raid, that his son-in-law was a prisoner at the Hammelburg camp. He claimed to have learned of Waters's presence there only after the raid. Hoge and Abrams would wait nearly two decades before setting the record straight.[31]

In all, Baum's task force lost nine men killed, thirty-two wounded, and sixteen missing in action.[32] The missing men were never accounted for and were presumed killed, bringing the total killed to twenty-five.[33] All of the task force's vehicles were destroyed or captured. Eventually, about half a dozen men of Task Force Baum who struck out on their own did succeed in finding their way safely back to American lines on foot.

TWENTY-NINE

RUMORS OF EVIL

General von Goeckel, now back in command at Oflag XIII-B, announced early on the morning of March 28 that the remaining prisoners would evacuate the camp in thirty minutes. Anyone refusing to leave would be shot. Todd's morale, like that of all the prisoners, sank to a new low.[1] Freedom had momentarily seemed so near, only to be lost so quickly and so violently.

With the recaptured American POWs and the newly captured men from Task Force Baum, the Germans had approximately 1,650 men to move southward. About 100 men remained in the camp hospital, wounded or too sick to be moved. Included in this group were Lieutenant Colonel John Waters and Captain Abe Baum. Another 50 men were still at large, as they had so far successfully evaded recapture and were trying to make their way to American lines.[2]

The Germans organized the men into three march columns and put another four groups of men on trains. Lieutenant Allan Todd and over three hundred other prisoners formed the first march column to leave the camp. The senior prisoner in the group, Colonel Cavender, organized the men into four companies, each led by a lieutenant colonel.[3] A forty-man guard force accompanied the march column, and although the guards walked along with the prisoners, the German colonel commanding this group rode in a staff car. Each day he would drive ahead to make arrangements for that night's billeting. A truck carried Major Hazlett, the mess officer, and his enlisted cooks to the next day's stopping point to prepare what little food they could for the prisoners. Trailing behind the column was a wagon hauling the guards' baggage.

By three that morning, the prisoners were on the road, marching nine miles through a densely wooded area until they reached Arnstein at ten o'clock. The column had been marching at an unusually slow pace, which the men attributed to the advanced age of the guards walking along with them. When a light rain began to fall, the guards moved the prisoners into the woods, where they sat as the rain continued to fall through much of the day. German soldiers issued a small piece of bread, a dab of canned meat, and three raw potatoes to each prisoner, and the men ate as they sat about. Later that evening, the column formed again and marched another four miles to the village of Schnackenwerth, about five miles west of Schweinfurt. Then the Germans began the old routine of feeding the prisoners an evening meal of a few boiled potatoes and some hot water and then billeting them in barns.

During the next day's march, the men filed across a bridge over the Main, in the middle of which lay two large bombs, rigged and ready to demolish the structure. On the far bank, they passed through the large town of Schweinfurt. Over the next few days, the column pushed on in a southeasterly direction through the picturesque countryside of Franconia.

One morning, the column was spotted by American fighter planes. Anticipating the danger of a bombing or strafing by Allied planes, the prisoners had prepared bedsheets torn into strips that could be used to form large letters reading "US PW." One fighter circled above and then flew ahead to join another plane; it looked as though the two might be preparing to strafe the column, mistaking it for a German army unit on the move. Prisoners broke out the bedsheets and quickly laid them out on the ground as the guards scampered to take cover under the nearest trees. As the planes flew in low, the prisoners tensed. Then, having recognized the letters spelled out on the ground, the pilots tipped their wings and flew off. The men cheered, but they would have to repeat the act later that morning.

On Easter Sunday, Father Cavanaugh got permission from Hauptmann (Captain) Stammler, a German officer whom Cavanaugh knew to be Catholic, to conduct Easter services. Stammler arranged for a church in the nearby village of Herchelheim to be made available for the POWs. At eleven on Sunday morning, around eighty prisoners crowded into the small, six-hundred-year-old church. Father Cavanaugh conducted the service, complete with gold vestments provided by the village priest, with two prisoner lieutenants serving as acolytes. Later that day, Gestapo officers arrived and inexplicably searched the prisoners.

In almost every way, the march from Hammelburg to the south was much like the one from Oflag 64 to Oflag XIII-B: long foot marches; scant rations of raw potatoes, watery potato or barley soup, bread, and ersatz coffee or hot water; and nights spent in barns. Two major differences were that the weather this time was much better and, if it was any consolation, the men were now walking through southern Bavaria, some of the most beautiful countryside Germany had to offer.

Guards continued to guide the weary men farther to the southeast, generally nine to fifteen miles a day. On some days, the men walked through forest thick enough to conceal the column from view by Allied planes. Whenever there was a break in the forest covering, the men could see contrails high above, left by Allied bombers, and they could hear the rumble of bombs impacting in the distance.

Sometimes, as the column filed through tiny rural Bavarian villages, small children came out to the road and greeted the Americans with a Nazi salute and a hearty *"Heil Hitler."*[4]

At two on the morning of Thursday, April 5, the column moved out under a fine drizzle, passing through the bomb-rubbled eastern outskirts of Fürth and Nuremberg. There the men saw that the city's I. G. Farben plant had been heavily damaged, though it was already back in limited operation. The rain had stopped and the skies had cleared by the time the column halted for lunch at eleven alongside a stretch of railroad next to a small stand of spruce.

Forty minutes later, as the men lunched on potato-and-barley soup and sipped ersatz tea, an air-raid siren wailed in the distance. Guards rushed to move the prisoners into the wood line, but before they could get the men organized, the siren blared a series of short blasts. High overhead, the men saw the contrails of a formation of bombers. Then some of the men noticed white flares falling, the flares used by bombers to mark targets. If they were meant to mark the Nuremberg railroad marshaling yards, they were falling about a mile short. The flares were coming down right in the area where the POWs had halted for their lunch break.

Thirty-four B-17s of the U.S. 100th Bomb Group (Heavy) released their bombs from an altitude of 24,700 feet.[5] Suddenly the prisoners found themselves on the receiving end of an American bombing. One stick of bombs, falling well short of the target, pummeled the road and the wood line where prisoners scattered to save themselves. Another group of bombers followed in a second wave and dropped its load of bombs on some nearby munitions factories. Flames and clouds of smoke soon poured from the buildings. In all, five flights of bombers came in quick succession, all bombing the same general area.[6] Then it was over.

When the dust settled, craters measuring fifteen to twenty feet in diameter and five feet deep lay near the stunned survivors. At least two dozen prisoners lay dead, and close to twice that number were wounded. Six Germans, including a captain who had been at Oflag 64, were also killed.[7]

As the shock of the incident subsided, German guards formed the survivors back into a column and, within an hour of the attack, marched the men out of the area. Fifteen prisoner of war chaplains and medical officers were allowed to stay behind to tend to the wounded, who were soon evacuated by truck to a German hospital. Throughout the evacuation, German Red Cross nurses administered morphine to those who needed it to help relieve pain. American prisoners of war from camps in the Nuremberg area buried the dead in a nearby cemetery the next day.

The column of Hammelburg POWs continued marching until they reached the town of Feucht, where the men were quartered in barns. Hours later, the chaplains and medical officers who had remained behind to see to the wounded rejoined the group.[8]

The prisoners, still recovering from the shock of the bombing, were allowed to rest most of the next day, and the Germans issued a Red Cross parcel to each man. Still, four more American officers died that day.[9] Father Cavanaugh judged that only four hundred men remained from the five hundred who had started the march from the Hammelburg camp.[10]

———

Reportedly, Sergeant John Austin of Jedburgh team Dudley, imprisoned in Holland since his capture in November 1944, never revealed to the Germans his true name or the names of his Jedburgh teammates, Major John Olmsted and Major Henk Brinkgreve. To his fellow prisoners, with whom he communicated secretly, he was known simply as "Tommy." The Germans listed him as Bunny Wyatt. At one point, after team Dudley's leader, Major Brinkgreve, had been killed, the Germans confronted Austin with a photo of Brinkgreve and asked him to identify the Dutch officer. Austin refused to do so.

In early April 1945, a month before the war in Europe ended, the German commander of the prison in Zwolle where Austin was being held received orders to select six prisoners to be shot. The prisoners were to be executed as a reprisal for the recent sabotage of a nearby railway. On the morning of April 4, the Germans selected Sergeant Austin and five imprisoned members of the Dutch resistance, took them to the IJssel dike at Hattem, and shot them. Austin was twenty-one years old at the time of his death.[11]

One of the last Jedburgh teams to be deployed in Europe during the war parachuted near Barneveld, Holland, on the night of April 3–4, 1945. Team Gambling included a British officer, Major A. H. Clutton; Captain Maarten J. Knottenbelt, the Dutch officer who had accompanied Jedburgh team Claude on Operation Market-Garden; and a British radio operator, Company Quartermaster Sergeant James S. Menzies. Operating in support of an SAS mission called Keystone, the Jedburgh team was there to prevent demolition by the Germans of bridges over the Apeldoorn Canal. The team's secondary mission was to arrange for the reception of additional SAS elements.

Shermans of the 47th Tank Battalion, 14th Armored Division, entered Oflag XIII-B at Hammelburg at four on the afternoon of April 6. Among the wounded American officers found in the camp hospital were Lieutenant Colonel John Waters and Captain Abe Baum. All the wounded, including Waters and Baum, were sent to a U.S. Army evacuation hospital near Frankfurt am Main.

Of the roughly 1,500 American POWs held at Oflag XIII-B at the time of the raid, it was later estimated that some 600 initially accompanied Task Force Baum as it set off on its return journey. Of those, around 400 returned to camp with Colonel Goode after the first skirmish, 50 remained with the task force, and about 150 took off immediately after the initial ambush in an attempt to evade recapture. Another

350 took off later in groups of 3 toward American lines. By early morning, around 500 men had returned to camp on their own or had been rounded up by the Germans.[12]

———

In Holland, paratroopers of the French 3rd and 4th Special Air Service jumped on the night of April 7–8, 1945, ahead of advancing Canadian forces. Teams of SAS troops spread throughout the Dutch province of Groningen to protect key facilities—dikes, drainage systems, and bridges—from demolition by the Germans. Along with the SAS, a Jedburgh team code-named Dicing jumped from a British Stirling to a field near Assen. Leading the team was a British officer, Major Robert Harcourt. Teamed with Harcourt and making his second jump into Holland was Captain Arie Bestebreurtje, who had earlier been George Verhaeghe's Dutch teammate on Jed team Clarence. Rounding out team Dicing were a British radio operator, Sergeant Claude Somers, and another Dutch officer, Captain C. Ruysch van Dugteren. Team Dicing's mission was to assist in the liberation of Camp Westerbork, near the village of Hooghalen. Westerbork was a transit camp for Jews destined for concentration camps in Germany. Once the camp was secured, the Jeds were to assist the Dutch underground in seizing key bridges in the northern provinces for the approaching Canadian 2nd Division. But things began going badly for the Jeds immediately upon landing.

Captain Bestebreurtje broke an ankle on the jump and narrowly escaped capture by the Germans. Major Harcourt was not as lucky; he was captured the day after their arrival. Van Dugteren and Somers found each other soon after the jump, but they were unable to locate either Harcourt or Bestebreurtje. The two proceeded with the mission, contacting the Dutch underground on their own.

Isolated behind enemy lines and unable to walk, Bestebreurtje began crawling toward the village of Hooghalen. Progress was painfully slow. He remained hidden during the daytime, sleeping amid the pine forests, under shrubs or heath plants or haystacks. Only during the hours of darkness did he crawl on his stomach toward the village. He was in terrific pain, and soon his growing thirst drove him to drink from mud puddles. His only food consisted of pieces of chocolate. Four days into his ordeal, he was discovered by a farmer named Jan Schutten, who, with the help of his son, loaded Bestebreurtje onto a horse-drawn cart and hauled him to their farmhouse. There he remained hidden in the attic, under the care of the Dutch family, until the area was liberated by Canadian troops on April 12, which happened to be Bestebreurtje's birthday. When he was evacuated from an emergency airfield, he learned that the plane was piloted by the same man who had dropped him and the other two members of Jed team Clarence with the 82nd Airborne Division near Nijmegen seven months earlier.[13]

Meanwhile, the POW column from Oflag XIII-B continued its southward march. As the men shuffled along on Friday, April 13, German guards told them the news of President Roosevelt's death. That evening, a German priest in the village of Zell confirmed the news. Understanding the impact this had on the Americans, the priest offered Father Cavanaugh the use of his church for a memorial service. Cavanaugh gratefully accepted and performed the service while the evening meal of potato soup was being prepared.

Over the next few days, the POWs marched through the rugged foothills of the Bavarian Alps, stopping to rest all day on the sixteenth as a light snow fell. Lieutenant Allan Todd relaxed with the other prisoners, unaware that only the day before, Canadian soldiers of Montgomery's Twenty-first Army Group finally captured the Dutch city of Arnhem.

By this time, like college roommates tiring of one another's annoying habits, many prisoners had grown weary of the behavior of some of their fellow POWs. Two captains had become particularly irksome. Butch and Ben were clearly pals, but they never seemed to be near each other. At night, in a barn, they would often find themselves at opposite ends of the loft, and all those trying to sleep would have to listen to their long-distance chats.

"Hey, Butch."

"Whaddaya want, Ben?"

"I got the hot water, bring the coffee."[14]

Such exchanges went on day and night, getting on everyone's nerves. Some prisoners became so tired of Butch and Ben's routine that they began mocking them. But the day would come when the prisoners would appreciate the humor of it.

At five on the morning of April 17, the column got under way and proceeded along forest trails for ten and a half miles to the southeast. Everyone hid among the trees whenever Allied planes were spotted overhead to avoid being mistaken for German troops and strafed. Soon they were walking on a modern highway that ran alongside the Danube. Here the river was fast-flowing and a hundred yards wide. It became clear that the Germans intended to cross the river, but the prisoners had seen no bridges.

Then the guards directed the column into a village off the main road, not far to the southwest of Regensburg and about sixty miles north of Munich. The men were taken in groups of sixty to the river, where they boarded a barge ferry guided by a heavy steel cable suspended between the river's banks. As the ferry inched its way across the river, the POWs stared down into the swirling, muddy water of the not-so-blue Danube.

On the opposite bank, the men dismounted and went ashore near the town of Weltenburg, overlooked by an impressive old Benedictine monastery atop a steep hill. Not much more than a day's march from here lay another large prisoner of war camp for Americans, Stalag VII-A. It was near the town of Moosburg, and most of the other groups of prisoners that had evacuated Oflag XIII-B marched or went by train to this camp, where they were then interned.

The Germans escorting Lieutenant Todd's march column, though, received word that there was no more room for prisoners at Stalag VII-A; the camp was already filled beyond its intended capacity. So Todd's group would have to continue marching southward, though no one knew what their destination was.

One day, during a halt in the march, a German pastor from a local church visited Father Cavanaugh and told him the latest news. American and Russian forces had met on the Oder River, and General Patton's Third Army had now turned southward, advancing in the general direction of the POW column's current location. That evening, the rumble of distant artillery could be heard.[15]

The column moved out again the following morning under a rainfall. When the rain stopped later that day, the men again heard the sound of artillery, and it seemed closer than it had the day before. Signs were all around them indicating that they would soon be engulfed by the combat zone. Enemy troops were seen digging machine-gun positions in the area. Prisoners saw carts delivering supplies to German troops, and the column marched across bridges rigged for demolition. Guards in the rear of the column were clearly in no mood for games as they pushed stragglers on. After walking ten and a half miles, the men halted for the night at the town of Obermarchembach.

The U.S. 14th Armored Division had crossed the Rhine on April Fools'
Day 1945. Three weeks later, the division was transferred from the Seventh Army to Patton's Third Army, and the 14th's tanks began driving
southward through Bavaria, led by the 94th Cavalry Reconnaissance
Squadron (Mechanized).[16] As early as April 19, the 94th began to encounter emaciated, dirty, unshaven GIs who wore strange mixtures of
uniform pieces—American, British, and German. The men turned out
to be former prisoners of war who managed to escape from march
columns as the Germans relocated captives from one camp to another.
Armored soldiers gave the repatriated men K-rations before sending
them to the rear in jeeps.[17]

As the division continued southward, it often advanced over roads
that Lieutenant Todd and the other American POWs had marched on
only days earlier. Lead elements of the 14th were still some fifty or sixty
miles behind the POW column when they ran into stiff enemy resistance on approaching the Danube. German forces in the area were scattered, largely unorganized, and they often consisted of young boys. But
along the Danube they fought stubbornly, and the Americans suffered
many casualties as the two sides pounded each other with mortar and
artillery fire. Just as the lead American tank was crossing a bridge over
the river, a squad of teenage Germans blew the bridge.

After a tough fight, the division crossed the Danube and, on April 28,
set out to seize a crossing over the next river obstacle, the Isar.[18] Almost
immediately, the division liberated thousands of British and American
POWs at a prison camp at Meilenhoffen.[19]

On the same day that the 14th Armored Division began their drive
toward the Isar, Lieutenant Todd's column began marching at three in
the morning under a full moon. After a ten-mile walk, the German
guards called a halt at the village of Averbach and issued a Red Cross
parcel to each prisoner.

A march of five and a half miles the next morning brought the men
to a church in the village of Inning. At this point, the guards discovered
that around thirty prisoners were missing; the men had slipped away
from the column to hide out and await the approaching U.S. forces.

An hour before noon on Sunday, April 29, troops of the 47th Tank Battalion and 94th Reconnaissance Squadron, both of the 14th Armored Division, entered Oflag VII-B, the prisoner of war camp near the town of Moosburg on the banks of the Isar. Among the thousands of American and British captives they freed were most of the POWs and soldiers of Task Force Baum relocated from Hammelburg. German SS troops paid dearly for their feeble attempt to defend the area. In all, the 47th and 94th liberated 110,000 Allied prisoners from a network of seven POW camps in the Moosburg area. Among the thirty thousand liberated American prisoners was Colonel Goode, the senior American officer at Moosburg, and Major Stiller, who was now free to return to General Patton's staff.

Another objective of the 14th Armored Division was a bridge over the Isar at Moosburg, but this the Germans blew at the last minute. On Monday, engineers erected a treadway bridge, and the division began crossing to the eastern bank while continuing to receive small-arms and mortar fire from scattered German forces. The division was now thirty miles northwest of Lieutenant Todd and the other prisoners in his column.

That same day, Todd's group, now numbering around two hundred men, continued its march southward from Nuremberg, walking eight miles to a town called Taufkirchen, about thirty miles east of Munich. As the men were served a supper of soup and boiled potatoes, guards informed them that the thirty POWs who had left the column near Inning had been recaptured and shot. Few of the prisoners believed this, and it did, in fact, turn out to be untrue. But other rumors were spreading among the POWs, including one speculating that the men were being marched to a remote Nazi headquarters high in the Bavarian Alps. Here, so the rumor went, they would become hostages of a desperate Third Reich.[20]

Allied intelligence, in fact, would have readily supported these rumors. For weeks, they had speculated on the existence of a Nazi "National Redoubt" in southern Bavaria, centered around Hitler's mountain retreat near Berchtesgaden, high in the Alps some seventeen miles from Salzburg. The Führer's fortified retreat was known to include a network of tunnels and stockpiles of supplies. Here, it was feared, desperate Nazi diehards would carry on a campaign of guerrilla warfare against the Allies.[21]

Such a redoubt had been proposed by some in the German military as early as September 1943, and the idea received serious consideration the following summer. U.S. Army intelligence reports developed the idea of a strong last-ditch defense of the Alpine region of southern Germany, and there was even some speculation that the Germans might move prisoners of war to the area and hold them as hostages. Enough of SHAEF's intelligence staff came to believe the reports that they were able to influence General Eisenhower in shifting his attention away from Berlin.

On March 21, the supreme commander issued a "Reorientation of Strategy" to Lieutenant General Omar Bradley, Twelfth Army Group commander. The new strategy's objective was to divide Germany, thus sealing off the suspected Alpine redoubt before additional forces could be moved there from the north. In late March and early April, Eisenhower increasingly shifted his main effort from Montgomery's drive in the north to the advance of Bradley's army group into southern Germany, naturally upsetting the British in the process.[22]

In late April, Hitler ordered Field Marshal Albert Kesselring to organize the defense of the Alpine fortress. But work on the Alpenfestung (Alpine Fortress) progressed slowly in the face of approaching Allied armies. American and French forces of the Sixth Army Group approached from the west and northwest; Patton's Third Army was pushing southward through Bavaria; and Russian units were moving into lower Austria from the east. Work on the Alpenfestung's machine-gun nests, observation posts, and tank obstacles along the western approaches were only partially completed, largely because of a shortage of skilled labor. Forces to man those positions never arrived. A few battered German units, pressed from all sides, straggled into the area but knew nothing of the planned Alpenfestung.

Once again, Allied planes threatened the POWs marching from Hammelburg. As the prisoners marched eastward down a hard-surfaced road under a clear and sunny sky, American fighters repeatedly swept over the area. To pilots high above, the POWs might appear to be just another column of enemy troops. Their sole means of protection from strafing and bombing were the strips of white sheeting that could quickly be spread on the ground in the form of the letters "US PW."

Four P-47s dropped out of the sky and circled the column, seemingly preparing for a strafing run. As the planes began their approach, prisoners hastily scattered, cursing as they ran in every direction. But curses turned to laughter when Ben's voice boomed, "Hey, Butch, bring the panels. I got the planes."[23]

The column was approaching the Inn River, and the men learned that they were to cross it the next day. Lieutenant Allan Todd didn't care for the idea of putting yet another water obstacle between him and the advancing U.S. forces. Every river crossing decreased his chances of liberation by the approaching Americans. Day and night now, the men heard the rumble of artillery and tank battles not far away, and some of them began discussing the prospects of escape. Local civilians, the prisoners speculated, probably didn't pose much of a threat to escapees. Their SS guards were the real and immediate danger. These hardened young Nazis were inclined to shoot any prisoners who in any way impeded their retreat into the mountains.[24]

Todd spoke with another prisoner, Captain Saul Dworkin, a St. Louis physician who had been captured in Belgium in December 1944 during the Battle of the Bulge, while serving with a surgical team in a field hospital supporting the 101st Airborne Division. Todd and the medical officer decided that they must attempt an escape that night, before reaching the river, if they were to have any chance of getting back to friendly lines.

The two officers had befriended Hauptmann Menner, the German captain who had once been a professor in Vienna.[25] Now they approached the German and shared with him their plans to slip away from the column. They urged the former professor to go with them. After several minutes of coaxing, the German officer agreed, but only on the condition that his sergeant major be allowed to join them. Todd and Dworkin indicated that the sergeant major was more than welcome to come along.

A plan quickly took shape. They would wait for the column to get under way the next morning, May 1. Just before daybreak, Todd and Dworkin would find the right opportunity to drop out of the column and slip away. The sergeant major would then feign discovery of their absence and leave the column on his bicycle to search for the missing prisoners. When the sergeant major failed to return after a short time, the German captain would volunteer to go back and look for all three. Meanwhile, the column would continue on its way. If all went as planned, First Lieutenant Allan Todd would soon be free.

THIRTY

FREEDOM

Guards roused the prisoners in the middle of the night as artillery rumbled to the north, illuminating the horizon the way a distant lightning storm does. German troops had been moving through the village of Moosen throughout the night as the front line grew nearer. The prisoners formed up in the dark and marched off in a southeasterly direction, slogging downhill on a forest trail.

For Lieutenant Todd and Dr. Dworkin, finding the right moment to drop out of the column proved more difficult than expected. With the sounds of approaching battle, the guards seemed exceptionally vigilant.[1]

At around five on that morning of Tuesday, May 1, 1945, the column snaked along a trail through thick woods. At times, wind rustled the tree branches above the silent column, causing wet snow to drop on the men. During the first rest stop, with the cover of darkness still on their side, Todd and Dworkin walked into the woods on the pretense of having to relieve themselves. Rather than return to the column, the two men quietly moved to a spot deeper in the woods. For forty-five minutes, they waited in hiding. Then, just as they had planned, the two Germans arrived. All four men remained hidden in the woods for another four hours as the column moved on down the trail.

LT. TODD'S MARCH TO FREEDOM, JANUARY 21–MAY 1, 1945

LEGEND

International border — · — · — · — · —
Todd's foot march, January 21–March 6, 1945 ------
Todd's rail movement, March 6–9, 1945 ············
Todd's foot march, March 28–May 1, 1945 — — — —

It was daylight when the men set out on foot in the direction of the approaching Third U.S. Army. A cold rain began to fall, and soon they spotted a farmhouse where they hoped to take shelter. When the four wet men entered the house, they were surprised to find three more Americans inside. Todd and Dworkin quickly learned that these three had left the column at about the same time they and the two Germans had. Now they were all glad to be together.[2]

The woman of the house, who spoke English, told the escapees that the family would hide and feed them and help them in any other way they could. The German farm family actually seemed happy to have the Americans in their home, even allowing the officers to sleep in their house while the family slept in the barn. From their vantage point in the barn, the family members could watch for approaching German soldiers and alert the escapees.

As they talked with the German woman, the escapees learned what the family's concerns were. Like German citizens everywhere, the family was apprehensive of the approaching Allied armies. The American officers quickly realized why the farm family had welcomed them so warmly: They were viewed by the family as a sort of insurance policy. If the family provided aid to Lieutenant Todd and the other American escapees, any U.S. forces arriving in the area were bound to treat them more kindly.

There was something else, though, that the family feared even more than the U.S. Army. Wandering German SS troops had been searching homes and farms throughout the area, often stealing anything of value and killing anyone, German or American, who got in their way.

Lieutenant Todd, Dr. Dworkin, and the other three Americans now collaborated with Hauptmann Menner and the German sergeant major on a contingency plan. The weapons carried by the two Germans were placed on a table in the farmhouse. If the family alerted them with news of approaching German soldiers, Menner and the sergeant major would pick up the weapons and the Americans would be escaped prisoners recently recaptured by the two Germans. If, on the other hand, U.S. forces were the first to arrive, the roles were to be reversed. The American escapees would pick up the weapons, and the German captain and sergeant major would be their prisoners.[3]

What Todd and the others needed most was rest and food. They had walked over two hundred miles in the past thirty-five days and had done so on scant rations. Including the earlier movement from Oflag 64 to

Oflag XIII-B, they had traveled nearly nine hundred miles, more than half of that on foot. In eighty-three days of walking since January, they had averaged almost seven miles a day.[4] Todd's weight during his captivity had dropped to just under 150 pounds, some 80 pounds less than when he'd entered service.[5]

Benefiting from the family's generosity, the escapees recovered quickly in the days to come, building their strength back on the hearty farm diet. A special treat came one day when the family provided a hog to be butchered. While the pork was being prepared, Dr. Dworkin warned the men not to eat much of the meat. After months of near starvation, large servings of fresh pork would make them sick. But none of the men, Dworkin included, could resist the rich and tasty meal. As the medical officer had predicted, all became violently ill for the next two days. But a regular diet of good food helped the men regain their strength in body as well as in spirit.[6]

Having crossed the Isar River against light resistance, the 14th Armored Division, now slowed by poor roads and snow flurries, struck out for the town of Mühldorf on the Inn River.[7] Townspeople along the way often hung bedsheets from windows signaling that no resistance would be offered. Surrendering German soldiers, no fight left in them, were simply waved to the rear by American troops as the division continued its advance.[8]

On Wednesday, the small group of escaped POWs in the German farmhouse were joined by two Hungarians, a Russian, and three German soldiers who surrendered their arms to the Americans.[9] The Russian joined the farm family in the barn to assist in keeping watch for approaching soldiers.

Thursday, May 3, was a cold day, threatening snow. Allan Todd and the other escapees passed the day eating and sleeping and listening to the approaching American artillery and tank guns.

Advance elements of the 14th Armored Division pushed southward toward their next objective, crossing over the Inn. Intermittent rain and snow transformed roads into muddy trails pockmarked with artillery craters. Often vehicles had to be pulled from the mire to continue on their way. Columns of American tanks and armored infantry rolled through countless towns and villages, where townspeople peered from windows or lined the streets to watch them pass by. German children sometimes waved to the troops. From time to time, though, the Americans had to fight through stubborn remnants of German combat units. At this stage of the war, many such units were manned with boys of sixteen or seventeen as well as old men and even a few young women.

At around two or three on the afternoon of May 4, an American reconnaissance unit—two jeeps and an armored reconnaissance car—approached a farmhouse. Suddenly, five men in American uniforms ran out on the road to meet them. One of the men was First Lieutenant Harvey Allan Todd.

The men learned that the recon element was from the 14th Armored Division. Regretfully, the soldiers in the jeeps said they were sorry that they did not have room to take the escapees back with them. But they assured the ex-POWs that they were safe right where they were and that their liberation was imminent. Before departing, the newcomers left a couple of pistols with Todd and the others and said they would send a truck for them in the morning.

As promised, a U.S. Army truck arrived at seven-thirty the following morning. Todd and the others climbed aboard and rode to Taufkirchen. From there, they found transportation back to Nuremberg. They were on their way home at last.

When U.S. soldiers finally broke through forward positions around Hitler's Berchtesgaden retreat, they were elated to find that the Alpenfestung was largely a myth.

EPILOGUE

Germany surrendered unconditionally on Monday, May 7, 1945. The following day was celebrated as V-E (Victory in Europe) Day. Allan Todd wrote to his parents, telling them that he had received no letters from them or from Mandy during his confinement as a prisoner of war. He wrote that he hoped he still had a wife and, perhaps unsure that his parents would recognize him, informed them that he had shaved off his mustache while a prisoner.[1]

From Nuremberg, Todd and the other newly freed prisoners were flown to Rheims, France, on May 12. Their next stop was Camp Lucky Strike, a sprawling tent city on a plateau north of the French port of Le Havre that served as a staging area for "recovered Allied military personnel," or RAMP, returning to the United States. A sign at the camp's entrance read simply RAMP CAMP.

Todd and the others enjoyed hot showers, received a new issue of clothing, and were served a hot meal. During debriefings they put down all they could recall of the circumstances of their capture, their confinement, and, for those like Todd, their escape. All the men underwent medical examinations and were given the opportunity to write V-mail letters home. A Red Cross tent provided the men many diversions, including reading material.[2]

As many as forty-eight thousand freed prisoners filled Lucky Strike at one point in May 1945, all of them waiting to be manifested on the next ship to the United States.[3] Because the camp was overwhelmed with a population of recovered POWs much larger than had been prepared for, conditions at the camp were, in some ways, worse than what the prisoners had experienced during their final days in German confinement. Returning prisoners considered the camp to be poorly administered and the food bad in quality and inadequate in quantity.[4]

The only solution for those running the camp was to get the men on ships back to the States as quickly as possible. Processing of former prisoners at the camp went on day and night. Repatriated POWs filled out forms, sat through a debriefing, went through delousing, received medical examinations, and tried to slowly adjust to a diet of three square meals a day.

Lieutenant Todd, though, would not board a ship at Le Havre. He was sent by train to Paris on May 21, where he checked into a room at the Hotel Francis on the rue de Lafayette. He reported to the Office of Strategic Services' Paris headquarters the following day, where arrangements were made for him to fly to England.

It was warm in London when Todd arrived on May 25 with orders to report to OSS headquarters. His debriefing there began four days later. In as much detail as possible, Todd completed reports recounting his actions in the Battle of Arnhem and his experience as a prisoner of war. In completing his report, Todd was able to accurately reconstruct his ordeal with the help of the diary he had kept throughout the battle in Arnhem and continuing through his captivity. With all processing completed, he was set to return to the United States.

Todd departed England on a military plane on June 23, arriving overnight at Fort Hamilton, New York. He was taken to OSS headquarters in Washington, D.C., the day after his return. After further debriefings and medical checkups, he was released on a thirty-day rest-and-recuperation leave to his home in Decatur, Illinois.

Unknown to Todd, his father had died one night after hearing a radio program in which the conditions in German POW camps and the treatment received by Allied prisoners were described. About an hour after the broadcast, Mr. Todd began having chest pains but dismissed them as indigestion. He was experiencing a massive heart attack. By the time he arrived at a hospital around midnight, he was dead.[5]

A month later, on July 27, Allan Todd was promoted to captain and his leave was extended for an additional thirty days.

Captain Todd reported for duty at the Pentagon near the end of August 1945. Amanda made arrangements with the school board to find a new teacher to replace her, and she accompanied Allan to Washington, where the couple found a small apartment close to Fort Myers. Allan had often written to her about his two closest friends in the service, Pappy Olmsted and George Verhaeghe. Amanda got to meet Pappy one night at dinner shortly after her arrival in Washington.[6]

At a small ceremony in front of OSS headquarters in Washington on September 24, Major General William J. Donovan, director of the Office of Strategic Services, pinned the Distinguished Service Cross and the Purple Heart with three Oak Leaf Clusters on Captain Todd.[7] Todd also received the European–African–Middle Eastern Campaign Medal with a Bronze Service Arrowhead to denote participation in an initial assault landing. The British War Office awarded him a Mentioned in Despatches for bravery in combat. The following award citations are found in Captain Todd's personnel records on file with the OSS records group at the National Archives in College Park, Maryland.

RESTRICTED

HEADQUARTERS
U.S. FORCES, EUROPEAN THEATER

GENERAL ORDER   31 August 1945
NUMBER 222

I—DISTINGUISHED SERVICE CROSS. By direction of the President, under the provisions of AR 600–45, 22 September 1943, as amended, the Distinguished Service Cross is awarded to:

First Lieutenant Harvey A. Todd (Army Serial No. 01291911), Infantry, United States Army, for extraordinary heroism in action, as an organizer with resistance groups, from 17 September 1944 to 1 May 1945. After being parachuted into Holland to take up resistance activities, Lieutenant Todd became involved in fierce fighting against overwhelming numbers of the enemy during the Arnhem bridge engagement. Although wounded, he remained heroically for three days on the roof of a target building, inflicted heavy casualties upon the enemy and rendering invaluable service. Later, he assumed command of badly disorganized groups and, working under conditions of appalling difficulty, brought order to the situation. Lieutenant Todd's extraordinary courage and leadership under heavy enemy fire were an inspiration to his associates and reflect great credit upon himself and the United States Army. Entered service from Illinois.

> BY COMMAND OF GENERAL EISENHOWER:
> W. R. SMITH
> Lieutenant General, USA, Chief of Staff

> **R E S T R I C T E D**

· · ·

By letter authority, War Department, Washington, D.C., 15 September 1945, for four wounds received in combat, Captain Harvey A. Todd is awarded the Purple Heart with three Oak Leaf Clusters for wounds received 18 September 1944, 20 September 1944, 26 September 1944, and 27 March 1945 in the European Theater of Operations.

A medical examination of Todd performed shortly after his return to the United States indicated that as a result of the mortar shell explosion on September 20, 1944, he had suffered a brain concussion and a rupture of the left ear with some loss of hearing.[8]

On October 1, 1945, Todd reported to the Regional Station Hospital at Fort Belvoir, Virginia, just south of Washington, D.C. Three weeks later, he was assigned to McGuire General Hospital in Richmond for observation and treatment. In late January 1946, he was transferred to Percy Jones Army Hospital at Fort Custer, Battle Creek, Michigan. In early August of that year, he was sent to Fort Sheridan, Illinois, where he was separated from the service on November 25. He began working for the Prudential Insurance Company in late December.

Around 1950, Allan, like most of the OSS veterans, received a letter from the new Central Intelligence Agency, asking him to join. Amanda told him he could go if he wanted to but that she would not accompany him. He declined the offer.

Allan and Amanda lived in Decatur, Illinois, and had three daughters—Allana, Cindy, and Cathy—and twelve grandchildren. Through his work with Prudential, he became a member of the Million Dollar Round Table, an estate-planning council, and was a chartered life underwriter. He served as a deacon and moderator in the First Baptist Church of Decatur and was a member of the Chamber of Commerce, the Lions Club, and a Decatur businessmen's organization called the Breakfast Club; he was a charter member and the first president of the Barbed-Wire Club, an organization of ex-POWs. For relaxation, he enjoyed fishing, hunting, and golf.

The Todds attended a Jedburgh reunion in Washington, D.C., in 1988. Allan died on June 15, 1993, and is buried at Graceland Cemetery in Decatur.

Jacobus Groenewoud, the Dutch officer on Jedburgh team Claude, was killed in action on September 19, 1944, during the battle at the Arnhem bridge. Based on a recommendation written by Allan Todd, the Dutch government awarded Groenewoud the Military Order of William, Knight 4th Class, the Netherlands' highest military award, posthumously.

Carl A. Scott, the American radio operator on Jedburgh team Claude, was among the wounded when last seen in Holland on September 20, 1944. He is believed to have been killed during the fighting in the British perimeter at Oosterbeek.

Maarten Jan Knottenbelt, the Dutch Commando attached to Jedburgh team Claude, settled in Australia for a time after the war and wrote on philosophy. He later returned to live in the Netherlands.

In July 1945, two months after V-E Day, Major John "Pappy" Olmsted, the American officer on Jedburgh team Dudley, received orders assigning him to the OSS mission to France. From there, he was sent on temporary duty to Holland to assist in accounting for and retrieving supplies dropped to the Dutch resistance and to help organize the new Dutch army.

Olmsted returned to the United States in October 1945 and was sent to the U.S. Army Separation Center at Fort Leavenworth, Kansas, having earned the number of points necessary for immediate discharge from military service. He was released in January 1946 but later served in the U.S. Army Reserve. He began graduate school at the University of Minnesota, attending classes while working as a laboratory assistant in the Botany Department. On August 22, 1948, he married Elisabeth Hed at the university chapel.

Olmsted returned to Holland and spent a year in graduate studies at the University of Utrecht, and in 1951 he received a master of science degree in botany from the University of Minnesota. In August 1952, he took a job with the Department of the Army as a civilian training adviser and evaluator. From 1953 through 1963, his work took him on assignments to England, Belgium, Germany, Sweden, Indonesia, the Philippines, Italy, Thailand, and India.

While assigned to the Southern European Task Force (SETAF) in Rome, he also worked with the United States Army's 10th Special Forces Group at Bad Tölz, Germany, and with the United States Navy's SEAL Team Two. From 1964 to 1968, Olmsted served in India, during which time he and Liz adopted a girl, Renu Teresa. After returning to the United States, he continued to make periodic job-related trips to Panama, Thailand, and Europe. He retired to Sun Valley, Idaho, in March 1973. The following year, the family moved to the Seattle area. There, he did volunteer work with several organizations, including helping children with learning disabilities. He also enjoyed his hobbies—photography, gardening, and environmental studies. He attended Jedburgh reunions in Paris, Fort Bragg, and Washington, D.C., and made a return visit to Holland. Pappy lived with his family in Bellevue, Washington, until his death on May 20, 2001, at the age of eighty-six.[9]

John Olmsted was awarded the Distinguished Service Cross, the Purple Heart, the European–African–Middle Eastern Campaign Medal with Bronze Service Arrowhead, and the bronze medal of the Order of the Netherlands Lion for his actions in Holland with Jedburgh team Dudley. The following award citations are taken from Major Olmsted's personnel records on file at the National Archives.

RESTRICTED

HEADQUARTERS
EUROPEAN THEATER OF OPERATIONS
UNITED STATES ARMY

[GENERAL ORDER] 56 8 Apr 1945

II—DISTINGUISHED SERVICE CROSS. By direction of the President, under the provisions of AR 600–45, 22 September 1943, as amended, the Distinguished Service Cross is awarded to:

SO—Major John M. Olmsted (Army Serial No. 0412128), Infantry, United States Army, for extraordinary heroism in connection with military operations against an armed enemy, as a member of the Special Operations Branch, Office of Strategic Services Detachment, European Theater of Operations, United States Army, from 11 September 1944 to 20 November 1944. Major Olmsted was parachuted into Holland to establish a central headquarters for the purpose of organizing, arming and directing partisans. In addition to arranging for the procurement of arms and munitions, he instructed the members of the underground in the most efficient method of procuring and reporting intelligence information, instituted a courier system throughout his area, established numerous dropping grounds, and designated reception committees therefore in order to facilitate the reception and distribution of supplies. Major Olmsted displayed courage and initiative in delivering valuable intelligence information concerning the disposition of enemy troops and installations to allied headquarters. Entered service from Nebraska.

BY COMMAND OF GENERAL EISENHOWER:
R. B. LORD
Major General, GSC, Deputy Chief of Staff

RESTRICTED

• • •

RESTRICTED

HEADQUARTERS
EUROPEAN THEATER OF OPERATIONS
UNITED STATES ARMY

[GENERAL ORDER] 37   15 Mar 1945

III—PURPLE HEART. By direction of the President, under the provisions of AR 600–45, 22 September 1943, as amended, the Purple Heart is awarded to:

Major John M. Olmsted (Army Serial No. 0412128), Infantry, United States Army, for wounds received as a result of enemy action on 18 and 19 November 1944 in Holland.

> BY COMMAND OF GENERAL EISENHOWER:
> R. B. LORD
> Major General, GSC, Deputy Chief of Staff

RESTRICTED

Henk Brinkgreve, the Dutch officer on Jedburgh team Dudley, was killed behind enemy lines on March 5, 1945. He is buried in a cemetery called the Oosterbegraafplaats in Enschede, Overijssel, about ten miles from the spot where he lost his life. An English translation of the inscription on his gravestone reads, "He kept the torch burning."

John Patrick "Bunny" Austin, the British radio operator on Jedburgh team Dudley, was executed by the Germans on April 4, 1945. His sister received the following letter, dated November 21, 1945, from SOE:

> Your brother performed very exceptional services, having volunteered to work behind the lines in enemy-occupied Holland. He was trained as a parachutist and wireless operator and was parachuted into Holland in September 1944. The officers with whom he worked

spoke very highly of his performance under conditions the difficulty of which can easily be imagined.[10]

The British government awarded Austin a Mentioned in Despatches posthumously. He is the only soldier buried in the graveyard at Hattem, near the Dutch town of Zwolle.[11]

———

Exactly one year after Operation Market-Garden began, September 17, 1945, the 82nd Airborne Division returned to Nijmegen to help the city's citizens celebrate the anniversary of their liberation. Homage was paid to the division's fallen troopers at the Molenhoek Cemetery, and when the crowd gathered to hear speeches by the mayor of Nijmegen and Major General James Gavin, it was Captain Arie Bestebreurtje, the Dutch officer of Jedburgh team Clarence, who introduced the American general.[12]

Arie Bestebreurtje received several gunshot wounds and a bayonet wound during the war. He joined his wife, Gertrude, and young daughter Hendriekje in New York in December 1946. He became a U.S. citizen and worked as an attorney for a New York firm, where his command of European languages made him invaluable in arranging European business agreements. In 1956, he graduated from the Union Theological Seminary in New York with a doctorate of divinity degree and became co-pastor at Asbury Church. He left for Kentucky the following year when he became pastor at the Calvin Presbyterian Church in Louisville.

Reverend Bestebreurtje moved his family to Charlottesville, Virginia, in 1966 and served as minister at the First Presbyterian Church there for fifteen years until his retirement in 1981. Few of his parishioners knew at the time of the role "Dr. B" had played in World War II. On May 10, 1970—a day after one hundred thousand people gathered in Washington, D.C., to protest the war in Vietnam—Dr. Bestebreurtje delivered a stirring sermon supporting the war effort. The sermon was broadcast by WINA and, because of the huge response, was rebroadcast a short time later.[13]

Arie's decorations included the Military Order of William, Knight 4th Class, the Netherlands' Bronze Cross, the Order of the British Empire, the French Croix de Guerre, the U.S. Legion of Merit, and the U.S. Purple Heart. The citation for his Legion of Merit reads:

LEGION OF MERIT

Captain Harry Bestebreurtje, Royal Netherlands Army

For exceptionally meritorious conduct in the performance of outstanding services in the United Kingdom and in Holland from 10 September to 13 October 1944. Serving with the Special Forces, British Royal Army, Captain Bestebreurtje, a native of Holland, was attached to the American 82d Airborne Division on 10 September to assist in operational planning and to direct liaison with Dutch resistance elements during the period of operations. Jumping by parachute with the division commander in the vicinity of Groesbeek, Holland, at 1300 hours, 17 September, he immediately made a personal reconnaissance of the area and secured valuable information from civilians which expedited the accomplishment of certain initial missions. That night while reconnoitering the German-held city of Nijmegen he was wounded in three places but succeeded in meeting the Dutch resistance leaders who furnished him vital information and assurances that the Underground would render the utmost aid to prevent demolition of the strategic Nijmegen bridge during assault operations to capture the city. During the subsequent bitter battle of Nijmegen, he established his headquarters within the city and organized the civilian populace to assist the Airborne forces in the consolidation of liberated communities. He expanded his activities to embrace the entire region south of the Waal River and established cells of underground resistance for operations in the area. His services to the Allied Forces during the entire operation are incalculable and the results of his efforts contributed materially to the success attained.

OFFICIAL

HEADQUARTERS, FORT JAY, N.Y.

Dutch actor Peter Faber played the role of Bestebreurtje in the 1977 film *A Bridge Too Far*. Reverend and Mrs. Bestebreurtje raised four children—daughters Hendriekje, Mary Anne, and Martha Jane and son Anton. They had three grandchildren. Arie Bestebreurtje died January 21, 1983, at the age of sixty-six, after falling through the ice and drowning while skating near Charlottesville, never once having spoken to his family about the Jedburghs because of the oath of secrecy he had taken before leaving the military.[14] He is buried at Monticello Gardens, within sight of Thomas Jefferson's home. Gertrude Bestebreurtje died in 2000.

George M. Verhaeghe, the American officer on team Clarence, was treated at an aid station in Holland for the serious wounds he suffered early in the battle. On September 21, 1944, he was evacuated from the aid station to the 192nd Base Hospital. Later, he was moved to the 4150th Hospital Plant.[15] Mr. Verhaeghe attended the Jedburgh reunion in Washington, D.C., in 1988. He is now deceased.

In addition to the Purple Heart and the European–African–Middle Eastern Campaign Medal with Bronze Service Arrowhead, Verhaeghe was awarded the Meritorious Service Cross from the Dutch government and a Mentioned in Despatches from the British government.

No. 57

We Wilhelmina, by the grace of God, Queen of the Netherlands, Princess of Orange-Nassau, etc., etc., etc.

On the recommendation of Our Ministers of War and for Foreign Affairs:
HAVE APPROVED AND ORDERED:

To award the MERITORIOUS SERVICE CROSS to:

Lieutenant G. VERHAEGHE,
United States Army,

For:

"Distinguishing himself by his gallant behavior and leadership in connection with enemy activities during the airborne operations near NIJMEGEN in September 1944."

Our Ministers of War and for Foreign Affairs are, each for his own part, in charge of the execution of this Decree.

Het Loo, 6th August 1946
(sgd.) WILHELMINA

The Minister of War,

(*sgd.*) A. H. J. L. FIEVEZ

The Minister for Foreign Affairs,

(*sdg.*) Mr. W. BARON VAN

BOETZELAER VAN OOSTERHOUT

· · ·

THE WAR OFFICE

DROITWICH SPA,

Worcestershire

The enclosed bronze Oak Leaf Emblem is issued by command of the King for wear by those who have been awarded a Mention in Despatches, or a King's Commendation, for brave conduct during the 1939–45 War. . . .

Awarded to: Lieutenant George M. VERHAEGHE (O-1322496)

Arm or Corps: American Army

Authorised: 25 May 1945

Willard W. "Bud" Beynon served as the American radio operator on two Jedburgh missions to Holland—Clarence and Stanley II. In November 1944, seeking further combat duty behind enemy lines, he volunteered for duty with the OSS in the Far East. He returned to the United States on leave on December 21 and was evaluated for continued service with OSS the following month. A medical officer examining Beynon on January 30, 1945, wrote that the young NCO was "buoyantly heedless of danger" and "contentedly accepts whatever lot befalls him, so long as it is a role of action."[16] By then a master sergeant, Beynon was transferred to Burma in March 1945. He jumped into China as a member of a five-man team called Baboon II, working with Chinese guerrillas against the Japanese. One day they heard over their radio that an atomic bomb had been dropped on Japan. Not long afterward, they heard that the war was over. By then, Beynon was down to ninety pounds because of malaria and dysentery.

Beynon was awarded the Bronze Star Medal and the European–African–Middle Eastern Campaign Medal with Bronze Service

Arrowhead by the United States Army,[17] a Mentioned in Despatches award with two bronze oak-leaf emblems from the British government, and two decorations from the government of the Netherlands: the Meritorious Service Cross, presented at the United States Military Academy, West Point, New York, in 1947, and the Dutch Resistance Cross, presented personally by Prince Bernhard of the Netherlands at the Army and Navy Club in Washington, D.C., in 1982. He also received the U.S. Army's Good Conduct Ribbon.

THE UNITED STATES OF AMERICA

TO ALL WHO SEE THESE PRESENTS, GREETING:
THIS IS TO CERTIFY THAT
THE PRESIDENT OF THE UNITED STATES OF AMERICA
AUTHORIZED BY EXECUTIVE ORDER, FEBRUARY 4, 1944
HAS AWARDED

THE BRONZE STAR MEDAL

TO
Technical Sergeant Willard W. Beynon, 13151112

FOR
MERITORIOUS ACHIEVEMENT
IN GROUND OPERATIONS AGAINST THE ENEMY
European Theater of Operations, 17 September 1944–1 October 1944
GIVEN UNDER MY HAND IN THE CITY OF WASHINGTON
THIS 3rd DAY OF February 1950

Gordon Gray
Secretary of the Army

After the war, Beynon attended the Pennsylvania Police Academy, graduating first in his class, and joined the Scranton Police Department. He served the department for forty-two years, working his way up from patrolman to the rank of captain before retiring in 1989. He made many contributions to the force, setting up its first bomb squad, its first SWAT (special weapons and tactics) team, and its first dive team. Mr. Beynon began working part-time as a security consultant for Procter & Gamble in 1968 and was still with them nearly forty years later. He graduated from Kings College and served the people of Lackawanna County as civil defense director for twenty years. He attended the reunion of the American Jedburghs at Fort Bragg, North Carolina, in 1985. Mr. Beynon's wife, Rachel, died in 1992. They had a son, Richard, a daughter, Linell, and two grandchildren. Bud still lives in Scranton, Pennsylvania.[18]

McCord Sollenberger, the American officer on Jedburgh team Edward, volunteered for duty in the Far East when his duty in Europe was completed, though he indicated a desire to transfer to a regular army unit, having become disenchanted with OSS.[19] His request for reassignment out of OSS was approved, and he was reassigned back to the Cavalry Replacement Training Center at Fort Riley, Kansas, in February 1945.[20] He remained in the army until 1954.

For his service in Holland during Operation Market-Garden, McCord Sollenberger was awarded the Bronze Star Medal and the European–African–Middle Eastern Campaign Medal with Bronze Service Arrowhead by the United States Army, the Cross of Merit from the Dutch government, and a Mentioned in Despatches from the British government.[21] The citation for the Bronze Star award reads as follows:

CITATION FOR BRONZE STAR MEDAL

Captain McCord Sollenberger, 01031210, Cavalry, United States Army, for meritorious service in connection with military operations while serving with the Office of Strategic Services, European Theater of Operations, from 17 September 1944 to 27 September 1944. During this period Captain Sollenberger, after having been infiltrated into Holland, established immediate contact with Resistance Forces located in key cities, obtaining operational information of great value to the Airborne Divisions with which he worked. Demonstrating exceptional initiative and resourcefulness, he coordinated the activities of Dutch Resistance Groups, which were of great assistance in

Allied operations in this area. Captain Sollenberger's display of courage and ability throughout this dangerous mission reflects high credit upon himself and the armed forces of the United States. Entered military service from Maryland.

GO 8, Hq USFET, 7 Jan 1946

James R. Billingsley, the American radio operator on Jedburgh team Edward, returned to New York from Europe on November 16, 1944, and was promoted to master sergeant the following month. The record of the interview conducted by OSS with Sergeant Billingsley upon his return from Europe describes him as a "cheerful extrovert who has made an excellent record in the field."[22] He volunteered for duty in the Far East and departed Miami for New Delhi, India, on February 3. As the radio operator on special operations team Leopard, Billingsley served behind enemy lines in China from May through August 1945.[23] He was separated from the service at Fort Meade, Maryland, in December and returned to his hometown of Watertown, New York. For his war service, Billingsley was awarded the Bronze Star Medal[24] and the European–African–Middle Eastern Campaign Medal with Bronze Service Arrowhead from the United States Army and the Cross of Merit from the Dutch Government.[25] The following is the citation for his award of the Bronze Star Medal.

CITATION FOR BRONZE STAR MEDAL

Technical Sergeant James R. Billingsley (Army Serial No. 6916249), Infantry, United States Army, for meritorious service in connection with military operations as a radio operator and assistant to the Jedburgh team "EDWARD," Special Operations Branch, Office of Strategic Services, European Theater of Operations, from 17 September 1944 to 27 September 1944. After having been infiltrated into Holland, Technical Sergeant Billingsley effectively maintained continuous radio communication with his headquarters in England, transmitting highly important operational information dealing with the airborne invasion of Holland, under constant shelling, strafing, and bombing. He was of the greatest assistance in contacting and recruiting Dutch resistance personnel for use with the airborne divisions. Technical Sergeant Billingsley's actions

throughout this mission reflect great credit upon himself and the armed forces
of the United States. Entered military service from Pennsylvania.[26]

One of the tragic consequences of the failure of Market-Garden was the
suffering that resulted for the Dutch people during the bitter winter of
1944–45. German reprisals for Dutch support to the Allies resulted in
many deaths, but even more died of starvation. In that part of northern
Holland still held by the Germans, people were cut off from food and
coal supplies and suffered terribly, most notably in the cities of Amsterdam, Rotterdam, and The Hague. In all, some fifteen thousand people
starved to death during the "hunger winter."[27] Relief finally came in the
form of Operation Manna in late April and early May 1945, when British
and American bombers dropped crates of food.

In addition to the thousands of Dutch citizens killed during the battles fought on their soil throughout the war and later from starvation
during the final winter of the war, two-thirds of the nation's prewar Jewish population of 140,000 perished. Material destruction included seventy thousand homes, more than three thousand farms, ten thousand
factories, and two hundred churches.[28]

The events described in the first chapter of this book, "The England
Game," affected how the Dutch Jedburgh teams were employed. During the time leading up to Operation Market-Garden, many in London
were still unsure of their Dutch resistance contacts. It was only shortly
before the operation that they became convinced it was possible to send
special operations teams into the country with a reasonable degree of as-
surance that they would link up safely with the resistance. In the brief
time still remaining before the launch of Market-Garden, the Allies
were able to insert some British Special Air Service parties and one Jedburgh team, Dudley, into Holland. Perhaps if there had been sufficient
time, more teams could have been inserted.

The Dutch teams were used in a manner quite different from what
they had been trained for. Teams had been dropped successfully
throughout France, well ahead of conventional ground forces, and most
of those teams conducted operations that were very beneficial to the
Allies. Had the Dutch teams been employed in this manner, it is possible the debacle at Arnhem could have been avoided. Field Marshal

Montgomery disregarded Dutch resistance reports on German forces. Would he have so easily dismissed reports coming from British, U.S., or Dutch officers in the field? One would hope not.

Even if the time had been available, though, it is likely that only a limited number of Jedburgh teams could have operated in Holland without becoming compromised. The terrain and the German security apparatus would have limited their activities to a great degree. Like team Dudley, they would have had to remain hidden for long periods of time, they would have had to move constantly, and they would have been able to move about the country only in civilian clothes, carrying false identity documents, which presents a whole new set of risks and dangers. The men of team Dudley were able to survive as long as they did because they followed security measures very closely. Still, two of them eventually were compromised and killed. At best, at least two more teams might have been able to successfully infiltrate the Market-Garden area of operations, begin preparation of the resistance groups, and provide intelligence reports on German force locations and activities. It could have made a difference.

Employed as they were, jumping into Holland with the airborne divisions, teams Daniel II, Clarence, and Claude were limited in what they could be expected to accomplish. Team Daniel II has been criticized for having done little or nothing in the way of arranging for support by the resistance to the 101st Airborne Division. In fairness to the men of Daniel II, there was little they could have been expected to accomplish given the brief time they were in the area before the British ground force arrived.

There is little question that much better use could have been made of the Dutch resistance. Montgomery's remark to Prince Bernhard—"I don't think your resistance forces can be of any help to us"[29]—was a clear indication that the resistance would not be allowed much opportunity to serve the Allied cause. Other commanders had very different opinions of the value of the resistance.

General Gavin described the work of the Dutch underground as "exemplary." Writing later about his division's success in capturing all of their assigned bridges, Gavin declared, "The underground played a major part in getting this done and they deserve a lion's share of the credit for saving the big bridge at Nijmegen."[30] These sentiments are echoed by World War II historian Charles MacDonald, who wrote, "The contributions of the Dutch underground not only to the operations of the 82nd Airborne Division but to those of other Allied units as well cannot be ignored."[31] General Frost, in his memoirs, wrote of how he was warned not to rely on the resistance because they had been penetrated by German collaborators and couldn't be trusted. "Here was yet another implement," Frost writes, "that could have been used to our advantage denied to those who were going to need every possible aid."[32]

The Dutch resistance, as well as the populace in general, provided information that was unavailable to the Allies from any other source. They also provided services for which soldiers would normally be required, thereby allowing more troops to fight, and they certainly were of tremendous value in their role as guides and interpreters for the combat forces.

The Dutch government, in 1980, struck a medal called the Cross of the Resistance to be awarded to all those who had served the cause of the Dutch underground during the war. Prince Bernhard, who had served as head of organized resistance from London, presented the medal to more than three hundred veterans of the resistance. In 1982, the prince traveled to Washington, D.C., where he presented the medal to sixteen OSS veterans, including those who had served on the Dutch Jedburgh teams.[33]

In May 1988, the Jedburghs held a reunion in Washington, D.C. The highlight of the reunion was a visit to the White House. After a brief tour, the crowd of Jeds and their families was ushered outside to the South Lawn. President and Mrs. Reagan were scheduled to depart shortly to spend the weekend at the presidential retreat in the Catoctin Mountain ridge of Maryland, where the American Jeds had trained some forty-five years earlier. Marine One, the presidential helicopter, would land on the South Lawn, where the First Couple would board it for the flight to Camp David.

Soon the president and Mrs. Reagan emerged from the White House and began shaking hands and chatting with a small crowd of people some distance away from where the Jeds and their families were standing. The day's busy schedule had taken a toll on Allan Todd, and it had been necessary for him to make use of a wheelchair that was provided by the White House staff. He sat in the chair, and he and Amanda sensed that they would not get close enough to speak with the president. Then Amanda had an idea. She shouted, "Eureka!" When President Reagan heard the name of his alma mater, he quickly turned and made his way over to the Todds. Allan had first met Mr. Reagan back at Eureka College in Illinois, and he and Amanda had met him again years later and had received one or two letters from him. But many years had passed since then, and the president might not have remembered who Allan was, but he did remember Eureka and the football coach for whom both he and Allan had played. The two men chatted for a few minutes about the school and the coach, and then the president and Mrs. Reagan were off to Camp David.[34]

The heavily damaged cities of Eindhoven, Nijmegen, and Arnhem have been rebuilt. Market-Garden veterans have revisited the battlegrounds and the cemeteries and the museums for many years, although their numbers have declined with each passing year.

In Oosterbeek, the Airborne Museum, devoted to Operation Market-Garden, is housed in the former Hartenstein Hotel (Huize Hartenstein) at Utrechtseweg 232. The building served as the head-quarters of General Urquhart, commander of the British 1st Airborne Division, in September 1944. In the cellar is a reconstruction of Urquhart's Market-Garden command post. The Liberation Museum is outside Groesbeek, at the spot where General Gavin and his 82nd Airborne Division landed during the war, and the National War and Resistance Museum is in the village of Overloon.

American bombers destroyed the bridge at Arnhem on October 7, 1944, at a time when it was still in German hands. When it was rebuilt to a nearly identical design after the war, the people of Arnhem named it John Frostbrug (the John Frost Bridge).

Every year, in September, children come to visit the graves of strangers. They gather quietly on a street called Van Limburg Stirumweg, in the northern outskirts of the village of Oosterbeek.

At a designated time, more than a thousand Dutch schoolchildren, bearing flowers in a rainbow of colors, pass between the tall brick piers and enter the cemetery. Row upon row of identical marble gravestones stand in rigid formation in the emerald clearing, cool and quiet, framed by soaring shade trees. With almost drill-team precision, the solemn youth file in, each taking a position at a grave site. On cue, the children raise the flowers above their heads, a salute to the fallen. Each vows, "I shall never forget you," and whispers the name of the soldier whose grave lies before him or her. Then the children lay the flowers at the graves of 1,754 men they never knew, in the clearing next to the farmer's field that once, on a bright Sunday afternoon long ago, was littered with parachutes.

This moving memorial service has taken place every year since 1945 at the Arnhem Oosterbeek War Cemetery—the final resting place for many of the Allied soldiers and airmen who lost their lives in the fierce battle that took place there more than sixty years ago. It is a singularly impressive legacy of remembrance, elegant in its simplicity, unabashedly sincere, passed from generation to generation of citizens of an eternally grateful nation; and today it is performed by children whose parents were not even born during the time the country lived under the oppressive heel of German occupation.

ACKNOWLEDGMENTS

Market-Garden witnessed dozens of heroic acts by Allied paratroopers and Jedburgh operators, including those of the men in this book. I have attempted to fill an important gap in the history of the war in Europe and, at the same time, honor these men by sharing their incredible stories before the distance of time further fades the memory. None of this, of course, would have been possible without the assistance and contributions of many people.

My most profound debt of gratitude is to the many former Jeds and their families who have given so freely of their time for interviews and correspondence and who have provided so much in the way of source documents and photographs. My thanks to Anton Bestebreurtje, Willard W. Beynon, Elisabeth H. Olmsted, and Amanda Todd; and to three subjects of the book who shared their memories and documents with me but passed on before completion of the project: John M. Olmsted, Harvey Allan Todd, and George M. Verhaeghe.

My research could not have been completed without the assistance of staff members at the following archives and libraries: the National Archives in College Park, Maryland; the United States Army Military History Institute Archives at Carlisle, Pennsylvania; the Combined Arms Research Library of the United States Army Command and General Staff College at Fort Leavenworth, Kansas; the Watson Library at the University of Kansas; the Hoover Institution at Stanford University; the United States Army Europe Library and Research Center in Heidelberg,

Germany; the RAND Corporation library in Santa Monica, California; the United States Special Operations Command Library at MacDill Air Force Base, Florida; and the public libraries in Redondo Beach, California, and Tampa, Florida.

I am grateful to Dr. Samuel J. Lewis for his assistance and mentorship during his time at the Combat Studies Institute of the United States Army Command and General Staff College, to Michael G. Leemhuis at the Congressional Country Club for permission to use photographs of the club, to Mary O'Dea for reading and editing parts of the manuscript, to Kevin Morrow for locating and copying documents at the National Archives, and to David Garver (Allan and Amanda Todd's son-in-law) for providing details on the children's remembrance ceremony at the Oosterbeek cemetery.

A special thank-you goes to my agent, John A. Ware, and to my editor, Jonathan Jao. Their tireless efforts, patience, and constant encouragement made this book possible.

I am forever grateful to my family and friends for their many sacrifices and for their steadfast support.

Any mistakes I have made in the process of writing this book are mine alone.

THE DUTCH JEDBURGH
TEAMS

RANK* AND NAME	NATIONALITY	REMARKS

TEAM CLARENCE

Deployed from Cottesmore, England, to Groesbeek, Holland, with the U.S. 82nd Airborne Division on September 17, 1944.

Capt. Arie Dirk Bestebreurtje	Dutch	Wounded in action
1st Lt. George M. Verhaeghe	American	Wounded in action
T/Sgt. Willard W. "Bud" Beynon	American	

* All ranks are as of the date of deployment and do not reflect later promotions. Rank abbreviations used in the table include Maj. (major), Capt. (captain), 1st Lt. (first lieutenant), 2nd Lt. (second lieutenant), Lt. (lieutenant), M/Sgt. (master sergeant), T/Sgt. (technical sergeant), Sgt. (sergeant), CQMS (British company quartermaster sergeant).

TEAM CLAUDE

Deployed from Barkston Heath, England, to Wolfheze-Arnhem, Holland, with the British 1st Airborne Division on September 17, 1944.

Capt. Jacobus "Jaap" Groenewoud	Dutch	Killed in action
1st Lt. Harvey Allan Todd	American	Captured, POW, escaped in 1945
Lt. Maarten Jan Knottenbelt	Dutch	Attached
T/Sgt. Carl A. Scott	American	Killed in action

TEAM DANIEL II

Deployed from Welford, England, to the St. Oedenrode–Son area, Holland, with the U.S. 101st Airborne Division on September 17, 1944.

Maj. R. K. Wilson	British	
Sgt. G. W. Mason	British	
Lt. Abraham "Bram" Dubois	Dutch	Attached
Sgt. Lykele Faber	Dutch	

TEAM DANIEL III

Deployed from England to the Overijssel region of Eastern Holland on the night of October 3–4, 1944 (Jedburgh Daniel II follow-on mission).

Maj. R. K. Wilson	British
Lt. Scherrer	French
Sgt. G. W. Mason	British

TEAM DICING

Deployed from England to the Drenthe region of northeast Holland on the night of April 7–8, 1945.

Maj. Robert Harcourt	British	Captured, POW, liberated in 1945
Capt. Arie Dirk Bestebreurtje	Dutch	Fractured ankle on jump
Sgt. Claude C. Somers	British	
Capt. C. J. L. Ruysche van Dugteren	Dutch	

TEAM DUDLEY

Deployed from Tempsford, England, to the Overijssel region of eastern Holland, on the night of September 11–12, 1944.

Maj. Henk Brinkgreve	Dutch	Killed in action
Maj. John M. "Pappy" Olmsted	American	Wounded in action
Sgt. John Patrick "Bunny" Austin	British	Captured, POW, executed in 1945

TEAM EDWARD

Deployed from Harwell, England, to Groesbeek, Holland, with British I Airborne Corps Headquarters on September 17, 1944.

Capt. Jaap "Jacob" Staal	Dutch/South African
Capt. McCord "Mac" Sollenberger	American
Capt. R. Mills	British
2nd Lt. Len R. D. Willmott	British
T/Sgt. James R. Billingsley	American

TEAM GAMBLING

Deployed from England to Barneveld, Holland, on the night of April 3–4, 1945.

Maj. A. H. Clutton   British

Capt. Maarten J. Knottenbelt   Dutch

CQMS James S. Menzies   British

TEAM STANLEY*

Deployed from England to the Nijmegen-Arnhem area of eastern Holland on October 3, 1944 (Jedburgh Clarence follow-on mission).

Capt. Arie Dirk Bestebreurtje   Dutch

Capt. Peter C. H. Vickery   British   Wounded in action
(replaced Lt. Verhaeghe)

T/Sgt. Willard W. "Bud" Beynon   American

* Because another Jedburgh team, which deployed to France on the last day of August 1944, had already been assigned the code name Stanley, the team deployed to the Netherlands is often referred to as Stanley II.

NOTES

PROLOGUE

1. Material for the prologue comes from Office of Strategic Services (OSS), "Report of Jedburgh Team Dudley," National Archives, Washington History Office, Record Group (RG) 226; and John M. Olmsted, "Team Dudley," 1946 (photocopy of unpublished personal account of war experience provided to the author by Mr. Olmsted).
2. Olmsted, "Team Dudley," 41.
3. Ibid., 41–42.

CHAPTER 1: THE ENGLAND GAME

1. Hubertus M. G. Lauwers, personal account provided in the epilogue to *London Calling North Pole,* by H. J. Giskes (New York: Bantam Books, 1982), 203.
2. British Broadcasting Corporation (BBC), "Englandspiel," *SOE: Special Operations Executive* series, television documentary, 1984.
3. Lauwers, 206; and BBC, "Englandspiel."
4. Lauwers, 208; and BBC, "Englandspiel."
5. Giskes, *London Calling,* 86–89; and Philippe Ganier-Raymond, *The Tangled Web,* trans. Len Ortzen (New York: Warner Paperback Library, 1972), 9–13.
6. Lauwers, 213–14.
7. Nigel West [Rupert Allason], *Secret War: The Story of SOE, Britain's Wartime Sabotage Organisation* (London: Hodder & Stoughton, 1992), 94.
8. BBC, "Englandspiel."
9. Leo Marks, *Between Silk and Cyanide: A Codemaker's War, 1941–1945* (New York: Free Press, 1998), 16, 98–102, 112–17.
10. West, *Secret War,* 97–100.

11. Ibid., 98.

12. OSS (European Theater of Operations), *Special Operations Branch and Secret Intelligence Branch War Diaries,* 1945, 13 vols. on eight reels of microfilm, ed. Paul Kesaris (Frederick, MD: University Publications of America, 1985), vol. 3, bk. 13, 151. Also found in National Archives Microfilm Publication M1623 and published by Garland Publishing (New York, 1988).

13. West, *Secret War,* 103.

14. Giskes, *London Calling,* 156.

15. West, *Secret War,* 99.

CHAPTER 2: THE MAN FROM WASHINGTON

1. OSS, Interview Report, John M. Olmsted, October 20, 1943, copy in the personnel file of John M. Olmsted, OSS records, National Archives, RG 226.

2. Ibid.

3. John Olmsted, letter to the author, January 13, 1989, and "Team Dudley," 6.

4. Harvey Allan Todd, personal account of wartime experiences, n.d. (photocopy of untitled and unpublished document provided to the author by Mrs. Amanda Todd); and Amanda Todd, interview with the author, February 25, 2005.

5. Amanda Todd, interview with the author, February 25, 2005.

6. Amanda Todd, telephone conversation with the author, January 6, 2006.

CHAPTER 3: HAZARDOUS DUTY

1. "Fannin Marker Tells Camp's Story," *Camp Fannin Guidon* (Tyler, TX: Camp Fannin Association, vol. 1, no. 1, spring 1993): 2; and George M. Verhaeghe, letter to the author, November 2, 1988.

2. M. R. D. Foot, *SOE: An Outline History of the Special Operations Executive, 1940–46* (London: British Broadcasting Corporation, 1984; Frederick, MD: University Publications, 1986), 11.

3. Peter Wilkinson, *Foreign Fields: The Story of an SOE Operative* (London: Tauris, 1997), 128.

4. Arthur Brown, "The Jedburghs: A Short History," April 1991, photocopy of unpublished manuscript provided to the author by Mr. Brown, 5.

5. War Department, paragraph 25, Special Orders no. 313, November 9, 1943; and Headquarters and Headquarters Detachment, OSS, Special Orders no. 259, November 13, 1943.

6. William L. Cassidy, ed., *History of the Schools and Training Branch, Office of Strategic Services* (San Francisco: Kingfisher Press, 1983), 72.

7. Willard Beynon, telephone interview with the author, February 26, 2006.

CHAPTER 4: HIGHLANDS INTERLUDE

1. The primary sources for this and all following chapters are Olmsted, "Team Dudley"; Harvey Allan Todd's unpublished and undated personal account of wartime experiences (photocopy provided to the author by Mr. Todd prior to his death); and the official after-action reports for all Jedburgh missions to Holland.

2. Corey Ford, *Donovan of OSS* (Boston: Little, Brown, & Co., 1970), 137–42.

3. Harvey Allan Todd, personal account of wartime experiences, 5.

4. Olmsted, "Team Dudley," 13.

5. Ibid., 19.

6. Jelle J. H. Hooiveld, "Sergeant John Patrick Austin, Jedburgh W/T Operator Team DUDLEY," posted on OSS Society, Inc., Digest at osssociety@yahoogroups.com, July 22, 2008.

7. OSS, Theater Service Record of T/Sgt. James R. Billingsley, October 11, 1944, in the personnel record of T/Sgt. Billingsley, OSS records, National Archives.

8. Willard Beynon, telephone interview, February 26, 2006.

9. Olmsted, "Team Dudley," 27.

10. Harvey Allan Todd, letter to his family, April 1944 (photocopy provided to the author by Amanda Todd).

11. Willard Beynon, telephone interview, February 26, 2006.

12. Ibid., December 27, 2007.

13. Olmsted, "Team Dudley," 34–35.

14. OSS (ETO), *Special Operations Branch War . . . Diary,* vol. 3, bk. 13, 350.

15. Ibid., vol. 3, bk. 13, 348.

16. Ibid., vol. 3, bk. 2, 360.

CHAPTER 5: FIRST JEDS INTO HOLLAND

1. James M. Gavin, *On to Berlin: Battles of an Airborne Commander, 1943–1946* (New York: Viking Press, 1978), 140.

2. Stephen E. Ambrose, *Eisenhower: Soldier, General of the Army, President-Elect, 1890–1952* (New York: Simon & Schuster, 1983), 336.

3. Gen. Dwight D. Eisenhower, personal cable to Gen. George C. Marshall, September 2, 1944, in *The Papers of Dwight David Eisenhower: The War Years,* vol. 4, ed. Alfred D. Chandler, Jr. (Baltimore: Johns Hopkins Press, 1970), 2112.

4. Edward M. Flanagan, Jr., *Airborne: A Combat History of American Airborne Forces* (New York: Ballantine Books, 2002), 237.

5. Allen L. Langdon, *"Ready": The History of the 505th Parachute Infantry Regiment, 82nd Airborne Division, World War II,* ed. George B. Wood (Indianapolis: 82nd Airborne Division Association, 1986), 86; and Charles B. MacDonald, *The Siegfried Line Campaign,* United States Army in World War II series (Washington, D.C.: Office of the Chief of Military History, 1963), 119.

6. Special Force Headquarters (SFHQ), "Preliminary Instructions, Operation 'Linnet,'" August 29, 1944, 1–2, 4; and amendment no. 1, August 30, 1944, 1.

7. SFHQ, "Preliminary Instructions, Operation 'Linnet,'" app. A.

8. SFHQ, "Instructions no. 1, Operation 'Comet,'" September 7, 1944, 1–2.

9. Dwight D. Eisenhower, *The Papers of Dwight David Eisenhower: The War Years,* vol. 4, ed. Alfred D. Chandler, Jr. (Baltimore: Johns Hopkins Press, 1970), 2120–22.

10. Norman Longmate, *The G.I.'s: The Americans in Britain, 1942–1945* (New York: Scribners, 1975), 109.

11. Harry C. Butcher, *My Three Years with Eisenhower: The Personal Diary of Captain Harry C. Butcher, USNR, Naval Aide to General Eisenhower, 1942 to 1945* (New York: Simon & Schuster, 1946), 658.

12. Bruce W. Nelan, "The V-2: Aiming for the Stars," *Time,* October 12, 1992, 35; and Cornelius Ryan, *A Bridge Too Far* (New York: Popular Library, 1977), 81.

13. Ryan, *A Bridge Too Far,* 83, based on Ryan's later interview with Eisenhower.
14. Ambrose, *Eisenhower,* 348, from an interview with Dwight D. Eisenhower.
15. Carlo D'Este, *Eisenhower: A Soldier's Life* (New York: Henry Holt & Co., 2002), 606.
16. Ibid., 350.
17. OSS, "Report of Jedburgh Team Dudley," 1; and Olmsted, "Team Dudley," 36.
18. Olmsted, "Team Dudley," 38.
19. OSS (ETO), *Special Operations Branch . . . War Diaries,* vol. 3, bk. 12, 1670.

CHAPTER 6: OPERATION MARKET-GARDEN

1. L. H. Brereton, "First Allied Airborne Army: Operations in Holland, September–November 1944," December 22, 1944, copy on file at the U.S. Army Military History Institute, Carlisle Barracks, PA, 9.
2. Floyd Lavinius Parks, "Diary: First Allied Airborne Army, September 1944," September 1, 1945, U.S. Army Military History Institute, Carlisle Barracks, PA, [Brigadier General] Floyd Lavinius Parks Papers, box 2, entry for September 10, 1944, 1–3.
3. 440th Troop Carrier Group History Project, *DZ Europe: The 440th Troop Carrier Group,* 2nd ed. (n.p., 2003), 60.
4. Matthew B. Ridgway and Harold H. Martin, *Soldier: The Memoirs of Matthew B. Ridgway* (New York: Harper, 1956), 108.
5. Robert Peatling, *Without Tradition: 2 Para, 1941–1945* (Barnsley, S. Yorkshire, UK: Pen & Sword Military, 2004), 143.
6. Stewart W. Bentley, Jr., *Orange Blood, Silver Wings: The Untold Story of the Dutch Resistance During Market-Garden* (Bloomington, IN: AuthorHouse, 2007), 32.
7. Robert E. Urquhart, *Arnhem* (Los Angeles: Royal Publishing Company, 1995), 4.
8. Bentley, *Orange Blood,* 41.
9. Gavin, *On to Berlin,* 147.
10. Willard Beynon, telephone interview with the author, February 26, 2006.
11. Dirk van der Heide, "Operation Yellow: The German Attack on Rotterdam, 10–11 May 1940," in *The Mammoth Book of Eyewitness World War II,* ed. Jon E. Lewis (New York: Carroll & Graf, 2002), 52.
12. Ronald Seth, *The Undaunted: The Story of Resistance in Western Europe* (New York: Philosophical Library, 1956), 169.
13. Bentley, *Orange Blood,* 8.
14. Ibid., 9.
15. Ibid., 11.
16. OSS (ETO), *Special Operations Branch . . . War Diaries,* vol. 3, bk. 12, 1673.
17. Ibid., 1672.
18. "It's No Dutch Treat in Holland," *Army Talks* 4, no. 20 (September 30, 1945): 26.

CHAPTER 7: GERMANS EVERYWHERE

1. OSS (ETO), *Special Operations Branch . . . War Diaries,* vol. 3, bk. 12, 1670.
2. Ibid., 1670–71; and Bentley, *Orange Blood,* 35.
3. MacDonald, *Siegfried Line Campaign,* 121.
4. Ryan, *A Bridge Too Far,* 78.
5. MacDonald, *Siegfried Line Campaign,* 122.

6. Walter Bedell Smith, *Eisenhower's Six Great Decisions* (New York: Longmans, Green, 1956), 218–19; and D'Este, *Eisenhower,* 614.

7. MacDonald, *Siegfried Line Campaign,* 136.

8. Floyd Lavinius Parks, "Diary," entry for September 16, 1944, 1.

9. Anthony Hibbert, letter to Amanda Todd, March 14, 1945 (copy provided to the author by Mrs. Todd).

10. Gavin, *On to Berlin,* 150.

11. Ibid.

12. Ibid.

13. Brereton, "First Allied Airborne Army," 14.

14. 440th Troop Carrier Group History Project, *DZ Europe,* 62.

15. Gavin, *On to Berlin,* 151.

16. Flanagan, *Airborne,* 25.

17. Martha Gellhorn, "Stand Up and Hook Up!," in *Saga of the All American,* ed. W. Forrest Dawson (Atlanta: Albert Love Enterprises, 1946).

18. OSS (ETO), *Special Operations Branch . . . War Diaries,* vol. 4, bk. 6, report of Jedburgh team Edward and report of Jedburgh team Clarence, 1.

19. Ibid., report of Jedburgh team Clarence, 1.

CHAPTER 8: SUNDAY, SEPTEMBER 17, D-DAY

1. William Colby and Peter Forbath, *Honorable Men: My Life in the CIA* (New York: Simon & Schuster, 1978), 24; M. R. D. Foot, *SOE: An Outline History of the Special Operations Executive, 1940–46* (London: British Broadcasting Corporation, 1984), 124–25; and OSS (ETO), *Special Operations Branch . . . War Diaries,* vol. 13, 2.

2. OSS (ETO), *Special Operations Branch . . . War Diaries,* vol. 4, bk. 6, report of Jedburgh team Daniel II, 1.

3. William G. Lord II, *History of the 508th Parachute Infantry* (Washington, DC: Infantry Journal Press, 1948), 41.

4. Allen L. Langdon, *"Ready": The History of the 505th Parachute Infantry Regiment, 82nd Airborne Division, World War II,* ed. George B. Wood (Indianapolis: 82nd Airborne Division Association, 1986), 87.

5. MacDonald, *Siegfried Line Campaign,* 137.

6. 440th Troop Carrier Group History Project, *DZ Europe,* 61; and Brereton, "First Allied Airborne Army," 16.

7. Brereton, "First Allied Airborne Army," 16.

8. MacDonald, *Siegfried Line Campaign,* 138.

9. Brereton, "First Allied Airborne Army," 16.

10. 440th Troop Carrier Group History Project, *DZ Europe,* 63–64.

11. Brereton, "First Allied Airborne Army," 16.

12. Gavin, *On to Berlin,* 152.

13. Langdon, *"Ready,"* 93.

14. Brereton, "First Allied Airborne Army," 16; and OSS (ETO), *Special Operations Branch . . . War Diaries,* vol. 4, bk. 6, report of Jedburgh team Daniel II, 3.

15. MacDonald, *Siegfried Line Campaign,* 137–38.

16. Stephen Badsey, *Arnhem 1944: Operation Market Garden* (London: Osprey Publishing, Ltd., 1993), 33–34.

17. Ibid.

18. Stars and Stripes, *Invaders: The Story of the 50th Troop Carrier Wing* (Paris: Desfosaés-Néogravure, 1944), 17.

19. John M. Taylor, *General Maxwell Taylor: The Sword and the Pen* (New York: Bantam Books, 1991), 111.

20. Ibid., 112.

21. MacDonald, *Siegfried Line Campaign,* 145–47.

22. Ross S. Carter, *Those Devils in Baggy Pants* (Canton, OH: Claymore Publishing Corporation, 1998), 179; and Langdon, "Ready," 93.

23. Quoted in Phil Nordyke, *The All Americans in World War II: A Photographic History of the 82nd Airborne Division at War* (St. Paul, MN: Zenith Press, 2006), 99.

24. MacDonald, *Siegfried Line Campaign,* 160.

25. William D. Mandle and David H. Whittier, *The Devils in Baggy Pants: Combat Record of the 504th Parachute Infantry Regiment, April 1943–July 1945* (Paris: Draeger Frères, 1945).

26. Langdon, "Ready," 93.

27. Bentley, *Orange Blood,* 63.

28. Barbara Gavin Fauntleroy, *The General and His Daughter: The Wartime Letters of General James M. Gavin to His Daughter Barbara,* ed. Gayle Wurst (New York: Fordham University Press, 2007), 131.

29. Gavin, *On to Berlin,* 154–55.

30. Bentley, *Orange Blood,* 64; and Gavin, *On to Berlin,* 155.

31. Willard Beynon, telephone interview with the author, February 26, 2006.

32. Col. James R. Forgan, memorandum from Headquarters and Headquarters Detachment, OSS (ETO), to the commanding general, European Theater of Operations, United States Army, subject: Recommendation of Award of Silver Star, March 14, 1945, 2.

33. Willard Beynon, telephone interview with the author, February 26, 2006.

34. OSS (ETO), *Special Operations Branch . . . War Diaries,* vol. 4, bk. 6, report of Jedburgh team Clarence, 1; and *Special Operations Branch . . . War Diaries,* Casualty Reports.

35. Lord, *History of the 505th,* 42.

36. MacDonald, *Siegfried Line Campaign,* 163.

37. Ibid., 163–64.

38. Ibid.

39. Ibid., 161.

40. Gellhorn, "Stand Up and Hook Up!"

41. MacDonald, *Siegfried Line Campaign,* 159.

42. Harvey Allan Todd, personal account of wartime experiences, 9–10; and Anthony Hibbert, letter to Amanda Todd, March 14, 1945.

43. Brereton, "First Allied Airborne Army," 27.

44. MacDonald, *Siegfried Line Campaign,* 170.

45. Peatling, *Without Tradition,* 143.

46. John Frost, *A Drop Too Many* (London: Leo Cooper, 1994), 201.

47. Harvey Allan Todd, personal account of wartime experiences, 11.

48. Urquhart, *Arnhem,* 39.

49. Frost, *A Drop Too Many,* 217.

50. OSS (ETO), *Special Operations Branch . . . War Diaries,* vol. 4, bk. 6, report of

Jedburgh team Claude, 5; and Harvey Allan Todd, personal account of wartime experiences, 11.

51. Frost, *A Drop Too Many,* 218.
52. Urquhart, *Arnhem,* 46.
53. MacDonald, *Siegfried Line Campaign,* 170.
54. Ibid., 138.

CHAPTER 9: MONDAY, SEPTEMBER 18, THE SECOND DAY

1. MacDonald, *Siegfried Line Campaign,* 150.
2. Stars and Stripes, *101st Airborne Division: The Story of the 101st Airborne Division* (Paris: Stars and Stripes, 1945), 14.
3. Brereton, "First Allied Airborne Army," 30.
4. MacDonald, *Siegfried Line Campaign,* 150–51.
5. Peatling, *Without Tradition,* 181.
6. OSS (ETO), *Special Operations Branch . . . War Diaries,* vol. 4, bk. 6, report of Jedburgh team Edward.
7. Gavin, *On to Berlin,* 165.
8. Ibid., 165–66; and Maj. Gen. James M. Gavin, letter to Gen. Williams, January 17, 1954, on file at the U.S. Army Military History Institute, Carlisle, PA.
9. Gavin, *On to Berlin,* 165–66.
10. Albert Balink, "Descent into Holland," *Knickerbocker Weekly,* May 28, 1945, 13; and Dawson, ed., *Saga of the All American.*
11. MacDonald, *Siegfried Line Campaign,* 167.
12. Ibid.
13. Ibid., 169–70.
14. Ibid, 142, 171; and Christopher Hibbert, *Arnhem* (New York: Phoenix Paperbacks, 2003), 47.
15. MacDonald, *Siegfried Line Campaign,* and G. G. Norton, "Arnhem," in *The Mammoth Book of Elite Forces,* ed. Jon E. Lewis (New York: Carroll & Graf Publishers, 2001), 459.
16. Frost, *A Drop Too Many,* 219.
17. Robert J. Kershaw, *"It Never Snows in September": The German View of Market Garden and the Battle of Arnhem, September 1944* (New York: Sarpedon, 1999), 127.
18. Ibid.
19. Frost, *A Drop Too Many,* 219.
20. E. M. Mackay, "Arnhem: At the Bridge, 18–29 September 1944," in *The Mammoth Book of Eyewitness World War II,* ed. Jon E. Lewis (New York: Carroll & Graf, 2002; first published in the United Kingdom by Robinson in 2002; selection extracted from *Royal Engineers' Journal* 68, no. 4), 421.
21. Olmsted, "Team Dudley," 48.

CHAPTER 10: TUESDAY, SEPTEMBER 19, THE THIRD DAY

1. Olmsted, "Team Dudley," 48.
2. OSS, "Report of Jedburgh Team Dudley," 49–50.
3. Ibid.

4. Olmsted, "Team Dudley," 50.

5. Stars and Stripes, *101st Airborne Division*, 12–13; and MacDonald, *Siegfried Line Campaign*, 152.

6. MacDonald, *Siegfried Line Campaign*, 152.

7. Donald R. Burgett, *The Road to Arnhem: A Screaming Eagle in Holland* (New York: Dell Publishing, 2001), 94.

8. OSS (ETO), *Special Operations Branch . . . War Diaries*, vol. 4, bk. 6, report of Jedburgh team Daniel II, 4; and MacDonald, *Siegfried Line Campaign*, 152–53.

9. Badsey, *Arnhem 1944*, 58; and MacDonald, *Siegfried Line Campaign*, 153.

10. Ibid., 174; and Brereton, "First Allied Airborne Army," 33.

11. Dawson, *Saga of the All American*; Mandle and Whittier, *Devils in Baggy Pants*; and Stars and Stripes, *All American: The Story of the 82nd Airborne Division*.

12. Mandle and Whittier, *Devils in Baggy Pants*.

13. MacDonald, *Siegfried Line Campaign*, 175.

14. Ibid., 175–76.

15. OSS (ETO), *Special Operations Branch . . . War Diaries*, vol. 4, bk. 6, report of Jedburgh team Clarence, 1.

16. MacDonald, *Siegfried Line Campaign*, 176.

17. Willard Beynon, telephone interview with the author, December 27, 2007.

18. OSS (ETO), *Special Operations Branch . . . War Diaries*, vol. 4, bk. 6, report of Jedburgh team Clarence, 2; and Capt. Jane M. Tanner, memorandum to Chief, Western European Section, OSS/London Special Operations Branch, subj.: "Jed Team 'CLARENCE' Field Activities," February 27, 1945.

19. 440th Troop Carrier Group History Project, *DZ Europe*, 69–70.

20. OSS (ETO), *Special Operations Branch . . . War Diaries*, vol. 4, bk. 6, report of Jedburgh team Claude, 5, 14; and Harvey Allan Todd, personal account of wartime experiences, 13–14.

21. Ibid.

22. Anthony Hibbert, letter to Amanda Todd, March 14, 1945 (photocopy provided to the author by Amanda Todd).

23. Digby Tatham-Warter, in Peatling, *Without Tradition*, 147.

24. Harvey Allan Todd, personal account of wartime experiences, 15.

25. Hilary St. George Saunders, *The Red Beret: The Story of the Parachute Regiment at War, 1940–1945* (Nashville: Battery Press, 1985), 248.

26. OSS (ETO), *Special Operations Branch . . . War Diaries*, vol. 4, bk. 6, report of Jedburgh team Claude, 2.

CHAPTER 11: WEDNESDAY, SEPTEMBER 20, THE FOURTH DAY

1. OSS, "Report of Jedburgh Team Dudley," 3; and Olmsted, "Team Dudley," 50–51.

2. Olmsted, "Team Dudley," 51.

3. Brereton, "First Allied Airborne Army," 37.

4. MacDonald, *Siegfried Line Campaign*, 187.

5. Ibid., 177–78.

6. Ibid., 180.

7. Delbert Kuehl, "Crossing of the Waal (Rhine) River," in 82nd Airborne Division Association, *82nd Airborne Division: America's Guard of Honor* (Nashville: Turner Publishing Company, 2004), 68.

8. Stars and Stripes, *All American;* and MacDonald, *Siegfried Line Campaign,* 180.

9. Kuehl, "Crossing of the Waal," 69.

10. MacDonald, *Siegfried Line Campaign,* 181.

11. T. Moffatt Burriss, *Strike and Hold: A Memoir of the 82d Airborne in World War II* (Washington, DC: Brassey's, 2000), 122–23; and MacDonald, *Siegfried Line Campaign,* 181–82.

12. MacDonald, *Siegfried Line Campaign,* 182.

13. Mandle and Whittier, *Devils in Baggy Pants;* Burriss, *Strike and Hold,* 144; and Dawson, *Saga of the All American.*

14. Burriss, *Strike and Hold,* 120–24.

15. Ibid., 164.

16. MacDonald, *Siegfried Line Campaign,* 185.

17. OSS (ETO), *Special Operations Branch . . . War Diaries,* vol. 4, bk. 6, report of Jedburgh team Clarence.

18. Ibid., report of Jedburgh team Edward, 3.

19. Karel Margry, ed., *Operation Market-Garden: Then and Now,* vol. 2 (London: Battle of Britain International Ltd., 2002), 485.

20. OSS (ETO), *Special Operations Branch . . . War Diaries,* vol. 4, bk. 6, report of Jedburgh team Claude, 7; and Harvey Allan Todd, personal account of wartime experiences, 17.

21. Ibid.

CHAPTER 12: THURSDAY, SEPTEMBER 21, THE FIFTH DAY

1. MacDonald, *Siegfried Line Campaign,* 185.

2. Ibid., 189.

3. OSS (ETO), *Special Operations Branch . . . War Diaries,* vol. 4, bk. 6, report of Jedburgh team Edward, 4, 11.

4. OSS, "Report of Jedburgh Team Dudley," 4.

5. OSS (ETO), *Special Operations Branch . . . War Diaries,* vol. 4, bk. 6, report of Jedburgh team Claude, 7; and Harvey Allan Todd, personal account of wartime experiences, 17–18.

6. Todd, personal account of wartime experiences, 17–18.

7. Ibid.

8. OSS (ETO), *Special Operations Branch . . . War Diaries,* vol. 4, bk. 6, report of Jedburgh team Daniel II, 5.

CHAPTER 13: FRIDAY, SEPTEMBER 22, THE SIXTH DAY

1. MacDonald, *Siegfried Line Campaign,* 191.

2. Ibid., 186.

3. Ibid., 196.

4. OSS, "Report of Jedburgh Team Dudley," 4; and Olmsted, "Team Dudley," 54.

CHAPTER 14: SATURDAY, SEPTEMBER 23, THE SEVENTH DAY

1. 440th Troop Carrier Group History Project, *DZ Europe,* 70.

2. MacDonald, *Siegfried Line Campaign,* 196.

3. OSS (ETO), *Special Operations Branch . . . War Diaries*, vol. 4, bk. 6, report of Jedburgh team Claude, 7; and Harvey Allan Todd, personal account of wartime experiences, 18.

4. OSS, "Report of Jedburgh Team Dudley," 4.

5. Olmsted, "Team Dudley," 56.

CHAPTER 15: SUNDAY, SEPTEMBER 24, THE EIGHTH DAY

1. OSS (ETO), *Special Operations Branch . . . War Diaries*, vol. 4, bk. 6, report of Jedburgh team Daniel II, 7.

2. MacDonald, *Siegfried Line Campaign*, 197.

3. Olmsted, "Team Dudley," 56.

4. Ibid., 61–62.

CHAPTER 16: WITHDRAWAL, THE LAST DAY

1. Den Portman, in Peatling, *Without Tradition*, 166.

2. MacDonald, *Siegfried Line Campaign*, 197.

3. Graeme Warrack, *Travel by Dark: After Arnhem* (London: Harvill Press, 1963), 50; and Bernard Law Montgomery, *The Memoirs of Field-Marshal the Viscount Montgomery of Alamein* (Cleveland, OH: World Publishing Co., 1958), 264.

4. OSS (ETO), *Special Operations Branch . . . War Diaries*, vol. 4, bk. 6, report of Jedburgh team Claude, 3 (p. 2 of Knottenbelt supplementary report).

5. Den Portman, in Peatling, *Without Tradition*, 167.

6. Ibid.

7. Peatling, *Without Tradition*, 143.

8. Saunders, *Red Beret*, 251.

9. MacDonald, *Siegfried Line Campaign*, 197–98; and Montgomery, *Memoirs*, 264.

10. OSS (ETO), *Special Operations Branch . . . War Diaries*, Casualty Reports.

11. OSS (ETO), *Special Operations Branch . . . War Diaries*, vol. 4, bk. 6, report of Jedburgh team Edward. This last statement seems odd after reviewing the Daniel II report, in which Lt. Dubois appears to be the most active member of the team. It may be that Lt. Dubois was a primary writer of the Daniel II report.

12. Ibid., report of Jedburgh team Clarence, supplementary report by T/Sgt. Beynon, 2; and report of Jedburgh team Edward, 14.

13. MacDonald, *Siegfried Line Campaign*, 199.

14. Dwight D. Eisenhower, quoted in Merle Miller, *Ike the Soldier: As They Knew Him* (New York: G. P. Putnam's Sons, 1987), 698.

15. Ibid.

16. Bernard Law Montgomery, *The Memoirs of Field Marshal Montgomery* (New York: Da Capo Press, 1982), 266.

17. Ibid., 267.

18. Frost, *A Drop Too Many*, xiii.

CHAPTER 17: PRISONER OF WAR

1. Harvey Allan Todd, personal account of wartime experiences, 19.

2. OSS (ETO), *Special Operations Branch . . . War Diaries*, vol. 4, bk. 6, report of

Jedburgh team Claude, 8; and Harvey Allan Todd, personal account of wartime experiences, 21.

3. Olmsted, "Team Dudley," 62.

CHAPTER 18: TODD'S JOURNEY BEGINS

1. Olmsted, "Team Dudley," 63.
2. Ibid., 65.
3. Harvey Allan Todd, personal account of wartime experiences, 22–23.
4. OSS (ETO), "Team Stanley II," report by Capt. Vickery, 1; and report by T/Sgt. Beynon, 1, RG 226, National Archives.
5. OSS (ETO), "Team Stanley II," report by Capt. Vickery, 1–2.

CHAPTER 19: DULAG LUFT

1. Olmsted, "Team Dudley," 66.
2. Harvey Allan Todd, personal account of wartime experiences, 23.
3. OSS (ETO), *Special Operations Branch . . . War Diaries,* vol. 4, bk. 6, report of Jedburgh team Claude, 9; Harvey Allan Todd, personal account of wartime experiences, 24; and Todd, personal chronology of activities from June 1939 to December 30, 1946, n.d. (photocopy of untitled and undated document provided to the author by Mr. Todd), 2.
4. Olmsted, "Team Dudley," 67.
5. Ibid., 67.
6. Ibid., 69–70.
7. Ibid., 70.
8. Ibid.

CHAPTER 20: THE INSUFFERABLE LORD HAW HAW

1. Olmsted, "Team Dudley," 73.
2. Ibid., 77–78.
3. Ibid., 75–76.
4. Ibid., 76.
5. Ibid., 77.

CHAPTER 21: SOLITARY CONFINEMENT

1. OSS (ETO), *Special Operations Branch . . . War Diaries,* vol. 4, bk. 6, report of Jedburgh team Claude, 9; and Harvey Allan Todd, personal account of wartime experiences, 25–26.
2. Ibid; and Harvey Allan Todd, personal chronology, 2. Additional details of prisoner life at Dulag Luft and at Stalag XII-A were taken from accounts written by Allied prisoners who were at the camps during the same time Todd was there. These accounts were by Lance Corporal John James Bird, Lance Sergeant Harold Padfield, and Sergeant Douglas Smithson, all members of the British 1st Airborne Division.
3. OSS (ETO), *Special Operations Branch . . . War Diaries,* vol. 4, bk. 6, report of

Jedburgh team Claude, 11; and Harvey Allan Todd, personal account of wartime experiences, 27.

4. OSS (ETO), *Special Operations Branch . . . War Diaries,* vol. 4, bk. 6, report of Jedburgh team Claude, 11 (p. 8 of Todd supplementary report); and Harvey Allan Todd, personal account of wartime experiences, 27.

5. OSS (ETO), *Special Operations Branch . . . War Diaries,* vol. 4, bk. 6, report of Jedburgh team Claude, 11; and Harvey Allan Todd, personal account of wartime experiences, 27–28.

6. Ibid.

CHAPTER 22: STOLEN PLANS TO BE DELIVERED

1. Olmsted, "Team Dudley," 80–81.
2. Ibid., 81–82.
3. Ibid., 83–84.
4. Ibid., 84.

CHAPTER 23: OFLAG 64

1. OSS (ETO), *Special Operations Branch . . . War Diaries,* vol. 4, bk. 6, report of Jedburgh team Claude, 10; Harvey Allan Todd, personal account of wartime experiences, 29; and Harvey Allan Todd, personal chronology, 2.

2. Clarence Ferguson, *Kriegsgefangener 3074: Prisoner-of-War* (Waco, TX: Texian Press, 1983), 191.

3. Clarence R. Meltesen, *Roads to Liberation from Oflag 64* (San Francisco: Oflag 64 Press, 1990), 174. In addition to the firsthand accounts of Harvey Allan Todd already cited, details of camp life at Oflag 64 and the experiences of Todd and other prisoners following their departure from the camp at Schubin are taken from the personal accounts of several veterans, some of which are available at the Oflag 64 veterans website: http://www.oflag64.org/index.html (accessed September 14, 2007) and the Doctor's Lounge website: http://www.graffagnino.com/doctorslounge/#war (accessed October 5, 2007). Personal accounts drawn from include those of Mays W. Anderson, Billy Bingham, Wright Bryan, Stanley W. Coburn, Robert L. Corbin, William R. Cory, John Culler, Jay Drake, Clarence Ferguson, Herbert L. Garris, Paul R. Goode, Dr. Peter Carl Graffagnino, Don Hartley, William P. Haynes III, Jonel C. Hill, Victor Kanners, Bob Keith, Brooks Kleber, James W. Lockett, Clarence R. Meltesen, Robert J. Miller, Lawrence Naab, Richard B. Parker, Dr. Walter S. Parks, Jr., Thomas J. Riggs, Jr., Bob Rivers, John P. Sandford, Robert T. Thompson, James H. Watts, C. A. Williamson, and Doyle R. Yardley.

4. OSS (ETO), *Special Operations Branch . . . War Diaries,* vol. 4, bk. 6, report of Jedburgh team Claude, 11; Harvey Allan Todd, personal account of wartime experiences, 30; and Harvey Allan Todd, personal chronology, 2.

5. American National Red Cross, "Reports on German Camps," *Prisoners of War Bulletin,* December 1944, 4.

6. J. Frank Diggs, *Americans Behind the Barbed Wire* (New York: ibooks, 2003), 31.

7. "Sixty Students, Ten Profs Pursue Higher Learning Inside Wire," *Oflag 64 Item,* November 1, 1944, 4. Available at the Oflag 64 veterans website: http://www

.oflag64.org/index.html (accessed September 14, 2007); and Diggs, *Americans Behind the Barbed Wire,* 31–32.

8. John Toland, *The Last 100 Days* (New York: Random House, 1966), 596.

9. Diggs, *Americans Behind the Barbed Wire,* 73–74; and Peter C. Graffagnino, "The Doctors' Lounge: Winter Scene, 1945," *Muscogee County* (Georgia) *Medical Bulletin* 20, no. 1 (1965): 20, available online at http://www.graffagnino.com/doctorslounge/#war (accessed October 5, 2007).

10. Robert Galloway, *Oflag 64: A P.O.W. Odyssey* (Galloway Productions, 2000), VHS video recording of public television documentary.

11. Harvey Allan Todd, personal account of wartime experiences, 30.

12. Ferguson, *Kriegsgefangener 3074,* 191–93.

13. Diggs, *Americans Behind the Barbed Wire,* 53, 103–4.

CHAPTER 24: GOODBYE TO BUNNY AND HENK

1. Olmsted, "Team Dudley," 85–87.

2. Ibid., 90.

3. Ibid., 91.

4. Ibid., 91.

5. Ibid., 94.

6. Ibid., 94.

7. Ibid., 96–97.

8. Robert Peatling, *Without Tradition,* 191.

9. Olmsted, "Team Dudley," 102.

CHAPTER 25: PAPPY'S RETURN

1. Olmsted, "Team Dudley," 102–5.

2. Warrack, *Travel by Dark,* 148.

3. Ibid.

4. Olmsted, "Team Dudley," 106.

5. Ibid.

6. Warrack, *Travel by Dark,* 149.

7. Ibid.

8. Olmsted, "Team Dudley," 108.

9. Ibid., 108.

10. Ibid., 110.

11. Ibid.

12. Ibid., 114.

13. Ibid., 115.

14. Ibid., 116.

15. Stars and Stripes, *101st Airborne Division,* 15–16.

16. Ibid., 2.

17. Ibid.

18. Ibid.

19. Ibid.

20. Stars and Stripes, *101st Airborne Division,* 3.

21. Hooiveld, "Sergeant John Patrick Austin."

CHAPTER 26: MISSING IN ACTION

1. Adjutant General's Office, War Department, Western Union telegram to Arville O. Todd, November 2, 1944 (photocopy provided to the author by Amanda Todd).

2. Ibid., November 24, 1944 (photocopy provided to the author by Amanda Todd).

3. Arville O. Todd, "Missing in Action" (poem, probably written in late 1944; photocopy provided to the author by Amanda Todd).

4. Ferguson, *Kriegsgefangener 3074*, 117.

5. Harvey Allan Todd, personal account of wartime experiences, 31; and Harvey Allan Todd, personal chronology, 3.

6. Ibid.

7. "Annual Minstrel, Swingland, Glee Club Program, Yule Festivities Celebrate Kriegy Christmas Season Here: Revamped Minstrel Opens Monday," *Oflag 64 Item*, December 1, 1944, 1. Available at the Oflag 64 veterans website: http://www .oflag64.org/index.html (accessed September 14, 2007).

8. Ferguson, *Kriegsgefangener 3074*, 128.

9. Harvey Allan Todd, personal account of wartime experiences, 31–32; and Harvey Allan Todd, personal chronology, 3.

10. Harvey Allan Todd, personal account of wartime experiences, 32.

11. Ferguson, *Kriegsgefangener 3074*, 223–38; and Diggs, *Americans Behind the Barbed Wire*, 101.

12. Harvey Allan Todd, personal account of wartime experiences, 32; and Harvey Allan Todd, personal chronology, 3.

13. Harvey Allan Todd, personal account of wartime experiences, 32–33.

14. Ibid.

CHAPTER 27: THE LONG MARCH

Towns within Poland are referred to in this chapter by the German name that was used during the war. The Polish names (in parentheses) for these towns are as follows: Exin (Kcynia), Wirnitz (Smogulec), Eichfelde (Polanowo), Charlottenburg (Falmierowo), Wirsitz (Wyrzysk), Lobsens (Lobżenica), Flatow (Złotów), Jastrow (Jastrowie), Zippnow (Sypniewo), Rederitz (Nadarzyce), Machlin (Machliny), Tempelburg (Czaplinek), Heinrichsdorf (Siemczyno), Zuelshagen (Suliszewo), Dramburg (Drawsko Pomorskie), Janikow (Jankowo), Gienow (Ginawa), Wangerin (Węgorzyno), Ruhnow (Runowo), Zeitlitz (Siedlice), Regenwalde (Resko), Plathe (Ploty), Lebbin (Lubin), Greifenberg (Gryfice), Stuchow (Stuchowo), Justin (Gostyń), Stresow (Strzezewo), Fritzow (Wrzosowo), Dievenow (Dziwnów), Leimbrink (Granik), Neuendorf (Wisełka), Misdroy (Międzyzdroje), and Swinemünde (Świnoujście).

1. Earl F. Ziemke, *The Soviet Juggernaut*, Time-Life World War II series (Alexandria, VA: Time-Life Books, 1980), 181.

2. Figures vary from source to source. According to Clarence R. Meltesen in *Roads to Liberation from Oflag 64* (self-published in San Francisco, 1990), 77, the Red Cross reported a total of 1,557 officers and enlisted men at Oflag 64 as of January 21, 1945.

3. James H. Watts, "Diary of a POW," unpublished ms., entry for January 20, 1945, available online at the Oflag 64 veterans website: http://www.oflag64.org/ index.html (accessed September 14, 2007), 13.

4. Victor Kanners, "Horseshit and Cobblestones," unpublished account by a former prisoner of war, 2, available online at the Oflag 64 veterans website: http://www.oflag64.org/index.html (accessed September 14, 2007).

5. Ibid.

6. According to the American Legation, Bern, enclosure no. 1 to dispatch no. 11619 (April 30, 1945), confidential report no. 755, "Special Report on Conditions of Transfer of American Officers from Oflag 64–Altburgund to Oflag XIIIB–Hammelburg," April 3, 1945 (available online at the Oflag 64 veterans website: http://www.oflag64.org/index.html, accessed September 14, 2007), a total of 1,471 officers and enlisted men departed Oflag 64 in the march column on January 21, 1945. Other accounts give slightly different numbers. John P. Sandford's account, for example, put the total at 1,391 (1,282 officers and 109 enlisted men).

7. Kanners, "Horseshit and Cobblestones," 7.

8. In addition to Harvey Allan Todd's personal account and diary, details of the march of American POWs from Oflag 64 to the south of Germany are taken from "The Diary of John P. Sandford," a prisoner of war diary available online at http://www.taskforcebaum.de/oflag64/march1.html, and from the public television documentary *Oflag 64: A P.O.W. Odyssey,* produced by Robert Galloway. The expanded account written later by Todd, 33, indicates the first day's journey ended at Wegheim; according to "The Diary of John P. Sandford," it ended at Exin (Kcynia).

9. Kanners, "Horseshit and Cobblestones," 32.

10. American Legation, Bern, enclosure no. 1 to dispatch no. 11619 (April 30, 1945), confidential report no. 755, 2.

11. Harvey Allan Todd, "POW March from Oflag 64 to Austria, 1-21 to 5-5-45," n.d. (photocopy of personal journal kept during the prisoner of war march from Oflag 64 to Austria, January 21 to May 5, 1945, provided to the author by Mr. Todd), 8; and "The Diary of John P. Sandford."

12. "Latvian Legion," Wikipedia, http://en.wikipedia.org/wiki/Latvian_Legion (accessed October 12, 2007).

13. Robert L. Corbin, "Prisoner of War Story," unpublished ms., 1988, available online at the Oflag 64 veterans website: http://www.oflag64.org/index.html (accessed September 14, 2007).

14. Meltesen, *Roads to Liberation,* 205. The pants-for-bread trade in Lobsens is recounted in several firsthand accounts of the march.

15. Harvey Allan Todd, "POW March from Oflag 64 to Austria," 8; and "The Diary of John P. Sandford."

16. Ziemke, *Soviet Juggernaut,* 182.

17. Harvey Allan Todd, "POW March from Oflag 64 to Austria," 8; and "The Diary of John P. Sandford."

18. American Legation, Bern, enclosure no. 1 to dispatch no. 11619 (April 30, 1945), confidential report no. 755, 2.

19. Harvey Allan Todd, personal account of wartime experiences, 33–34; and Harvey Allan Todd, "POW March from Oflag 64 to Austria," 8.

20. Ziemke, *Soviet Juggernaut,* 182.

21. Harvey Allan Todd, "POW March from Oflag 64 to Austria," 8; and "The Diary of John P. Sandford."

22. Toland, *The Last 100 Days,* 62.

23. Ziemke, *Soviet Juggernaut,* 186–87.

24. Harvey Allan Todd, "POW March from Oflag 64 to Austria," 9.

25. Ibid.; and "The Diary of John P. Sandford."

26. Meltesen, *Roads to Liberation,* 261.

27. American Legation, Bern, enclosure no. 1 to dispatch no. 11619 (April 30, 1945), confidential report no. 755, 2.

28. Kanners, "Horseshit and Cobblestones," 42.

29. Ibid., 46.

30. Lloyd R. Shoemaker, *The Escape Factory: The Story of MIS-X* (New York: St. Martin's Press, 1990), 187. Shoemaker cites a report prepared in February 1945 by a Swiss representative of the International Committee of the Red Cross when he provides the figure of 1,444 POWs evacuated from Oflag 64. Other sources, including documents prepared by the War Department, put the total at anywhere from 1,392 to slightly more than 1,500.

31. John M. Olmsted, conversation with the author in Washington, D.C., May 11, 1988; and Hooiveld, "Sergeant John Patrick Austin."

CHAPTER 28: PATTON'S HAMMELBURG RAID

1. American Legation, Bern, enclosure no. 1 to dispatch no. 11619 (April 30, 1945), confidential report no. 755, 2. Clarence Meltesen indicates that two other accounts provide differing totals: 480 (412 officers and 68 enlisted men) and 495.

2. Meltesen, *Roads to Liberation,* 382.

3. Anthony Hibbert, letters to Amanda Todd and Mr. Arville Todd, March 14, 1945 (photocopies provided to the author by Amanda Todd).

4. OSS (ETO), *Special Operations Branch . . . War Diaries,* vol. 4, bk. 6, report of Jedburgh team Claude, 13; Harvey Allan Todd, personal chronology, 3; and "The Diary of John P. Sandford."

5. Meltesen, *Roads to Liberation,* 386.

6. Ibid., 389–90.

7. Gen. George S. Patton, Jr., letter quoted in Martin Blumenson, *The Patton Papers, 1940–1945* (Boston: Houghton Mifflin Co., 1974), 664.

8. Karel Margry, "The Hammelburg Raid," *After the Battle,* no. 91 (1996): 2.

9. Patton, letter quoted in Blumenson, *Patton Papers,* 665.

10. Kenneth Koyen, *The Fourth Armored Division from the Beach to Bavaria: The Story of the Fourth Armored Division in Combat* (Munich: 4th Armored Division, 1946), 107–8.

11. Eric Niderost, "A Fool's Errand," *World War II* (July–August 2006): 31.

12. Jonathan F. Keiler, "Top Secret: A Costly Raid to Liberate General George S. Patton's Son-in-Law from a German Prison Camp Failed with Heavy Losses," *WWII History* (March 2004): 24.

13. Richard Baron, Abe Baum, and Richard Goldhurst, *Raid: The Untold Story of Patton's Secret Mission* (New York: Berkley Books, 1984), 21.

14. Toland, *Last 100 Days,* 290.

15. OSS (ETO), *Special Operations Branch . . . War Diaries,* vol. 4, bk. 6, report of Jedburgh team Claude, 11; and Meltesen, *Roads to Liberation,* 390–91.

16. Report prepared by Capt. Abraham J. Baum upon his return to headquarters, 4th Armored Division, on April 10, 1945.

17. OSS (ETO), *Special Operations Branch . . . War Diaries,* vol. 4, bk. 6, report of Jedburgh team Claude, 12.

18. Toland, *Last 100 Days,* 292.

19. Ibid.

20. Ibid.

21. Ibid.

22. Ibid.

23. OSS (ETO), *Special Operations Branch . . . War Diaries,* vol. 4, bk. 6, report of Jedburgh team Claude, 12; and Harvey Allan Todd, personal account of wartime experiences, 35.

24. Toland, *Last 100 Days,* 295.

25. OSS (ETO), *Special Operations Branch . . . War Diaries,* vol. 4, bk. 6, report of Jedburgh team Claude, 12; and Harvey Allan Todd, personal account of wartime experiences, 35–36.

26. Harvey Allan Todd, statement about medical care received during his time as a POW (photocopy provided to the author by Amanda Todd).

27. Brooks Kleber, in an interview by Alexander S. Cochran, Jr., "Trauma of Capture," *Military History* (February 1985): 48.

28. Toland, *Last 100 Days,* 297.

29. Koyen, *Fourth Armored Division,* 117, 124.

30. Ibid., 124, 138.

31. Toland, *Last 100 Days,* 299.

32. Ibid., 602.

33. Baron, Baum, and Goldhurst, *Raid,* 270.

CHAPTER 29: RUMORS OF EVIL

1. OSS (ETO), *Special Operations Branch . . . War Diaries,* vol. 4, bk. 6, report of Jedburgh team Claude, 12; and Harvey Allan Todd, personal account of wartime experiences, 36.

2. Meltesen, *Roads to Liberation,* 420.

3. Ibid., 420, 426.

4. Ibid.

5. Jesse Wofford B-17 Crew Web page at http://www.100thbg.com/mainpages/history/history5/wofford_crew.htm.

6. Toland, *Last 100 Days,* 362.

7. Meltesen, *Roads to Liberation,* 442. Meltesen's account lists 25 killed, 23 wounded, and 13 walking wounded. The figures shown in the Jedburgh team Claude mission report are 29 killed and 40 wounded. In his personal journal, Lieutenant Allan Todd notes the figures at 40 killed and 16 wounded.

8. OSS (ETO), *Special Operations Branch . . . War Diaries,* vol. 4, bk. 6, report of Jedburgh team Claude, 12; Harvey Allan Todd, personal account of wartime experiences, 36; Harvey Allan Todd, "POW March from Oflag 64 to Austria," 11; and Meltesen, *Roads to Liberation,* 442.

9. Harvey Allan Todd, "POW March from Oflag 64 to Austria," 11; and "The Diary of John P. Sandford."

10. Meltesen, *Roads to Liberation,* 450.

11. Hooiveld, "Sergeant John Patrick Austin."

12. Meltesen, *Roads to Liberation,* 419.

13. Balink, "Descent into Holland," and Hans Vanderwerff, "The Story of Arie Bestebreurtje," 2005, available online at http://www.cympm.com/bestebreurtje.html (accessed January 28, 2006).

14. Meltesen, *Roads to Liberation,* 453.

15. Ibid., 462.

16. Joseph Carter, *The History of the 14th Armored Division* (Atlanta: Albert Love Enterprises, 1945), ch. 14.

17. Vernon H. Brown, Jr., *Mount Up! We're Moving Out!: A World War II Memoir of D Troop, 94th Cavalry Reconnaissance Squadron (Mechanized) of the 14th Armored Division* (Bennington, VT: Merriam Press, 2003), 134.

18. Carter, *History of the 14th Armored Division,* ch. 14.

19. Brown, *Mount Up!,* 140.

20. OSS (ETO), *Special Operations Branch . . . War Diaries,* vol. 4, bk. 6, report of Jedburgh team Claude, 12; Harvey Allan Todd, personal account of wartime experiences, 36.

21. Rodney G. Minott, *The Fortress That Never Was: The Myth of Hitler's Bavarian Stronghold* (New York: Holt, Rinehart & Winston, 1964), 3–5.

22. Ibid., 11–15, 47–57.

23. Meltesen, *Roads to Liberation,* 465.

24. OSS (ETO), *Special Operations Branch . . . War Diaries,* vol. 4, bk. 6, report of Jedburgh team Claude, 12; Harvey Allan Todd, personal account of wartime experiences, 36–37.

25. Ibid.; and Harvey Allan Todd, "POW March from Oflag 64 to Austria," 13. Although Todd did not mention the German captain by name in his account, Clarence R. Meltesen, in *Roads to Liberation,* identifies him as Hauptmann Menner.

CHAPTER 30: FREEDOM

1. OSS (ETO), *Special Operations Branch . . . War Diaries,* vol. 4, bk. 6, report of Jedburgh team Claude, 12.

2. Ibid.; and Harvey Allan Todd, personal account of wartime experiences, 37.

3. Ibid.

4. Harvey Allan Todd, "POW March from Oflag 64 to Austria," 14.

5. Harvey Allan Todd, information provided to the Veterans Administration on VA Form 10-0048, "Former POW Medical History," October 19, 1987 (photocopy provided to the author by Amanda Todd).

6. OSS (ETO), *Special Operations Branch . . . War Diaries,* vol. 4, bk. 6, report of Jedburgh team Claude, 13; and Harvey Allan Todd, personal account of wartime experiences, 38.

7. Brown, *Mount Up!,* 144.

8. Minott, *Fortress That Never Was,* 3–5.

9. Harvey Allan Todd, "POW March from Oflag 64 to Austria," 13.

EPILOGUE

1. Harvey Allan Todd, letter to Mr. and Mrs. Arville Todd, May 7, 1945 (photocopy provided to the author by Amanda Todd).

2. Meltesen, *Roads to Liberation,* 480.

3. Ronald H. Bailey, *Prisoners of War,* Time-Life World War II series (Chicago: Time-Life Books, 1981), 176.

4. Brooks Kleber, in an interview by Cochran, "Trauma of Capture," (February 1985): 49.

5. Amanda Todd, telephone conversation with the author, May 6, 2006.

6. Amanda Todd, interview with the author, February 25, 2005.

7. OSS, letter, subject: Presentation of Decoration, dated September 24, 1945, National Archives (copy in the author's possession).

8. OSS, letter, subject: Physical Examination, dated September 12, 1945, from the examining physician, Major (Dr.) Louis Lostfogel, to the Adjutant General, National Archives (copy in the author's possession).

9. John Olmsted, correspondence with the author (author's possession); and obituary, *Eastside Journal* (Bellevue, WA), May 24, 2001; "De oorlog wordt nooit meer dichtgeslagen boek," *Regio,* May 3, 1985.

10. Hooiveld, "Sergeant John Patrick Austin."

11. Ibid.

12. Dawson, *Saga of the All American.*

13. "1970 Pro-Vietnam War Sermon," article online at http://www.cvillenews.com/2005/12/22/bestebreurtje-sermon (accessed January 28, 2006).

14. Fred L. Borch and Robert F. Dorr, "Dutch Spy Helped 82nd Take Town from Germans," *Army Times,* July 17, 2006, 37.

15. OSS (ETO), Special Orders no. 8, January 10, 1945, personnel records of George M. Verhaeghe, OSS Records, National Archives; and OSS (ETO), *Special Operations Branch . . . War Diaries,* Casualty Reports.

16. 1st Lt. J. G. Miller, Medical Corps, "Interviewer's Report," January 30, 1945, personnel file of Willard W. Beynon, OSS records, National Archives.

17. Headquarters, U.S. Forces, European Theater, General Order 218, August 30, 1945, copy in the personnel file of James R. Billingsley, OSS records, National Archives.

18. Willard Beynon, telephone interviews with the author, February 26, 2006, and December 27, 2007; "Britain Awards Beynon Emblems, Citation for Distinguished Duty," *Scranton Times,* August 6, 1948; and Joseph Nieroda, "40 Years of Silence: Elite Heroes of 'Secret War' Come Out of Closet," *Scranton Times,* July 5, 1985.

19. G. Colket Caner, MD, record of OSS return from overseas interview, January 24, 1945, copy in personnel file of Capt. McCord Sollenberger, OSS records, National Archives.

20. Office of the Adjutant General, War Department, Special Orders no. 30, February 3, 1945, copy in personnel file of Capt. McCord Sollenberger, OSS records, National Archives.

21. Headquarters, United States Forces European Theater, Citation for Bronze Star Medal [to Capt. McCord Sollenberger], General Order no. 8, January 7, 1946; Headquarters and Headquarters Detachment, OSS/European Theater of Operations, letter, subj.: Status of Recommendation for the Award of the Dutch Cross of Merit to Captain Sollenberger and T/Sgt. Billingsley, February 8, 1945; and Headquarters, U.S. Forces, European Theater, letter, subj.: Foreign Award [to Capt. McCord Sollenberger], March 23, 1946. All documents in personnel file of Captain McCord Sollenberger, OSS records, National Archives.

22. OSS, Interviewer's Report, T/Sgt. James R. Billingsley, December 30, 1944, copy in the personnel records of James R. Billingsley, OSS records, National Archives.

23. Headquarters, OSS/China Theater, letter, subj.: Recommendation for Award [to M/Sgt. James R. Billingsley], September 10, 1945.

24. Headquarters, U.S. Forces, European Theater, General Order no. 218, August 30, 1945, copy in the personnel file of James R. Billingsley, OSS records, National Archives.

25. Headquarters and Headquarters Detachment, OSS/European Theater of Operations, letter, subj.: Status of Recommendation for the Award of the Dutch Cross of Merit to Captain Sollenberger and T/Sgt. Billingsley, February 8, 1945.

26. Copy of citation in the personnel file of M/Sgt. James R. Billingsley, OSS records, National Archives.

27. Teresa Machan, ed., *The Netherlands* (London: Insight Guides, 2004), 59.

28. Ibid., 58.

29. Quoted in Bentley, *Orange Blood*, vii.

30. MacDonald, *Siegfried Line Campaign*, 183–84.

31. Ibid., 184.

32. Frost, *A Drop Too Many*, 200–201.

33. "The Prince and the O.S.S.," *New York Times*, October 16, 1982, available online at http://select.nytimes.com/search/restricted/article (accessed October 31, 2005).

34. Amanda Todd, interview with the author, February 25, 2005.

BIBLIOGRAPHY

I. RECORDS AND OTHER UNPUBLISHED DOCUMENTS

Adjutant General's Office. War Department. Western Union Telegram to Arville O. Todd, November 2, 1944. Photocopy provided to the author by Amanda Todd.

——. Western Union Telegram to Arville O. Todd, November 24, 1944. Photocopy provided to the author by Amanda Todd.

American Legation, Bern. Enclosure no. 1 to dispatch no. 11619 (April 30, 1945), confidential report no. 755, "Special Report on Conditions of Transfer of American Officers from Oflag 64-Altburgund to Oflag XIIIB-Hammelburg." April 3, 1945. Available online at the Oflag 64 veterans website: http://www.oflag64.org/index.html (accessed September 14, 2007).

American National Red Cross. Map, "Location of German Camps and Hospitals Where American Prisoners of War and Civilian Internees Are Held (Based on information received to December 31, 1944)."

——. *Prisoners of War Bulletin* 2, no. 12 (December 1944).

Brereton, L. H. "First Allied Airborne Army: Operations in Holland, September–November 1944." December 22, 1944. U.S. Army Military History Institute, Carlisle Barracks, PA.

Brown, Arthur. "The Jedburghs: A Short History." April 1991. Photocopy of unpublished manuscript provided to the author by Mr. Brown.

Browning, F. A. M. "Operation Market: Instructions No. 1" to Maj. Gen. R. E. Urquhart, Commander, 1 British Airborne Division. September 13, 1944.

Corbin, Robert L. "Prisoner of War Story." Unpublished manuscript. 1988. Available online at the Oflag 64 veterans website: http://www.oflag64.org/index.html (accessed September 14, 2007).

Gavin, James M. Letter to Gen. Williams, January 17, 1954. U.S. Army Military History Institute, Carlisle Barracks, PA.

Hibbert, Anthony. Letter to Amanda Todd, March 14, 1945. Photocopy provided to the author by Mrs. Todd.

Kanners, Victor. "Horseshit and Cobblestones." Unpublished and undated manuscript. Available online at the Oflag 64 veterans website: http://www.oflag64.org/index.html (accessed September 14, 2007).

Office of Strategic Services. "Report of Jedburgh Team Dudley." National Archives, Washington History Office, Record Group (RG) 226.

Office of Strategic Services (European Theater of Operations). *Special Operations Branch and Secret Intelligence Branch War Diaries.* 1945. Edited by Paul Kesaris. 13 vols. on eight reels of microfilm. Frederick, MD: University Publications of America, 1985. Also found in National Archives Microfilm Publication M1623. Also published in New York by Garland Publishing, Inc, 1988.

Office of Strategic Services, London Office, Special Operations Branch. "Coordination of Activities Behind the Enemy Lines with the Action of Allied Military Forces Invading N.W. Europe." April 1943. In Office of Strategic Services, London Office, *Special Operations Branch War Diary,* vol. 2, pp. viii, xxvii; and vol. 12, p. 118.

Office of Strategic Services and the United States Army. Personnel records of George M. Verhaeghe. National Archives, Washington History Office, RG 226, entry 101, box 1, folder 8; entry 128, box 10, folder 94; and entry 224, box 803, folder "Verhaeghe."

———. Personnel records of Harvey A. Todd. National Archives, Washington History Office, RG 226, entry 92A, box 115, folder 2473; and entry 224, box 780, folder "Todd, Harvey."

———. Personnel records of John M. Olmsted. National Archives, Washington History Office, RG 226, entry 128, box 11, folder 101; and entry 224, box 572, folder "Olmsted."

———. Personnel records of Willard W. Beynon, James R. Billingsley, Carl Scott, and McCord Sollenberger. National Archives, Washington History Office, RG 226.

Olmsted, John M. "Team Dudley." 1946. Unpublished personal account. Photocopy of unpublished manuscript, written in the spring of 1946, provided to the author by Mr. Olmsted.

Parks, Floyd Lavinius. "Diary: First Allied Airborne Army, September 1944." September 1, 1945. U.S. Army Military History Institute, Carlisle Barracks, PA. Floyd Lavinius Parks Papers, box 2, entry for September 10, 1944.

Royal Air Force Station Tarrant Rushton. Transcription of Operations Record Book, Summary of Events from June through September 1944. Downloaded from the website http://www.tarrant-rushton.ndirect.co.uk.

Sandford, John P. "The Diary of John P. Sandford." Unpublished diary kept during time as a prisoner of war at Oflag 64. 1945. Available at Task Force Baum website, http://www.taskforcebaum.de/main10.html.

Special Force Headquarters (SFHQ). "SFHQ G-3 Periodic Reports," published and submitted daily to Supreme Headquarters, Allied Expeditionary Force (SHAEF) G-3 from June 5, 1944, through May 7, 1945. Photocopies, declassified from top secret in 1989, in the author's files. Photocopies are also on file at the Combat Studies Institute, U.S. Army Command and General Staff College, Fort Leavenworth, KS. Originals are in the National Archives, Washington History Office, RG 226.

Special Operations Executive. SOE Activities Summaries for the Prime Minister for the

Quarters of April through June 1944 and July through September 1944. Public Record Office, London. Catalogue Reference HS 8/899.

Special Operations Executive/Special Operations (SOE/SO) Headquarters. "Basic Directive on Jedburghs, Prepared Jointly by SOE/SO." December 1943. Copy in Office of Strategic Services, London Office, *Special Operations Branch War Diary,* vol. 12, pp. 38–42.

———. "Coordination of Activities of Resistance Groups Behind the Enemy Lines with Allied Military Operations in an Opposed Invasion of Northwest Europe." N.d. Copy in Office of Strategic Services, London Office, *Special Operations Branch War Diary,* vol. 12, pp. 54–64.

Supreme Headquarters Allied Expeditionary Force. SHAEF Directive 17240/Ops: "Open Title for Headquarters, SOE/SO." May 1, 1944. Copy in Office of Strategic Services, London Office, *Special Operations Branch War Diary,* vol. 12, p. 85; vol. 1, p. 4; vol. 4, bk. 1, p. 14.

Todd, Arville O. "Missing in Action." Poem, probably written in late 1944. Photocopy provided to the author by Amanda Todd.

Todd, Harvey Allan. Letter to his family from Milton Hall, April 1944. Photocopy provided to the author by Amanda Todd.

———. Letter to Mr. and Mrs. Arville Todd, May 7, 1945. Photocopy provided to the author by Amanda Todd.

———. Personal account of wartime experiences. N.d. Photocopy of untitled and unpublished document provided to the author by Amanda Todd.

———. Personal chronology of activities from June 1939 to December 30, 1946. N.d. Photocopy of untitled document provided to the author by Mr. Todd.

———. "POW March from Oflag 64 to Austria, 1-21 to 5-5-45." N.d. Photocopy of personal journal kept during POW march from Oflag 64 to Austria, January 21 to May 5, 1945, provided to the author by Mr. Todd.

Twelfth Army Group. *Report of Operations, 12th Army Group (Final After Action Report).* Vol. 5, *Office of the Assistant Chief of Staff, G-3.* [1945]. Photocopy in author's files.

War Department, *U.S. American Prisoners of War in Germany: Dulag Luft.* Report prepared by the Military Intelligence Service. July 15, 1944.

———. *U.S. American Prisoners of War in Germany: Dulag Luft.* Report prepared by the Military Intelligence Service. November 1, 1945.

———. *American Prisoners of War in Germany: Oflag 13B (Transit Camp for Evacuees).* Report prepared by the Military Intelligence Service. November 1, 1945.

———. *American Prisoners of War in Germany: Stalag Luft 1.* Report prepared by the Military Intelligence Service. July 15, 1944.

———. *American Prisoners of War in Germany: Stalag Luft 1 (Air Force Officers).* Report prepared by the Military Intelligence Service. November 1, 1945.

———. EX-Report No. 61, Col. Paul R. Goode. Prepared by CPM Branch, Military Intelligence Service, General Staff G-2. May 17, 1945.

———. EX-Report No. 600, Lt. Col. James W. Lockett. Prepared by CPM Branch, Military Intelligence Service, General Staff G-2. April 25, 1945.

———. "Name, Rank, Serial No., Plus." *Intelligence Bulletin,* June 1946.

Watts, James H. "Diary of a POW." Unpublished manuscript. January 20, 1945. Available online at the Oflag 63 veterans website, http://www.oflag.64.org/index.html (accessed September 14, 2007).

II. OFFICIAL UNIT HISTORIES

Carter, Joseph. *The History of the 14th Armored Division*. Atlanta: Albert Love Enterprises, 1945.

Critchell, Laurence. *Four Stars of Hell*. 1947. Nashville: Battery Press, 1982.

Dawson, W. Forrest, ed. *Saga of the All American*. Atlanta: Albert Love Enterprises, 1946. Reprint, Nashville: Battery Press, 1978, 2004. Citations are to the 2004 Battery Press edition.

82nd Airborne Division Association. *82nd Airborne Division: America's Guard of Honor*. History section written by Steven J. Mrozek. Nashville, TN: Turner Publishing Company, 2004.

440th Troop Carrier Group History Project. *DZ Europe: The 440th Troop Carrier Group*. 2nd ed. N.p., 2003.

Griesbach, Marc F., ed. *Combat History of the Eighth Infantry Division in World War II*. Baton Rouge: Army & Navy Publishing Company, 1945.

Koyen, Kenneth. *The Fourth Armored Division from the Beach to Bavaria: The Story of the Fourth Armored Division in Combat*. Munich: Herder-Druck, 1946. Reprint, Nashville: Battery Press, 2000. Citations are to the Battery Press edition.

Langdon, Allen L. *"Ready": The History of the 505th Parachute Infantry Regiment, 82nd Airborne Division, World War II*. Edited by George B. Wood. Indianapolis: 82nd Airborne Division Association, 1986.

Lord, William G., II. *History of the 508th Parachute Infantry*. Washington, DC: Infantry Journal Press, 1948. Reprint, Nashville: Battery Press, 1977. Citations are to the Battery Press edition.

Mandle, William D., and David H. Whittier. *The Devils in Baggy Pants: Combat Record of the 504th Parachute Infantry Regiment, April 1943–July 1945*. Paris: Draeger Frères, 1945. Reprint, Nashville: Battery Press, 1977, 2004. Citations are to the 2004 Battery Press reprint edition.

Mrozek, Steven J., ed. *Prop Blast: Chronicle of the 504th Parachute Infantry Regiment*. Fort Bragg, NC: 82nd Airborne Division Historical Society, 1986.

Phillips, David J. *The Epic of the 101st Airborne: A Pictorial Biography of the United States 101st Airborne Division*. Auxerre, France: 101st Airborne Division Public Relations Office, 1945.

Rapport, Leonard, and Arthur Northwood, Jr. *Rendezvous with Destiny: A History of the 101st Airborne Division*. Washington, DC: Infantry Journal Press, 1948. Reprint, Old Saybrook, CT: Konecky & Konecky, 2001. Citations are to the Old Saybrook edition.

Stars and Stripes. *All American: The Story of the 82nd Airborne Division*. Paris: Desfosaés-Néogravure, 1945.

———. *Ever First: The Story of the 53rd Troop Carrier Wing*. Paris: Desfosaés-Néogravure, 1945.

———. *The 4th Armored: From the Beach to Bastogne, the Story of the 4th Armored Division*. Paris: Desfosaés-Néogravure, 1945.

———. *Invaders: The Story of the 50th Troop Carrier Wing*. Paris: Desfosaés-Néogravure, 1944.

———. *101st Airborne Division: The Story of the 101st Airborne Division*. Paris: Desfosaés-Néogravure, 1945.

Third United States Army. *A Souvenir Booklet for the Officers, Enlisted Men and*

Civilians Who Made History with the Third U.S. Army in the European Theater of Operations, 1944–1945. Bad Tolz, Germany: Third United States Army, 1945.

United States Army. *Now It Can Be Told: 14th Arm'd Div*. N.p.: 14th Armored Division, n.d.

Wallace, Brenton G. *Patton and His Third Army*. Harrisburg, PA: Military Service Publishing, 1946. Reprint, Mechanicsburg, PA: Stackpole, 2000. Citations are to the Stackpole edition.

III. BOOKS

Advertiser Company. *The History of Fort Benning [GA]: Diamond Jubilee, 1918–1993*. Columbus, GA: Advertiser Company, 1994.

Alanbrooke, Lord. *War Diaries, 1939–1945*. Edited by Alex Danchev and Daniel Todman. Berkeley: University of California Press, 2001.

Alcorn, Robert Hayden. *No Banners, No Bands: More Tales of the OSS*. New York: McKay, 1965.

———. *No Bugles for Spies: Tales of the OSS*. New York: McKay, 1962.

Allen, Robert S. *Lucky Forward: The History of Patton's Third U.S. Army*. New York: Vanguard, 1947.

Alsop, Stewart, and Thomas Braden. *Sub Rosa: The OSS and American Espionage*. New York: Harcourt, Brace & World, 1964.

Ambrose, Stephen E. *Band of Brothers: E Company, 506th Regiment, 101st Airborne from Normandy to Hitler's Eagle's Nest*. New York: Simon & Schuster, 1992.

———. *Citizen Soldiers: The U.S. Army from the Normandy Beaches to the Bulge to the Surrender of Germany, June 7, 1944–May 7, 1945*. New York: Simon & Schuster, 1997.

———. *Eisenhower*. Vol. 1, *Soldier, General of the Army, President-Elect, 1890–1952*. New York: Simon & Schuster, 1983.

———. *Ike's Spies: Eisenhower and the Espionage Establishment*. Jackson: University Press of Mississippi, 1999. Originally published in Garden City, NY, by Doubleday, 1981.

———. *The Supreme Commander: The War Years of General Dwight D. Eisenhower*. Garden City, NY: Doubleday, 1970.

———. *The Victors: Eisenhower and His Boys: The Men of World War II*. New York: Simon & Schuster, 1998.

Ammerman, Gale R. *An American Glider Pilot's Story*. Bennington, VT: Merriam Press.

Badsey, Stephen. *Arnhem 1944: Operation Market Garden*. London: Osprey, 1993.

Bailey, Ronald H. *Partisans and Guerrillas*. Time-Life World War II Series. Alexandria, VA: Time-Life Books, 1978.

———. *Prisoners of War*. Time-Life World War II Series. Alexandria, VA: Time-Life Books, 1981.

Bando, Mark. *101st Airborne: The Screaming Eagles at Normandy*. Osceola, WI: Motorbooks International, 2001.

Bank, Aaron. *From OSS to Green Berets*. Novato, CA: Presidio, 1986.

Baron, Richard, Abe Baum, and Richard Goldhurst. *Raid: The Untold Story of Patton's Secret Mission*. New York: Berkley Books, 1984. Originally published in 1981 by G. P. Putnam's. Citations are to the Berkley edition.

Barrett, Walter Horace. *My Story: Every Soldier Has a Story*. Boonville, NC: Whiteline Ink Book Design & Production, 2004.

Bauer, Cornelis. *The Battle of Arnhem: The Betrayal Myth Refuted*. New York: Stein and Day, 1967. Originally published in London by Hodder & Stoughton, 1966.

Beavan, Colin. *Operation Jedburgh: D-Day and America's First Shadow War*. New York: Viking, 2006.

Bentley, Stewart W., Jr. *Orange Blood, Silver Wings: The Untold Story of the Dutch Resistance During Market-Garden*. Bloomington, IN: AuthorHouse, 2007.

Berkeley, Roy. *A Spy's London*. London: Leo Cooper, 1994.

Bishop, Chris, ed. *Combat Guns and Infantry Weapons*. Shrewsbury, UK: Airlife, 1996.

Blake, Lord, and C. S. Nicholls, eds. *The Dictionary of National Biography, 1971–1980*. Oxford: Oxford University Press, 1986.

Blumenson, Martin. *Breakout and Pursuit*. United States Army in World War II Series. Washington, DC: Center of Military History, 1961, 1984.

———. *Liberation*. Time-Life World War II Series. Alexandria, VA: Time-Life Books, 1978.

———. *Patton: The Man Behind the Legend, 1885–1945*. New York: Morrow, 1985.

———. *The Patton Papers: 1940–1945*. Boston: Houghton Mifflin Co., 1974.

Bowen, Robert M. *Fighting with the Screaming Eagles: With the 101st Airborne from Normandy to Bastogne*. Edited by Christopher J. Anderson. Mechanicsburg, PA: Stackpole, 2001.

Bowman, Martin W. *The Bedford Triangle: U.S. Undercover Operations from England in World War 2*. Somerset, UK: Stephens, 1988.

———. *The B24 Liberator, 1939–1945*. New York: Rand McNally, 1980.

Bradley, Omar N. *A Soldier's Story*. New York: Henry Holt & Co., 1951.

Bradley, Omar N., and Clay Blair. *A General's Life*. New York: Simon & Schuster, 1983.

Brammal, R. *The Tenth: A Record of Service of the 10th Battalion, the Parachute Regiment*. Ipswich, UK: Eastgate, 1965.

Brereton, Lewis H. *The Brereton Diaries*. New York: Morrow, 1946.

Brinkley, David. *Washington Goes to War*. New York: Knopf, 1988.

Brown, Anthony Cave. *"C": The Secret Life of Sir Stewart Menzies, Spymaster to Winston Churchill*. New York: Macmillan, 1987.

———. *The Last Hero: Wild Bill Donovan*. New York: Times Books, 1982.

Brown, Vernon H., Jr. *Mount Up! We're Moving Out! A World War II Memoir of D Troop, 94th Cavalry Reconnaissance Squadron (Mechanized) of the 14th Armored Division*. Bennington, VT: Merriam Press, 2003.

Bruce, David K. E. *OSS Against the Reich: The World War II Diaries of Colonel David K. E. Bruce*. Edited by Nelson D. Lankford. Kent, OH: Kent State University Press, 1991.

Burgett, Donald R. *Currahee!* Boston: Houghton Mifflin, 1967.

———. *The Road to Arnhem: A Screaming Eagle in Holland*. Novato, CA: Presidio, 2001. New York: Dell Publishing, 2001. Citations are to the Dell edition.

Burne, Alfred H. *Strategy in World War II*. Harrisburg, PA: Military Service Publishing, 1947.

Burns, Dwayne T., and Leland Burns. *Jump into the Valley of the Shadow: The War Memories of Dwayne Burns, Communications Sergeant, 508th Parachute Infantry Regiment*. Philadelphia: Casemate, 2006.

Burriss, T. Moffatt. *Strike and Hold: A Memoir of the 82d Airborne in World War II*. Washington, DC: Brassey's, 2000.

Butcher, Harry C. *My Three Years with Eisenhower: The Personal Diary of Captain Harry C. Butcher, USNR, Naval Aide to General Eisenhower, 1942 to 1945*. New York: Simon & Schuster, 1946.

Butler, Daniel Allen. *Warrior Queens: The Queen Mary and Queen Elizabeth in World War II.* London: Leo Cooper, 2002. Mechanicsburg, PA: Stackpole, 2002.

Calvocoressi, Peter. *Top Secret Ultra.* New York: Pantheon, 1980.

Cannicott, Stanley M. *Journey of a Jed.* Cheddar, UK: Cheddar Valley Press, 1986.

Carter, Ross S. *Those Devils in Baggy Pants.* Canton, OH: Claymore Publishing Corporation, 1998. Originally published in 1951.

Casey, William. *The Secret War Against Hitler.* Washington, DC: Regnery Gateway, 1988.

Cassidy, William L., ed. *History of the Schools and Training Branch, Office of Strategic Services.* San Francisco: Kingfisher Press, 1983.

Chalou, George C., ed. *The Secrets War: The Office of Strategic Services in World War II.* Washington, DC.: National Archives and Records Administration, 1992.

Churchill, Winston S. *Blood, Sweat, and Tears.* New York: Putnam, 1941.

———. *The Second World War.* 6 vols. Boston: Houghton Mifflin, 1948–53.

Cline, Ray S. *Secrets, Spies and Scholars.* Washington, DC: Acropolis, 1976.

Codman, Charles R. *Drive.* Boston: Little, Brown, 1957.

Colby, William, and Peter Forbath. *Honorable Men: My Life in the CIA.* New York: Simon & Schuster, 1978.

Cookridge, E. H. [Edward Spiro]. *Set Europe Ablaze.* New York: Crowell, 1967. Originally published as *Inside S.O.E.* in London (by Arthur Barker, 1967).

———. *They Came from the Sky.* New York: Crowell, 1967.

Cronkite, Walter. *A Reporter's Life.* New York: Knopf, 1996.

Crosby, M. G. M. *Irregular Soldier.* United Kingdom: XB Publications, 1993.

Deane-Drummond, Anthony. *Return Ticket.* London: Collins, 1953.

Dear, Ian. *Sabotage and Subversion: The SOE and OSS at War.* London: Cassell, 1999.

de Guingand, Francis. *Operation Victory.* London: Hodder & Stoughton, 1947. New York: Scribners, 1947.

Deighton, Len. *Blood, Tears, and Folly: An Objective Look at World War II.* Vol. 1. New York: HarperPaperbacks, 1996.

de Jong, Louis. *Holland Fights the Nazis.* London: Drummond, 1942.

Delarue, B. Jacques. *The Gestapo: A History of Horror.* New York, 1964. Published in London as *The History of the Gestapo* and in Paris as *La Gestapo,* 1965.

de Launay, J., ed. *European Resistance Movements, 1939–1945.* 2 vols. London: Pergamon, 1960–64.

D'Este, Carlo. *Eisenhower: A Soldier's Life.* New York: Henry Holt & Co., 2002.

Diggs, J. Frank. *Americans Behind the Barbed Wire.* New York: ibooks, 2003. Originally published in Clearwater, FL, by Vandamere Press, 2000. Citations are to the ibooks edition.

Dolan, Anne Reilly. *Congressional Country Club, 1924–1984.* Baltimore: MacLellan and Associates and Wolk Press, n.d.

Doubler, Michael D. *Closing with the Enemy: How GIs Fought the War in Europe, 1944–1945.* Lawrence: University Press of Kansas, 1994.

Dourlein, Pieter. *Inside North Pole: A Secret Agent's Story.* Translated by F. G. Renier and Anne Cliff. 2nd ed. London: Kimber, 1954.

Dreux, William B. *No Bridges Blown.* Notre Dame: University of Notre Dame Press, 1971.

Duvall, John S. *North Carolina During World War II: On Home Front and Battle Front, 1941–1945.* Fayetteville, NC: Airborne and Special Operations Museum Foundation, 1996.

Ehrman, John. *Grand Strategy.* Vol. 5, *August 1943–September 1944.* Edited by J. R. M. Butler. London: Her Majesty's Stationery Office, 1956.

Eisenhower, David. *Eisenhower at War, 1943–1945.* New York: Vintage Books, 1987. Originally published by Random House in 1986.

Eisenhower, Dwight D. *Crusade in Europe.* Garden City, NY: Doubleday, 1948.

———. *D Day to VE Day, 1944–45: General Eisenhower's Report on the Invasion of Europe.* London: Stationery Office, 2000. First published as *Report by the Supreme Commander to the Combined Chiefs of Staff on the Operations in Europe of the Allied Expeditionary Force, 6 June 1944 to 8 May 1945.* London: His Majesty's Stationery Office, 1946. Washington, DC., 1946.

———. *The Eisenhower Diaries.* Edited by Robert H. Ferrell. New York: Norton, 1981.

———. *The Papers of Dwight David Eisenhower: The War Years.* 5 vols. Edited by Alfred D. Chandler, Jr. Baltimore: Johns Hopkins Press, 1970.

Eisenhower, John D. *Allies: Pearl Harbor to D-Day.* Garden City, NY: Doubleday, 1982.

Elson, Aaron. *A Mile in Their Shoes: Conversations with Veterans of World War II.* Maywood, NJ: Chi Chi Press, 1998.

Esposito, Vincent J., ed. *A Concise History of World War II.* New York: Praeger, 1964.

———, ed. *The West Point Atlas of American Wars.* Vol. 2, *1900–1953.* New York: Praeger, 1959.

Farago, Ladislas. *Patton: Ordeal and Triumph.* New York: Obolensky, 1964.

Farmer-Hockley, Anthony. *Airborne Carpet: Operation Market-Garden.* New York: Ballantine, 1969.

Fauntleroy, Barbara Gavin. *The General and His Daughter: The Wartime Letters of General James M. Gavin to His Daughter Barbara.* Edited by Gayle Wurst. New York: Fordham University Press, 2007.

Ferguson, Clarence. *Kriegsgefangener 3074: Prisoner-of-War.* Waco, TX: Texian Press, 1983.

Flanagan, Edward M., Jr. *Airborne: A Combat History of American Airborne Forces.* New York: Ballantine Books, 2002.

Foot, M. R. D. *Resistance: European Resistance to Nazism, 1940–1945.* New York: McGraw-Hill, 1977.

———. *SOE: An Outline History of the Special Operations Executive, 1940–46.* Frederick, MD: University Publications, 1986.

———. *SOE in the Low Countries.* London: St. Ermin's, 2001.

Foot, M. R. D., and J. M. Langley. *MI-9: Escape and Evasion, 1939–1945.* Boston: Little, Brown, 1979.

Ford, Corey. *Donovan of OSS.* Boston: Little, Brown, 1970.

Ford, Corey, and Alastair MacBain. *Cloak and Dagger: The Secret Story of OSS.* New York: Random House, 1945.

Forty, George. *U.S. Army Handbook, 1939–1945.* United Kingdom: Alan Sutton, 1995.

Fowler, Will, and Mike Rose. *Their War: German Combat Photographs from the Archives of "Signal."* Conshohocken, PA: Combined Publishing, 2000.

Frankel, Nat, and Larry Smith. *Patton's Best: An Informal History of the 4th Armored Division.* New York: Hawthorn Books, 1978.

Frisch, Franz A. P., and Wilbur D. Jones, Jr. *Condemned to Live: A Panzer Artilleryman's Five-Front War.* Shippensburg, PA: Burd Street Press, 2000.

Fritz, Stephen G. *Frontsoldaten: The German Soldier in World War II.* Lexington: University Press of Kentucky, 1995.

Frost, John. *A Drop Too Many*. London: Leo Cooper, 1994. Originally published by Cassell in 1980.

Gabel, Christopher R. *The U.S. Army GHQ Maneuvers of 1941*. Washington, DC: Center of Military History, 1991.

Ganier-Raymond, Philippe. *The Tangled Web*. Translated by Len Ortzen. New York: Warner Paperback Library, 1972. New York: Pantheon, 1968. Originally published in Paris as *Le Réseau Étranglé* by Librairie Arthème Fayard, 1967. Citations are to the Warner paperback edition.

Gann, Lewis H. *Guerrillas in History*. Stanford, CA: Hoover Institution Press, 1971.

Garrison, Gene, with Patrick Gilbert. *Until Victory Comes: Combat with a Machine Gunner in Patton's Third Army*. Havertown, PA: Casemate, 2004.

Gavin, James M. *On to Berlin: Battles of an Airborne Commander, 1943–1946*. New York: Viking Press, 1978.

Gilbert, Martin. *In Search of Churchill*. Newport Beach, CA: Books on Tape, 1996.

Giskes, H. J. *London Calling North Pole*. New York: Bantam, 1982. Originally published in London by Kimber, 1953. Published in Paris as *Londres Appelle Pole Nord* by Plon, 1958. Citations are to the Bantam edition.

Greenfield, Kent Roberts. *American Strategy in World War II: A Reconsideration*. Westport, CT: Greenwood, 1979. Originally published in Baltimore by Johns Hopkins Press, 1963.

———, ed. *Command Decisions*. Washington, DC: Center of Military History, 1987.

Griess, Thomas E., ed. *Atlas for the Second World War: Europe and the Mediterranean*. The West Point Military History Series. Wayne, NJ: Avery, n.d.

———, ed. *The Second World War: Europe and the Mediterranean*. West Point Military History Series. Wayne, NJ: Avery, 1984.

Grossjohann, Georg. *Five Years, Four Fronts*. Translated by Ulrich Abele. Bedford, PA: Aegis Consulting Group, 1999.

Guard, Julie, ed. *Airborne: World War II Paratroopers in Combat*. Oxford, UK: Osprey Publishing, 2007.

Guderian, Heinz Günther. *From Normandy to the Ruhr: With the 116th Panzer Division in World War II*. Edited by Keith E. Bonn. Translated by Ulrich Abele, Esther Abele, and Keith E. Bonn. Bedford, PA: Aberjona, 2001.

Hackett, John Winthrop. *I Was a Stranger*. Boston: Houghton Mifflin, 1978.

Hagen, Louis. *Arnhem Lift*. London: Hammond Hammond, 1953.

Hall, Roger. *You're Stepping on My Cloak and Dagger*. New York: Norton, 1957.

Harding, Steve. *Gray Ghost: The R.M.S. Queen Mary at War*. Missoula, MT: Pictorial Histories, 1982.

Hastings, Max. *Victory in Europe: D-Day to V-E Day*. Boston: Little, Brown, 1985.

Heaps, Leo. *Escape from Arnhem*. Toronto: Macmillan, 1945.

———. *The Evaders*. New York: Morrow, 1976.

Heck, Alfons. *A Child of Hitler: Germany in the Days When God Wore a Swastika*. Frederick, CO: Renaissance House, 1985.

Heilbrunn, Otto. *Partisan Warfare*. New York: Praeger, 1962.

———. *Warfare in the Enemy's Rear*. New York: Praeger, 1963.

Hibbert, Christopher. *Arnhem*. New York: Phoenix Paperbacks, 2003. First published in London by Batsford, 1962.

Hirshson, Stanley P. *General Patton: A Soldier's Life*. New York: HarperCollins, 2002.

Hogg, Ian V., and John S. Weeks. *Military Small Arms of the 20th Century*. 4th ed. Northfield, IL: DBI Books, 1981.

Höhne, Heinz. *The Order of the Death's Head: The Story of Hitler's SS*. Translated by Richard Barry. New York: Ballantine, 1971. Originally published in Hamburg as *Der Orden unter dem Totenkopf* by Spiegel, 1966.

Horrocks, Brian, ed. *The Red Devils: The Story of the British Airborne Forces*. London: Leo Cooper, 1971.

Howarth, Patrick. *Undercover: The Men and Women of the SOE*. London: Phoenix Press, 2000. Originally published by Routledge & Kegan Paul, 1980.

Hugh Lauter Levin Associates. *The "Stars and Stripes": World War II Front Pages*. New York: Hugh Lauter Levin Associates, 1985.

Hutchison, James. *That Drug Danger*. Montrose, Scotland: Standard Press, 1977.

Hutton, Clayton. *Official Secret: The Remarkable Story of Escape Aids—Their Invention, Production—and the Sequel*. New York: Crown, 1961.

Hymoff, Edward. *The OSS in World War II*. New York: Ballantine, 1972.

Iddekinge, P. R. A. van. *Arnhem: September 1944*. Arnhem, Netherlands: Gemeentearchief, 1969.

Ingersoll, Ralph. *Top Secret*. New York: Harcourt, Brace, 1946.

International Conference on the History of the Resistance Movements. *European Resistance Movements, 1939–45: Proceedings of the Second International Conference on the History of the Resistance Movements Held at Milan, 26–29 March 1961*. New York: Macmillan, 1964.

Irwin, Will. *The Jedburghs: The Secret History of the Allied Special Forces, France 1944*. New York: PublicAffairs, 2005.

Jablonski, Edward. *A Pictorial History of the World War II Years*. Garden City, NY: Doubleday, 1977.

Jakub, Jay. *Spies and Saboteurs, 1940–45: Anglo-American Collaboration and Rivalry in Human Intelligence Collection and Special Operations*. New York: St. Martin's, 1999.

Kahn, David. *Hitler's Spies: German Military Intelligence in World War II*. New York: Macmillan, 1978.

Keegan, John. *Intelligence in War: The Value—and Limitations—of What the Military Can Learn About the Enemy*. New York: Vintage, 2004.

Keitel, Wilhelm. *The Memoirs of Field-Marshal Keitel*. Edited by Walter Gorlitz. Translated by David Irving. New York: Stein and Day, 1966. Originally published in Gottingen, Germany, by Musterschmidt, 1961.

Kelso, Nicholas. *Errors of Judgment: SOE's Disaster in the Netherlands, 1941–44*. London: Hale, 1988.

Kennett, Lee. *G.I.: The American Soldier in World War II*. New York: Scribners, 1987.

Kershaw, Robert J. *"It Never Snows in September": The German View of Market Garden and the Battle of Arnhem, September 1944*. New York: Sarpedon, 1999.

Kesselring, Albrecht. *The Memoirs of Field-Marshal Kesselring*. Novato, CA: Presidio, 1989. Originally published in London by Kimber, 1953; in New York by Morrow, 1953; and as *Soldat bis zum letzten Tag* in Bonn, Germany, by Athenaum, 1953.

Kimball, Warren F., ed. *Churchill and Roosevelt: The Complete Correspondence*. Vol. 1, *Alliance Emerging, October 1933–November 1942*. Princeton, NJ: Princeton University Press, 1984.

Knox, Bernard. *Essays Ancient and Modern*. Baltimore: Johns Hopkins University Press, 1989.

Koskimaki, George. *Hell's Highway: Chronicle of the 101st Airborne Division in the Holland Campaign, September–November 1944*. Havertown, PA: Casemate, 1989.

Kraus, Rene. *Europe in Revolt*. New York, 1942.

Ladd, James, and Keith Melton. *Clandestine Warfare: Weapons and Equipment of the SOE and OSS*. London: Blandford, 1988.

Lamb, Richard. *Montgomery in Europe, 1943–1945: Success or Failure?* New York: Watts, 1984.

Laqueur, Walter. *Guerrilla: A Historical and Critical Study*. Boston: Little, Brown, 1976.

———. *The Guerrilla Reader: A Historical Anthology*. New York: New American Library, 1977.

Larrabee, Eric. *Commander in Chief: Franklin Delano Roosevelt, His Lieutenants, and Their War*. New York: Harper & Row, 1987.

Lebenson, Len. *Surrounded by Heroes: Six Campaigns with Division Headquarters, 82d Airborne Division, 1942–1945*. Philadelphia: Casemate, 2007.

Lemmon, Sarah McCulloh. *North Carolina's Role in World War II*. Raleigh: Division of Archives and History, North Carolina Department of Cultural Resources, 1964.

LeVien, Jack, and John Lord. *Winston Churchill: The Valiant Years*. New York: Scholastic Book Services, 1963.

Levy, Bert. *Guerrilla Warfare*. Boulder, CO: Paladin Press.

Lewin, Ronald. *Montgomery as Military Commander*. New York: Stein & Day, 1971.

———. *Ultra Goes to War: The First Account of World War II's Greatest Secret Based on Official Documents*. New York: McGraw-Hill, 1978. London: Hutchinson, 1978.

Liddell Hart, B. H. *The German Generals Talk*. New York: Morrow, 1948.

———. *History of the Second World War*. New York: Putnam, 1970.

Linderman, Gerald F. *The World Within War: America's Combat Experience in World War II*. New York: Free Press, 1997.

Lloyd, Mark. *The Guinness Book of Espionage*. London: Guinness, 1994. New York: Da Capo, 1994.

Longmate, Norman. *The G.I.'s: The Americans in Britain, 1942–1945*. New York: Scribners, 1975.

Lorain, Pierre. *Clandestine Operations: The Arms and Techniques of the Resistance, 1941–1944*. New York: Macmillan, 1983.

Lovell, Stanley. *Of Spies and Stratagems*. Englewood Cliffs, NJ: Prentice-Hall, 1963.

MacDonald, Charles B. *Airborne*. New York: Ballantine, 1970.

———. *The Siegfried Line Campaign*. United States Army in World War II Series. Washington, DC: Office of the Chief of Military History, 1963.

MacDonald, John. *Great Battles of World War II*. Foreword by General Sir John Hackett. New York: Macmillan, 1986.

Machan, Teresa, ed. *The Netherlands*. London: Insight Guides, 2004.

Mackenzie, W[illiam] J. M. *The Secret History of SOE: The Special Operations Executive, 1940–1945*. London: St. Ermin's, 2000.

Macksey, Kenneth. *The Partisans of Europe in the Second World War*. New York: Stein & Day, 1975.

Manvell, Roger. *SS and Gestapo: Rule by Terror*. New York: Ballantine, 1969.

Manz, Bruno. *A Mind in Prison: The Memoir of a Son and Soldier of the Third Reich*. Washington, DC: Brassey's, 2000.

Margry, Karel, ed. *Operation Market-Garden: Then and Now*. 2 vols. London: Battle of Britain International Ltd., 2002.

Markham, George. *Guns of the Elite: Special Forces Firearms, 1940 to the Present*. London: Arms & Armour, 1987.

Marks, Leo. *Between Silk and Cyanide: A Codemaker's War, 1941–1945*. New York: Free Press, 1998.

Marshall, Bruce. *The White Rabbit*. Boston: Houghton Mifflin, 1952.

Marshall, George C. *General Marshall's Report: The Winning of the War . . . Biennial Report . . . July 1, 1943 to June 1945*. New York, 1945.

Marshall, George C., H. H. Arnold, and Ernest J. King. *The War Reports of General of the Army George C. Marshall, General of the Army H. H. Arnold, and Fleet Admiral Ernest J. King*. New York: Lippincott, 1947.

Masaryk, Jan, et. al. *The Sixth Column: Inside the Nazi-Occupied Countries*. New York: Alliance Book Corporation, 1942.

Matloff, Maurice, ed. *American Military History*. Washington, DC: Office of the Chief of Military History, 1969.

———. *Strategic Planning for Coalition Warfare, 1943–1944*. United States Army in World War II Series. Washington, DC: Office of the Chief of Military History, 1959.

Megellas, James. *All the Way to Berlin: A Paratrooper at War in Europe*. New York: Ballantine, 2003.

Mellenthin, F. W. von. *Panzer Battles: A Study of the Employment of Armor in the Second World War*. Edited by L. C. F. Turner. Translated by H. Betzler. New York: Ballantine, 1971. Originally published by the University of Oklahoma Press, 1956.

Meltesen, Clarence R. *Roads to Liberation from Oflag 64*. San Francisco: Oflag 64 Press, 1990. First published in 1987.

Melton, H. Keith. *OSS Special Weapons and Equipment: Spy Devices of WWII*. New York: Sterling, 1991.

Mendelsohn, John, ed. *Covert Warfare: Intelligence, Counterintelligence, and Military Deception During the World War II Era*. New York: Garland, 1989.

Michel, Henri. *The Shadow War: European Resistance, 1939–1945*. Translated by Richard Barry. London: Andre Deutsch, 1972. New York: Harper & Row, 1972. First published in France as *La Guerre de l'Ombre*.

Miksche, F. O. *Secret Forces: The Technique of Underground Movements*. London: Faber & Faber, 1950.

Milkovics, Lewis, ed. *"The Devils Have Landed" ("Die Teufel Sind Gelanded"), WWII: With the Fighting U.S. Airborne*. Longwood, FL: Creative Printing and Publishing, 1993.

Miller, Merle. *Ike the Soldier: As They Knew Him*. New York: G. P. Putnam's Sons, 1987.

Miller, Russell. *Behind the Lines: The Oral History of Special Operations in World War II*. London: Secker & Warburg, 2002.

———. *The Resistance*. Time-Life World War II Series. Alexandria, VA: Time-Life Books, 1979.

Miller, William H., and David F. Hutchings. *Transatlantic Liners at War: The Story of the Queens*. New York: Arco, 1985.

Minnery, John A., and Joe Ramos. *American Tools of Intrigue*. Cornville, AZ: Desert Publications, 1980.

Minott, Rodney G. *The Fortress That Never Was: The Myth of Hitler's Bavarian Stronghold*. New York: Holt, Rinehart & Winston, 1964.

Mitcham, Samuel W., Jr. *Retreat to the Reich: The German Defeat in France, 1944*. Westport, CT: Praeger, 2000.

Mitchell, George C. *Matthew B. Ridgway: Soldier, Statesman, Scholar, Citizen.* Mechanicsburg, PA: Stackpole Books, 2002.

Mollo, Andrew. *A Pictorial History of the SS: 1923–1945.* New York: Stein and Day, 1977.

Molnar, Andrew R., et al. *Undergrounds in Insurgent, Revolutionary and Resistance Warfare.* Published as Department of the Army Pamphlet 550–104. Washington, DC: Special Operations Research Office, American University, 1963.

Montgomery, Bernard Law. *The Memoirs of Field Marshal Montgomery.* New York: Da Capo Press, 1982.

———. *The Memoirs of Field-Marshal the Viscount Montgomery of Alamein.* Cleveland, OH: World Publishing Co., 1958.

Moody, Sidney C., and the Associated Press. *War in Europe.* Novato, CA: Presidio, 1993.

Moon, Tom. *This Grim and Savage Game: The OSS and the Beginning of U.S. Covert Operations in World War II.* New York: Da Capo, 2000.

Moore, Bob, ed. *Resistance in Western Europe.* Oxford: Berg, 2000.

Mosley, Leonard. *Marshall: Hero for Our Times.* New York: Hearst, 1982.

Murray, Williamson, and Allan R. Millett. *A War to Be Won: Fighting the Second World War.* Cambridge, MA: Belknap Press of Harvard University Press, 2000.

National Military Publications. *Home of the Airborne.* El Cajon, CA: National Military Publications, 1985.

Neave, Airey. *Saturday at M.I.9: A History of Underground Escape Lines in Northwest Europe in 1940–1945.* London: Hodder & Stoughton, 1969.

The New Yorker Book of War Pieces: London, 1939, to Hiroshima, 1945. New York: Reynal & Hitchcock, 1947.

Nichol, John, and Tony Rennell. *The Last Escape: The Untold Story of Allied Prisoners of War in Europe, 1944–45.* New York: Viking, 2003.

Nordyke, Phil. *All American All the Way: The Combat History of the 82nd Airborne Division in World War II.* St. Paul, MN: Zenith Press, 2005.

———. *The All Americans in World War II: A Photographic History of the 82nd Airborne Division at War.* St. Paul, MN: Zenith Press, 2006.

———. *Four Stars of Valor: The Combat History of the 505th Parachute Infantry Regiment in World War II.* St. Paul, MN: Zenith Press, 2006.

Nütt, Hans, with Larry Harris and Brian Taylor. *Escape to Honour.* London: Hale, 1984.

Obolensky, Serge. *One Man in His Time: The Memoirs of Serge Obolensky.* New York: McDowell, Obolensky, 1958.

O'Donnell, Patrick K. *Beyond Valor: World War II's Ranger and Airborne Veterans Reveal the Heart of Combat.* New York: Free Press, 2001.

———. *Operatives, Spies, and Saboteurs: The Unknown Story of the Men and Women of World War II's OSS.* New York: Free Press, 2004.

Office of Strategic Services. *OSS Sabotage and Demolition Manual.* Reprint. Boulder, CO: Paladin Press, n.d.

———. *Provisional Basic Field Manual, Strategic Services.* Washington, DC: Office of Strategic Services, 1943.

———. *Strategic Services Field Manual No. 3, Simple Sabotage Field Manual.* Washington, DC: Office of Strategic Services, 1944.

———. *Strategic Services Field Manual No. 4, Special Operations Field Manual.* Washington, DC: Office of Strategic Services, 1944.

Office of Strategic Services Assessment Staff. *Assessment of Men: Selection of Personnel for the Office of Strategic Services.* New York: Rinehart, 1948.

Oliver, David. *Airborne Espionage: International Special Duties Operations in the World Wars*. Stroud, UK: Sutton Publishing, 2005.

Parnell, Ben. *Carpetbaggers: America's Secret War in Europe*. Austin, TX: Eakin, 1987.

Patton, George S. *War as I Knew It*. Boston: Houghton Mifflin, 1947.

Pawle, Gerald. *The Secret War, 1939–1945*. New York: W. Sloane Associates, 1957.

Peatling, Robert. *Without Tradition: 2 Para, 1941–45*. Barnsley, S. Yorkshire, UK: Pen & Sword Military, 2004.

Perret, Geoffrey. *There's a War to Be Won: The United States Army in World War II*. New York: Ivy Books, 1991.

Persico, Joseph E. *Piercing the Reich: The Penetration of Nazi Germany by American Secret Agents During World War II*. New York: Viking, 1979.

———. *Roosevelt's Secret War: FDR and World War II Espionage*. New York: Random House, 2001.

Pogue, Forrest C. *George C. Marshall: Ordeal and Hope, 1939–1942*. Foreword by General Omar N. Bradley. New York: Viking, 1966.

———. *The Supreme Command*. United States Army in World War II Series. Washington, DC: Office of the Chief of Military History, 1954.

Pöppel, Martin. *Heaven and Hell: The War Diary of a German Paratrooper*. Staplehurst, UK: Spellmount, 1988. Also published in Munich.

Powell, Geoffrey. *The Devil's Birthday: The Bridges of Arnhem, 1944*. London: Leo Cooper, 1992. Originally published by Buchan & Enright, 1984.

———. *Men at Arnhem*. London: Leo Cooper, 2003.

Province, Charles M. *Patton's Third Army: A Daily Combat Diary*. New York: Hippocrene, 1992.

Reader's Digest Association. *Secrets and Spies: Behind-the-Scenes Stories of World War II*. Pleasantville, NY: Reader's Digest Association., 1964.

Reitlinger, Gerald. *The SS: Alibi of a Nation, 1922–1945*. London: Heinemann, 1956.

Ridgway, Matthew B., and Harold H. Martin. *Soldier: The Memoirs of Matthew B. Ridgway*. New York: Harper, 1956.

Ritgen, Helmut. *The Western Front 1944: Memoirs of a Panzer Lehr Officer*. Translated by Joseph Welsh. Winnipeg: Fedorowicz, 1995.

Rogers, James Grafton. *Wartime Washington: The Secret OSS Journal of James Grafton Rogers, 1942–1943*. Edited by Thomas F. Troy. Frederick, MD: University Publications of America, 1987.

Roosevelt, Franklin D., and Winston S. Churchill. *Roosevelt and Churchill: Their Secret Wartime Correspondence*. Edited by Francis L. Loewenheim, Harold D. Langley, and Manfred Jonas. New York: Saturday Review Press/Dutton, 1975.

Roosevelt, Franklin D., Joseph Stalin, and Winston S. Churchill. *The Secret History of World War II: The Ultra-secret Wartime Letters and Cables of Roosevelt, Stalin and Churchill*. Edited by Stewart Richardson. New York: Richardson & Steirman, 1986.

Roosevelt, Kermit. *The Overseas Targets: War Report of the OSS (Office of Strategic Services)*. Vol. 2. History Project, Strategic Services Unit, Office of the Assistant Secretary of War, War Department. Washington, DC: Carrollton, 1976. New York: Walker, 1976.

———. *War Report of the OSS*. New York: Walker, 1976.

Russell, Francis. *The Secret War*. Time-Life World War II Series. Alexandria, VA: Time-Life Books, 1981.

Rutledge, Brett. *The Death of Lord Haw Haw*. New York, 1940.

Ryan, Cornelius. *A Bridge Too Far*. New York: Popular Library, 1977. Originally published by Simon & Schuster, 1974.

———. *The Last Battle*. New York: Simon & Schuster, 1966.

Sage, Jerry. *Sage*. Wayne, PA: Miles Standish Press, 1985.

Saunders, Hilary St. George. *The Red Beret: The Story of the Parachute Regiment at War, 1940–1945*. Nashville: Battery Press, 1985. Originally published in London by Michael Joseph, 1950.

Saunders, Tim. *Operation Market Garden: Nijmegen, Grave and Groesbeek*. London: Leo Cooper, 2001.

Schreider, J. *Das War Das England Spiel*. Munich: Stutz, 1950.

Second International Conference on the History of the Resistance Movements. *European Resistance Movements, 1939–45: Proceedings of the Second Intl. Conf. on the History of the Resistance Movements*. New York: Macmillan, 1964.

Sefton, George William. *It Was My War: I'll Remember It the Way I Want To!* Manhattan, KS: Sunflower University Press, 1994.

Seth, Ronald. *How the Resistance Worked*. London: Bles, 1961. Published as *The Noble Saboteurs: The Resistance Against Hitler's Forces* in New York by Hawthorn, 1966.

———. *The Undaunted: The Story of the Resistance in Western Europe*. London: Muller, 1956. New York: Philosophical Library, 1956.

Shirer, William L. *The Rise and Fall of the Third Reich: A History of Nazi Germany*. New York: Simon & Schuster, 1960.

Shoemaker, Lloyd R. *The Escape Factory: The Story of MIS-X*. New York: St. Martin's Paperbacks, 1992. Originally published by St. Martin's in 1990.

Simons, Gerald. *Victory in Europe*. Time-Life World War II Series. Alexandria, VA: Time-Life Books, 1982.

Simpson, John, with Mark Adkin. *The Quiet Operator: Special Forces Signaller Extraordinary*. London: Leo Cooper, 1993.

Singlaub, John K., and Malcolm McConnell. *Hazardous Duty: An American Soldier in the Twentieth Century*. New York: Summit, 1991.

Smith, Bradley F. *The Shadow Warriors: OSS and the Origins of the CIA*. New York, 1983.

Smith, Michael. *Station X: Decoding Nazi Secrets*. United Kingdom: Boxtree, 1998.

Smith, Richard Harris. *OSS: The Secret History of America's First Central Intelligence Agency*. Berkeley: University of California Press, 1972.

Smith, Walter Bedell. *Eisenhower's Six Great Decisions*. New York: Longmans, Green, 1956.

Sorley, Lewis. *Thunderbolt: From the Battle of the Bulge to Vietnam and Beyond: General Creighton Abrams and the Army of His Times*. New York: Simon & Schuster, 1992.

Sosabowski, Stanislaw. *Freely I Served*. London: Kimber, 1960.

Special Operations Executive. *Secret Agent's Handbook: The WWII Spy Manual of Devices, Disguises, Gadgets and Concealed Weapons*. Introduction by Mark Seaman. Reprints of SOE's *Descriptive Catalogue of Special Devices and Supplies* (1944) and vol. 2 (1945). Richmond, UK: Public Record Office, 2000. Guilford, CT: Lyons Press, 2001.

———. *SOE Secret Operations Manual*. Reprint, Boulder, CO: Paladin Press, 1993.

———. *SOE Syllabus: Lessons in Ungentlemanly Warfare, World War II*. Richmond, UK: Public Record Office, 2001. Reprint, Public Record Office, 2004.

Special Operations Research Office. *Human Factors Considerations of Undergrounds in Insurgencies*. Washington, DC.: Special Operations Research Office, American University, 1966.

Stafford, David. *Britain and European Resistance, 1940–1945*. Toronto: University of Toronto Press, 1980.

———. *Secret Agent: The True Story of the Covert War Against Hitler*. New York: Overlook Press, 2001.

Stein, George H. *The Waffen SS: Hitler's Elite Guard at War, 1939–1945*. Ithaca, NY: Cornell University Press, 1966.

Steinhoff, Johannes, Peter Pechel, and Dennis Showalter. *Voices from the Third Reich: An Oral History*. New York: Da Capo, 1994.

Stevenson, William. *The Secret War*. New York: Ballantine, 1977.

Sweet-Escott, Bickham. *Baker Street Irregular*. London: Methuen, 1965.

Sydnor, Charles W., Jr. *Soldiers of Destruction: The SS Death's Head Division, 1933–1945*. Princeton, NJ: Princeton University Press, 1977.

Taylor, John M. *General Maxwell Taylor: The Sword and the Pen*. New York: Bantam Books, 1991. Originally published by Doubleday in 1989.

Terkel, Studs. *"The Good War": An Oral History of World War Two*. New York: Pantheon, 1984.

Thompson, Julian. *The Imperial War Museum Book of War Behind Enemy Lines*. London: Sidgwick & Jackson, 1998.

Tickell, Jerrard. *Moon Squadron*. Garden City, NY: Doubleday, 1958. Originally published in London by Wingate, 1956.

Tieke, Wilhelm. *In the Firestorm of the Last Years of the War: II SS-Panzerkorps with the 9 and 10 SS-Divisions "Hohenstaufen" and "Frundsberg."* Translated by Frederick Steinhardt. Winnipeg: Fedorowicz, 1999. Originally published as *Im Feuersturm letzer Kriegsjahre: II. SS-Panzerkorps mit 9. und 10. SS-Division "Hohenstaufen" und "Frundsberg"* in Osnabrück, Germany, by Munin, 1975.

Time-Life Books, ed. *The Heel of the Conqueror*. Third Reich Series. Alexandria, VA: Time-Life Books, 1991.

———, ed. *The Shadow War*. Third Reich Series. Alexandria, VA: Time-Life Books, 1991.

———, ed. *The SS*. Third Reich Series. Alexandria, VA: Time-Life Books, 1989.

Toland, John. *Adolf Hitler*. Garden City, NY: Doubleday, 1976.

———. *The Last 100 Days*. New York: Random House, 1966.

True, William, and Deryck Tufts True. *The Cow Spoke French: The Story of Sgt. William True, An American Paratrooper in World War II*. Bennington, VT: Merriam Press, 2002.

Truesdale, David, Paul Rea, and Joseph F. Barlow. *Just Ordinary Men: Reminiscences from the Battle of Arnhem/Oosterbeek, 1944*. Newtownards, Northern Ireland: Airborne Battle Study Group, 1990.

Tucker, William H. *Parachute Soldier: Based on the 1942 to 1945 Diary of Sergeant Bill Tucker*. 2nd ed. Harwichport, MA: International Airborne Books, 1994.

United States Military Academy. *The War in Western Europe*. Part 1, *June to December, 1944*. West Point, NY: Department of Military Art and Engineering, 1949.

Urquhart, Robert E. *Arnhem*. Los Angeles: Royal Publishing Company, 1995. Originally published in London by Cassell, 1958; and in New York by Norton, 1958.

Voss, Johann. *Black Edelweiss: A Memoir of Combat and Conscience by a Soldier of the Waffen-SS*. Bedford, PA: Aberjona, 2002.

Wallace, Brenton G. *Patton and His Third Army*. Harrisburg, PA: Military Service Publishing, 1946. Reprint, Mechanicsburg, PA: Stackpole, 2000.

War Department, U.S. *Field Manual 100–5: Field Service Regulations—Operations*. Washington, DC: War Department, 1941.

———. *Pocket Guide to the Cities of the Netherlands*. Washington, DC: War Department, [1944].

Warner, Philip. *The Secret Forces of World War II*. London: Granada, 1985.

———. *World War Two: The Untold Story*. London: Bodley Head, 1988.

Warrack, Graeme. *Travel by Dark: After Arnhem*. London: Harvill Press, 1963.

Webster, David Kenyon. *Parachute Infantry: An American Paratrooper's Memoir of D-Day and the Fall of the Third Reich*. New York: Delta Trade Paperbacks, 2002.

Weeks, John S. *Infantry Weapons*. New York: Ballantine, 1971.

Weidinger, Otto. *Comrades to the End: The 4th SS Panzer-Grenadier Regiment "Der Führer," 1938–1945; The History of a German-Austrian Fighting Unit*. Translated by David Johnston. Atglen, PA: Schiffer Military History, 1998.

Weinberg, Gerhard L. *A World at Arms: A Global History of World War II*. Cambridge: Cambridge University Press, 1994.

Wellard, James Howard. *General George S. Patton, Jr.: Man Under Mars*. New York: Dodd, Mead, 1946.

West, Nigel [Rupert Allason]. *MI6: British Secret Intelligence Service Operations, 1909–45*. New York: Random House, 1983. Originally published in London by Weidenfeld & Nicolson.

———. *Secret War: The Story of SOE, Britain's Wartime Sabotage Organisation*. London: Hodder & Stoughton, 1992.

Whiting, Charles. *48 Hours to Hammelburg: The True Story of Patton's Bloodiest Mission*. New York: PBJ Books, 1982.

———. *Hunters from the Sky: The German Parachute Corps, 1940–1945*. London: Leo Cooper, 1974.

Widder, Arthur. *Adventures in Black*. New York: Harper & Row, 1962.

Wilkinson, Peter. *Foreign Fields: The Story of an SOE Operative*. London: Tauris, 1997.

Wilkinson, Peter, and Joan Bright Astley. *Gubbins and SOE*. London: Leo Cooper, 1993, 1997.

Williams, Eric. *The Tunnel Escape*. New York: Berkley, 1952.

———. *The Wooden Horse*. New York: Abelard-Schuman, 1958.

Williamson, Gordon. *Loyalty Is My Honor*. Osceola, WI: Motorbooks International, 1995.

Wilmot, Chester. *The Struggle for Europe*. New York: Harper, [1952].

Winterbotham, F. W. *The Nazi Connection*. New York: Harper & Row, 1978.

———. *The Ultra Secret*. New York: Harper & Row, 1974.

Wistrich, Robert. *Who's Who in Nazi Germany*. New York: Bonanza, 1984.

Wurst, Spencer F., and Gayle Wurst. *Descending from the Clouds: A Memoir of Combat in the 505 Parachute Infantry Regiment, 82d Airborne Division*. Havertown, PA: Casemate, 2004.

Yardley, Doyle R. *Home Was Never Like This: The Yardley Diaries; A World War II American POW Perspective*. Edited by Charles A. Turnbo. Evergreen, CO: Yardley Enterprises, 2002.

Zee, Henri A. van der. *The Hunger Winter: Occupied Holland, 1944–1945*. London: Jill Norman & Hobhouse, 1982.

Zeno [pseud.]. *The Cauldron*. London: Macmillan, 1966.

Ziemke, Earl F. *The Soviet Juggernaut*. Time-Life World War II Series. Alexandria, VA: Time-Life Books, 1980.

IV. ARTICLES

"Airborne Army Lands in Holland." *Times* (London), September 18, 1944.

"Armada Flew in Fighter 'Tunnel.'" *Daily Mail* (London), September 18, 1944.

"Armored Drive Into Holland." *Daily Mail* (London), September 18, 1944.

Associated Press. "D-Day Chutists Rate as Heroes: South Bend Officer One of International Secret Unit." Unidentified Indiana newspaper, September 27, [1945?].

———. "Emotional Ceremony Opens Resistance Museum." *Stars and Stripes,* October 16, 1992.

———. "Soldiers Remember Life Behind Enemy Lines." *Middletown (NY) Times Herald Record*, May 12, 1988.

Balink, Albert. "Descent into Holland." *Knickerbocker Weekly*, May 28, 1945.

Bentley, Stewart. "Of Market-Garden and Melanie: The Dutch Resistance and the OSS." *Studies in Intelligence*, Spring 1998. Available online at http://www.odci.gov.

Bishop, Stanley. "'Going Well' Reports Are Coming In." *Daily Herald*, September 18, 1944.

Blumenson, Martin. "The Hammelburg Affair." *Army,* 1965.

Borch, Fred L., and Robert F. Door. "Dutch Spy Helped 82nd Take Town from Germans." *Army Times*, July 17, 2006.

"Britain Awards Beynon Emblems, Citation for Distinguished Duty." *Scranton (PA) Times,* August 6, 1948.

"British Armour Reaches Airborne Troops." *Times* (London), September 19, 1944.

"British Reach the Rhine." *Times* (London), September 21, 1944.

"British 2nd in Holland." *Stars and Stripes,* September 19, 1944, Mediterranean edition.

"British Tanks Driving on to Arnhem." *Times* (London), September 22, 1944.

Brooks, William. "Black Tuesday." *World War II*, September 2004.

Bruske, Ed. "For 'Jeds,' No Mission Impossible." *Washington Post*, May 13, 1988.

———. "The Spirit of the Jeds." *Washington Post*, May 14, 1988.

Cherry, Niall. "Arnhem's Alamo." *World War II*, September 2006.

Coburn, Stanley W. "The Last Train from Danzig." *Ex-POW Bulletin*, March 1994.

Cochran, Alexander S., Jr. "Trauma of Capture." *Military History*, February 1985.

"Corridor into Holland Reopened." *Evening Star* (Ipswich, UK), September 26, 1944.

"De oorlog wordt nooit meer dichtgeslagen boek." *Regio,* May 3, 1985.

"Dutch Towns Taken in First Hours: Fierce Fighting." *Daily Mail* (London), September 18, 1944.

"Enemy Retreat in Holland Begins." *Daily Mail* (London), September 28, 1944, Continental edition.

"Epic of the Sky Men." *Daily Mail* (London), September 28, 1944, Continental edition.

"Fannin Marker Tells Camp's Story." *Camp Fannin Guidon* (Tyler, TX: Camp Fannin Association) 1, no. 1 (Spring 1993): 2.

"First Link with Troops North of Rhine." *Times* (London), September 25, 1944.

Galen Last, Dick van. "The Netherlands." In *Resistance in Western Europe,* edited by Bob Moore, 189–221. New York: Oxford, 2000.

Graffagnino, Peter C. "The Doctors' Lounge: The Rail Yards of Berlin." *Bulletin of the Muscogee County (GA) Medical Society* 27, no. 2 (February 1980): 10, available online at http://www.graffagnino.com/doctorslounge/#war (accessed October 5, 2007).

———. "The Doctors' Lounge: Winter Scene, 1945." *Muscogee County (GA) Medical Bulletin* 20, no. 1 (1965): 20, available online at http://www.graffagnino.com/doctorslounge/#war (accessed October 5, 2007).

———. "Of General Interest: Winter Scene, continued." *The Bulletin of the Muscogee County (GA) Medical Society* 12, no. 4 (April 1965): 14, available online at http://www.graffagnino.com/doctorslounge/#war (accessed October 5, 2007).

"Great Sky Army Opens Battle for Rhine." *Daily Mail* (London), September 18, 1944.

Hall, Norley. "Living Hell: The True Story of Mays W. Anderson and His Life as a German P.O.W." Available online at the Oflag 64 veterans website: http://www.oflag64.org/index.html (accessed September 14, 2007).

Hanlon, John. "Lt. Col. Tom Riggs' Remarkable WWII Odyssey." *Providence Journal*, December 30, 1985. Available online at the Oflag 64 veterans website: http://www.oflag64.org/index.html (accessed September 14, 2007).

Heide, Dirk van der. "Operation Yellow: The German Attack on Rotterdam, 10–11 May 1940." In *The Mammoth Book of Eyewitness World War II*, edited by Jon E. Lewis, 52–54. New York: Carroll & Graf, 2002.

Hughes, Les. "The Special Force Wing." *Trading Post*, July–September 1988.

"It's No Dutch Treat in Holland." *Army Talks* 4, no. 20 (September 30, 1945): 26–31.

Kamps, Charles T., Jr. "The Partisans." In *Soldiers of Freedom*, 26–31, 92–93. Boulder, CO: Omega Group, 1987.

"Keeping Posted." *Saturday Evening Post*, March 23, 1946.

Keiler, Jonathan F. "Top Secret: A Costly Raid to Liberate General George S. Patton's Son-in-Law from a German Prison Camp Failed with Heavy Losses." *WWII History*, March 2004.

MacDonald, Charles B. "The Decision to Launch Operation Market-Garden." In *Command Decisions*, edited by Kent Roberts Greenfield, 429–42. Washington, DC: Center of Military History, 1987.

Mackay, E. M. "Arnhem: At the Bridge, 18–29 September 1944." In *The Mammoth Book of Eyewitness World War II*, edited by Jon E. Lewis, 420–24. New York: Carroll & Graf, 2002. First published in the UK by Robinson, 2002. Selection extracted from *Royal Engineers' Journal* 68, no. 4.

Margry, Karel. "The Hammelburg Raid." *After the Battle*, no. 91 (1996): 1–39.

———. "The Market Garden Corridor Tour." *After the Battle*, no. 86 (1994): 32–41.

Matloff, Maurice. "Allied Strategy in Europe, 1939–1945." In *Makers of Modern Strategy: From Machiavelli to the Nuclear Age*, edited by Peter Paret, 677–702. Princeton, NJ: Princeton University Press, 1986.

McMillan, Richard. "230 Hours of Hell." *Daily Mail* (London), September 28, 1944, Continental edition.

Meltesen, Clarence R. "From Schokken to Wugarten." *Ex-POW Bulletin,* January 1993.

Murphy, Frank. "The Liberation of Moosburg." Edited by Cindy Goodman. *Splasher Six* 33, no. 2 (Summer 2002), available online at http://www.100thbg.com/splasher/moosburg.htm (accessed August 10, 2005).

Nelan, Bruce W. "The V-2: Aiming for the Stars." *Time*, October 12, 1992.

"New Drive, Air Action Dovetailed." *Stars and Stripes,* September 19, 1944, Mediterranean edition.

Niderost, Eric. "A Fool's Errand." *World War II,* July–August 2006.

———. "Gallant Defense at Arnhem Bridge." *World War II,* January 1997.

Nieroda, Joseph. "40 Years of Silence: Elite Heroes of 'Secret War' Come Out of Closet." *Scranton (PA) Times,* July 5, 1985.

Norton, G. G. "Arnhem." In *The Mammoth Book of Elite Forces,* edited by Jon E. Lewis, 459. New York: Carroll & Graf Publishers, 2001.

"The Prince and the O.S.S." *New York Times,* October 16, 1982, available online at http://select.nytimes.com/search/restricted/article (accessed October 31, 2005).

Ramsey, Winston G., ed. "Arnhem." *After the Battle,* no. 2 (November 1973): 1–25.

Reavis, Ed. "Jedburghs: Elite Teams Fought Behind the Lines." *Stars and Stripes,* June 6, 1994, D-Day+50 commemorative edition.

Rollings, Charles. "Dulag Luft." *After the Battle,* no. 106 (1999): 3–27.

Ross, Bernie. "Training SOE Saboteurs in World War Two." BBC. http://www.bbc.co.uk/history/.

Royal Air Force WWII 38 Group website, http://www.raf38group.org.

"Second Army near the Rhine." *Times* (London), September 20, 1944.

"Second Army's Battle of the Corridor." *Times* (London), September 26, 1944.

"Second Army's Corridor Widened." *Times* (London), September 27, 1944.

"Skyborne Army Rescued." *Stars and Stripes,* September 23, 1944.

"Tank Battle 5 Miles from Arnhem." *Times* (London), September 23, 1944.

"2,000 Men Return from Arnhem." *Times* (London), September 28, 1944.

"2,000 Men Safe Out of 8,000." *Daily Mail* (London), September 28, 1944, Continental edition.

Wilson, William. "Ambitious Airborne Assault." *World War II,* September 1994.

Winfree, Marie. "Bragg Was Training Site During WWII." *Fayetteville (NC) Observer-Times,* May 20, 1988.

Wood, Alan. "'Break-out' Order to Survivors." *Daily Mail* (London), September 28, 1944, Continental edition.

Woodward, Stanley. "Airborne Army Captures Dutch Towns Near Reich Border." *Daily Herald,* September 18, 1944.

V. AUDIO AND VIDEO RECORDINGS

British Broadcasting Corporation. "Englandspiel." *SOE Special Operations Executive* series. Television documentary. 1984

Galloway, Robert. *Oflag 64: A P.O.W. Odyssey.* VHS. Galloway Productions, 2000.

INDEX

ABOUT THE AUTHOR

WILL IRWIN retired from the United States Army in January 2000 after a career of more than twenty-eight years, half of that in Special Forces. He received a B.A. in history from Methodist College and a master of military arts and sciences degree from the U.S. Army Command and General Staff College. He has served as a research fellow at the RAND Corporation and now works as a defense consultant.